Georgina Sarah Godkin

Life of Victor Emanuel II, First King of Italy

Georgina Sarah Godkin

Life of Victor Emanuel II, First King of Italy

ISBN/EAN: 9783337230081

Printed in Europe, USA, Canada, Australia, Japan

Cover: Foto ©ninafisch / pixelio.de

More available books at **www.hansebooks.com**

LIFE OF

VICTOR EMMANUEL II.

FIRST KING OF ITALY

BY

G. S. GODKIN

NEW EDITION

London
MACMILLAN AND CO.
1880

PREFACE.

MANY MEMOIRS have been written of Victor Emmanuel since his death, but none of them would answer for the purpose of translating into our language. The best work on the subject is one lately issued from the press, entitled '*La Vita ed il Regno di Vittorio Emanuele*,' by Signor Massari, and to it I am much indebted in the composition of this work. It is full of reliable information, and ably written; but too comprehensive and diffuse for English readers, who cannot be supposed to take the same interest in all the particulars of contemporary events in Italy as the natives of the country.

Ghiron's brief Memoir is charming as far as it goes, but it does not pretend to be a regular biography. And the author is a true hero-worshipper; he is on his knees at the opening sentence, and never rises from that reverential attitude to the close of the book.

But it is hardly reasonable to expect at the present moment an impartial work on the subject from an Italian, any more than it would be to look for an impartial biography from a son of a loved father whom he had just laid in the grave. While the heart of the nation was still vibrating with a sorrowful emotion, some writers felt impelled to vent their excited feelings in eulogistic Memoirs of the deceased; and at the same time the Papal party let loose a flood of foul invective—not so much in the press, for fear of popular indignation, as by private means and verbal reports, sent floating through society—particularly foreign society—in Italy.

I confess that I have been partly induced to undertake a Life of the Honest King, in whose career England has always taken a warm interest, by observing how English and American travellers, who do not read Italian books, and who see only the surface of things, receive as undoubted facts every false report set on foot by the malignity of a party whose defeat naturally renders them bitter.

Victor Emmanuel, from the day he succeeded his father on the field of Novara, distinguished himself by a rectitude of purpose, so strikingly at variance with the conduct of the other Italian princes, that his subjects dubbed him *Rè Galantuomo*—a title soon endorsed by the rest of Europe.

How did the Honest King *par excellence*, who would have resigned every foot of ground he possessed rather than break his word to his people, ever merit the title —equally widespread in the Catholic world—of Robber King? There may be difference of opinion with regard to a man's appearance, manners, or abilities; but surely there ought to be but one with regard to his honesty. Can black ever be white, or white black? Can a man be an honest, a remarkably honest man, and a robber, a very great robber? He can, and is so, in the sincere opinion of those who so designate him. It all depends on the sort of spectacles through which he is regarded. I have tried to look through both spectacles with as fair an eye as possible. If I have seen unreal distorted visions through one, which vanish or change their character on investigation, I may be pardoned for preferring the glass which in the main is true, though given overmuch to beautify the object under consideration.

I believe that a perfectly impartial biography is an extremely difficult, almost impossible, thing to find. The sympathy which a writer naturally feels, and ought to feel, for his subject, is apt to increase as he studies his life in all its bearings, and his motives of action. To be on his guard against this sympathy, and not let it bias his judgment, is the duty of the conscientious biographer. I have tried, in this simple record of facts, to do justice to the memory of Victor Emmanuel, without doing injustice to the opposing party.

G. S. GODKIN.

SIENA: *December* 19, 1878.

CONTENTS.

		PAGE
INTRODUCTION		xi

CHAPTER		
I.	PARENTAGE	1
II.	BIRTH, EDUCATION, MARRIAGE. A.D. 1820-42	28
III.	THE YOUNG SOLDIER. A.D. 1848.	35
IV.	THE HONEST KING. A.D. 1849	48
V.	PIO NONO AND THE PAPAL POWER. A.D. 1848-49	58
VI.	THE KING AND CONSTITUTION. A.D. 1849-50	68
VII.	THE BEGINNING OF THE QUARREL WITH ROME, AND CONTINUATION OF THE QUARREL WITH AUSTRIA. A.D. 1850-53	81
VIII.	THE ALLIANCE WITH ENGLAND AND FRANCE.—DOMESTIC AFFLICTIONS. A.D. 1854-55.	91
IX.	RATTAZZI'S LAW.—CRIMEAN WAR.—VISIT TO PARIS AND LONDON. A.D. 1855.	101
X.	THE CONGRESS—THE PEACE. A.D. 1856	110
XI.	CONTINUED DISAGREEMENTS WITH AUSTRIA.—MACHINATIONS OF THE CLERICALS AND SECTARIES. A.D. 1857-58	118
XII.	'J'ATTENDS MON ASTRE.' A.D. 1858-9	130
XIII.	THE FIRST SOLDIER OF ITALIAN INDEPENDENCE. A.D. 1859	142
XIV.	'ITALY SHALL BE FREE FROM THE ALPS TO THE ADRIATIC!' A.D. 1859.	152
XV.	THE PEACE OF VILLAFRANCA. A.D. 1859	166
XVI.	THE VOTE OF THE ITALIAN PEOPLE. A.D. 1859	177
XVII.	THE ROBBER KING. A.D. 1860	186
XVIII.	KING OF ELEVEN MILLION SUBJECTS. A.D. 1860	203

CONTENTS.

CHAPTER		PAGE
XIX.	The Revolution of Naples. A.D. 1860	210
XX.	King of Italy. A.D. 1860	217
XXI.	By the Grace of God and the Will of the Nation. A.D. 1861	231
XXII.	Death of Camillo Benso Cavour. A.D. 1861	238
XXIII.	Italy without Cavour. A.D. 1862-3	243
XXIV.	The Seat of Government transferred to Florence. A.D. 1864-5	256
XXV.	The Final Expulsion of the Foreigner. A.D. 1866	265
XXVI.	The King and Pope.—Financial Difficulties.—Marriage of Prince Amedeo. A.D. 1867	277
XXVII.	Mentana. A.D. 1867.	282
XXVIII.	Marriage of the Crown Prince.—Anecdotes of Victor Emmanuel's Charity.—Spanish Revolution. A.D. 1868	293
XXIX.	Birth of Amedeo's Son.—Dangerous Illness of the King.—Birth of Umberto's Son. A.D. 1869	301
XXX.	Franco-Prussian War. A.D. 1870	307
XXXI.	M. Thiers' Appeal to the King.—Amedeo accepts the Crown of Spain.—Last Parliament in Florence. A.D. 1870	317
XXXII.	Italian Unity finally accomplished. A.D. 1871-76.	322
XXXIII.	Victor Emmanuel in Private Life. A.D. 1877.	334
XXXIV.	Drawing to a Close. A.D. 1877.	344
XXXV.	The Last Days of Victor Emmanuel. A.D. 1878	348
XXXVI.	The Funeral	351

INTRODUCTION.

'ITALY is one sole nation: the unity of customs, of language, of literature—in some future, more or less distant—will unite all its inhabitants under one sole government. . . . Rome is undoubtedly the capital which one day the Italians will select. . . . It is necessary to the happiness of Europe that Italy should form one sole State which will maintain the equilibrium on the Continent between France and Austria, and on the sea between France and England.'

The man who on a desert rock thus meditated on the destinies of nations, says the historian La Farina, 'was not a poet guided by imagination and sentiment; not a solitary philosopher, little practised in human affairs; he was a man who had learned by experience how empires are made and unmade—who had studied peoples, observing them from the most humble grades in society and from the loftiest throne that for ten centuries had ever been supported in Europe; who had experienced victories and defeats, who had overrun the world as master—from the arid deserts of Egypt, to the snowy plains of Russia.'

While the idea of Italian unity was thus working in Napoleon's brain, Italy was sunk in abject slavery under a host of petty tyrants, who, overawed and supported by Austria, dared not, if they would, institute any reforms in their respective governments. All the sovereigns without exception were despots pure and simple—their subjects at the mercy of their good or bad impulses, or the suggestions of their ghostly advisers. The rulers were divided into two classes: those conscienceless princes to whom the possession of a throne only means superior facilities of enjoyment; and those whose consciences were in the keeping of the Jesuit Fathers, and who carried out their views in the administration of State affairs. It would be difficult to say under which of these *régimes* the community suffered most.

When a people were permitted to live in peace without any

intolerable exactions or injustices, as in Tuscany and Piedmont, it was the effect of the sovereign's goodness, and he was much praised for abstaining from harassing his subjects by imprisonments, confiscations, tortures. And where, as in the Romagna, Naples, Parma, Modena, and Lucca, the princes indulged in rapacity, cruelty, and caprice, their subjects had no remedy but hopeless rebellion; for these petty tyrants were supported by the great military power of Austria, which not only ruled Lombardy and Venetia with a rod of iron, but prevented any change of government in the other States.

In Piedmont there reigned Victor Emmanuel I.—good, honourable, and brave, but wedded to the past, and much under priestly influence; consequently opposed to any reforms, even to a mitigation of the barbarous laws which his humanity rarely allowed to be carried out to the letter. His cousin, Charles Albert, Prince of Carignano-Savoy, heir presumptive to the throne, was known to have liberal sympathies, hated Austria, and was hated by the Austrians, who wished to break the Salic law, hitherto in force in Sardinia, and cut him off from the inheritance, in order to give the crown to the Duke of Modena, in virtue of his connection by marriage with the House of Savoy.

Francis IV., Duke of Modena, was a Bourbon prince, with all the vices of his race, and perhaps an extra grain of savage cruelty. The prisons of Modena in his reign were worthy of the days of the Borgias. The loathsome dungeons in which the unhappy Liberals languished without a trial were not the worst infliction. They were drugged so as to produce delirium just before they were brought out to be examined, and everything they said in this state was noted down and used against them. An officer died of an over-dose of the poison; and a barrister went violently mad, and had to be chained to prevent him killing himself; while countless numbers of the most intelligent, high-minded, and well-disposed citizens perished on the scaffold, or endured the prolonged martyrdom of the galleys, without any positive evidence against them. This ferocious prince spared neither sex nor age; and not even the sacred office of priesthood could protect the unhappy man, no matter what his virtues, who was once suspected of Liberalism. One instance will serve to show the sort of justice that was then administered in Modena. Two prisoners were sentenced to die on the same day—the one for the murder of his father; the other, a priest, accused of Liberalism, a man of great talent, and such excellent character that he was universally beloved and respected. The parricide received the sovereign grace;

INTRODUCTION.

while the good priest was pitilessly sent to the block, though his bishop begged on his knees for his life to be spared, and refused to *unpriest* the condemned, which was necessary before the sentence could be executed. Another less scrupulous bishop was found to perform the office, and the victim died with the calm resignation of a Christian. The clergy were almost always on the side of despotism, and were the chief supporters and instigators of every act of tyranny perpetrated throughout the peninsula. But there were not wanting noble exceptions; every State in Italy counts some reverend names among its martyrs of liberty, and with them must be numbered this poor Andreoli di Correggio.

In Parma the Austrian Duchess, Maria Luisa, acting in obedience to orders from Vienna and her Jesuit advisers, pursued the same course, persecuting with unrelenting animosity all enlightened thought, as tending towards disaffection.

Passing over the Duchy of Tuscany, which enjoyed a mild rule under the house of Lorraine—except when, occasionally bullied and threatened by Austria, the Grand Duke was forced into some act of severity, such as surrendering a political refugee to a neighbouring government—we come to the vast and fertile provinces stretching across Central Italy from the Mediterranean to the Adriatic. These were under the Pope's sway, and were in as miserable a condition as a government founded on corruption, and nurtured in abuses, could make them. Pius VII. was personally a respectable character, with a reputation for learning; and he was undoubtedly an encourager of art. But he was never capable of governing the Papal States with any efficiency, and his great age left him in a state of ineptitude for years before his death.

It is anticipating the narrative somewhat to mention his successor Leo XII., who ascended the Papal throne 1823; but, as we are now taking a general glance at the state of the peninsula in our hero's infancy, we may as well here give a few brief words to describe the most remarkable and powerful enemy to progress that Italy had then to struggle against. Pope Leo appeared to be in a hopeless state of health at the time of his election, and it was confidently believed that he would not survive many months. But, like Richelieu, the possession of power had a revivifying effect on him, and the new Pontiff began to display extraordinary energy as soon as the tiara was on his brow. He was a ferocious fanatic, whose object was to destroy all the improvements of modern times, and force society back to the government, customs, and ideas of mediæval days. In his insensate rage against progress he stopped vaccination; consequently, small-pox devastated the Roman provinces during his reign, along with many other curses which his brutal ignorance and misgovernment brought upon the inhabitants of those beautiful and fertile regions. He curtailed the old privileges of the municipalities, granted new privileges to the religious communities, and enlarged the power of the clergy to the extent that bishops and cardinals had the power of life and death in their hands. He set the Inquisition to work with new vigour; and though torture had been nominally abolished in 1815, new kinds of torment were invented, quite as effectual as the cord, the thumbscrew, and the rack of old times. He renewed the persecutions of the Jews; drove them back into the *Ghetto* from whence they had begun to emerge, rebuilt its walls, and had them locked in at night like wild beasts; and issued an edict ordering all Israelites to sell their goods within a given time on pain of confiscation. On the first day of the Carnival they were obliged to come in a deputation to the Capitol, kneel at the foot of the throne of the Senator of Rome, and petition to be let live. The Senator made a motion of his foot as if to spurn them, with the words: 'Go; for this year we will tolerate you.'

The Christians fared little better; to use a vulgar but expressive phrase, they literally 'could not call their souls their own.' The Pope put all educational establishments into the hands of the Jesuits, and no other means of instruction were permitted to his holiness's subjects. He instituted a system of espionage by which he could be accurately informed of the private sins of the people, and punish them as crimes against the State. Whoever did not observe the fasts of the Church, or neglected to attend religious service on prescribed days, or failed to confess once a month—the confessors being appointed by government—or committed any offence against morality, was subject to whatever castigation the bishop or the Holy Office of the Inquisition chose to inflict. One instance will serve to show the severity of those sentences. One of the Noble Guards was accused of a misdemeanour with a woman of light fame; without a trial he was deprived of his rank, and ordered to be imprisoned for seven years. At the same time the clergy, whose good example might have done more than these harsh laws to reform the morals of the laity, were leading scandalous lives; but no one dared accuse *them*. And the real felons who preyed upon society escaped with impunity by bribing the officers of justice. Brigandage was rife throughout the States of the Church, and it was in this reign that the famous chiefs De Cesaris and Gasparone flourished. At the head of a numerous following of malefactors they fortified themselves in the wooded mountains, making raids on the neighbouring towns and villages, committing indescribable outrages on the inhabitants, and sparing neither convents, schools, nor monasteries. The fear and horror that reigned in those neighbourhoods induced the unfortunate citizens to supplicate the Pope to put a stop to the infliction. But the Papal Government, strong to persecute, was powerless to protect. It had resort to such means as the princes of the Saxon Heptarchy tried in order to extirpate wolves from Britain; that is, it offered a reward for a certain number of brigands' heads. It is unnecessary to point out the incentive given to crime and treachery by this irregular mode of executing justice. The system which answered very well for wild beasts could not be applied with equal success to men, inasmuch as a wolf's head could not be mistaken for anything but a wolf's head; but who could tell whether a human head had belonged to a brigand or an honest man? The cardinal sent by the Pope to find a remedy for these ills became infected himself with the spirit of brigandage, and was discovered in such nefarious practices that Leo hastily recalled and sent him into retirement, despatching another in his stead. This prelate opened negotiations with the bandit chief, with the view of coming to terms. After long discussion, the preliminaries of a treaty of peace were agreed upon, and the brigands capitulated on honourable conditions; that is, life, liberty, and a pension. While these abandoned criminals were set free of all punishment, honest, brave men were dying on the gibbet, or languishing in the dungeons of the Inquisition. The papal legates who ruled the provinces were worthy representatives of their sovereign; particularly Cardinal Rivarola in Ravenna, who decimated the surrounding country of its most intelligent and virtuous inhabitants. In one month, August 1825, the following condemnations—nearly all capital—were passed in Ravenna, all for the offence of Liberalism —Thirty nobles, one hundred and fifty farmers and shopkeepers, two priests, seventy-four *employés*, thirty-eight military men, seventy-two doctors, lawyers, and men of letters, and many artisans. As may be imagined, a brief experience of this rule embittered the spirit of the Liberal party, who threw themselves without reserve into the ranks of the secret societies, and planned acts of desperate revenge. Many attempts were made on the life of Cardinal Rivarola, who at last had to fly Ravenna, and was succeeded by another, as bad if not worse. The prisons could not hold all the accused; and they had to be crammed into monasteries and such-like edifices, where they were secretly examined, condemned, and sent where their relatives might never know what had become of them.

The famous Society, or, as the Italians call it, *Sect*, of the Carbonari, which had been introduced into Naples some time before, was now spreading northwards, and gaining importance and influence, as the tyranny of the governments hardened and embittered the populations. The Carbonari now counted amongst their numbers scions of the oldest families in Italy, and some of the noblest and most single-minded men that any country ever produced, who, under more favourable circumstances, would have been useful and honoured members of society. It was, however, composed for the most part of the sons of the people. The word *Carbonaro*, coal-man, signifies that its founder was a man of humble rank; and it continued to have the character of a very democratic institution, in spite of the admixture of noble blood which by degrees had been infused into it. The middle classes supplied large numbers to the society, and the professional men who belonged to it were not few. It is unnecessary to say that there were attached to this as to all such combinations a goodly number of worthless characters; self-seeking adventurers who made a trade of politics; light-minded, erratic youths who wanted the excitement and importance attaching to the character of *conspirator*; vain and unprincipled ones, who loved to hear themselves holding forth on the subject of Liberty, and were ready for any deed that would bring them notoriety.

This faction had ramifications in all parts of Italy, but it took deeper root in the Papal States than elsewhere—the natural result of persecution. For every member immolated by the Holy Office seven sprang into existence, more fierce and reckless than he, more determined on revenge. To assassinate a tyrant became an act of sublime public virtue in their eyes, and the perpetrator was regarded as a magnanimous hero, a modern Brutus.

Many suffered, however, who were innocent of any offence against the law, and who died professing the Christian faith, but protesting against its unworthy ministers. One of these, going to the scaffold, was exhorted by his confessor to reconcile himself to the Pope, 'Christ's minister on earth;' to which he replied, 'It is a long time since Christ has had any ministers on earth, and certainly he is none such who has transformed himself into an executioner.' He kissed the crucifix and exclaimed, 'Lord, save me, and I shall be safe!'

The Papal Government being unable to cope with the Carbonari, a counter-secret society was instituted, in order to overcome them by espionage. The members called themselves Sanfedisti, Holy Faithists. The following initiatory oath will sufficiently explain the object of this combination:—

Sanfedist Oath.

'In the presence of Omnipotent God, Father, Son, and Holy Spirit, of Mary, Immaculate Virgin, of all the celestial host, and of thee, my honoured father, I swear to let my right hand be cut off, or my throat be cut, to die of hunger, or perish in the midst of terrible torture, and I pray the Lord God to condemn me to eternal pains, sooner than I should betray one of the honoured fathers or brothers of the Catholic Apostolic Society, to which in this moment I subscribe myself, and if I do not scrupulously obey its laws and assist my brothers in need. I swear firmly to maintain and defend the holy cause I have embraced, and to spare no individual appertaining to the infamous sect of Liberals, whatever be his birth, parentage, or fortune; to have no pity either on children or old men, and to shed the last drop of the Liberals' blood without regard to sex or rank. I swear, in short, implacable hatred to the enemies of our holy Roman Catholic and only true religion.'

The oath was taken, kneeling, upon the Eucharist, and a blessed dagger was put into the hand of the neophyte.[1]

Adjoining the States of the Church was the kingdom of Naples, under the Bourbon sway. Ferdinand I. had already been driven from his kingdom by the aid of French arms, when he was reseated on the throne by the English, who compelled him to restore the ancient privileges and liberties of which he had deprived Sicily, and institute some reforms in Naples; but he soon returned to the old *régime* again. He was coarse, illiterate, heartless, and mindless, given up to the grossest pleasures. When his dying brother, who had shown him much kindness, sent repeated messages requesting his presence, he refused to sacrifice a hunting-party or feast with his favourites to gratify the fraternal wish. And while the funeral obsequies were going on, he was revelling with shameless indecency in his favourite amusements. The English minister, having received at this time a royal invitation, replied to the effect that he had

---

[1] See La Farina, *Storia d'Italia*, vol. I.

to assist at the mournful ceremony of an august funeral, and therefore could not accept it.

In 1820 an outbreak of Carbonarism shook the throne of the Two Sicilies to its foundations. Almost all the population of Naples except the old nobility attached to the Court were Carbonari; a great part of the army fraternised with the revolutionists, and many priests and monks were seen marching in their ranks. The king and all his family made a virtue of necessity, and pretended to be quite charmed with the novel idea of a Liberal Constitution. They made a great *fête* to celebrate the event, the princes and princesses standing on a balcony, waving their handkerchiefs to the cries of *Viva il Rè e la Constituzione*, and showering tricoloured cockades amongst the people. The hoary king walked at the head of a procession to church, and, taking his place at the altar with his hand on the Bible, swore to maintain the Constitution, invoking the Deity to strike him that moment with a thunderbolt if he spoke falsely. His sons also swore, and kept the oath in the same manner as their sire.

Soon after this he fled to Laybach, at the invitation of the Emperor, and sent an Austrian army to reduce his subjects to submission. When they were utterly crushed, and King Ferdinand *absolute* was proclaimed through the streets, he returned to his capital. We have already described how Carbonarism was punished in the States of the Church and the Duchies of Modena and Parma. We will now return to Piedmont, where all the hopes of the revolutionists began to centre, after the overthrow of the Neapolitan rebels. The King of Sardinia was absolute like all the other princes; but he was Italian, descended from a long line of Italian fathers, while all the others were more or less foreign, and under the influence of Austria to a greater extent than he was. The heir presumptive was well known to be Liberal, and it was hoped that he would take the lead of the national party. The Carbonari *were* national in their aspirations, though they had but a vague plan for the future of their country when all the tyrants should be extinguished. They were not Red Republicans, being quite willing to follow the standard of any hereditary prince who would grant a free constitution, and engage in a war for the expulsion of the Austrians from the peninsula, as it was that Power only which held the petty tyrants on their respective thrones.

The national party in Piedmont felt their hopes of a reform rise when the enlightened and highly cultivated Count Prospero Balbo came into power. But when he proposed some necessary reforms in the administration, he was overborne by the clerical party and the old nobility, who warned the king to beware of innovations, 'which always brought misfortunes in their train.' The Spanish revolution and the outbreak in Naples had produced a profound impression in Piedmont; every class was penetrated with the desire for a reform in the government, though they were all loyal to the House of Savoy. In March 1821 a general rising of the people in Turin simultaneously with one in Alessandria led by the Carbonari, in which the military joined, forced Victor Emmanuel I. to look the question straight in the face. It is probable that he would have yielded to the just desires of his people, and granted the constitution they asked, but for his fatal promise to the Emperor of Austria not to make any change in the existing order of things. He abdicated in favour of his brother, Charles Felix, making Charles Albert regent in the absence of the new king. The regent, who was at the same time loyal and liberal, was much puzzled as to his duty in the trying circumstances in which he was placed. He yielded to the popular demand, proclaimed the Spanish Constitution, adding on his own account an oath of fealty to the new king.

Carlo Felice was a strong upholder of absolute power, and devoted to Austria. He banished his young cousin from the kingdom in return for his fidelity, and visited the revolutionists with the severest punishments. The rebellion of Piedmont had been the result of a concerted plan with the nationalists of other States. The Lombards, particularly, were deeply involved in the conspiracy, and when it fell to the ground the terrible price of the daring attempt had to be paid in blood and tears. The trials, sentences, and executions were going on at the same time in Lombardy and Piedmont; and there were few families in either State who were not torn with anxiety and grief, if not for relatives at least for friends who had come under the law, so widespread was the sympathy with the movement in Sardinia, and so deep-rooted in Lombardy the hatred of the Austrian rule.

The Austrian Government was rather more civilised and enlightened than that of the other States in Italy—that is, as long as there was no suspicion of disaffection towards the Imperial power; but any offence that came under the head of treason was punished with merciless severity. Everyone has read Silvio Pellico's '*Le Mie Prigioni*;' but perhaps everyone does not know that it is entirely free from exaggeration, that the author was scrupulously truthful in all his statements. Orsini's 'Austrian Prisons,' published in England and in the

English language, shortly before his death, is intensely interesting, and gives a fair idea of the treatment which political prisoners received under the government of Austria. It would seem incredible, if such accounts were not corroborated by hundreds of trustworthy authorities. The acts of gratuitous brutality which Austrian soldiers perpetrated in the discharge of their duty was not the worst infliction which the poor prisoners had to complain of. Horrible calumnies were circulated about them, so as to destroy all sympathy for their fate in the hearts of the people. This, doubtless, was the work of the Jesuits, whose influence was all-powerful at Vienna; and it was also to them the prisoners owed certain refined cruelties, such as depriving them of a valuable book, or precious *souvenir*, removing the spectacles of those whose sight was defective; and telling them bad news of their companions in misfortune or of their families. They were deprived of light and air, almost starved, allowed no water to wash themselves, or any appliance of civilisation; their miserable sleep was interrupted by gaolers who came to conduct them to midnight examinations, presided over by judges who took pleasure in augmenting their unhappy condition. Of the many touching instances of Lombard courage and constancy then displayed we will cite one.

The Count Confalonieri, a young enthusiast in the cause of liberty and nationality, was in the thick of the conspiracy, and, after a prolonged and cruel imprisonment, was condemned to death with many other noblemen and gentlemen, among whom was Silvio Pellico, October 1823. The count's young wife was broken-hearted; during her husband's trial and imprisonment she touched the hearts of the severest Austrian judges by her grief. When the sentence was at last pronounced, she set out for Vienna, accompanied by her husband's father and brother, to plead his cause at the feet of the emperor. They all threw themselves on their knees, and, with tears and sobs, the old count implored grace for his unhappy son. The emperor replied that mercy was impossible; examples must be made; the sentence of death was already signed and on its way to Milan. The father fell insensible to the ground on hearing this, and the wife with passionate entreaties tried to touch the heart of the emperor; but to no purpose. She almost went mad with grief that night. The empress had her carried to her own apartments, where she showed her the greatest attention, and, in compliance with her piteous appeals, went repeatedly to try to change the resolution of her husband. All night she stayed with the unhappy lady, going to and fro between the emperor and her guest. At last she prevailed on him to commute the sentence. The countess and her father instantly set out for Milan, and never stopped day or night till they reached it, fearing that the sentence might be executed before the arrival of the pardon. The Count Confalonieri was separated from his companions, and conducted alone to Vienna, where he was put under a searching examination; but nothing could be extracted from him which could compromise anyone. He was proof against every temptation and every falsehood told him in order to shake his faith in his companions. At last Prince Metternich himself came to visit him in prison, and, expressing sympathy and regret to see the count in such a condition, said it depended on himself to make the chains fall from his hands and those of his friends. He had only to tell who it was who had conspired along with them (the Lombard rebels), who it was who had encouraged them to the attempt. What he would not tell the judges he could tell him in confidence. Confalonieri knew whose name it was that he was expected to reveal. Evidence of treason in the Prince of Carignano would have been worth the lives of a score of Carbonari leaders; for the Austrians desired above all things to cut him off from the succession, and give the throne of Sardinia to an obedient vassal who would carry out their policy—that is, the Duke of Modena.

'I see you have no confidence in me, count,' said Prince Metternich, on the prisoner's repeated declaration that he had nothing more to say. 'If you wish to confide your secrets to the most august person in the empire, that person will come to see you.'

'Tell that august person that I have nothing to reveal more than what I have told the judges,' was the firm reply. The Count Confalonieri was thrown into prison, chained and subject to the worst treatment; he was told he must consider himself dead to the world for evermore. All communication was cut off from his family, from whom he never heard. Twice a year they were informed that he was 'well' or 'ill,' as the case might be. His devoted wife, who was a woman of superior mind and character, lived only to accomplish his freedom. For ten years she gave herself with untiring zeal to this work, and then died, when the hope of saving him died in her heart. One day the prisoner No. 14 was called out of his cell, and thus addressed: 'No. 14, the emperor has ordered me to announce to you that your wife is dead;' and without another word he was led back to his dungeon.

'The Austrian Government,' says La Farina, 'not content

with punishing the conspirators in the provinces subject to her domination, stimulated to severity the other Italian Governments whose subjects had committed no acts of rebellion; and the most of them needed no stimulus.'

This brief sketch will give an idea, though an imperfect one, of the general state of Italy when Victor Emmanuel II. was born in 1820—a state of things which continued for nearly forty years after, with very little mitigation.

LIFE

OF

VICTOR EMMANUEL II.

CHAPTER I.

PARENTAGE.

A MODERN Italian writer says: 'Few families in Europe have flourished so long as the Sabaud, and among its members we do not count one tyrant.'[1] It is a proud boast, that is, if it were absolutely true. But the word *tyrant* is a plastic term, and there are other Italian historians who would be inclined to dispute this statement of the Marquis Gualterio, who is an enthusiastic admirer of the Savoy family. But if it is saying too much to state that it does not count one tyrant, it might be safely said that few dynasties could count so many heroes, famous for their daring deeds, against whom no charge of cowardice could be brought; false dealing and treachery were also alien to the blood of the Sabauds; but they were men of fierce ungovernable passions and great ambition.

Legendary records of the Sabaud family date back to the tenth century. Old chronicles relate that in 998 a foreign prince of Northern extraction, exiled from his own country, settled in Burgundy, where, by his military prowess and administrative ability, he rose to power and

[1] Gualterio, *Ultimi Rivolgimenti Italiani*.

influence. This prince, so the story ran, was of Saxon birth, the nephew of the Emperor Otho III., banished from his native soil for having slain the empress in a moment of uncontrollable anger, when he detected her infidelity to his uncle. But these early records are no more than tradition, and we are sure of nothing about this gallant prince, not even his name. He first appears to go under the designation of Berold, but in 1003 there is mention made of him as 'Humbert of the White Hand.' It is possible that the Saxon Berold may have changed his name to elude the pursuit of his enemies, or that it may have been changed by the people he lived amongst to a more familiar appellation; but it would appear that Berold and Humbert were one and the same person, and the founder of the Sabaud family.

Humbert of the White Hand is spoken of as the possessor of large territories, and as having erected his family seat or castle at the narrow pass called Morienne on the frontier of Savoy; hence the title assumed later of Count Moriana. In the course of time these brave, gifted, ambitious counts became Dukes of Savoy (1238), intermarried with the most powerful royalties of Europe, and commanded extraordinary respect and consideration, the smallness of their state taken into account.

The growing power and prosperity of the dukes, and the geographical position of their states, drew upon them the enmity of their powerful neighbours. In the reign of Charles III., 1536, Savoy and Piedmont were invaded by the Swiss, Spanish, and French; and for several years the dukedom remained the battle-ground of foreign powers, while the legitimate prince, by degrees despoiled of all his possessions, died in absolute want, and with him the Sabaud monarchy seemed to have come to a termination. But the wonderful vitality of that dynasty enables it, as we have seen in our days, to survive misfortunes which would extinguish an ordinary race. Charles III. had left one son, who was destined to restore and re-invigorate the family fortunes, and whose courage, genius, and force of character won from his contemporaries the surname of Testa di Ferro (head of iron). He had been early destined for the Church because of the weakness of his legs, and was usually called 'the little Cardinal,' the Pope having promised him such preferment when he came of age. But his elder brother dying, and the succession so devolving upon him, the boy threw off the monk's frock, buckled on the sword, and added to his classic and philosophic studies the arts of war and government. Emmanuel Philibert showed great aptitude and talent in the various branches of learning to which he gave his attention, but his genius was essentially military.

When still a mere boy he had attached himself to the Emperor Charles V., and followed his standard through all the wars that then desolated Europe, serving him faithfully, but never losing sight of the interests of his own unhappy and oppressed country, for the relief of which he never ceased to implore the emperor, though with little or no result. Emmanuel Philibert won for himself, by the might of his sword, and by the genius of his statecraft, the restitution of his ancestral dominions, the people of which had always remained faithful to their legitimate prince. He was offered the hand of Elizabeth Tudor of England; but hearing that the princess herself was not quite agreeable to the match, he declined. He then married the Duchess de Berry, sister of the King of France—this marriage being part of the treaty by which his dominions were restored—and had one son, who succeeded him. Emmanuel Philibert was great in peace as in war; he brought his *testa di ferro* to bear upon the management of his state; and if this early part of his reign had not been darkened by the persecutions of the Waldensians, he might have been called a model prince. These persecutions, however, were far less cruel than those of the other Catholic princes, by whom Emmanuel Philibert was driven to take severe measures in order to prevent a foreign intervention for the purpose of eradicating the heresy. He was not a bigot by any means, and adopted these repressive measures more from reasons of state than fanaticism. He found that his subjects, Protestant and Catholic, when left to themselves, were constantly making war upon one another, and he thought it best to compel the minority to conform, and live '*Cattolicamente*,' in order to maintain peace. When he found that did not answer, he became more tolerant, and granted certain privileges to the proscribed sect.

The Testa di Ferro remains to this day a most popular hero in Piedmont; for the people, feeling that to his courage and genius they owe their national existence, overlook the loose morality of the gifted and patriotic chief, as incident to the times in which he lived. 'All his good qualities were his own, the bad ones he drew from the age,' says Ricotti, the historian of the Piedmontese monarchy.

Somewhat different from the description of this famous prince given by Italian writers is the picture drawn by the masterly pen of the Anglo-Saxon republican, Motley, who seems to delight in stripping sixteenth century heroes of the virtues with which the popular voice of their respective countries had endowed them. The glorious Count Egmont, the flower of Flemish chivalry, the Bayard of the Netherlands, shrinks into a rude soldier, vain, ignorant, and arrogant. The good Coligny, who had 'more elevated views than many of his contemporaries,' is introduced in the act of surprising a sleeping city in time of truce. In fact, William the Silent is the only one of the popular heroes of the day whom this merciless iconoclast leaves standing on his pedestal. It is not to be expected, then, that a soldier of fortune like Emmanuel Philibert should be described as other than 'unscrupulous;' had he been scrupulous, he would have had no business to take part in the councils of European princes as they then stood. Here is his portrait at twenty-seven years of age, when he was appointed Governor of the Netherlands.

> The Duke of Savoy had become one of the most experienced and successful commanders of the age, and an especial favourite of the emperor. He had served with Alva in the campaigns against the Protestants of

Germany, and in other important fields. War being his element, he considered peace as undesirable, although he could recognise its existence. A truce, however, he held to be a senseless paradox, unworthy of the slightest regard. An armistice, such as was concluded on the February following the abdication, was in his opinion only to be turned to account by dealing insidious and unsuspected blows at the enemy, some portion of whose population might repose confidence in the plighted faith of monarchs and plenipotentiaries. He had a show of reason for his political and military morality, for he only chose to execute the evil which had been practised on himself. His father had been beggared, his mother had died of spite and despair, he had himself been reduced from the rank of a sovereign to that of a mercenary soldier, by spoliations made *in time of truce*.

He was reputed a man of very decided abilities, and was distinguished for headlong bravery. His rashness and personal daring were thought the only drawbacks to his high character as a commander. He had many accomplishments; he spoke Latin, French, Spanish, and Italian with equal fluency, was celebrated for his attachment to the fine arts, and wrote much and with great elegance. Such had been Philibert of Savoy, the pauper nephew of the powerful emperor, the adventurous and vagrant cousin of the lofty Philip, a prince without a people, a duke without a dukedom, with no hope but in warfare, with no revenue but rapine; the image in person of a bold and manly soldier, small, but graceful and athletic, martial in bearing, wearing his sword under his arm like a corporal, because an internal malady made a belt inconvenient, and ready to turn to a swift account every chance which a new series of campaigns might open to him. With his new salary as governor, his pensions, and the remains of his possessions in Nice and Piedmont, he had now the splendid annual income of one hundred thousand crowns, and was sure to spend it all.[1]

[1] *The Rise of the Dutch Republic.*

Victor Amadeus, the second of that name, and fifteenth Duke of Savoy, was the first prince of the family who assumed the title of King, 1703. He was a sickly, inert youth, who allowed his mother to rule as regent, even after he had attained his majority. Suddenly, however, he seems to have awakened from his lethargy, and shaken off the tyranny of the duchess. With the sovereign power once in his hands, he developed a surprising energy of character, tact, and firmness. He married the niece of Louis XIV. of France; but this alliance, instead of being an advantage to the young duke, proved a misfortune, since it gave the 'Grand Monarque' a pretext for meddling in the affairs of Savoy and treating the prince as his vassal. At last the overbearing haughtiness of King Louis drove Victor Amadeus to declare war, with the hope of succours from Spain. 'But more than to my allies I trust to the valour and loyalty of my nobility and my people; to these a Prince of Savoy has never yet appealed in vain,' he said, addressing the council.

The war was long and disastrous for Savoy, but year after year the indomitable courage of the duke led him to renew it, rather than submit to humiliating conditions. No sooner was this over than other wars succeeded, the Duke of Savoy being sometimes on the side of France, sometimes on the side of Germany, but almost always the sufferer. The last great contest, in which the enemy had carried his arms to the walls of Turin, ended favourably for Victor Amadeus, who displayed extraordinary skill and courage during the siege, and for the time overturned the Bourbon power in Italy. The treaty which followed made him King of Sicily, 1703, afterwards exchanged for Sardinia, and some other territories adjoining his frontier.

This prince's reign marks a long step in the rising fortunes of the House of Savoy, and so deserves the brief notice which we cannot afford to give to his successors, though some of them were very distinguished. He was pious like all his family; and in gratitude for the deliverance of his country from the French yoke, he erected the church of Superga, used as a royal mausoleum, on the spot where he defeated the enemy. The stain upon his fame is the painful fact that for a time he bowed to the dictates of the French king, and allowed a war of extermination to be waged against the unhappy Huguenots and Waldensians who had fortified themselves in the mountains of Savoy. At that time, however, he had not made up his mind that he had the power to resist Louis' authority; after he had once taken up arms against the French, these persecutions were not renewed.

The princes of Savoy generally left a goodly number of sons to perpetuate their name and honours. In the beginning of the present century, however, this robust and long-lived family came very near extinction, when no less than six brothers died without leaving male issue. Three of these died unmarried; the other three succeeded each other to the throne, took wives and lived to be old, but left only female offspring. The eldest, Charles Emmanuel IV., was deceived by his French allies, and tricked into concessions, till at last he was compelled by the republican government to abdicate and seek refuge in Tuscany, where he became a Jesuit monk.

Victor Emmanuel I. succeeded his brother, was persecuted by the French emperor, and driven into the island of Sardinia, where he remained till Napoleon was himself confined to the narrower limits of Elba, when he returned to his capital, to the great joy of the Piedmontese people. Victor Emmanuel was a brave, honest, good-hearted man, but of limited intellect, with prejudices which had their roots firmly fixed in mediæval soil. He was a conscientious despot, and to change the ways of his house would have seemed to him sacrilege. He might, nevertheless, have listened to reason, and come to see what the present century required, if it had not been for Austrian influence. The emperor had extorted a promise from him that he never would grant a free constitution, and that promise held him so firmly as a man of honour that he chose to lay down his crown rather than break it.

He was succeeded by his last brother, Charles Felix, a man in no way more enlightened, and with a less kindly nature. With Charles Felix the House of Savoy would have come to an ignominious termination had there not been a collateral branch, descended in seven generations from Charles Emmanuel I., of which one young scion was in existence, the sole hope of the Savoy dynasty, his father having died when he was two years old, and left no other son.

Thomas, fifth son of Charles Emmanuel I., born in 1596, was invested by his father with a rich inheritance of 'castles, territories, and jurisdictions, with the title of Prince of Carignano, for himself and his descendants.' The seventh Prince of Carignano-Savoy in direct line was Charles Albert, born 1798, and left an orphan two years later to the guardianship of his mother, a princess of Saxony, who kept him far from his cousins, and gave him a much more liberal education than he would have received at their hands. It was a grief to the royal brothers that their heir should not have been reared according to the traditions of the family. The Austrian rulers also were distressed about the education of the future King of Sardinia; and Prince Metternich, having intercepted letters from the Princess of Carignano to her son, wrote to King Victor advising him to remove the boy from the influence of one whom he described as a lady of 'detestable political principles, fomenting liberal ideas in the mind of Charles Albert.'

The young prince spent some time at a military school in Paris, and at the age of sixteen was made lieutenant of dragoons by Napoleon. His education was completed at Geneva under the direction of a very learned Protestant divine.

For all his liberal education, Charles Albert was as devout a Catholic as any of his predecessors. He was by nature profoundly religious, and his faith was firmly, indissolubly fixed in the Catholic Church. His political principles were liberal, just, generous, his love of country sincere. The conflicting elements of love of liberty and love of the Church warring in his soul, made him melancholy, reserved, inconsistent, 'incomprehensible'[1]—wore out his mortal frame, and before he was past the meridian of life brought him to a premature grave. The noble, chivalrous character of this prince, and the pathetic story of his unhappy reign, make him personally quite as interesting as his successful son, whose stronger and tougher fibre was able to bear the strain which broke the father's heart.

Prince Charles Albert married the daughter of the Grand Duke of Tuscany and had a son, who was only a year old at the time of the rising in Piedmont in 1821. The Prince of Carignano was then in his twenty-third year, very tall, and of noble, dignified aspect, with a face pale, grave, thoughtful, almost severe. His manners were reserved and cold, but gentle; he had a sweet low voice, and when he spoke there was some subtle fascination in his bearing which excited interest and sympathy. Though not on good terms with his cousin, Charles Felix, who disliked and distrusted him because of his Liberalism, he had completely won the affection of his distant cousin, King Victor, whom he called 'Uncle,' and to whom he was faithfully attached. For this reason the young prince was much beloved by the people; the Liberals of Piedmont being loyal to the king, and very anxious to secure his heir as their leader, and so cut him off from Austrian influence. The Carbonari had gained a strong footing in the Sardinian States, and though all the Constitutionalists were not connected with the society, they were willing to work in concert with it to effect their object. The Piedmontese army was full of the idea of a grand military *coup*, by which they would liberate Lombardy, and annex it to the kingdom of Sardinia. But they all reckoned without their host; the sovereign's consent was wanting to this agreeable arrangement. The Liberals presented a petition to him; and a false report was spread that he had said, that if his people asked a constitution he would not deny it. The joy caused by this report was

---

[1] 'Is it not true that I am an incomprehensible man?' he said once to a friend.

quickly quenched when the people saw military preparations going on to resist any movement that might be made.

Just at this critical and exciting moment some foolish students appeared at the theatre with red caps, and were arrested by the police. Their companions attempted a rescue and were themselves dragged to prison. Next morning great excitement prevailed, and a cry was raised about university privileges. The students barricaded the college, and vowed they would not open it till the prisoners were released. A body of grenadiers assaulted the college, broke it open, and charged the helpless students, who were found wounded in all parts of the building. Great indignation was felt throughout the city, for almost all the respectable inhabitants had some member of their family in the university. Among those who paid a consolatory visit to the wounded youths was the Prince of Carignano; the news flew like lightning through Turin, and immensely increased his popularity. The conspirators of Lombardy and Piedmont felt that the moment for action had arrived, and Charles Albert must be secured to them.

The famous Count Santorre Santa Rosa, the leader of the Piedmontese 'federates,' opened the matter to Prince Charles, explaining how entirely loyal their intentions were towards the king, and that all they wanted was that he should separate himself from Austria, and become nationalist. The prince did not utterly reject nor yet accept the proposition. The Marquis Gualterio and Count Cibrario, and all the admirers of Charles Albert who have written narratives of those events, declare that he declined to lead the movement; he would never lend himself to anything like a rebellion against his sovereign. The Carbonari, on the other hand, branded him as a traitor, who deserted them in the last moment. He himself left a narrative in which he protested his innocence of treason, either towards his king or the revolutionists. La Farina, who is, on the whole, just and true, and not by any means blinded by affection for the

Sabaud family, says that after half consenting, he got frightened and withdrew his assent, and then hesitated so long that the revolutionists were induced to precipitate the movement in order to cut off his retreat. Santa Rosa, who was the leading spirit of the party, and the medium of negotiations, says in his account of the transaction, that 'he would, and he would not.'

This is most likely true. Charles Albert was as brave as a lion when his duty was clear before him; but he had an unhappy conscience, which was constantly giving him contradictory counsels, and dragging him in opposite directions. At one moment doubtless he was dominated by his love of liberty and justice, while at another he shrank from what would appear to stain his ancient name with a spot of disloyalty to his kinsman and sovereign. He was alike incapable of treason to the king who trusted him implicitly, or to the revolutionists who had confided in him. A less conscientious man would have stuck to the conservative party, cried 'Viva il Rè assoluto!' and won honour by so doing; or he would have silenced the claims of kindred, told himself that the interests of his country were paramount to all others, and sailed into power on the wave of popular enthusiasm. He did neither, and 'between the two stools he fell to the ground.'

The Count Santa Rosa printed an address to the Piedmontese calling on them to rise, with the war-cry, 'Viva Italia e la Costituzione! Guerra all' Austria!' In Alessandria, a great military depôt, the Carbonari proclaimed the Spanish constitution, and declared war against Austria 'in the name of the Kingdom of Italy.' The soldiers thought it no violation of their oath to take part in this movement; for their king should still be their king; they only wanted to make him great and powerful in spite of himself. On the arrival of this news at Turin there was great disturbance and excitement. Victor Emmanuel hastened from his country seat to the capital, and called a council in which the queen and Prince Charles Albert took a part. He issued a proclamation to the effect that there was nothing in the movement, and that it did not deserve any serious notice.

'Tranquillity is not the least disturbed in our capital, where we are with our family and our beloved cousin the Prince of Savoy-Carignano, who has given us proofs of his constant fidelity.' That sentence must have hurt Prince Charles's delicate conscience, and perhaps helped to make him break utterly with the revolutionists.

But the capital was not tranquil; next day some of the military, uniting with the students and citizens, marched through the streets with the red, white and green banner, crying 'Viva la Costituzione! Viva l'Italia!' The guards flew to arms, and one officer was killed when trying to force his way through the people with drawn sword. Prince Charles was then sent, in the king's name, to ask the people what it was they desired. He came on horseback, unattended by military escort, and was received with warm applause. 'Our hearts are faithful to the king,' was the reply of the Turinese, 'but we wish to withdraw him from perfidious counsels. The Spanish constitution, war with Austria, these are our desires.'

Victor Emmanuel did not think any reforms were likely to be beneficial; but his mind would have gradually opened to the necessities of the times, and he would then and there have acceded to his people's wish, but for the fatal promise which the Emperor of Austria had extorted from him—

> His honour, rooted in dishonour, stood;
> And faith, unfaithful, kept him falsely true.

But he would not shed his subjects' blood. He abdicated in favour of his brother, Charles Felix, then in Modena, and appointed Charles Albert regent with full regal powers.

The abdication of Victor Emmanuel was a great grief to the Constitutionalists. Santa Rosa wrote: 'The night of March 13, 1821, was fatal to my country. So many swords raised in defence of liberty dropped, so many dear hopes vanished like a dream. The country, it is true, did not fall with the king; but the country was for us *in* the king; Victor Emmanuel himself personified it; and the young promoters of that military revolution often exclaimed, "Perhaps some day he will pardon us for having made him king of six millions of Italians."'

The new king, Charles Felix, was devoted to the House of Austria, a firm upholder of absolutism, an enemy to liberty, and inferior to his brother in point of feeling. Even the devoted adherents of the Savoy family find little to admire in this prince, except that he was a man of his word, and did not perjure himself, as the custom was among Italian sovereigns.

If Charles Albert had been the self-seeking man that some writers have represented him, he had now a grand opportunity of seizing the reins of power, and establishing a popular government without a shadow of dishonour, his oath of allegiance to the abdicated king being dissolved, and all the authority of the state vested in his hands. But instead, he made desperate efforts to reconcile the monarchy with liberty; he wanted to be faithful alike to king and people, and he displeased both. Great agitation reigned in Turin on the night of the abdication of Victor Emmanuel I., with intense impatience to hear the regent's programme. The ministers of the late king counselled him to declare the Spanish constitution, and so save the country from a bloody revolution. The people stood all night round the regent's palace, and sent a deputation to him to explain their wishes. They disliked and distrusted Charles Felix, and they wished to have the revolution carried into effect before he had time to come from Modena, or send any express commands. 'How can I proclaim the constitution in the king's absence?' said the regent; and, when urged to it in order to avoid bloodshed, he replied proudly, 'I am ready to die for him I represent.' The liberal counsels prevailed, however, and Charles Albert came on the balcony and proclaimed the constitution, in the midst of intense agitation, and at the same time swore fidelity to the new king, Charles Felix. In his proclamation he said :—

Our respect and submission to his majesty Carlo Felice, to whom the throne belongs, would have hindered us making any fundamental change in the laws of the realm till the sovereign's intentions were known ; but as the force of circumstances is manifest, and we desire to render to the new king his people safe, uninjured, and happy, and not in a civil war,— having maturely considered everything, and with the advice of our council, we have decided—in the hope that his majesty, moved by the same considerations, will give his approval,—that the constitution of Spain shall be promulgated.

Charles Felix did not give his approval; he showed his disapprobation very strongly, and ordered his young cousin to quit Turin and go to Novara. He immediately obeyed ; and the secrecy of his departure awakened the suspicion of treason in the minds of the revolutionists. On his arrival in Novara another letter met him, requiring him on his allegiance to betake himself instantly to Florence, where his family should speedily join him.

Carlo Felice took possession of his capital shortly after, when the leaders of the revolution, and particularly the officers of the army, were visited with the heaviest punishments. Massimo Azeglio says he did not merit the name the Liberals gave him of 'Carlo Feroce,' but there is no doubt he was very severe.

The Prince of Carignano, distrusted and hated by his cousin the king because of his liberalism, maligned and execrated by the revolutionary party because of his loyalty, took up his abode with his father-in-law, the Duke of Tuscany. Conscious rectitude of purpose may sustain an old man, who has learned by experience what the gratitude of princes and peoples is worth ; but it could not and did not sustain Charles Albert under this double trial. He was only twenty-three, a young soldier, full of generous, chivalrous sentiments ; and to be so wronged by his king and country, for both of whom he was ready to die, was more than he could bear. He desired to return to Turin, and be tried by court-martial. But his friends, particularly the French ambassador in Florence, strongly dissuaded him from putting himself into the hands of his enemies so entirely. Austria was using all her secret influence against him; and Charles Felix contemplated cutting him off from the succession, and appointing a regent during the minority of the little Prince Victor. The bitterness of the exile's life at Florence became insupportable, and he begged permission to travel, which prayer was answered immediately by a commission to serve in the Spanish war, where he distinguished himself by extraordinary bravery.

In accepting this commission, and engaging to fight in the French army against the liberties of Spain, Charles Albert committed the only inexcusable mistake of his life; and we know not how to account for it, except that he was in a desperate frame of mind and wished to meet death, which would appear from the reckless manner in which he exposed himself to danger.

He was a man of strange contradictions, and it is probable that the violence of the Carbonari, and their bitter vituperations of himself, had thrown him back into the arms of the retrograde party; and the clergy, to whose influence he had always been subject, had worked upon his mind so as to win him over to see things from their point of view. It was a fatal step, which divorced him from the national party, and made him disliked and distrusted, even in his own Piedmont, where he had once been held so dear.

Charles Albert was recalled to Sardinia by Charles Felix in 1824, and a reconciliation took place later, shortly before the king's death, which occurred in 1831, when the Prince of Carignano ascended the throne peacefully, but with no demonstrations of joy.

Charles Albert seems to have been born under an unlucky star, for he invariably took the wrong road in the turning points of life; and with the best and most disinterested intentions he ruined the cause he most wished to serve. He was always destined to be misjudged and misunderstood. Half his honesty and justice, and a third of his morality, would have sufficed to carry an ordinary prince through life with a pretty fair reputation, while he was branded as a traitor, a tyrant, an executioner. When he ascended the throne, Mazzini had instituted a new secret society called *Giovane Italia* (Young Italy), which put the Good Cousins and all the rest quite out of fashion. The society did not begin as republican, at least did not so profess itself. The great conspirator who set the machine to work, and directed its movements with such consummate skill, made overtures to most of the crowned heads, or those nearest the thrones, in Italy, before he declared war against monarchies. To Charles Albert he wrote a long letter, offering his services to him if he would consent to lead the Liberal cause. And here again, if Charles Albert had not been conscientiously conservative, he would have been tempted by the dazzling prospects so ably depicted.

'Sire,' wrote the great revolutionist:—

> All Italy waits for one word—one only—to make herself yours. Proffer this word to her! Place yourself at the head of the nation, and write on your banner: 'Union, Liberty, Independence.' Proclaim the liberty of thought. Declare yourself the vindicator, the interpreter of popular rights, the regenerator of all Italy. Liberate her from the barbarians. Build up the future; give your name to a century; begin a new era from your day. All humanity has declared that kings do not belong to it; history bears out the sentence with facts. Contradict humanity and history. Compel it to write under the names of Washington and Kosciuszco, born citizens, another name greater than these: to say, There was a throne erected by twenty million free men, who wrote on its base: 'To Carlo Alberto, born king, Italy regenerated by him . . .' Select the way that accords with the desire of the nation; maintain it unalterably; be firm, and await your time; you

have the victory in your hands. Sire, on this condition we bind ourselves round you, we proffer you our lives, we will lead to your banner the little states of Italy. We will paint to our brothers the advantages that are born of union; we will promote national subscriptions, patriotic gifts; we will preach the word that creates armies. . . . Unite us, Sire, and we shall conquer.

To this stirring appeal Charles Albert would not listen; he seemed completely transformed into the legitimist sovereign of the old school. Then *Giovane Italia* lost all confidence in kings, became republican, and made war on Charles Albert with the bitterness of a suitor scorned. Seditious publications were circulated through his realm, exciting his subjects against him—the officers of the army in particular Mazzini tried to seduce from their allegiance. A conspiracy was discovered, and the promoters put on their trial. The bad feeling between sovereign and people was fanned into a flame by the Jesuits, who were then, as always, the creatures of the Austrian government, though Charles Albert did not know it. They carried the most alarming reports to the king's ears; they gave him information of a frightful plot to overturn the monarchy and the altar by means of the most diabolical crimes.

These stories were for the most part inventions, got up to frighten the king, and drive him into severe repressive measures, and thus sever him for ever from the Liberal party. It was afterwards discovered that the head of the police was in the pay of Austria; but, unfortunately, too late to prevent certain military executions which might with advantage have been commuted to a lighter punishment, and which filled the king with remorseful sadness.

In 1833 conspiracies broke out in the other states of Italy, simultaneously with that in Piedmont, and were punished much more severely. In Naples there reigned Ferdinand II.—quite a different character from his grandfather, Ferdinand I. He was neither immoral, intemperate, nor extravagant; on the contrary, he began his reign by an edifying simplicity, economy, and piety, which led his subjects to hope that better days than they had been accustomed to were in store for them. But a few years of his reign made them cry out, 'Better the rule of the Turks.' In fact, this prince's Christianity was no better than his grandfather's paganism. He was a morose bigot, given up to superstition; a slave to the Jesuits, who made him model his government on that of Pope Leo XII. In character he resembled Louis XI. of France, but without his ability. There was no falsehood, cruelty, or treachery he was not capable of. Religious persecutions, such as we have described as existing in the papal states, were carried on with vigour. Accusations of heresy were frequent, and for every small offence against the Church's laws the sinner was subject to corporal punishment, more or less severe, according to the nature of his offence. It is recorded that 'many citizens died under the infliction of the lash, as much from shame as suffering,' the sentences being carried out in the open squares. When private sins were visited with such severity, we can imagine how the great crime of rebellion would be treated in the Neapolitan states. The executions and proscriptions which took place there, and in the pontifical possessions, reduced the populations considerably; and, as generally happens in such cases, the most promising young men were those who fell victims to the tyranny of the government. In Modena the duke, having trifled with the Liberal leader, Menotti, in order, it is thought, to draw him into a snare, had to fight for his life in a sudden outburst of rebellion. The same night in which he had overcome this treasonable attempt, he despatched the following characteristic note :—

> A terrible conspiracy against me has broken out to-night. The conspirators are in my hands. Send me the hangman.
>
> FRANCIS.

The Austrians, always at hand to crush any rising, swarmed all over Central Italy and Naples, assisting energetically in the punishment of the rebels, and in the work of restoring order, or what they called order. The kingdom of Sardinia alone was not visited by this infliction, its sovereign reserving to himself the right of punishing his own subjects without foreign assistance.

The secret hatred which King Charles nourished toward Austria he was obliged to smother, for he had no means to resist her power. Keeping therefore his plans and desires buried in his own breast, he devoted himself to reforming the semi-barbarous laws still existing in his state—those relating to prison regulations, cruel punishments, disabilities of Jews and Protestants, etc.—and to improving the state of the army. But the sad, silent king, who lived like an anchorite, devoted to business, rigorous in the performance of religious duties, became more and more of a puzzle to everyone, and was not regarded either with confidence or affection by his subjects. What unhappy years those were to the friendless, lonely monarch, his subjects have since learned, and shed tears of remorse upon the tomb of him whom they justly call 'the martyr of their liberties.'

The desire for national unity, as the only safeguard of liberty, began to be felt more and more by thinking men. Giusti, in his famous poem called 'The Boot' (1836), makes Italy describe herself as made up of patches, and beg her next possessor to have her remade all of 'one piece and one colour;' but this owner must not be a foreigner—

> Non Tedesca s'intende, nè Francese;
> Ma una gamba vorrei del mio paese.

The book which perhaps best describes the growth of the national spirit in Italy, during the seven years that preceded the great revolutionary era of 1848, is D'Azeglio's *I Miei Ricordi*. This distinguished man may be said to have presided at the birth of that spirit; he certainly watched over its diseased infancy with indefatigable care and patience, and was rewarded by seeing it grow up with a certain robustness of constitution, though it never quite realised his ideal. D'Azeglio travelled north, south, east, west, trying to sow in the different populations the seeds of national life. It was grievous and discouraging to find the youth of the educated classes generally given up to pleasure, or burning with that patriotic fervour which consisted chiefly in shouting '*Fuori il barbaro! Fuori lo straniero!*' while the more earnest ones were members of secret societies.

There was, however, a considerable party of moderate men like D'Azeglio himself, who desired reform if it could be effected without war, and if it could not, were prepared to push matters to the last extremity when a favourable moment arrived. This party went on increasing and gathering new force every year, and at last it became evident that the nation was preparing itself for some grand movement. The premonitory symptoms were felt by the rulers of the land, like the rumbling thunder that precedes a volcanic outburst.

D'Azeglio, who loved law and order, trembled for what might come. He had endeavoured to educate the youth of Italy in a higher political creed than the assassination of tyrants. He desired that the war should be solely for the expulsion of the foreigner, and his earnest wish was that the national forces should be united and led by a native sovereign. And where in Italy was there what might be called a native sovereign? They were all satraps of Austria, with the exception of the Pope and the King of Sardinia. The Pope was out of the question, and D'Azeglio naturally turned his thoughts to his own king, who, if a despot, was at least an Italian, and maintained the independence of his little state against Austrian encroachments.

The bad reputation which he had among the Liberal party made it difficult for D'Azeglio to persuade his friends to share his hopes. 'What is it you want?' he said, trying to argue his Roman colleagues into a practical view of the case. 'You wish to drive the Austrians out of Italy, and to check the power of the priests. If you tell them to go, it is probable they will refuse. You must force them, and what force have you? None.

Then you must unite with those who have, that is, with Piedmont. She at least has an independent life, and money, and an army.'

'What, Carlo Alberto! would you have us hope in him?' asked his Roman friend.

'If you will not hope, don't hope. But you must then resign yourselves, and hope in nothing.'

'But '21 and '33?' persisted the Roman.

"'21 and '33 are not pleasing memories to me any more than to you. Nevertheless there is something to be said in his defence. But, admitting the worst, I repeat that in him you must trust, or in no one. Were we inviting Charles Albert to engage in a scheme contrary to his interests, for pure heroism and to serve Italy, then you might ask, "Shall we confide in the traitor of '21 and the executioner of '33?" But we only ask him, when an opportunity offers, to let us aid him to become more great and powerful. If you invite a thief to become an honest man, you may doubt his promise to do so; but if you invite a thief to rob, I see no reason to think he would fail in his promise.'

D'Azeglio adds, 'Poor Charles Albert! Time proved that you did not deserve so harsh a judgment. When I think of my comparison, I am bitten with remorse.'

D'Azeglio did not make much head in Tuscany, so deep-rooted was the prejudice against the Sardinian king. One gentleman quoted the example of a Roman legion, the soldiers of which killed their general when they found him unfaithful to his duty. 'What sort,' he asked, 'are the Piedmontese soldiers, who suffer Charles Albert to live?' D'Azeglio tried to excuse the poor Piedmontese soldiers for not having executed their king, urging in their defence that the times and ideas were so changed since the days of the pagan republic. But he felt the unlucky Roman legion had put him to the rout, and he could make no impression on the mind of the sanguinary Tuscan. Finally, having made the round of all Italy, D'Azeglio arrived in Turin (1845), and demanded an audience of his sovereign.

We have said that Charles Albert had a fascination

for those who approached him. D'Azeglio had armed himself against this influence, and while the king, who had not seen him for a long time, was courteously inquiring after his welfare, he said to himself, ' Massimo, trust him not!'

'Whence do you come now?' asked the king.

D'Azeglio then seized the moment to explain his mission. He said he had been travelling in all parts of Italy, and if his majesty permitted he would like to tell him the state of public affairs. Charles Albert said, ' Pray speak ; I shall be glad to hear you.'

D'Azeglio spoke at some length. He began by alluding briefly to the rebellions, their causes and effects. Then he passed on to the present disturbed state of the nation ; dwelt on the danger of a revolution at the Pope's death ; but said that for the most part the people were convinced of the folly of such attempts. They desired a new and more moderate plan of action, and they looked to Piedmont only for a leader. He then related all he had done in concert with the reform party, and assured the king that he had never been a member of a secret society.

' And now,' he concluded, ' your majesty will tell me whether you approve or disapprove of what I have done.'

He paused for a reply ; and, according to his preconceived idea of Charles Albert's doubleness, expected an evasive one. Instead of that, the king, without a moment's hesitation, fixed his eyes frankly on those of D'Azeglio, and said in a calm, resolute tone :—

' Let those gentlemen know that for the present they must remain quiet ; but when the time comes, let them be certain *my life, the lives of my sons, my arms, my treasures—all shall be freely spent in the Italian cause.*'

D'Azeglio, whose loyalty till now had been of the coldest, was touched by the king's heroic sentiments, and thanked him with emotion for his confidence. When they both rose to their feet, Charles Albert laid his hands on D'Azeglio's shoulders, and touched first one cheek and then the other with his own. There was something so solemn, almost funereal, in this embrace, that it somewhat chilled D'Azeglio's enthusiasm. In after years he said he could never see without a thrill those green silk chairs in the bay-window where they sat while the king offered, through him, to his country, all he possessed—even his life.

D'Azeglio communicated the result of his interview with the king, in cypher, to his correspondents; and, in obedience to a suggestion of his majesty, began to write a pamphlet for the furtherance of their scheme. It was to be a vast society extending over all Italy; its proceedings carried on in open day, without arms, or oaths, or concealment; its object the gradual redemption of the whole peninsula from the hands of the foreigner. He felt painfully how difficult it was to rouse a population sunk in misery and ignorance to a feeling of citizenship; and part of the reform scheme was to improve the condition of the people, and educate them. 'Before forming Italy, we must first form the Italians,' he often said.

Great secrecy was observed on the part of the Liberal party so as not to compromise the King of Sardinia; but in spite of this it crept out that he was giving them his adhesion, and he began to be received with warm demonstrations when he appeared at the reviews. Austria's suspicions were aroused; but Charles Albert's spirits were raised and sustained by the joyful news of the accession to the papal throne of the reforming liberal Pio Nono.

D'Azeglio, who had been banished from Rome for his attack on the late popes, wheedled himself into the good graces of the new pontiff, and used all his arts to bind him to the reform party. He writes thus to his wife:—

> I found Rome completely changed—joyous, full of hope and confidence in the future. The old party falls lower and lower every day; it still works mischief, however.

He evidently thought he could lead the good-natured pontiff by the nose; and he conciliated him in every possible way, while he worked hard by speeches and meetings to make the people loyal to their new sovereign, trusting altogether to gentle persuasion to obtain the desired reforms. He writes again to his wife:—

> The Pope was much pleased, and in dismissing me said, 'Marchese d'Azeglio, I bless you. Continue always in the moderate course you have chosen.' I have now the approbation of Pio Nono, which is no little thing. We are forming a society called *Concordia*, which I hope will extend over all Italy; objects: to improve the condition, moral, civil, and social, of the nation; means: law, moderation, absolute publicity, absolute absence of secrets and mysteries. We shall combat the excesses of both parties; and in the people, gambling in the lotteries, and drink. We shall promote education and establish schools. We shall send into the provinces agents to propagate our doctrines. Amongst its founders are monsignori and citizens of the highest class. The Duke Cesarini gives funds, and his palace, provisionally, for our meetings.

D'Azeglio and his colleagues had their hands full, preaching patience and moderation to the Romans, promising that the Pope would institute all needful reforms—and at the same time urging Pio Nono forward, while the powerful retrograde party were pulling him back.

The people believed the leaders of the moderate party; they believed in the reforming Pope, who was at that moment the most popular sovereign in Europe. The 'Hymn of Pio Nono' was sung at the theatre amidst rapturous applause, the audience standing and waving their handkerchiefs. In short, the enthusiastic Romans were wild with loyalty to their priest-king, under whose beneficent rule religion and liberty were to be at last reconciled. The Pope's charming manners, and benevolent, handsome face, did a great deal to win the faith of the people; and they followed him in thousands to his palace to receive the papal benediction from the balcony. This ceremony of marching to the Quirinal, and calling out the Pope, became a regular institution at Rome. D'Azeglio describes it as a soul-stirring scene, the vast piazza filled with thousands and thousands of people, who, at the sight of the noble figure and beaming face of the Pontiff, dropped on their knees, while in a voice of thrilling sweetness he gave the Benediction.

But there was another power at work besides the Moderates and the Retrogrades, who were tearing Pio Nono in opposite directions. There were the members of the Society of Giovane Italia, who, acting under the directions of Mazzini, were exciting the people to violent demonstrations, in order to goad the Pope to sweeping reforms, and make him commit himself irretrievably to an advanced liberal policy. These agents of Mazzini gathered the people together on every possible pretext, and by degrees began to introduce national cries such as '*Viva l'Italia! Fuori lo straniero!*' mixed up with applause and loyal exclamations for the sovereign. Still, though one secret society thus worked upon the people, and played upon the vanity of the Pontiff, there is no just reason to believe that the great bulk of the Romans were insincere in the affection that they professed for Pio Nono, or that Pio Nono was insincere in his professions of affection for his subjects, and his earnest desire to improve their condition. He had been an excellent bishop, and he would have made an excellent Pope, if circumstances had not rendered it next to impossible. The writings of Balbo, and the philosopher-priest Gioberti, had made a deep impression on him, and he had come to the throne with the noblest aspirations of regenerating not the Roman states only, but all Italy. On the other hand, the subjects of Leo XII. and Gregory XVI. might well be fascinated by such a man as Pius IX., whose many virtues shone with all the more lustre from the contrast presented by the character of his predecessors. The fact that this mutual good-will did not last is not a reason to believe it feigned. There were causes enough in the great divergence of opinion which afterwards arose between the Pope and his subjects to create the breach which ended so unhappily, without accusing either party of unusual fickleness.

In the beginning of 1847 the Romans began to feel restive and impatient. For nearly a year they had been fed on smiles, benedictions, and a few trifling concessions. D'Azeglio writes to his brother:—

> You can tell the king, if a favourable opportunity occurs—I do not care to write it by post, but I want you to know it as soon as possible—I am convinced—it wrings my heart to say it—but I am convinced *the magic of Pio Nono will not last.* He is an angel, but is surrounded by demons; he has a disordered state and corrupt elements, and he will not be able to combat the obstacles.

Meantime Charles Albert was making preparations which could no longer be concealed. He had medals struck with his image, and the motto, which he had taken from the shield of a remote ancestor, *J'attends mon astre*, and secretly distributed them amongst the Liberals. D'Azeglio's pamphlets were also circulated by royal permission in the Sardinian states, though he did not dare to print them there for fear of compromising the king before the moment for action arrived.

Although Pio Nono had done little more than smile, and bless the Liberals when they put themselves strikingly under his notice, yet he had offended the despotic power of Austria, and in the summer of 1847 she proceeded to the hostile step of violating the papal territory and occupying Ferrara. All the Roman provinces were ready to rush to arms to resent the indignity. Money and arms poured in from all quarters to the holy father, with ardent protestations of devotion. Charles Albert despatched a letter to say he regarded the quarrel as his own, it being a violation of the independence of the Italian princes. But the Pope held back and vacillated, putting off taking any decided step beyond sending an indignant protest to the Austrian general, until the Romans rose and threatened to burn the cardinals' palaces if troops were not sent to defend the provinces. Then,

THE CONSTITUTION GRANTED. 27

unwillingly, he gave his consent, but faltered again, and wished to recall them when they arrived at their destination, declaring he never meant to *make war*, only to *protect* his states against aggression.

Charles Albert meanwhile was bracing his nerves for the death-struggle with Austria; and as a preliminary step he decided on granting the constitution so long desired by the Piedmontese people. This important act would, he knew, give mortal offence to Austria, and cut him off from all kinship with the other Italian princes. But he had the Pope on his side; and he said in the council, 'If Austria is against us, Italy will be with us.' Next day, February 7, 1848, a royal proclamation made public his consent to the much-desired *Statuto*. The citizens of Turin, wild with joy, but still doubting, ran to the palace, singing the 'Hymn of Pio Nono,' then a national song. The pale face and tall form of Charles Albert appeared on the balcony, with his sons by his side, holding the tricolour in his hands. The people shouted, wept, embraced each other, and swore eternal fealty to the House of Savoy.

What the conscientious King of Piedmont granted voluntarily, the sovereigns of Tuscany and Naples were compelled to cede to the unanimous demand of their people.

All Italy was on fire. Lombardy and Venice were already in arms, and the Milanese, after five days of terrible fighting, drove the Austrian troops out of the city. The declaration of the War of Independence could be no longer delayed. The last grand act of the drama in which Charles Albert played the part of hero began with that declaration of war; the rest of his life is so bound up with that of his son, whose story we have undertaken to relate, that we will pursue it no further in this chapter.

CHAPTER II.

BIRTH, EDUCATION, MARRIAGE. A.D. 1820–42.

ON March 14, 1820, in the Carignano Palace, Turin, the eldest son of Charles Albert of Savoy-Carignano first saw the light. The child was born a little after midnight, and next day he was received into the bosom of the Catholic Church,—King Victor Emmanuel and his queen assisting at the ceremony, in which the august godfather bestowed on his little cousin his own name, and a liberal supply of other appellations. The child was baptised, Vittorio Emanuele Maria Alberto Eugenio Ferdinando Tommaso.

Before a year passed the Carbonari revolution, and the consequent change of sovereigns, drove the Prince of Carignano into exile. The infant years of Victor Emmanuel were passed in a villa outside of Florence, called Poggio Imperiale, and there, when he was two years old, the life on which Italy's destinies hung was all but extinguished. His nurse, Teresa Bacca, a Turin woman, having accidentally set fire to his bed-curtains, only with difficulty saved him from the flames. He was slightly burned, and the unfortunate nurse died a few days after of the injuries she received. A tablet placed on the spot by the Provisional Government of Tuscany commemorates the accident.

In this same year, 1822, was born Charles Albert's second son, the Duke of Genoa. This baby brother was the object of intense interest and affection to the little Victor, who used to run every minute to the nursery, which adjoined his own room, to look at him and kiss him. His mother writes of him :—

My little Victor is very docile; I have, however, some
   difficulty in teaching him, for he wants to be always

running or jumping, but when he once learns a thing he rarely forgets it.

The future hero's chief delight in infant years was playing at war—constructing armies of little wooden soldiers, and putting them through military evolutions. The child felt with his parents, that he was an exile from the paternal abode, and at four years old he said to his mother, 'I am impatient to see papa's house.'

Very soon after this they returned to Piedmont, and lived in retirement in their castle of Racconigi, where Charles Albert devoted himself to the mental and physical training of his sons. He wished to give them a high intellectual education, but also to familiarise them with a soldier's duties, so that they should not be inferior to their ancestors in courage, strength, and daring. So, between learned bishops and professors in the classroom, and military tutors and drill-sergeants out of doors, the young princes had a pretty hard time of it, and not a minute to spare to get into mischief, from morning till night. They were up at five o'clock in the morning, when they began their studies, and continued them till late in the day, only broken by the hours allotted for meals, and diversified by a fencing lesson, a long walk, or a six hours' ride on horseback. The Princess of Carignano did not like to see her little boys kept under such severe soldierly discipline, and often reproached her husband for his excessive rigour.

But notwithstanding this severity, and the strict court etiquette which always accompanies an absolute monarchy, and which obliges the son of the prince to maintain towards his sire an attitude of distant respect, —Victor Emmanuel understood and appreciated his good father, whom he loved devotedly, and regarded as an ideal hero.

When Prince Victor was fifteen his father succeeded to the throne; and just about that time he wrote a life of one of his ancestors, Amadeus VI., surnamed Conte Verde. This juvenile production is dedicated 'A Papa' on one side of the page, and 'Au Roi' on the other, and signed 'P. Victor de Savoie,' in a bold clear hand. The letter, which is prettily composed in the French language, begins 'Sire,' and concludes with these words:—

Deign, my very dear father, to throw a kind glance on this effort of your son Victor, full of the desire to please you, and to give you some proofs of his tender and respectful attachment, proofs which he would have wished to render more worthy of you.

Almost all the compositions of the Duke of Savoy at this period treat of military subjects, such as the arrangement of an army in a plain, the siege of a fortress, the passage of a river, the defence of a wood, etc. One is entitled, 'The History of the Treaties between the different Powers of Europe, in which reference is made to the Savoy Dynasty.' The subjects were suitable studies for the heir to the throne which must be held by the sword.

Every Wednesday morning in Turin, in spite of burning sun, or pouring rain, or drifting snow, the drums beat and the trumpets blew for the military to repair to the Piazza d'Armi, where the King held a grand review, in which he was always assisted by his sons. An extraordinary sympathy and friendship had always united these brothers from infancy. They were inseparable as twins; no boyish emulation, no ambitious rivalry in manhood, ever cooled the fraternal affection, which is a beautiful trait in the character of the Savoy family. The brothers were equally brave, generous, kind-hearted, but Victor's fiery, impetuous nature, and overflowing animal spirits, were tempered by the prudent counsels of the graver, calmer Ferdinand, who resembled his father in character much more than did the elder son. Prince Victor's fine, manly qualities, and pleasant, genial manners endeared him to all his teachers and masters; in a special manner to two—Monsignor Charvaz, afterwards Archbishop of Genoa, and Colonel Dabormida, afterwards general and minister of state. The general's affection for his royal pupil surpassed the common devotion of a faithful subject, and was fully returned by the prince. Having received one day from the king, his father, an intimation of his friend's promotion, he writes thus :—

> Carissimo,—I experienced the greatest pleasure in receiving this note that his majesty sends me, while I listen to the relations of the Minister of War, *J'ai signé la patente de Dabormida*, and I hasten to announce it to you. I do not know, dear friend, and dear lieutenant-colonel, how I can express to you the gratification this gives me, but you know how I love you, and that everything that gives you pleasure gives me a great deal. . . . We have here (at Genoa) the third son of Prince ———. He is a handsome youth, tall as my brother, but very *efflanqué*. We are always together; he asks me everything he ought to do, and seems much embarrassed with his person, which ought not to be after ten years' travelling in all parts of the globe. He is about my age, and knows nothing of the usages of the world. One evening he was in company at the Lady ———'s, and sat opposite to her before a roasting fire, without knowing how to take himself away. Monday we must manœuvre with seventeen battalions before the prince. I shall command the Savona regiment and Royal Marines, forming a reserve.

The Duke of Savoy had now reached his twenty-first birthday; and on the whole Charles Albert was not disappointed in the heir on whom he had lavished such care and affection. His father's training had not succeeded in making him a learned man, for his natural bent was towards action rather than study; but he was a keen observer of men and things, had a large endowment of good sense, wide sympathies, and shared to the full his father's generous ambition to liberate Italy from the foreign yoke, and bring fresh lustre to the ancient race from which he sprang.

This *ancestry worship*, with other chivalrous ideas of bygone times, is a striking characteristic of the House of Savoy. The children of that house have always been nourished and fed upon the traditions of ancestral heroes, and taught that they ought to endeavour to resemble them to the utmost of their ability. The religious reverence which every son of the Sabaud family entertains for the early founders of the house, as much as for his immediate progenitors, has always acted as a powerful incentive to their daring deeds. 'A people,' says Macaulay, 'who take no pride in the noble achievements of remote ancestors will never achieve anything worthy to be remembered by remote descendants.' Without a particle of personal vanity, this pride of race was a passion in Victor Emmanuel. An exiled Neapolitan general once said to him that there were two sovereigns in Europe who might serve as a warning and example for a young prince—Ferdinand of Naples, and Leopold of Belgium; to which Victor replied with a proud smile and flashing eye, 'General, I need not go out of my own family for examples of loyalty and heroism. Enough for me to remember the deeds of my ancestors.'

The prince was of middle stature, broad shouldered, powerfully built, with a brown complexion, snub nose, and a heavy underjaw; his full brown beard, and fierce-looking moustache curling upon his cheek, were not then such striking characteristics as afterwards. Notwithstanding this homely exterior, the intelligence, good sense, and good feeling expressed in his broad open brow and kindly smile, won confidence and sympathy at a glance. His ardent, dauntless spirit might be read in the steady unflinching glance of his piercing dark eye, which was never seen to quail for an instant in the presence of any earthly peril. His manners were frank and simple, but not wanting in a certain soldierly dignity.

Such was Victor Emmanuel of Savoy in his twenty-second year, when he began to pay court to his fair cousin, Maria Adelaide, daughter of the Archduke Ranieri, Viceroy of Lombardy-Venice. The mother of the princess was the only and beloved sister of Charles Albert, and the frequent intercourse of the families led to an intimacy between the young people. Victor's cousinly affection quickly grew into love, and he did not fail to inspire in Adelaide a corresponding sentiment, which, if less ardent, proved more constant than his. The only possible objection to an alliance with the archduchess was her Austrian birth; it was a strong one to Charles Albert at that moment, and would make the marriage very unpopular in Piedmont. But as she was Italian and Sabaud on her mother's side, the king overcame the difficulty, and yielded to the wishes of his son. The marriage took place in 1842, when the duke was twenty-two years old, and his bride nineteen. King Charles Albert celebrated the event with all sorts of fêtes, and among other diversions was the novel one of a tournament, not so strange at the Savoy court as it would have been elsewhere, for in no other country have old chivalric customs and ideas lingered so long as in the Sardinian states. The people looked coldly on these festivities, disapproving of the marriage, as a new tie to bind their sovereign to Austrian interests. In a very short time, however, the charming qualities of the Princess Adelaide completely gained the hearts of the Piedmontese, and the manly loyalty of this brave people won the affection of the princess, who had cast in her lot with them for weal or woe. She must have imbibed from her mother some of the sentiment of Italian nationality; and even if it were not so, the gentle young wife could not have resisted the overwhelming influence of a husband to whom she was so deeply attached. *His* soul was so permeated with the idea of national independence that she could hardly love Victor without loving Italy.

The Princess Adelaide was very pious; but neither the Austrians nor the Jesuits were able to make use of her influence to the prejudice of Italian interests. When it came to a question of war between her husband and father it nearly broke her heart; but she was still true to Victor and to Italy. A Neapolitan gentleman records that just before the battle of Novara he was seated beside the Duchess of Savoy, who asked him the news of his country. He replied that they would

D

denounce the armistice and appeal once more to arms. 'We also denounce the armistice. Fatal necessity!' said the princess, and her eyes filled with tears.

Maria Adelaide was a princess of boundless charity. She kept an exact register of the poor of the city; she knew their names, occupations, maladies, etc., and sacrificed her time, and many luxuries of dress and jewels, to supply their wants. When her husband brought her a magnificent present, she said it was too handsome for her, the money would have done so much for her poor pensioners. 'She was a most excellent wife and mother,' says Ghiron, 'giving constant care to the education of her children, being herself their teacher, ever present at their studies, their recreations, their meals; and in educating them she followed the principles of the House of Savoy, which requires its sons to be robust and courageous. We have the results in those two brave princes who exposed their lives on the field of battle like common soldiers; in Prince Amedeo, who sustained such a bitter struggle on the throne from which he retired only when it was necessary to use force; in Queen Maria Pia of Portugal, who threw herself into the waves to save her son; in the Princess Clotilde, who proclaimed the incontestable truth that "Fear and Savoy had never yet met."'

The friends of Victor Emmanuel assert that he was a loving husband, and deeply attached to his sweet young queen, whose noble qualities he fully appreciated. His enemies, on the other hand, pronounce him a brute, a monster, a demon, who broke the heart of his saintly wife and brought her to an early grave. Neither of these stories is strictly true, but the least false is that told by the Liberal party. It is true that he was very fond of and kind to his wife, and that he retained her affection to the latest hour of her existence. She died of an acute disease, not of a broken heart; but that he was guilty of certain gallantries during her lifetime, which must have caused her deep pain, is equally true. We do not mean to chalk over the spots on our hero's fame. He had his faults, but they were redeemed by many noble qualities.

CHAPTER III.

THE YOUNG SOLDIER. A.D. 1848.

THE Duke of Savoy, as we have said, was liberal to the heart's core, and hailed with intense joy his father's adoption of the national cause. When the news arrived of the rising of Milan on March 18, 1848, and the famous Five Days that followed, ending in the expulsion of the Austrians, Turin was convulsed with joyful excitement, and the citizens crowded in the piazzas, demanding arms from the government to go to the aid of their Lombard brothers. The king and princes were deeply agitated; though war was pending, they did not expect such a sudden explosion. A Cabinet council was held, and orders were given that the military were to be put in motion as soon as possible to cross the Ticino. Another council was held to make the necessary military appointments. The prince was not present at the council, and though he was burning to flesh his maiden sword in Austrian breasts, did not know but the government might forbid his going to the seat of war. Count Cesar Balbo, the historian, was then at the head of affairs; and as he was returning home from the council he was conscious of some one following his steps. At last he turned round and faced a gentleman wrapped in a mantle so as to disguise his face.

'What do you want of me?' he asked.

'Don't you recognise me?' asked a well-known voice, and the prince threw back his mantle. 'I am come to pray you not to forget me when forming the divisions of the army that is to cross the Ticino.' Then he said in a voice of concentrated, intense anxiety, 'Am I to have a command? I entreat you, speak to my father immediately.'

Count Balbo replied, 'It is the intention of his majesty to give you a command. Be tranquil; the

Duke of Savoy could not be, and has not been forgotten.'

Victor caught his hand and pressed it warmly; then wrapped himself in his mantle, and bounded away joyously.

'During the campaign the young general comported himself valorously,' says Massari. 'Without using a profusion of words, it is enough to say that under the canvas or in the battle-field he showed himself worthy of his race. He who knows the story of the Savoy dynasty knows that there is no higher eulogium than this.'

Apart from the sentiments of patriotism which he felt so strongly, the danger of war had as romantic a fascination for Victor Emmanuel as for any young knight of mediæval days. In the hunting excursions amidst Alpine snows and glaciers he was famous for the reckless daring of his wild exploits, in which he seemed to court danger for its own sake. When he first heard the rattle of musketry and booming of cannon on the battle-field, and knew the enemy was in front of him, he cried out, 'Ah, *this* is the music that pleases me!'

His first taste of war was at Santa Lucia, May 6, where he gallantly led his brigade, and behaved so well that he was awarded a silver medal for valour. Those who have seen Victor Emmanuel on his war-horse in moments of danger say that there was something soul-stirring in his aspect. He looked such a perfect soldier, and displayed such a reckless gallantry in his impetuous charges, that he inspired the wildest enthusiasm in the troops. He was a good general in every respect. He guarded against surprises, looked after the comforts of his men, particularly the sick and wounded, and bore any amount of fatigue and hardship uncomplainingly.

At Goito, however, the experienced Austrians outwitted the Piedmontese, coming upon them at a moment when they were weary after a long march, and had laid down their arms to prepare themselves some refreshments. The prince, who was just retiring to his tent when the firing began, sprang to the saddle and galloped to the spot. The Piedmontese, weary, hungry, and surprised unarmed, had not recovered their presence of mind, and were making but a feeble resistance to the fresh and vigorous Austrian troops. One regiment was beginning to break up, and give way, when the Duke of Savoy threw himself before the soldiers, and addressing them with that generous indignation which makes men ashamed of weakness, forced them to turn and face the enemy. His own dauntless courage communicated itself to his followers, who contested the field most heroically.

An eye-witness, the Duke of Dino, thus describes the crisis :—

> There was a moment when victory seemed to smile on the Austrians. Then I saw pass before me like a whirlwind a young general, his Arab horse covered with foam, his spurs stained with blood. The cavalier with eyes flashing fire, and moustache bristling on end, precipitated himself, sword in hand, towards a splendid regiment of the guards; he pulled up opposite to it, and cried out, 'With me, guards, to save the honour of Savoy!' A general shout responded to the chivalrous invitation. The regiment put itself in motion instantly, and the fight was more desperate than ever. The Austrians paused, retreated; received new reinforcements, and then returned to the attack. They were on the point of overpowering the guards, whose officers gave the greatest proof of valour. In the midst of the smoke and fire the young general appeared and disappeared from my sight like lightning. He galloped up and down the field, encouraging the soldiers with voice and gesture, and though wounded by a ball in the thigh, still stood firm in the fiercest struggle. At last General d'Arvillars ordered a light battery to advance. When this opened fire the Austrians paused, and became confused, and then the Cuneo Brigade rushing into the combat, they soon sounded a retreat. I asked an officer who passed me, wounded, 'Who is that general

who so courageously exposed his life?' 'The Duke of Savoy.'

'Viva Casa Savoya!' cried the Duke of Dino; 'the descendants of Emanuele Filiberto have not degenerated.'

While this desperate fight was going on, King Charles Albert, pale and immovable, sat on his horse like the statue of an ancient cavalier, giving his orders with a calm and stately dignity, as if he were on the parade. As the Duke of Savoy had just driven the Austrians from their last stand-point, and they were in full retreat, the king received a despatch, and turning to his officers, said: 'Gentlemen, Peschiera is ours. My son, the Duke of Genoa, gives me news of its surrender.' At that moment the crown prince rode up, with blood-stained garments and radiant face. 'Majesty,' he said, with a military salute, 'the battle of to-day shall be called the victory of Goito.' It was a proud and happy moment for the king and father, who had few such in his life, and whose feelings were all the more intense because of the habitual restraint in which he held them; a moment of delirious joy to the crown prince, and of true, deep-felt enthusiasm on the part of the army, who with acclamations long and loud saluted Charles Albert as the liberator of Italy.

'Viva l'Italia! Viva Carlo Alberto! Viva Vittorio!' were the cries that rang from regiment to regiment, then taken up, and repeated again and again, throughout the camp. Victor Emmanuel was intoxicated with delight. The rare honour of a gold medal for valour was awarded to him; but his wound was more precious still. It was, fortunately, not so serious as to disable him from active service, but enough to give him the delicious sensation of having shed his blood for Italy. He did not conceal his boyish delight in the fact, and said to his attendants, 'How the Duke of Genoa will envy me this!'

Alas! it was a short-lived triumph. The glory of Goito was doomed ere long to be extinguished in blood and tears.

'Twere long to tell, and sad to trace,'

the causes of the disastrous issue of this campaign. It was meant to be a national war. Charles Albert believed, as many others did, that he was to lead an Italian, not a Piedmontese army, for the expulsion of the foreigner from Italian soil. The Romagna, Tuscany, Lombardy, Venice, and Naples had all declared their determination to unite in one great effort to liberate the whole country from Austrian oppression. The Pope had an army already in the field near Ferrara to combat Austrian aggression, the Lombards were actually in arms before the King of Sardinia had crossed the Ticino. He had said in his proclamation: 'I will do my best to further your just desires, aided by that Providence which has given to Italy a Pio Nono.' The Pope had proposed a league between the Italian princes for the protection of the peninsula, which he hoped would soon bring matters to a peaceful solution; he meant to go to Lombardy himself, and throw the weight of his spiritual authority into the scale of Italian independence, which—added to the united arms of all the principalities—would bring Austria to see the matter from a just and Christian point of view. There can be little doubt that the Pope was honestly patriotic in his intentions, though the republican writers will not acknowledge it, and invariably class him with the other princes who acted so false a part on this occasion. All the sovereigns declared themselves disposed to follow the lead of the good Pope in everything. They granted constitutions all round with a great flourish of trumpets, and loudly declared they shared the sentiments of their 'beloved subjects,' in their hatred of the foreign yoke. Ferdinand II.'s patriotic fire burned stronger than that of any other. 'War with Austria,' he said, was his soul's desire. He had always 'detested Austria.' One can hardly take in the full depth of this man's treachery without reading his long proclamation to his 'most beloved people,' on the occasion of the declaration of war, in which he says, 'Our brothers await us on the field of honour, and we shall not fail them,' and concludes with these words:—

Union, abnegation, firmness—and the independence of our beautiful Italy shall be accomplished. Let this be our only thought; so generous a passion silences all other less noble ones. Before long 24,000,000 Italians will have a country—a common and rich patrimony of glory, etc., etc.

The Grand Duke of Tuscany was not behind his royal brothers; and it must be owned that they had all learned the language of the Nationalists admirably. Leopold's address to his soldiers is so short that we are tempted to quote it.

Soldiers!—The holy cause of the independence of Italy is to be decided now on the fields of Lombardy. Already the citizens of Milan have bought—with their blood, and by a heroism the like of which history offers few examples—their liberty. Already the Sardic army moves to the field, led by its magnanimous king, under whose orders fight the royal princes. Sons of Italy, heirs of the glory of their ancestors, the Tuscans cannot, must not, remain in shameful ease at such a solemn moment. Fly then, unite yourselves to the valiant citizens who as volunteers are ranging themselves under our banner—fly to the succour of our Lombard brothers, etc., etc.

The little Dukes of Modena and Parma were drawn along in the wake of their powerful neighbours. They expressed great repentance for having yielded so long to Austrian domination—because they could not help it; henceforth they should put themselves under the direction of his holiness the Pope, the King of Sardinia, and the Grand Duke of Tuscany. *They* also made out a *statuto*, and swore to it; and sent forth their little contingents to aid in the national war. The wildest enthusiasm prevailed in every part of Italy; the great sacrifices that were made by the poor as well as the rich attested the sincerity of the sentiment which burned in the breasts of all Italians who deserved to be called such. The young women who had no ornaments to give sold their abundant tresses to contribute to the expenses of the volunteers.

Led by their princes, blessed by the Pope, the people felt they were going to fight in the holiest of causes. 'And holy it was, because it was a war of independence,' says Farini.

> Imprudent or no, it was holy. Holy, because a war of independence is always holy. A war of defence only is always legitimate, because to repulse and expel a foreign invader from our country is to defend our welfare, our honour, our sepulchres—all that a man holds dear and sacred, from the altar of God to the kiss of his beloved. And the foreigner is always a domineering tyrant. He cannot be other than a tyrant. Even his civilisation, his gentleness, his liberality are refinements of tyranny. Holy, then, was the war of independence; holy the enthusiasm that kindled the population in the Roman State, in the spring of 1848; holy the gifts and the sacrifices that they made.[1]

But the glorious hopes of the Italian nation were blasted by the weakness and treachery of the sovereigns. The army of the King of Naples took as long to reach Lombardy as they would have taken to go to the Holy Land. They never went farther than Bologna, where the commander, Pepe, received an order to return to Naples with the troops. This he could not bring himself to do, so resigned his post to an inferior, who, in obedience to secret orders from the king, had undermined and thwarted him all through the march. The officers and men were filled with shame and grief; some deserted and volunteered in the Sardinian army, but most of them submitted to the authority of their superiors. One officer is said to have died, literally of grief,

---

[1] *Lo Stato Romano dal* 1815 *al* 1850. The illustrious author, Luigi Carlo Farini, is a most trustworthy historian of the events in which he took an active and important part. He was a Moderate, high in favour with Pio Nono in the Pontiff's liberal days, and one of the few whose attachment to him seems to have survived his apostasy. His book has the additional interest to the English reader of being dedicated to William E. Gladstone.

and it is certain that another committed suicide. The grand duke's army was similarly rendered useless by secret orders to hoodwink and delude the Sardinians with the false hope of aid.

The Lombards, who had begun the war with such heroism as was displayed in the Five Days' struggle, did not maintain the same noble bearing throughout; they were divided among themselves and failed to support the Piedmontese as the king had been led to expect. They and the Venetians spent the precious time in disputing as to what form of government they would have, while the Austrians were still in possession of Italian soil. The Mazzinians were busy haranguing against monarchies, and circulating libellous stories about the Savoy family, while that family were doing more than any other in Italy to defend the rights and liberties of the nation.

The Romans, on whom King Charles had been taught to rely much, were rendered almost useless by the extraordinary indecision of Pius IX., who, as soon as he had committed himself to a straightforward course of action, directly after stultified himself by some contradiction. Though he protested against Austrian outrages on the frontier, and sent troops to defend it, he did away with the effect of these proceedings by saying that he did not mean to make war. Radetsky knew how to avail himself of this weakness, and issued a proclamation saying that as the holy father had said repeatedly that he would not make war, he regarded the Roman soldiers as outlaws, and would shoot every man he found bearing arms; which he accordingly did. This naturally had a demoralising effect on the troops, and all the more because they were not allowed to cross the Po and meet the Austrians in honourable warfare. General Durando could not wring a consent from the Pontiff, and he found himself in the position of making war on his own account, till at last the fear of a popular rising in Rome obliged the Pope to put his troops under the command of Charles Albert. But the papal army was very much inferior in spirits and numbers then to what it had been when it marched out of Rome, and did not render very effectual aid in the contest.

Thus, in point of fact, if we except the volunteers, gallant little Piedmont was left alone to fight the battle of Italian independence. Marshal Radetsky, having made short work of the papal troops at Vicenza, collected his forces, and concentrated them on the point where he could most easily come upon the Sardinian army, small in numbers, exhausted by heat, fatigue, and fevers. The first reverse they had was at Sommacampagna, the royal family not being present at the engagement. They hastened forward and encountered the enemy at Staffala, and attacked them with such vigour that they drove them from the field, taking 2,000 prisoners, arms, colours, etc. Victor Emmanuel was the leading spirit of this battle. For the past two months, during which the army had suffered much from fever and other causes, the prince, by his admirable discipline, the kindly interest he took in the men, and the soldier-like manner in which he shared their hardships, had endeared himself more and more to them.

The victory of Staffala was won under great difficulties; a wasted army, encamped in a low, hot plain, under a burning July sun, was not equal to another such effort. But on the morrow the Piedmontese were called to defend themselves from a fresh attack, and they did it gallantly, desperately, but all in vain. The Austrian officers bore testimony to the valour of the Duke of Savoy and his brother, who led their men again and again to the assault, and were finally driven back only when all hope was over. This battle, fought at Custoza, near Villafranca, left the Italian army almost crushed, morally and physically.

Charles Albert was advised to retreat across the Po, and fortify himself in Piacenza. But the evil genius which had presided over all his public acts did not forsake him now. His generous disposition led him to neglect this prudent counsel, and betake himself to the aid of Milan. D'Azeglio said:—

Since Lombardy and Venice will not unite, I told the

king that his duty, the good of Italy, the welfare of the cause, required that he should retreat to Piedmont and defend it, where he could preserve an Italian army for a better occasion. Another defeat will render this occasion hopeless for centuries; and with one sole army we should not risk it.

But Charles Albert did risk it; he threw himself into Milan. Badly provisioned and badly defended against a powerful victorious army, the struggle became hopeless, and he capitulated. It was then that the Milanese populace effaced the glory of the Five Days by their cruel ingratitude to the too-generous king, who had all but sacrificed his own state to protect them. Goaded by the Mazzinians, they cried out that he was a traitor, and might have taken his life if he had not escaped from the city before his sons had come to his rescue.

The populace of Milan were saved from the infamy of personal outrage towards the king by the daring feat of a young Piedmontese major, who with a few followers came under his balcony at midnight, and carried him off out of the city. This brave officer had already given evidence of the noblest gifts of heart and mind, and he was destined in the future to win immortal honour for the Italian arms, and cover with new glory the ancient name of La Marmora.

The unhappy Charles Albert, whose destiny it was still to be misunderstood, recrossed the Ticino with the firm intention of resuming the war. The advice of England and France was strongly against a renewal of the contest, as was that of many brave, wise men in Italy. But the heedless people demanded it, and called everyone a traitor who opposed it; and the poor king, feeling his honour and the honour of Piedmont to be at stake, went almost without hope to his doom.

On March 20, 1849, the war was renewed, and was ended in three days by the utter overthrow of the Italian arms at Novara, a defeat which postponed the work of independence for ten years. The Piedmontese army as well as the king, expected defeat, for they were utterly broken in spirits and health. Even the sanguine, high-spirited Victor Emmanuel went sadly with clouded brow to this last campaign. 'We were unfortunate,' said he to a friend, 'but we were also betrayed by many persons.' The prince probably meant the secret adherents of Austria; but the republicans helped largely to ruin the national cause for the time. The one conspicuous person who was openly false to his duty, and who suffered the just punishment of his treachery, was General Ramorino. He was ordered to hold the passage of the Po against the Austrian army, while the king was collecting his forces at Magenta. He left the passage open, the enemy passed into the country, and cut off the Piedmontese from their basis of operations.

At Sforzesca the Italians met with a success, but at Mortara the great body of the Austrian army was concentrated; and there General Durando and the Duke of Savoy encountered them, and after a long-contested, bloody battle, were utterly defeated. The Italians and Austrians fought through the streets of Mortara after night fell, and committed fearful havoc not only on one another but the unfortunate citizens. General Durando fought his way inch by inch out of the town, and joined the Duke of Savoy and La Marmora, who were trying to collect together the miserable remains of the army. The divisions of Durando and the prince, which had been the flower of the army, were no longer in existence. With heart oppressed by grief, Victor set out for his father's quarters, where the fatal news had preceded him. Charles Albert had received his son with sedate composure when he rushed up to him with the cry of victory on his lips; but now his paternal heart was moved by the young man's misfortune. He embraced him with emotion, and told him that he knew he had comported himself as became a son of the Savoy family.

The king never raised his head after this; he knew he must be defeated in the last great encounter, and was resolved to seek death. Throughout the march to Novara his aide-de-camp heard him murmur broken-hearted words, unconscious that anyone was listening. '*C'est tout fini pour moi,*' he said repeatedly. March 23 was the fatal day which extinguished for so many years all hope of Italian independence. The morning broke gloomily in a drizzling rain, and soon came to a heavy fall which lasted all day, mingling with the streams of blood, which, hopeless though they knew it was, the Italians did not shrink from pouring out like water. To die in vain, seemed to the king and his brave followers all that was left for them to do. We have heard innumerable touching stories of individual heroism displayed on the field of Novara, and these were only in keeping with the general conduct of the whole army. Radetsky said the Piedmontese 'fought like devils,' and there were moments when he feared that he must give way before them.

General Perron, heading a desperate assault, had his skull broken. He begged the men who supported him to lay him at the king's feet, and with his last convulsive breath he said, 'Sire, I offered to you and my country the last days of my life. My duty is accomplished.' A captain of artillery having an arm shot off, never left his post, but rallied his men and rushed again to the assault. A young boy pointing a cannon had his hand taken away. His father seeing him look pale asked him was he wounded? He raised the bleeding stump, and cried, *Viva il Rè!* This heroic boy, Carlo di Robilant by name, is now Italian ambassador at Vienna. Count Balbo had sent his five sons to the war, and all were engaged in this last combat; one of them fell by too strict obedience to his commander's orders. These deeds of vain heroism only wrung the heart of the unhappy king, who, wherever he turned his haggard eyes, saw his brave people overwhelmed by fresh reinforcements, falling thick and fast upon the field. He was fighting for more than life, for that without which life would be insupportable; and seeing it hopeless, he sought in the thickest fire to meet the death for which he longed. But the balls passed him by as if by a miracle. Indeed the Savoy family seemed on that day to have charmed lives. The Duke of Genoa had three horses killed under him. The Duke of Savoy, having performed deeds of valour greater far than at the famous victory of Goito, covered the slow retreat of the Italian forces when night put a stop to the vain combat.

A flag of truce was sent to the Austrian camp to demand an armistice; but the conditions offered by the Marshal were too dishonourable to accept, even then; the first being the immediate expulsion of all Italian exiles from the state of Piedmont. It was only a few hours after the combat had ceased that the embassy returned with this reply. Charles Albert had previously notified to his generals that they were to meet him in council; and when he had communicated to them the answer of Marshal Radetsky, he said, 'Gentlemen, we cannot accept these conditions. Is it possible that we can resume hostilities?'

All replied with one voice, 'No.'

Then Charles Albert addressed his generals in the following pathetic words, his last speech as king:—

> From eighteen years till now I have always made every effort possible for the benefit of the people. I am deeply afflicted to see that my hopes have failed, not so much for my own sake, as for the country's. I have not been able to find death on the field of battle, as I had desired; perhaps my existence is now the only obstacle to obtaining from the enemy reasonable terms. And since there remain no further means of continuing hostilities, I abdicate this moment, in favour of my son Vittorio, in the hope that, renewing negotiations with Radetsky, the new king may obtain better conditions, and procure for the country an advantageous peace. Behold your king!

The prince turned pale, and in an agitated voice tried to dissuade his father from the step he proposed, the Duke of Genoa and all present uniting with him. But in vain; Charles Albert was resolute. He shook hands with his generals, and dismissed them, remaining alone with his sons. The princes were receiving his last advice and counsel, when the officers deputed to carry the message of the change of sovereigns to the Austrian camp presented themselves, saying they wanted more minute instructions from the king.

'Certainly,' said Charles Albert. 'Victor, speak to those gentlemen, give them your instructions.'

At midnight the uncrowned king set out in a small carriage with one sole attendant, under the title of Count Barge, to seek an obscure home in the friendly state of Portugal. Charles Albert had warm devoted friends who would have followed him, had he permitted it, in poverty and exile to the ends of the earth. But he chose to live in absolute privacy in Oporto, where he tried in vain to forget the dream of his life, the glorious dream of being the liberator and uniter of Italy. All that now remained to him for the few short months of his existence was to watch, from a distant shore, his Victor, all unaided, bravely buffeting the waves of adverse fortune, under which he himself had sunk exhausted.

CHAPTER IV.

THE HONEST KING. A.D. 1849.

'PER DIO, Italia sarà!' cried Prince Victor, shaking his sword in the direction of the Austrians, as he followed in the rear of his shattered army at Novara. It seemed a mad boast at that moment, and doubtless would have made Marshal Radetsky smile, had he heard it; yet, insuperable as the obstacles seemed to be, he lived to overcome them all, and fulfil his vow.

His first taste of sovereign power was bitter; a more miserable inheritance could hardly have been handed from father to son than that which he received on the evening of the fatal day which seemed to have extinguished the last hope of Italian liberty. 'I did not desire to be king,' he said a short time after to Sir Ralph Abercrombie, and there is every reason to believe that he spoke sincerely. 'I have no taste for the profession, which seems to me a miserable one, and in the present day very difficult.'

It was indeed a gloomy prospect. Surrounded by enemies in all the Italian princes, forsaken by the Pope, Lombardy and Venice crushed, the Jesuits and Mazzinians working to their utmost for the destruction of his dynasty, England and France looking on in strict neutrality, he stood alone in presence of a powerful and victorious army, which threatened his little state with annihilation. But he manfully took up the broken sceptre which had fallen from his father's grasp, and nerved himself to encounter the terrible difficulties that beset his way.

The first thing to be done was to arrange an armistice, so as to give time to consider a treaty of peace. Marshal Radetsky requested a personal interview with the king, hoping to win him by threats and bribes to abandon the Liberal cause. He was young and inexperienced, had not yet sworn to the Constitution, and perhaps had suffered enough to show him the folly of adhering to so hopeless a cause as popular government in Italy. If he could be brought to exchange his new-fangled ideas for the good old despotic rule of the House of Savoy, then Austria would be his friend and ally, and hold him on the throne in spite of a rebellious and discontented people.

But the young king was faithful to his subjects and to his principles. He knew how to resist the cunning old general's threats and blandishments alike. 'Marshal,' said he with a fierce energy, 'sooner than subscribe to such conditions I would lose a hundred crowns. What my father has sworn I will maintain. If you wish a war to the death, be it so! I will call my nation to arms once more, and you will see what Piedmont is capable of in a general rising. If I must fall, it shall be without shame. My house knows the road of exile, but not of dishonour.'

The manly firmness of the loyal-hearted king in his misfortune stirred a little sympathy in the grizzled old soldier who was trying to stamp his principles and his nation out of existence. At least, he always professed an admiration and esteem for Victor Emmanuel, and spoke of him as a 'noble fellow.'

On March 26, 1849, the armistice was concluded. The King of Sardinia was to break up all the military corps composed of Lombards, Poles, Hungarians, etc., retaining only the few who chose to remain his subjects for ever; a heavy war indemnity was to be paid to Austria; and meantime the troops were to occupy Piedmontese territory between the Po, the Sesia, and the Ticino; half the fortress of Alessandria was to be given up to the foreign army.

These were the best terms that King Victor Emmanuel could wring from the conquerors; and though something was ceded in compliment to him personally, they were hard conditions. A writer who saw him come away from this trying interview thus describes him:—

> Victor Emmanuel II. passed at a gallop, followed by his staff officers, in the midst of the serried battalions; but in that rapid glance his appearance was impressed on the mind of everyone who saw him. His countenance was grave, severe, firm, his gaze fixed before him as of one who reflects deeply; in it we noted the resoluteness of a strong soul, that accepts events, but does not sink under them. In the expression of his face there was dignity mingled with a noble, proud grief—the grief of a son, citizen, and king.[1]

Marshal Radetsky wanted to make a great display of military homage to the king, and had ordered that all the Austrian troops on the road to Turin were to turn out to do him honour. Victor Emmanuel absolutely refused to permit it, as he wished to return to his capital in the most private manner.

When a prince leads forth an army amidst the ac-

---

[1] Bersezio, *I Contemporanei Italiani*.

clamations of the citizens to expected victory, and returns defeated, with a shattered remnant of that army, what welcome does he look for from his countrymen? If he has read history to any purpose, he may know that a leader who comes back alive under these circumstances must be made a scapegoat. The 'many-headed monster' called the People, who at times have as little generosity as reason or gratitude, but an immense amount of vanity, cannot conceive how *their* army could be defeated by any just means. Nothing but treason or gross mismanagement on the part of the commander could account for the humiliating fact. So they make him a scapegoat.

The republican element, which had ruined the national cause in Lombardy and Venice, had not been without effect in Piedmont. Slanderous insinuations had been set afloat about Victor Emmanuel as well as his father, so that the news of the overthrow of the Italian army set Turin in a flame of anger against the prince, who had a large share in the conduct of affairs. Of course it was for the most part the *basso popolo* who felt so. The sober-minded, well-informed citizens knew enough of the difficulties of the war question to understand how the Italian army, with all its courage and enthusiasm, could be defeated. Yet even the minds of the better classes were influenced by false reports.

Victor Emmanuel on his way to the capital received a private letter from the queen consort, acquainting him with the state of public feeling, and begging him to enter Turin privately. He did so; and the day after issued a proclamation, and received the oath of the troops. The queen assisted at the ceremony in a carriage, accompanied by the two children Humbert and Amadeus, the one five and the other four years old. The royal party were received with the coldest courtesy by the citizens. Not a cheer welcomed the unfortunate prince to the throne of his ancestors, except what was given by his faithful soldiers who had followed him through the war. The king was deeply wounded by the injustice and ingratitude of his people, and, naturally, his wife felt with him. They went home miserable and disconsolate.

The royal proclamation was to the following effect:—

Citizens,—Untoward events and the will of my most venerated parent have called me, long before my time, to the throne of my ancestors. The circumstances under which I hold the reins of government are such that nothing but the most perfect concord in all will enable me, and then with difficulty, to fulfil my only desire, the salvation of our common country. The destinies of nations are matured in the designs of Providence, but man owes to his country all the service he is capable of, and in this debt we have not failed. Now all our efforts must be to maintain our honour untarnished, to heal the wounds of our country, to consolidate our constitutional institutions. To this undertaking I conjure all my people, to it I will pledge myself by a solemn oath, and I await from the nation the exchange of help, affection, and confidence.

VICTOR EMMANUEL.

The proclamation was not countersigned by any minister; but his adviser was Cadorna, whom he had empowered to form a ministry on the resignation of the late one.

On the evening of March 27 the new ministers presented themselves to the Chamber of Deputies, to make known the terms of the armistice which had been agreed to on the 24th, that is, the day after the battle. At 8 o'clock the Chamber was opened, and the house was crowded to excess by an anxious, agitated assembly. The Minister of the Interior, Pinelli, rose to read the articles of the capitulation. His face was pale with suppressed emotion as he looked round at his hearers and began the humiliating recital. He was listened to in gloomy silence till he came to the third article, which provided that the Austrian troops, 18,000 infantry and 2,000 cavalry, were to occupy Piedmontese territory and part of the fort of Alessandria. Then there was a general burst of indignation, and a cry against the Austrians and the traitors. 'It is an infamy,' was shouted from the benches of the deputies and the galleries simultaneously. The tumult lasted for some minutes, and it was some time before the minister could resume his reading, which he was hardly able to do because of his own agitation and that of his hearers. He was interrupted by fierce exclamations at every article, which came to a climax when it was stipulated that the Sardinian fleet should be removed from the Adriatic, and brought into the Ligurian ports within fifteen days.

The minister felt it his duty to add that these conditions would have been much heavier if the earnest insistance of the king had not obtained considerable modifications.

When the ministers betook themselves to the palace, they found the king waiting in intense anxiety to hear how the armistice had been received, and they described the scene in the Chamber. He had borne up bravely throughout the miserable week, but when he knew the Parliament was hostile to him his spirits gave way. The suppressed grief of the past five days found vent in tears and sobs, as he repeated again and again that he had nothing to reproach himself with; he had done his utmost for the country, and that was his only consolation.

Next day a deputation from the Chamber of Deputies waited on the king, and addressed him in terms of respectful remonstrance, as though their sovereign held their liberty in the hollow of his hand, and had but to issue an order and they would immediately be rid of the incubus of Austrian occupation. The deputation, after bitterly lamenting the grievous state of things, hoped that their monarch would follow the example of his magnanimous predecessor, who was a firm upholder of the Italian cause. The king was put on his defence, and, though very much agitated, he did defend himself boldly and ably. He began by saying that he wished to be, like his father, an upholder of Italian independence, and he had already given some proofs of his fidelity to the cause. He then related the story of the disastrous campaign from beginning to end. The deputation was impressed by the narration from the lips of the king, whose truth they could not doubt, and they reported the facts to the assembly.

Next day, the 29th, the king took the oath to the constitution. As he was ascending the stairs of the palace, on his way to the Chamber, he narrowly escaped a sudden death. An enormous beam fell from the roof close to him, striking the epaulet of the gentleman beside him, Menabrea, who was horrified at the danger; but the king did not give it the least attention. 'Come on, we have other things to think of,' he said to his minister, and moved forward without a moment's delay.

The senators, deputies, and spectators were very numerous. Victor Emmanuel, dressed in military uniform, took his seat upon the throne, while the Keeper of the Seals announced the Chambers opened. When the formula of the royal oath, which is the twenty-second article of the famous *Statuto*,[1] for which his father had suffered so much, was presented, the king stood up, uncovered his head, and after casting a significant glance around the assembly, spoke in a loud, sonorous voice :—

> In the presence of God, I swear to observe loyally the *Statuto*: not to exercise the royal authority but in virtue of the laws and in conformity with them; to see that full justice is rendered to everyone according to his rights; to comport myself in all things with the sole view of the interest, the prosperity, and honour of the nation.

He placed his signature to the document, reseated himself on the throne, and said :—

> In assuming the government of the state in the present circumstances, of which I more than any other feel the weight and bitterness, I have already expressed to the nation what my intentions are. The consolidation of our constitutional institutions, the welfare and

---

[1] For particulars of the Sardinian Constitution, now that of all Italy, see *Monarchia Rappresentativa in Italia*, by Count Cesare Balbo.

honour of our common country, form the constant subject of my thoughts, and I trust I shall be able to accomplish them with the aid of Providence and your accordance. In taking this solemn oath, I am profoundly sensible of the gravity of my duties, which must shorten my life.

In returning from the legislative assembly, Victor Emmanuel had recovered his usual composure. The agitation of his mind was calmed by the grandeur of the oath and the consciousness that he meant to maintain it at any cost. It was only a week since the battle of Novara, yet he had lived through so many important scenes and events in that time, that the Duke of Savoy seemed quite a different person from the King Victor Emmanuel II.

The new ministry was formed by General Delaunay, who chose for one of his colleagues Gioberti, who had been in the Cabinet of Charles Albert. Signor Nigra, a rich banker, much esteemed for his spotless probity, consented, from pure devotion to the king and country, to be Minister of Finance, at a moment when the treasury was empty and the nation reduced to a state of penury.

The first thing the king and his ministers agreed upon was to dissolve the Parliament and have a general election. It was an unpractical and scatter-brained assembly, elected on the war-cry, when no candidate would have had a chance who was not 'sound' on that question; when such men as Camillo Cavour were rejected, and sometimes denounced as traitors, because they were opposed to it. It was, in fact, an impossible Parliament to do sober, sad work with, for it could not be persuaded to accept the inevitable consequences of defeat. The Chambers were dissolved on the 30th, and the day for the general election was not named, because the government thought it well to give time for turbulent passions to calm down, while the peace negotiations were going forward.

These negotiations were prolonged into the summer, and seemed never likely to come to a peaceful solution. The King of Sardinia had recourse to the friendly powers of France and England to use their influence on his behalf. In a private conversation with the respective ambassadors of these states, Victor Emmanuel spoke to the following effect :—

I have done my duty as a soldier, and now I will serve my country in another way, because I love her sincerely. I will tell you the truth always, and I wish my ministers to do the same. If we think it necessary to follow a line of conduct, once it is adopted, I will say so frankly. This shall always be my policy, internal and external. As to you, gentlemen, you can tell your governments that I desire peace, frankly, loyally, without any ambitious second ends. Say, also, to Marshal Radetsky that I am willing to follow the armistice, or even to modify it in the interest of peace. I do not pretend to elude the fulfilment of the conditions I have signed. I shall be very grateful to you for what you do for us; be sure I shall never compromise you, for I never fail in my word.

The city of Genoa had been the seat of republican intrigues in 1848, and after the overthrow of the royal army in 1849 the people, incited by some unprincipled demagogues, broke into open anarchy. General Alfonzo la Marmora was sent to restore order to the distracted city, and he fulfilled his mission with ability and discretion. He was, however, obliged to hold it in a state of siege for some time. An amnesty was granted to the insurgents, with a few exceptions; and amongst those few was the Marchese Pareto, formerly Minister of Foreign Affairs in Charles Albert's reign. His case was a bad one; but when the paper was presented to the king, he said,—

'I do not wish this exception made. I will not have it said that I have used rigour towards a man who was once my father's minister.'

The ministry soon broke up, divided on the peace question, and Delaunay resigned; on this the king thought of Massimo d'Azeglio, who, still suffering from the wound received at Vicenza, and deeply afflicted in spirit, was wandering up and down the Riviera. If Victor Emmanuel did not like the 'profession of king,' D'Azeglio liked that of minister quite as little. The king's message found him at Genoa, and it was earnestly backed up by his brother Roberto, Marchese d'Azeglio, and one of the ministers, who came to his room early in the morning, before he was out of bed, and entreated him to accept the difficult charge. He could not refuse, though the office was most distasteful to him. On May 10, he sent forth an address to his constituents confirming what the king had already said. 'The misfortunes, the errors of the past, render war impossible,' said he; 'but for the nation, for the king, for us, we proclaim it in the face of the world, dishonour is quite as impossible.'

The king was much pleased with his new minister; their political opinions exactly coincided; they both had a large fund of good sense and keen observation, as well as an uncompromising candour and honesty of character; and though Victor Emmanuel was not a polished man of letters, he could appreciate D'Azeglio's varied talents and charming manners. He made him his friend and confidant; and when D'Azeglio's wound obliged him to lie on a sofa all day, used to go to see him, and talk over affairs public and private. D'Azeglio, being so much older than the king, and having had such a large experience of life, beside being nothing of a courtier, gave his opinions and advice with unusual frankness.

One day talking alone with his sovereign, he said, there have been so few honest kings in the world, it would be a grand thing to begin the series.

And Victor, looking at him with a smile, asked,—

'Have I to play the part of honest king?'

'Your majesty has sworn to the *Statuto*, and has thought of all Italy, and not of Piedmont only. Let us continue in this path, and hold always that a king, as well as an obscure individual, has one word only, and by that he must stand.'

'Well, in that case,' replied the monarch, 'the profession seems easy to me.'

'And the *Rè galantuomo*, we have him,' concluded the minister.

His majesty was pleased with the title, and proud of it. When the register of the census of Turin was brought, and he was asked to sign his name, he wrote, under the head 'Profession,' '*Rè galantuomo*.'[1]

CHAPTER V.

PIO NONO AND THE PAPAL POWER. A.D. 1848-49.

THERE were no people in Italy in whom the feeling of nationality was stronger, or the desire for a change of government so intense, as the Romagnuoli. And indeed when one reads the history of modern Rome, the wonder is how a brave, high-spirited people could have submitted so long to the papal government. They did not submit very patiently, it is true, for they were much given to conspire and rebel; but these conspiracies and rebellions were nipped in the bud by a system of espionage and terrorism quite unique—a system in which were united the temporal and spiritual powers. Anyone suspected of liberal thought in religion or politics was hunted down, not so much by means of the police as by means of the priests. The confessional was a ready way of obtaining the secrets of every family; and the aged or dying persons were refused absolution

---

[1] A critic in the *Pall Mall Gazette*, among some other misstatements, contradicted this story and substituted the following:—'The title of *Rè galantuomo* was not given him by any minister. The story runs that when some one was blaming the errors of the preceding reign he replied—*But I am an honest man.*'

All we have to say concerning this is that the critic should have some better proof than 'the story runs' when he undertakes to correct; and that no one who knows anything about Victor Emmanuel would believe that he could insinuate that his father was *not* an honest man. His father's honour was an article of faith with him. *Our* version is so well known in Italy that we did not think it necessary to cite any of the numerous authorities which we might on so trivial a matter.

See D'Azeglio's *Letters to Torelli*, published at Milan; Massari's *Life of Victor Emmanuel*, etc., etc.

unless they betrayed the haunts of their suspected friends and relations. The information thus obtained was grossly abused, and men were dragged before the Inquisition, tortured and imprisoned on the pretext of heresy, who were perfectly orthodox, and desired nothing but some reform in the administration of justice.

The immediate predecessors of Pius IX. were so detestable, that they made him appear, by force of contrast, an angel from heaven. His benevolent disposition, the purity of his private life, and the reforms with which he began his reign—for he too granted a representative form of government—raised the wildest hopes in the hearts of the people; they persuaded, caressed, and adored him to such an extent that he was carried along on the wave of popularity, and landed in Liberalism before he knew what he was about. But suddenly he awoke as if from a delirium, and finding he had drifted unconsciously away from the fixed principles of the papacy, tried to get back as best he could.

He had initiated the reform movement before Charles Albert had dared to unfurl the tricolour; but before that unfortunate monarch had well entered into the desperate struggle, Pius IX. was beginning to recover from the liberal fever; he was quarrelling with his ministers, contradicting his own utterances, sending orders to his generals not to fight, and trying every means to avoid a rupture with Austria—Austria who all the time hated him as a demon of revolution, and had the clergy preaching against him and threatening a schism. This was what he feared; and though not devoid of courage and patriotism, the *priest* was stronger in him than the *citizen*. Still some reforms from time to time he granted, and he had fresh accesses of Liberalism when Austrian aggression made him feel for the moment like a man and an Italian. His subjects, who were truly attached to him, prostrated themselves at his feet, and implored permission to fight his enemies—to defend the sacred confines of the Church's States. They offered money, arms, jewels—all they possessed—if he would only give them the blessed privilege of dying in his cause, and let that cause and Italy's be one. He was touched by the pathetic appeal, and seemed to yield for the time. He would bless them and their banner, and write an indignant protest to the Austrian general against outrages in Ferrara, or brutalities in Bologna; and then his patient subjects would thank him with an excess of gratitude, for having protested against the violation of his own territories.

The Romans were all the time burning to take their part in the national war into which they had helped to drive Charles Albert. He had said:—

> I will do my best to further your just desires, aided by that Providence which has given to Italy a Pio Nono —that Providence which is visibly with us, and has given Italy strength to stand alone.

They thought it would be an everlasting disgrace if Piedmont and Lombardy were left to fight the battle of liberty all unaided, after having been misled by so many promises; and there were those who felt such generous shame at the idea, that they did not wait for any permission, but volunteered under the banner of the King of Sardinia.

The wildest joy pervaded the city of Rome when the first Piedmontese successes were announced, but the defeat of Custoza threw her into mourning. The deputies of the Consulta—a sort of parliament which the Pope had instituted—framed an address to the sovereign in the most passionate language of entreaty, concluding thus:—

> We wish to save the state from the discord and horrid turmoil by which she is threatened, and we cannot do so unless we direct to a good end the extraordinary popular enthusiasm, and unless you uphold us with your authority. Listen, O blessed Father, to the sorrowful cry of your devoted children! Oh, do not *will* that in the reign of Pio Nono a great disaster to the Italian arms should weigh down our consciences with remorse!

The Pope still hesitated; he wanted time to consider, he said. The citizens became desperate. Time! they exclaimed, time! while their Piedmontese and Lombard brothers were pouring out their best blood! while Italy was being assassinated!

Even the priests—many of them, at least—shared the popular enthusiasm. They harangued the people, blessed the banners, and offered to march north with the army. Amongst these warlike priests was the Barnabite *frate*, Gavazzi, a very eloquent, but a turbulent and injudicious preacher, who subsequently left the Church of Rome. When General Durando, accompanied by Massimo d'Azeglio, at last marched to the seat of war, he was not permitted to cross the Po, and the discontent at this inactivity of the papal government was increased by various other incidents. Gioberti had just issued his book against the Jesuits, who were detested in Rome as the deadly enemies of liberty, and the Romans received the work with unmeasured praise.

The Pope grew angry, and accused everyone of ingratitude; the people insulted the Jesuits and forced them to leave Rome, threatened to burn cardinals' palaces, crying, 'Live Pio Nono *alone*! Death to Lambruschini!' The Pope grew more angry; he went about guarded, and showed a want of confidence in the citizens, even alluding to the national aspirations as 'insane hopes.' All this time a continual change of ministers went on, as liberal or clerical counsels prevailed, or rather as the pressure of the popular will was brought to bear upon the sovereign. The people were becoming more violent and unreasonable in their demands, and the Pope was gradually receding from the position of reformer, frightened of schism and anarchy. The breach was widening rapidly, and the people, under the pernicious influence of violent demagogues, had been worked into the worst frame of mind, when Pellegrino Rossi came into office. He was an excellent man, and an able statesman; but he pleased nobody, because he courted neither clergy nor people, but set about his duty with a stern resolve to put down riotous disorder in the city, and corrupt practices in high places. His brutal murder, which is an everlasting disgrace to the people of Rome, gave Pio Nono a great shock, and threw him back into the arms of the retrograde party. He was bitterly disappointed and grieved to find that the Utopia of his poetic imagination was but an impossible dream. Disaffection daily increased, and the Romans began to regard their once adored Pontiff as a false, capricious, tyrannical ruler.

D'Azeglio had said truly when he wrote, 'The magic of Pio Nono will not last.' The fact is, that he never had been the phœnix they took him for at first, nor was he, even at his worst, a heartless tyrant, though the acts of his government might well cover his name with odium. He was weak and vacillating, and lent an ear now to the words of one party, now of another. The clerical party was the most powerful, and by the most cunning and artful means managed to inspire in him such a fear of anarchy and schism that he shrank from the simplest and most necessary reforms as dangerous. His great fault was an extravagant idea of his own self-importance. He believed in himself as Pope as firmly as he did in the Madonna; an offence against him was an offence against religion, and deserved the severest punishment. This will account for what sometimes seemed evidence of a vindictive nature, but was not really so. He never meant to deceive his subjects. They deceived themselves by imagining that the Pope was a man of such transcendent genius, force of character, and sublime virtue, that he could overturn and remodel at his will such a powerful institution as the Church government, the abuses and corruptions of which had their roots deep fixed in far-back ages.

When at last the mutinous citizens bombarded the Quirinal palace—the Pope being inside—he ceded, but with a protest. 'I cede to force alone,' he said; and in a few days he left Rome secretly by night, disguised as a common priest. November 25, 1848, Pio Nono abandoned his capital, a prey to contending parties, and took refuge with the King of Naples at Gaeta. It was a most unhappy choice, and cut off all hope of a reconciliation with his people. The liberal ministers, lately called to office by compulsion, established a provisional government, and sent a deputation to Gaeta to entreat his holiness to return to Rome. The deputation was stopped on the frontier by order of the King of Naples, and not allowed to approach the Pope.

Meanwhile, the Austrian Jesuits had come round him, and were doing their utmost to make the breach wider. In an evil hour he appealed to the Catholic powers for help against his subjects—an evil hour for him, Pio Nono, and the temporal power—not for Italy. He had left his capital without a leader, and one of his deadliest enemies, Garibaldi, had taken possession of it, and was disseminating his heretical views in a very fruitful soil, giving a republican bias to all the liberal movements. The reception the deputation met with broke the last tie between the Pope and his subjects.

Carlo Alberto was cut to the heart by the defection of Pio Nono from the Liberal cause. He was really his only ally, and he valued him more than all the other princes put together, because of his spiritual authority. He tried repeatedly to reconcile the Romans and their sovereign, but in vain. On January 1, 1849, Conte di San Martino, envoy of the Sardinian king, arrived at Gaeta. The Pope refused to see him, though the king had given him no offence whatever. At last, after much trouble, he consented to receive him as a private individual. They talked of his return to Rome, and the count hinted at the advisability of conciliatory measures; but the Pope gave him to understand that he trusted entirely to foreign aid for his restoration. The count started and looked reproachfully at the Pope, who was himself a little disturbed. '*Che vuole?* they would have it,' said he.

The Austrian and Bavarian ambassadors laboured incessantly to circumvent San Martino, but he remained for some time at Gaeta, and pleaded the cause of the Romans, which was the cause of Italy, with great earnestness. There were moments when the Pope's better nature was in the ascendant; and once he seemed moved by San Martino's arguments; but he said again, 'What would you have? It is too late,' and sighed.

It was doubtless a sigh from the depth of his soul, a sigh for his better self, the lost Pio Nono of 1846, beloved and reverenced as he never could be again. Perhaps at that moment a vision flashed across his mind of himself on the balcony of the Quirinal, with hands outstretched over thousands of upturned faces, all breathing love and trust, while he blessed the Italian cause, and they vowed fidelity to their pastor and king. And now he was about to let loose upon them a foreign soldiery; henceforth he must hold his throne by the sole force of arms. Well might Pio Nono sigh.[1]

King Ferdinand and the Austrian ambassador persuaded the Pope that nothing but Austrian intervention could reseat him on the throne. France and Spain, equally eager to get hold of him, were profuse in offers of services. Poor Count San Martino had no chance against such odds, but he spoke boldly nevertheless. Gioberti, once much admired by Pio Nono, was then Charles Albert's minister, and he addressed a letter to Gaeta on the subject of a reconciliation between the Pope and the Romans which concluded thus:—

[1] Early in 1848, the Pope had issued a proclamation blessing the Italian cause. Some misunderstandings had previously arisen between the Pontiff and citizens about the Civic Guard; but these differences having been accommodated for the moment, the proclamation was issued, and the people surrounded the Pope's carriage, holding up a placard with the words: '*Holy Father, confide in your people*'—and then followed him in great numbers to the Quirinal. He came on the balcony, and spoke, in the midst of a profound silence:—

'Before the benediction of God descends upon you, on the rest of my states, and—I repeat it once more—on *all Italy*, I pray you to be of one accord, and to maintain that faith which you have vowed to your Pontiff.'

The silence was broken by a tumultuous, agitated cry from the multitude: 'I swear.'

The Pope raised his hand to consecrate this solemn compact by calling God's blessing upon it.

Who broke faith—the Pope or the people? To be quite just, we should say neither party observed the compact, both feeling themselves justified in breaking it.

I hope the Court of Gaeta is about to return to sentiments more evangelical, more worthy of Pio Nono. I am sorry to have to say that the Court of Gaeta, repudiating the doctrine of conciliation, and adopting that of vengeance and blood, does not seem to know that it is repudiating the maxims of Christ, and putting in their stead those of Mahomet.

It is necessary to bear these events of Charles Albert's reign in mind, in order to judge fairly of the quarrel between his successor and the Holy See.

The respectable portion of the city of Rome thought they had done their duty in trying to make peace, and now, under the influence of Garibaldi and Mazzini, just then arrived, they felt inclined to use their liberty, and establish a different form of government. In February 1849, a meeting of Parliament took place, in which it was resolved that Pope Pius IX. had fallen from the temporal power in fact and in right, but that his independence as Pontiff should be strictly guaranteed. Galletti, the late minister of Pio Nono, accepted office. The Romans inaugurated their republic with religious observances, for they were anxious to show that they adhered to the Christian faith, and that liberty did not mean atheism. Among the first measures of the new government was the abolition of the Holy Office of the Inquisition.

The populace would have levelled it with the ground, but the ministers decided to put the building to some charitable purpose; before making any alteration in it, they thought it well to leave it open for a few days, to let the citizens see with their own eyes the secret mechanism of the papal system. They did not need any evidence to know that the only crime of serious moment in the States of the Church was liberal thought in religion and politics. That their friends and relations had been spirited away, and immured in prison, they also knew too well. And when the prison doors were open these emaciated heretics had a sad tale to tell of cruel suffering and ingenious torture, and that without any visible instruments, for these had been abolished by law in 1815. But worse than anything that had come to their knowledge was discovered in the dungeons, and in the archives where the criminal records were kept.[1]

The following account by one of the prisoners, a foreigner, will give an idea of the excitement of Rome at the opening of the Inquisition.

> It was the 27th of March, 1849, near sunset, when a great tumult and rushing of feet at a rapid pace, and a noise of many voices made themselves heard in the corridor. Ignorant of what had happened, I did not know the cause of the noise, and thought my last hour was come, and throwing myself on my knees, I commended my soul to God. Then the door of my prison opened, and there entered a man of short stature, who fell upon my neck and embraced me, while tears fell abundantly from under his green spectacles. It was the minister Sterbini, author of the abolition of the Holy Office. 'You are free,' he said. I was excessively weak from long confinement in the narrow, damp prison, and had almost lost the power of walking. But the men who accompanied him took me by the arms and carried me across a court, through a crowd who cried, 'Down with the Pope!' 'Live the Republic!' I was put in a room with other prisoners, where the good people, so different from their priests, took great pains to restore me with soups, wine and cordials. When Sterbini had visited all the prisoners, he asked each where he would like to be sent. I replied that, being a foreigner, I had no friends in Rome, and prayed him to conduct me to the consul of my nation.
>
> 'You shall go to your consul,' he said, 'but not in your present state; wait till you are a little recovered.' Then one of the gentlemen present entreated me to accept his hospitality, which I did with gratitude. I

---

[1] See Fiorentino, *La Vita di Pio Nono*.

was put in a carriage and carried to the house of this good Roman, where I now am.

It was just three days after the battle of Novara, which plunged Rome and Italy in the deepest mourning. There were rejoicings at Gaeta when the news arrived, and Pio Nono showed his chameleon-like character in its worst aspect at this time. His old ally, Carlo Alberto, who was a devoted son of the Church, had been overpowered in a last desperate stand against his enemies. Lombardy was being trampled to death by Austrian dragoons, under a general at whose name humanity shudders. Venice was still making a gallant but utterly hopeless defence against the enemy, having addressed the most touching appeals for help to the holy father, before his flight.

At the time that the war was raging in the north of Italy, Naples was a prey to the same misfortune. The Two Sicilies were in open rebellion; having decided to depose for ever the Bourbon race, they invited to the throne Ferdinand of Savoy, Charles Albert's younger son. But Piedmont could not spare one gallant arm from her service, much less a prince of the blood. Garibaldi, with 5,000 volunteers, lent able assistance to the Neapolitan insurgents, and defeated the royal troops repeatedly. He hastened back to defend Rome from the French, who, in answer to the Pope's appeal, had landed at Civitavecchia, April 1849. Though they came in friendly guise, promising to respect the liberties of the people, the Romans thought it well to prepare for defence, and the bells of the Capitol rang out calling the citizens to arms. On April 29 there were within the walls 9,000 soldiers ready for battle, in two divisions, one commanded by Garibaldi, the other by Bartolucci.

The gallant conduct of the Romans during the siege redeemed their character from the stain which their previous excesses and follies had left upon it. The best men came to the front in this moment of dire distress, while the citizens, aided by some northern volunteers, not only performed acts of great valour, but displayed a constancy and heroism worthy of ancient days. The siege lasted four months. Then, utterly worn out, the city capitulated, and General Oudinot entered on July 3. The Pope sent him a warm letter of thanks, and benedictions for himself and his soldiers.

> When he fled from Rome [says Guerrazzi], with the locket of Pius VI. in his bosom, and the woman Spaur by his side, he never ceased to supplicate the Divine Redeemer for the health of his enemies—whom later he sent openly to the gallows.

The same author records the fact that at the time of the numerous trials for high treason which followed the Pope's restoration, he used to lay the death warrant at the foot of the cross, and when no heavenly inspiration or sign came from it, he ordered the sentence to be executed.[1]

CHAPTER VI.

THE KING AND CONSTITUTION. A.D. 1849-50.

EARLY in May, a month after Victor Emmanuel had come to the throne, it was decided between him and his advisers to make one more effort to restore peace to the distracted peninsula by addressing an earnest appeal to the three exiled sovereigns at Gaeta, more particularly to the Pope, who would naturally have more influence than the others if he could be won over to a policy of conciliation.

The ambassador chosen for this delicate mission was Cesare Balbo, a man of superior intellect, great personal worth, and much public spirit. He was one of those rare men whom it was Victor Emmanuel's good fortune to find round him in his hour of bitterest trial—men whose truth and loyalty could not be doubted, for

---

[1] *L'Assedio di Roma.*

nothing but disinterested patriotism could bind them to *his* service at that moment. Count Balbo was Azeglio's cousin and very dear friend, and like him he felt that all personal feeling must give way before the public interests, so he accepted the mission.[1]

The king had charged Count Balbo with reverent messages for the Pope, and told him to exhort him to re-establish a constitutional government in his states, send away the French, and conciliate his people. As the two other dispossessed sovereigns, the Grand Duke of Tuscany and the King of Naples, were also at Gaeta, the count was instructed to drop a word of advice to them also. The mission failed utterly, no one of the three giving any ear to the Sardinian envoy. But it is right to record every effort made by Victor Emmanuel's government to reconcile the Pope with the spirit of the nation. These attempts at establishing a good understanding are not usually mentioned by clerical writers, nor do they generally take much note of the proscriptions and executions which followed the Pope's restoration.

Victor Emmanuel had not been yet two months on the throne, when his life, which had already had so many hair-breadth escapes, was threatened by a dangerous illness, the same sort of fever which ultimately proved fatal. For nearly a month his family and friends were held in a state of suspense, hope and fear alternating as the fever abated or increased. It was a time of harrowing anxiety for those who understood the situation of affairs. His death at that moment would have been a calamity for the country which had no parallel. A letter from General Dabormida, the king's aide-de-camp, to General La Marmora at Genoa, will explain the state of feeling at the time.

[1] Azeglio writes to his wife on March 28 :—' I have just heard that one of Balbo's sons is killed ; I do not know which. Poor Balbo ! He had five sons in the field, and it seems that our people contested that battle like lions. . . . Poor Balbo ! Noble heart! While I write to you I am thinking of him, and that poor youth—I do not know which—but I loved them all, and I cannot restrain my tears.'

May 29, 1849.

Dearest Friend,—I delayed some days replying to your letter, hoping to have some good news about the king, and it is with a sad heart I must tell you that the disease does not draw to a favourable conclusion, but on the contrary increases, so as to put us in fear of his life. Riberi at first seemed confident of a favourable issue, but now he begins to be frightened, and the Prince Carignano, who sees the king often, yesterday was much afflicted. Grief perhaps makes us see the danger greater than it is, but the danger exists.

Just think, my friend, of the dreadful consequences of such a loss. How could we in these times sustain a regency which would last over thirteen years?[1] I shrink from the thought; and I fear more than ever that we are destined for some terrible crisis. Believe me, I do not grieve for the king as much as for the country. He would cease to suffer, and be spared the future miseries, which threaten to embitter his life, of party conflicts. You cannot imagine how much this poor young man suffers in seeing himself so villanously maligned in the journals, and threatened and insulted by anonymous letters. I have always believed his disposition good, but I never imagined him so excellent as since I have seen him groan under the weight of undeserved calumnies, but never heard issue from his lips a single threat, a desire for revenge, or a word of hate. He is, I repeat, excellent, and his death would be a great calamity to the country. I do not doubt that when the present troubles are passed his fine character will be appreciated, and he will be loved in the end. But before he arrives at that point, how much he has to suffer! If you were here I might relieve my heart to you, and I have much need to do so, because my friends who do not know the king well do not sympathise with my grief.

The queen is an angel; she never abandons her husband, and I fear that her health cannot hold out

---

[1] The crown prince, Humbert, was five years old.

much longer under the fatigues of nurse-tending. The Duke of Genoa comes from the camp every day to visit the king and take his orders.

The duke, who filled the king's place with ability, was the most devoted of subjects. 'How good my brother is!' he said to General Dabormida, on coming out of the sick-room. 'Confess, General, that even you doubted Vittorio would have turned out so good?'

Happily for Italy Victor Emmanuel did not die; and General Dabormida's words, that he had much to suffer, but would conquer in the end, were fulfilled.

As soon as the king was recovered he issued a proclamation to the people. He thanked everyone for the trouble and anxiety they had had about him; said he was grateful to Providence for such a brother and friend as the Duke of Genoa; spoke with tender sadness of his father, who 'had so loved Italy and her people, who had laboured and suffered so much for them, and now found himself in a distant land in infirm health;' alluded to the peace still unsigned, saying it never should be, unless the terms were honourable and worthy of the nation.

While the king was ill, General Ramorino, who had assisted as much as was in him to the overthrow of the Italian arms, was tried by court-martial, and being found guilty of disobedience to his commander's orders, which was plainly tantamount to treason, was sentenced to be shot. He appealed to the royal clemency; but the king being too ill to attend to the affair, his advisers felt that Ramorino was not a fit subject for grace, and the sentence was executed. Everything that the government did in those days was criticised and cavilled at. While the case was pending, D'Azeglio said to a friend with a bitter smile :—

Certain journals have their articles already prepared for each of the two hypotheses : if it be the first, they will leave the one and print the other; and if the second, they will do the opposite. In both cases their aim will be reached, which is to put the 'traitor' king and his ministers in the wrong.

The negotiations for peace dragged their weary length far into the summer, and seemed as if they never would come to a conclusion. The Sardinian government held out for an amnesty for Lombardy. 'We never will abandon the brothers who fought by our side—not to save Piedmont from annihilation,' said Azeglio. 'Peoples, like individuals, should prefer death to dishonour.' These noble sentiments were fully shared by the king.

But there was another point on which he was even more sensitive, and where he felt the responsibility to be his alone: this was the *Statuto*, which the Austrians again attacked, threatening to break off the negotiations unless it were modified. But Victor was inexorable; in public and private he vowed he would resign his kingdom sooner than touch it. 'I have promised,' said he, 'to maintain the constitution *intact*, and I never will violate my oath; sooner than submit to foreign dictation on the subject, we will all go to America.'

The general election took place on July 15, and the Parliament opened on the 30th. The country was in a miserably distracted, impoverished state, full of discontent, everyone blaming someone else for the public misfortunes. Many of the electors had abstained from voting, out of weariness and disgust with politics. Those who did vote were the 'Reds,' who sent many of the Radical agitators who had composed the late Parliament back again. One person, even, who had been excluded from the amnesty for open rebellion in Genoa—the Marchese Pareto, who owed it to the king's special grace that he was not in prison—was duly elected deputy to the Chamber. Notwithstanding this the Turin people were coming to their senses, and beginning to see the king's conduct in a clearer and juster light. He was welcomed more warmly on his way to the Legislative Assembly than ever before, and the royal discourse was well received. Victor seemed happier than he had been since his accession; and on his return to the palace he said to D'Azeglio in a gay tone, 'Don't you think the Tyrant did his part well to-day?' He used to call himself 'the Tyrant' jestingly to his friend. But the happiness was short-lived. Even while he was delivering the speech from the throne, his beloved father was already dead. Victor, who had constantly corresponded with the late king, felt his loss deeply, and made arrangements for the transfer of his body to the family mausoleum at Superga, near Turin. Over and above this private trouble, he found himself all at variance with the new Parliament, which seemed as impracticable and difficult to get on with as the last. In fact it represented 'Giovane Italia,' which 'being young,' said Azeglio, 'cannot be expected to have much sense, and certainly has little.'

The treaty of peace was signed August 6, 1849—a treaty which Balbo pronounced an *armistice* which would last ten years. It was near coming to an end much sooner. In November a fierce debate, which lasted several days, took place in the Chambers on the subject of the treaty, particularly the provisions relating to the Lombard and Venetian refugees. The government had every intention of protecting them; but the opposition party were not content with reasonable assurances, they wanted a revision of the treaty. The king and the ministry were of one accord that it was necessary to dissolve the Assembly, and appeal once more to the country. In his proclamation the king strongly defends himself and his ministers, severely blames the Chamber for its unreasonable and ill-timed opposition to the Crown, and reproaches the electors for their neglect of duty in not going to the poll. Cavour thought the bold, firm action of the government at this crisis saved the country, but others thought that it was too arbitrary a measure. As the royal proclamation of Moncalieri has become an historical document, we will quote a paragraph or two from it.

By the dissolution of the Chambers the liberties of the

country run no risk whatever. They are guarded by the venerated memory of King Charles Albert, my father; they are confided to the honour of the House of Savoy; they are protected by the religion of my oaths. Who dares fear for them?

Before assembling the Parliament, I addressed to the nation, and particularly to the electors, some frank words. In my proclamation of July 3 I admonished them to bear themselves so as to render the *Statuto* possible. But only a third, or little more, went to the elections. The remainder neglected to exercise that right, which is a strict duty in every free country. I have fulfilled my duty; why have they not fulfilled theirs?

In the speech from the throne I made known the sad conditions of the State. I demonstrated the necessity of giving a truce to party passions, in order to resolve the vital questions of the day. My words were the result of profound love of my country, and fearless loyalty. What fruit did they obtain? The first acts of the Chamber were hostile to the Crown. . . . I signed a peace with Austria, honourable, and not ruinous. The public good required it. The honour of the country and the religion of my oath demanded that it should be faithfully followed out, without duplicity or equivocation. . . .

I have sworn to maintain justice and liberty. I have promised to save the nation from the tyranny of factions, whatever be the name, objects, or rank of the men who compose them. These promises I fulfil by dissolving a Chamber whose existence had become impossible; I fulfil them by calling another immediately. But if the country, if the electors, deny me their support, not on me will fall the responsibility of the future.

If I have believed it my duty to give utterance to severe words, I confide in the sense and justice of the public to understand that they are dictated by a profound love of my people and of their true interests; that they arise from my firm will to maintain their liberty, and to defend them from foreign as well as internal enemies.

The country responded to the king's earnest appeal, which aroused in the electors a sense of duty and citizenship. The new Parliament was composed of different elements from the last—moderate, sensible men, who had the true interests of the country at heart. The Chambers were opened on December 20. The ceremony was more cheerful than the last. The king began to win the confidence of the people; his last frank proclamation had done much to bring about a better understanding. He was received with warm applause, as was also Queen Adelaide, who appeared in one of the galleries leading the little Prince Humbert, dressed as a national guardsman. The king's speech was cheerful in tone. He warmly thanked the electors for having listened to his voice, and performed the duty of good citizens.

The new Chamber approved of the treaty with Austria, and amicable relations were resumed between the two countries. '*Votre roi est un bon enfant,*' said Radetsky to the Piedmontese plenipotentiaries. '*Nous l'aimons beaucoup; nous sommes ses meilleurs amis: nous avons toujours à sa disposition quarante mille baïonnettes.*' The Piedmontese ambassadors thanked the Marshal for his praises of their sovereign, but declined the proffered aid of bayonets, saying the King of Sardinia had no need of foreign soldiers to hold him on his throne; he confided in the affection of his subjects.

The ambassador who was sent to represent Austria at the Court of Turin was very well selected for the position. Count Appony was a Hungarian of much ability, tact, and delicacy, and all these qualities were needed in the very sore state of Sardinian feelings at that time. The peace being finally settled, it was necessary to turn the attention of Parliament to the civil institutions of the country. The famous *Statuto*, which had been the cause of so much quarrelling, was still a mass of undeveloped laws. It is true that some legal reforms had been under discussion in the late Assembly, but they had not passed into acts, having excited the bitterest and most strenuous opposition even in the royal household.

To put the new Constitution in working order was a task of incalculable difficulty. Piedmont had hitherto been not only an absolute monarchy, but in an extraordinary degree under clerical domination; so that this order retained certain privileges which had been long abolished in other principalities of Italy. Everyone knows how much it goes against the natural inclination of man to resign a power or privilege inherited from ancestors or predecessors of any sort, however founded in injustice. Charles Albert, called by his subjects the Magnanimous, voluntarily resigned his absolutism: but his profound reverence for the Church, and his deep religious feeling, would not let him touch the privileges of the clergy; and these privileges were on the whole much more objectionable than the sovereign's power. There was a constant war going on in the king's mind between his religious convictions and his sense of political justice; and it is said that the Jesuits took advantage of his perturbed state to terrify his soul by awful midnight visions, so that he was sometimes found insensible on his chamber floor in the morning.

But the *Statuto* which he at last promulgated struck indirectly at those privileges, by providing that 'all subjects should be equal in the eyes of the law;' and when Victor Emmanuel's government came to apply the articles of the *Statuto*, they had, amongst other abuses, to deal with the important question of the *Foro Ecclesiastico*. The *Foro Ecclesiastico* was a powerful tribunal over which the clergy only presided. A council of three bishops had the right to pronounce sentence of death on any ecclesiastic. The pain of death for offences against religion was part of the penal code; to the Church was still permitted that relic of mediæval lawlessness—the right of asylum for criminals; to the parish priest were left all civil registers; to the Jesuits the right to penetrate everywhere—to rule the royal household, the private homes of citizens, the public institutions, the schools, etc.; so that the country was absolutely subject to the priestly power.

In the new Chamber the Minister of Grace and Justice, Count Aveta, boldly asserted that by the 24th and 68th articles of the *Statuto*—the first of which declared all subjects equal before the laws, while the second provided that justice should be administered in the name of, and by judges chosen by, the king—the ecclesiastical tribunal should cease to exist. His successor, Sclopis, said that the existence of a privileged jurisdiction, independent of the royal authority—regarding affairs entirely temporal—was quite irreconcilable with the provisions of the Statute Book.

The clergy were naturally up in arms; they protested against the sacrilege and impiety of touching their ancient privileges; they denounced in the grossest language the promulgators of these wicked laws, particularly Siccardi, a man of great probity and learning, who had given many years of his life to the study of jurisprudence, and was energetic in carrying out the reforms. Count Siccardi was sent on an embassy to the Pope to ask his consent to the abolition of the above-mentioned abuses, and to beg him to put a check on the insolence of the Piedmontese bishops, who were trying to excite civil dissensions in the realm. Antonelli replied that 'the holy father was willing to please the King of Sardinia as far as going into the antechamber of the devil, but into his very chamber he would not go.'

The Sardinian king and Parliament, indignant at the insult, set about abolishing the clerical privileges and immunities without further ceremony. They were branded as infidels who wanted to overturn the altar, and destroy all religion. Victor Emmanuel did not like this reputation; he protested to the French ambassador that he was not 'a bad Christian,' as he had been falsely represented, and tried in every way possible to conciliate the irate priesthood. He had had a hard trial in the opposition of the queen dowager, who wearied him with entreaties and exhortations not to give his sanction to the anti-clerical acts. But however grieved he was at his mother's distress, he never dreamed of letting any consideration interfere with his public duty. When he put his signature to the act, he looked at Siccardi with a smile, and said, ' Look to it, Count ; if this law leads those who have made it to the *inferno*, you will have to go alone.'

It was followed by a burst of rage from the clergy—protestations from Rome, and protestations from the Piedmontese bishops. Two of these violated the law of the realm and were consequently punished, a delicate intimation that the *Statuto* had begun to work, and the clergy were to be treated like any other delinquents.

Victor Emmanuel was consoled for the abuse which the clergy poured out upon him, and which caused him acute pain, by the ever-increasing affection of his subjects. The abolition of the *Foro Ecclesiastico* made him immensely popular throughout Piedmont ; his triumph was shared by his minister Siccardi, to whom the nation decided on immediately building a monument. When the king went in the summer-time on a tour in the Alps he took Siccardi with him, that they might do some work from time to time in their resting-places. The following characteristic letter is addressed to D'Azeglio :—

Dear Friend,—In this Alpine retreat I never forget my friend. Thanks for your two letters. We arrived here on Saturday at eleven, after a week of terrible fatigues over the glaciers of Dondenaz and Cogne. I traversed the valleys of Bard, Champorcher, Fenils, Saint Julien, and Cogne, and found everywhere proofs of true affection from these hardy sons of the Alps. On Sunday I received almost the whole town of Aosta, which came to compliment me in a truly cordial manner. Some of these discourses I will send you, because they are really fine. In the replies I was aided by the sincerity of my sentiments and my small poetic vein.

I had good fortune in the chase, too. I killed six chamois and two stags of the rare kind. I astonished the hunters of these mountains by the length of my shots, and we have left a good impression of ourselves also, because Barba Vittorio makes money circulate a little.

To-day (Monday) is a very sad day for us, for me in particular. It is the anniversary of my poor father's death. I ordered a high mass to be said, and almost all the national guards of Aosta came in uniform to assist at it with great decorum. They have asked that my second son, who is duke of these regions, should be enrolled as one of them, and my consent gave them great pleasure. But, dear Massimo, I am very sad, and I do nothing all day but shed tears, thinking of him I loved so dearly, and of the mournful past. . . .

Write to me, dear friend. Take care of your health ; and think sometimes of Barba Vittorio, who loves you from his heart, and who never deceives.

Your affectionate
VITTORIO EMANUELE.

July 29, 1850.

To the Noble Man, Chevalier Massimo d'Azeglio,
   President of the Council, &c.

Barba Vittorio means 'uncle Victor' in the Piedmontese dialect, and was probably a name given to the king by some of the little mountaineers, with whom he loved to converse familiarly, and play the part of 'special Providence.' There are many anecdotes told of his adventures in the Alps, which show his genial, sympathetic nature. One time he asked a little girl if she had ever seen the king ? The child replied that his majesty often came to her father's cottage to eat *polenta* with them. 'You little story-teller,' said Victor, giving her a piece of money. 'Here is his portrait, and don't tell fibs any more.' Another day he met a little barefooted boy in a wood, carrying his shoes in his hand. The king asked him why he did not put on his shoes. 'They wear out,' was the reply. 'And the soles of the feet, don't they wear ?' 'Yes, but the skin grows again, and costs nothing.' 'What is your name ?' asked Victor. 'Albert.' The king took out a gold piece and put it in his hand.

'You bear my father's name, my boy,' said he; 'buy a pair of new shoes with this.'

One evening descending from the mountain, after a hard day's sport, with one attendant, he met a peasant farmer who accosted him thus:—'You seem brave hunters, gentlemen; you would do me a great kindness if you would kill a fox which destroys all my property.' 'To-day our ammunition is exhausted,' replied the royal sportsman; 'but we will pass this way to-morrow.' On the morrow he pursued and killed the animal, bringing its head in triumph to the peasant, who thanked the king, and gave him two francs for his trouble. Victor put the francs in his pocket, saying to his friend, 'These are the only moneys I ever really earned.' Soon after, the peasant was summoned to the royal villa, and, to his amazement, recognised in King Victor Emmanuel, the Alpine hunter, who returned him his two francs with enormous interest.

In this year, 1850, the Duke of Genoa married Elizabeth of Saxony, and the king and queen made a tour through Savoy to meet the bride and bridegroom, and fête them on their return. While the royal family travelled by the easiest routes in carriages to Courmayeur, the king and his brother made an excursion across the mountains in hunting costume; and after the usual fatigues, adventures, and enjoyments, joined the ladies in their rustic retreat. While sojourning in the mountains all court etiquette was laid aside, and the royal family lived in the utmost simplicity. The primitive inhabitants of those wild regions did not even know the king by sight. One day a woman came to the door of the royal villa with eggs, and met on the threshold a roughly dressed individual, who saluted her graciously, and asked her what she had in her basket. This man took the basket, brought it into the kitchen, and then returned it to her empty, with a piece of money. Seeing him so polite, the woman confided to him her desire to see the king,—the queen she had already seen.

'I am he,' said Victor, who with his thick boots, gaiters, conical hat, and rough sun-burnt features, was not the peasant's *beau idéal* of regal majesty. 'You!' she exclaimed with a derisive laugh. 'Oh, you won't get me to believe that! A nice, pretty woman like the queen would never marry such an ugly man.'

The king related the story to the queen, laughing heartily, and often repeated it to his friends when telling of his first trip to Courmayeur.

CHAPTER VII.

THE BEGINNING OF THE QUARREL WITH ROME, AND CONTINUATION OF THE QUARREL WITH AUSTRIA. A.D. 1850–53.

ONE of the king's ministers, who had assisted at the passing of the Siccardi bill for the abolition of clerical privileges, was the Cavaliere Santa Rosa, a gentleman of excellent private character, and a pious Catholic.[1] He was dying of consumption, even while he sat in the council; and soon after the prorogation of Parliament he succumbed to the fatal disease. His confessor had no power to administer the sacrament without the concurrence of the parish priest, who refused it, at the command of his bishop. The dying man protested that he was a true Catholic, that he was conscious of no sin in taking part in the late acts of the government, and implored his confessor to procure for him the last consolations of religion. The confessor, moved with pity, returned once more to the curate, and used all his persuasions to change his resolution. Instead of yielding to the prayer, the brutal priest entered the sick chamber and reviled the dying man so grossly, that his wife, weeping hysterically, implored him to quit the house, and not torture her husband in his last agonies. The good Santa Rosa expired without receiving the sacrament; and all Pied-

[1] Cousin of the revolutionist Santorre Santa Rosa.

mont was stirred to its depths with indignation, and cried out that the law must be vindicated. The bishop by whose authority this outrage had been committed was imprisoned, and another also for some similar offence.

Naturally the Court of Rome protested against this outrage to the sacred persons of the bishops. An envoy was sent to explain the case to his holiness, and further beg of him to put a restraint on the rebellious language of the clergy. The Pope refused to listen to the Piedmontese ambassador. Later, another was sent, with whom he seemed disposed to treat; but as he demanded a restitution of the immunities the clergy enjoyed in the reign of Charles Albert, the negotiation ended in smoke. The next move was an autograph letter addressed by Victor Emmanuel to the holy father, couched in the most respectful terms, asking him again to restrain the insolence of the clergy, who did not hesitate to insult him and the laws of his realm. The Pope, not to be outdone in politeness, replied in an autograph letter, in which he said the priests had only done their duty, and begged his majesty to put a restraint on the excessive liberty of the press, 'boiling over with blasphemies and immoralities—to the end that the clergy should not be persecuted, calumniated, and derided.' The irate Pontiff adds, 'Because they defend pure religion and the principles of truth, is this a reason why they should come under your majesty's displeasure?'

And so these exchanges of royal compliments went on with ever-increasing acerbity.

D'Azeglio could restrain himself no longer: he rushed to the front of the battle, and wrote a pamphlet in his own name, attacking the papal government under Pio Nono, as he had so often done under his predecessors, but in dignified and measured language.

The death of Santa Rosa, which had given rise to these disputes, gave occasion also to the Premier to call to the vacant post of Minister of Agriculture and Commerce another bold spirit, whose statesmanlike genius far surpassed his own in grand design and daring execution. 'Take care,' said the king, when D'Azeglio proposed the appointment. 'Cavour will rule you all; he will send you away; *he* must be Prime Minister.'

In this year, 1851, a fourth son was born to King Victor, whom he called Charles Albert; and in the same year was born also the Duke of Genoa's eldest child, Margherita, now Queen of Italy.

Victor Emmanuel at this time had need of all the affection of his subjects, for he had little sympathy from the outer world. He was the only constitutional monarch in Italy. The position of the Lombardo-Venetian provinces was a perpetual thorn in his side, and a continual source of irritation between the governments of Vienna and Turin. The subjugated provinces would rebel from time to time; and these rebellions being put down with great severity, the Piedmontese, having a free press, would express their feelings without reserve. Hence arose complaints and counter-complaints. All the other states of Europe were either coldly neutral or critical, with the sole exception of England, 'whose friendship for the House of Savoy and Piedmont was of ancient date, and her sympathy for Italy profound,' says Massari.

The governments both of Berlin and Vienna sent to Victor Emmanuel dictatorial, menacing messages, thinly veiled under the form of friendly advice. In Italy the petty princes were one and all his enemies, his constitutional government being a standing reproach to them, who had violated their oaths. But the greatest enemy of liberal institutions was Ferdinand, King of Naples, who, in 1848, after having sworn upon the Bible to grant a constitution and to join the national war, proceeded to slaughter, imprison, and banish innumerable citizens, for no other offence than taking part in the movement. This old tyrant hated Victor Emmanuel and Piedmont, and was most anxious to put an end to what he called 'the bad example of the King of Sardinia,' or 'the Sardo,' as he designated him in private.

Massari, who is Neapolitan, says he was discontented with his ambassador at the Court of Turin, and recalled him for the following reason: A princess of the Bourbon family asked the Count Grifeo to narrate to her the disorders which had taken place in Turin. He looked amazed at the question, and said no disorders had been known during his residence there. This was enough to excite the distrust of the suspicious sovereign, and Grifeo was recalled. His successor, Cavaliere Ramirez, better understood what was expected of him.

On presenting his credentials to the Sardinian king he was received courteously; and after the usual exchange of compliments, he began to read an address written in French. The king, who was quite unprepared for an 'allocution' from the Neapolitan ambassador, was not attended by any of his ministers on the occasion. 'The king, my august master,' said Ramirez, reading from the paper, 'has ordered me to explain to your majesty the wishes he has formed for the conservation of your majesty's country, threatened by so many dangers.'

'What are the dangers, M. le Chevalier?' asked the king, interrupting him. The ambassador was not prepared for the question; he hesitated, stammered, and at last spoke of the wicked press, secret societies, and such like. Victor Emmanuel replied with dignity,—

'I have nothing to fear, M. le Chevalier. Behind *my* throne there is neither treason nor perjury.'

When Massimo d'Azeglio heard of this cutting reply, he felt very proud of his young king, who knew how so well to maintain his own dignity. 'Everyone knows,' said he, with that charming frankness which was a striking characteristic of his, 'that I can always find appropriate phraseology to clothe my thoughts; but indeed I should hardly have been able to give such a telling, pointed reply as that of the king. It is a fact that an honest man has the secret of true eloquence.' The Neapolitan complained to the Austrian ambassador of the king's rudeness, but Count Appony held that he had provoked the offence, and had better pass it by.

At this time the philosopher Gioberti, tired of political life, was living in Paris, where he published his famous book, 'Rinnovamento Civile d' Italia,' which excited much attention. In treating of Piedmont, he said :—

Except the young sovereign who rules Piedmont, I see no one in Italy who could undertake our emancipation. Instead of imitating Pius, Ferdinand, and Leopold, who violated their sworn compacts, he maintains his with religious observance—vulgar praise in other times, but to-day not small, being contrary to example.

The king was much pleased with Gioberti's book, and while reading it often said, 'I will do what Gioberti says.'

He had enough of trouble and danger to contend with still, but he was more resigned since he knew he had the sympathy of his own people. 'I am not sad,' he said in a letter. 'Dangers threaten me, but one must be a fatalist and say, "God is great," and nothing more.'

Victor Emmanuel, whatever his faults may have been, had a very noble trait of character, which in a prince is particularly admirable—a magnanimity of soul which set him above petty considerations, and made him ignore all personal injuries and offences. He could not bear to have sentences for treason carried out, unless the peace of the country demanded it; and he made a regular habit of setting at liberty all the seditious priests condemned by the courts of law. 'You have done your duty in condemning them,' said he; 'that is enough to vindicate the law; I do mine in pardoning them.' He never knew what it was to harbour malice against any human being, even when groaning under the weight of undeserved calumnies. 'I am not angry,' he writes to a friend in 1851, 'neither was I ever. I am accustomed to everything; and I know we cannot shut people's mouths, and that malicious persons attack virtue, or those that they think better than themselves, for rage against good, or because they cannot attain their perverse ends. I believe at this moment I know the world well, and nothing can astonish me more.'

One of the calumnies which struck Victor most

severely—and which his enemies, knowing this weakness, persisted in reiterating loudly—was that directed against his religious belief. He was said to be an impious scoffer at religion, who laughed to scorn every sacred thing in heaven and earth. The fact was that Victor, who had been brought up by most devout parents, had a profound reverence for religion. It is true he was not, like Charles Albert, an anchorite; on the contrary, he was a pleasure-loving man. But this does not, so far as we know, hinder a man being a pious Catholic—else the Bourbon princes and princesses would not have been such favourites with the holy father, or have enjoyed such a reputation for piety as they did.

Victor Emmanuel firmly believed the Italian cause was under the protection of Divine Providence; and in the royal speech for the opening session of 1852, he insisted on inserting the words, 'Providence, which has plainly blessed our work.' His majesty delivered these words with emphasis as he looked round at the assembly, and was much disappointed to see they did not produce the lively impression he expected.

The king had had for preceptor, when a youth, a very learned divine to whom he was much attached. This Monsignor Charvaz had the courage to espouse the Liberal cause, and stand by his sovereign in the disputes between Church and State—which, it is well known, cost Victor Emmanuel, as well as his father, bitter mental struggles. 'Stick to the Constitution,' said Charvaz, 'and let the ignorant and the fanatical scold and shout.' He was a great comfort and support to the king, who used to say that he never saw Monsignor Charvaz without hearing a sermon from him; but, so far from complaining of his severity, took it as a proof that his old governor's affection for him had not diminished. One day the king sent for Charvaz, wishing to convey to him personally the news of his elevation to the Archbishopric of Genoa. When the Monsignore presented himself, Victor sprang forward with boyish glee, and threw his arms round his neck. 'Monsignore, no sermon to-day, I entreat,'said he, holding him tightly in his strong embrace. 'I know I am a sinner, but I have a good heart, and I will not let you go till you promise not to preach to me to-day.'

Meantime fresh offences were given to Rome by almost every act of the Sardinian Government. There were then going on very warm debates on the subject of civil marriages, which excited the bitterest feeling amongst the clergy. D'Azeglio and Cavour had been disagreeing for some time; finally there was a split in the Cabinet, and the ministry resigned. The king accepted the resignation; but directed D'Azeglio to form a new ministry, excluding Cavour and other discordant elements. 'Later we will want Cavour, but not yet,' said the king, who probably feared that he would push matters to extremes prematurely, and so prevent the possibility of a reconciliation with Rome.

While the marriage law was in abeyance during the prorogation of Parliament, the king once more addressed a letter to the Pope, giving all his arguments in favour of it. He hesitated before bidding the clergy defiance on this point. When there was placed before him an elaborate statement on the question, he read it carefully, and then said: 'It is well. Those are the learned arguments of lawyers; but I must also think how it will be regarded above'—pointing heavenward.

Massimo d'Azeglio, weary and disgusted with state affairs, and in poor health, resigned office in a few months after he had formed his second ministry, advising the king to call to office his rival Cavour, whom he disliked but admired. Cavour hesitated, and said that in the face of the extravagant pretensions of Rome he could not accept the responsibility. The king said he would not take his refusal, and sent him to talk with Monsignor Charvaz, who had just come back from an embassy to the Pope. The result of the conversation confirmed the count in his opinion that he could not get on peaceably with the Holy See. He accordingly recommended the king, in the present excited state of public feeling, to send for Count Balbo, who was more moderate and conservative. After further negotiations, finding that concessions did not conciliate the Court of Rome, Victor Emmanuel thought it useless to deprive himself of Cavour's able counsel; and this time the count yielded to the royal invitation, and took upon him the conduct of affairs. It was a fortunate day for the king, for Piedmont, for Italy, when this great, wise, far-seeing patriot seized the helm of the state, and guided her over the stormy waters which so often threatened to engulf her, to a safe anchorage.

The bitterness of feeling between Austria and Piedmont broke out from time to time in mutual accusations and complaints. An abortive rebellion in Milan, February 6, 1853, gave occasion for a diplomatic conflict, which threatened to end in actual warfare. The Austrian Government accused Piedmont of encouraging and hatching conspiracies in Lombardy. Piedmont replied that the Lombards were driven to rebellion by an oppressive and cruel government; and indignantly denied having anything to do with conspiracies. Austria responded in injurious terms, speaking of the Piedmontese as 'traitors.' The king, very indignant, addressed a memorandum to the Court of Vienna. 'We must show,' said he to Cavour, 'that the House of Savoy must not be vilified by any power.' The ambassadors of England and France, feeling the justice of the king's angry message, supported it. Austria was more enraged than ever; and the quarrel arrived at the dangerous point of breaking off diplomatic relations. Count Appony, having vainly remonstrated with his own government, left Turin at the same time that the Sardinian ambassador started from Vienna. It began to be clear to everyone that the Peace of Milan was, what Count Balbo had said, an armistice that would last about ten years. This illustrious author and statesman died on June 3, 1853, and

> The world was poorer of a noble man.

Cesare Balbo was one of that brilliant set to which the brothers D'Azeglio belonged, who united the polish and enlightenment of modern times with the knightly spirit of loyalty and patriotism of the antique Piedmontese gentlemen.

The financial difficulties of Piedmont ever since the war—the indemnity was eighty million francs—were not the least of her troubles. In this year much discussion on the question had been carried on in the Chambers, and great difference of opinion existed on the subject of taxation. Cavour then shared the common lot of all men in his difficult position. The country was poor, the treasury empty, money was required to keep the machinery of the state in motion, and he had no magic treasure house to draw upon, so had to resort to taxes, and was consequently unpopular for a time. His liberalism had previously given offence to the aristocratic conservative party, to which he belonged by birth and antecedents, and this offence was increased by his seeking support from the Left when he found the Right would not advance at his pace.

But Cavour knew how to balance himself between extremes of party, and make use of politicians of every shade of opinion. He was often attacked by the extreme Left, particularly by Brofferio, a clever journalist and dramatist of republican tendencies, whose bitterest satires were directed against the count, and who was never tired of sneering at him. Cavour's admiration of England had won for him the nickname of 'Lord Camillo' amongst this party. Once when he quoted English institutions in terms of praise—as he often did—there was laughter from the opposition benches. The count said in parenthesis, without losing the thread of his discourse: 'That laughter can only proceed from someone whose name has never reached England.' It was impossible to put out or confuse Cavour, in spite of a certain defect in his speech which he had laboured hard to overcome. But he often put his adversaries to the rout by the ironical smile which he wore while they were speaking. Bonghi says of him :—

His speech was not fluent nor elegant; his voice was sharp and sometimes harsh; the words stopped in his mouth; and although he hid the defect by a cough, which he invoked for the occasion, this would have tired his hearers if their spirit were not sustained by the hope, constantly satisfied, of a lucid idea which shone before them at the end of the period, interrupted always, never broken. The hesitation of his tongue never made him lose the thread of his discourse—much less the interruption of his adversaries, whom he provoked rather than feared—feeling sure of his response.

Once Brofferio called him an 'Ultra-Moderate,' and in his reply he said:—

In truth, I have found the words used by the Hon. Brofferio rather too indulgent than severe; and I feel due gratitude for the exquisite courtesy which distinguishes him in calling me only an 'Ultra-Moderate,' and not having employed the word 'Retrograde,' or the more vulgar, but more expressive '*Codino*.'

Cavour was a man of imperious will, and loved power; the consequence was that his will and that of his royal master sometimes clashed. But he was good-tempered, and both were large-minded, sensible men, who felt the necessity of mutual support in the great work of developing their liberal institutions, to which they were equally devoted; and so they not only worked well together, but became personally attached to each other. Though Victor Emmanuel was scrupulously conscientious not to stretch his authority beyond constitutional limits, he did not, on that account, throw all the care and responsibility of affairs on his ministers. He took an active part in all the Cabinet discussions, and sometimes his simple straightforward policy was found more effective than Cavour's diplomatic play. In the royal speech of December 1853, the words 'restored finances' occurred. The king, reading it over, said: 'Stop; it seems to me we promise too much. Let us put in an "almost." It will be more true, and not spoil the sense of the sentence.'

In this year the king and queen being at Spezia for sea-bathing, with the royal family, all went on an excursion in a man-of-war. The ship struck on a rock, sprung a leak, and was foundering rapidly, when another vessel came in time to rescue the precious freight from imminent death. When the news arrived in Turin of how near extinction had been the dynasty of Savoy, the people cried, 'God protects Italy!'

CHAPTER VIII.

THE ALLIANCE WITH ENGLAND AND FRANCE. DOMESTIC AFFLICTIONS. A.D. 1854-55.

AMONGST other modern improvements set on foot by Victor Emmanuel's government was railway communication. The line was just completed between Genoa and Turin, and at Count Cavour's suggestion the king and queen went to Genoa to inaugurate it. That once rebellious city, now become intensely loyal, greeted them enthusiastically.

Soon after this pleasant trip troubles came. The little prince Charles Albert died, to the great grief of his mother and father, who were both devotedly fond of their children. Cholera broke out with fearful virulence in the Riviera; but the great populous city of Genoa suffered most in this visitation. The mortality was so great that it was almost impossible to give the most necessary attention to the sick, much less decent burial to the dead. The king felt it his duty to be with his afflicted subjects; so he sent the Duke of Genoa to represent him at the opening of the Novara line of railway, and hastened to the plague-stricken city, where he distributed large sums of money for the relief of the sick, visiting the hospitals, and taking an active part in all the works of charity; for he did not shrink from death in its most repulsive form.

In this year, 1854, the famous Silvio Pellico, author of the book describing Austrian prisons, died at Turin.

In the month of April the treaty of alliance between England and France to defend Turkey against Russian aggression was signed; and Cavour conceived the bold idea of securing the friendship of those two powerful states by joining in the alliance. The king was more than willing, he was eager for war, if it could be reconciled to the good of Italy. He had said, in 1849, to the English and French ambassadors, that, having done his duty as a soldier, he meant to serve his country in other ways; and he had honestly done so for the following five years. But his pride as a king and soldier had been too deeply wounded for him to content himself with peaceful occupations the rest of his life. The burning desire to retrieve his lost glory, and wipe out the defeat of Novara, though concealed, had never been extinguished in his breast. 'Our defeat was too ignominious; we have need of a little glory to raise us up,' he said. In addition to this, Russia and Sardinia had been on very bad terms for a long time; so he caught at the idea of the alliance, saying, 'If I cannot go to the war myself, I will send my brother.'

The friendship between England and Piedmont had become warmer since 1851, from which time her Britannic Majesty had been represented by Sir James Hudson, a gentleman for whom Victor Emmanuel conceived the highest esteem and regard. He was in very friendly relations with France also; and there seemed no impediment to the conclusion of the proposed alliance, except Cavour's natural love of diplomatic mystery. The stir of military preparations in Piedmont excited suspicions of hostile intentions against Austria; and to quiet these alarms the wily premier had to show his hand a little to the ambassadors, and say that if England or France called on Piedmont for help, she felt bound to send a contingent to the war. He had no immediate designs on Austria; though the chief object of this Anglo-French alliance was to put Piedmont in a position to settle that old score. Cavour was probably held back from committing himself definitely by the uncertainty of what part Austria was about to take in the quarrel. It was likely at that time that she might join in the alliance, but nothing was concluded. King Victor writes to the Minister for Foreign Affairs as follows :—

Cher Dabormida.—Faites votre possible pour savoir les conditions secrètes stipulées par l'Autriche dans l'adhésion à la triple alliance.

Je ne voudrais pas qu'il y eût quelque article concernant la conservation de l'intégrité du territoire Italien, guerre finie ; cela changerait bien notre affaire dans l'alliance, et il faut en être bien sûr avant.

Ciao, cher ami. En avant, marche, et soyez gai.
          Votre tres-affectionné,
                    VICTOR EMMANUEL.

The official announcement of the Anglo-French alliance, made to the Sardic government in the month of April, was replied to in a friendly spirit, but without committing Piedmont to any positive engagement. This was disappointing to the ambassadors, and not quite in accordance with the king's wishes, as he would have preferred a more straightforward course of action. He took occasion to ask the Duke of Gramont to pay him a private visit. 'Come, *sans cérémonie*, in an overcoat, about five o'clock,' said the king, and the ambassador did so.[1] The king was in his hunting-dress, standing by a table, writing, when the ambassador entered. He received him kindly, offered him a cigar, and immediately entered on the subject that was occupying his mind, asking him what he thought of the note which his minister had addressed to him on June 2, and telling him to speak frankly. The duke spoke frankly. He said they had expected something different from a cold expression of sympathy, particularly after what the Conte di Cavour had said six weeks

---

[1] The Duke of Gramont communicated the particulars of this interview to Signor Massari. See *La Vita ed il Regno*, etc.

before. He confessed that he thought the note rather diplomatic.

The king said that in his opinion the note was stupid, and he would have written it differently. The duke then asked if his majesty meant to say that he would stand by the overtures of M. de Cavour. 'What do you mean by Cavour's overtures?' asked Victor. 'It is better to call things by their names. Il n'y a pas d'ouvertures de Cavour; c'est moi qui ai parlé. Je lui ai dit de vous offrir 25 mille hommes. C'est tout ce que nous pouvons donner maintenant, sans quoi j'aurais dit 30 mille.'

'Then, sire, if the proposition came from you, how is it that all has ended in smoke?' asked the ambassador.

The king explained how Cavour had been checked by the attitude of Austria, that he feared the war might not be popular, and that he was greatly influenced by his Lombard friends, and wound up by saying that he knew beyond all doubt that Austria would *not* enter into the alliance, and he was resolved that Piedmont should.

'Sire,' returned the Frenchman, 'I have only to say that I share your opinions, and I heartily wish you may do as you say.'

'Do you doubt it?' said the king, fixing his piercing eyes upon him with an angry light in them.

'No, sire, no; I do not doubt it, and I am only too happy to believe it.'

The king shook hands with him at parting, and told him to keep his own counsel, but not to forget what he had said.

As time wore on Cavour saw clearer what was best for the interests of his country, and earnestly desired as much as did Victor Emmanuel to conclude the treaty; but he was strongly opposed by all his colleagues, particularly Dabormida and La Marmora, both military men, whose opinion on a question of war was not to be despised.

There was at the same time a discussion going forward, as to whether Piedmont was bound in honour to make it a condition of entering into the alliance, that the confiscated property of the Lombards who had made themselves Victor Emmanuel's subjects should be restored to them. England and France objected to the introduction of the question, and some of the ministry were for breaking off the negotiations. But a Lombard refugee, called Achilles Mauri, wrote in his own name and those of his fellow exiles to the effect that they would not let their private interests stand for a moment in the way of any benefit that might accrue to their common country from the Anglo-French alliance; and this disinterested declaration was a help to Cavour in his long and tedious struggle with his colleagues. The year 1854 drew to a close without any decision. The conferences were renewed early in January, but the ministers were still divided. 'Well, uncle,' said Cavour's niece, the Countess Alfieri, one evening at a party, 'shall we go to the Crimea or not?'

'Who knows?' was the reply. 'England solicits us to enter the alliance, and would permit our soldiers to join her army, and wash out the defeat of Novara. But all the Cabinet is hostile to the project. Even Rattazzi, and my best friend, La Marmora, say they will resign on it. But the king is with me, and we may prevail.'

Hearing of the divisions in the Cabinet, the Duke of Gramont, remembering the words of the king six months before, asked for a private audience on January 9. He found him in low spirits; for, over and above the worry of state affairs, his mother and wife were both very ill at the time. He said he was grieved at the result of the conference the evening before; the ministers were all against him, save only Cavour. But he had pledged his word to the emperor, and he was resolved to keep it. 'If we are beaten in the Crimea, why, we must retire; but if we conquer, it will serve the Lombards more than all the fine articles that have been written about them. I am weary of telling them this; as yet they will not listen to me. But, *pazienza*, all will be well in a little while. You know I told you I have one word only; and if these generals will not march, I must find others who will march. The Chambers and the country are with me.'

The king urged the ministers to a decision, and next day another conference was held; but the foreign ambassadors refusing to give a written compact, the meeting, which lasted till midnight, broke up without any result. Count Cavour, who for four hours had carried on the discussion, now with the foreign ministers, and now with his colleagues, was quite exhausted at the close, and his usual serene temper gave way.

'I hope you will tell the king what I have said,' remarked the Duke of Gramont.

'I am the best judge of what I ought to tell the king,' replied Cavour brusquely.

It was an hour past midnight when he arrived at the palace and demanded an immediate audience. His advice was to sign the treaty at once, or withdraw altogether from the position. The king did not hesitate a moment; he had had his mind made up long ago, and so now when Cavour pronounced it safe, he took his own way. Dabormida resigned, and the other ministers yielded to the powerful united will of Victor and Cavour. It was all settled, and Cavour installed as Minister of Foreign Affairs, between twelve at night and four in the morning. At seven o'clock the English and French ambassadors received a note inviting them to an interview. They found Count Cavour serene and smiling. Dabormida, overcome with the fatigues of office, had resigned in the night, he said, and the king had confided to him (Cavour) the vacant post. They were all of one accord now, and the treaty should be signed that evening, if the gentlemen were agreeable. Then he begged the Duke of Gramont to forget his rudeness the evening before, saying they were like advocates, doing the best they could for their clients, and now that the cause was ended they would all dine together to-morrow.

It was a solemn moment for the king (says Massari), and decided the fate of his country: that treaty was the fortune of Italy. To overcome so many difficulties the genius of Cavour was not enough; there was needed also the firmness of purpose of Victor Emmanuel, for without him the treaty would not have been concluded.

And it is quite true. Foreigners have not fully appreciated how much was due to Victor Emmanuel's indomitable courage, firmness, and sound judgment. With another sort of sovereign the great statesman might not have been able to carry out his designs; while with a less able minister the patriot king could not have conquered all the difficulties, external and internal, that beset his path. Without taking from the merit of either, we may say that Victor Emmanuel was necessary to Cavour, Cavour to the king, and both to Italy.

During the long and anxious negotiations about the Crimean war, Victor Emmanuel's soul was harrowed by an accumulation of domestic troubles. His mother was hopelessly ill; Queen Adelaide had had an unfortunate confinement, from which she had not recovered, and the state of her health caused the doctors the gravest apprehensions; the Duke of Genoa, who was to have represented his brother in the Crimea, was in a precarious state, though soldier-like he refused to give way to his weakness, saying always he should be well when once the order was given to march. 'The poor duke,' said his aide-de-camp, 'he will die if he goes to the Crimea, and he will die if he does not go.'

Victor's affectionate heart was wrung with pity as he went from one sick chamber to another, trying to cheer and comfort his invalids, while he was himself oppressed with care and anxiety of all kinds. He was a devoted son; he loved and reverenced his mother sincerely, and he would sooner have dared the wrath of the whole Catholic world than encounter the prayers and tears of this pious mother, who entreated him not to sanction the anti-clerical laws. Hers was the only remonstrant voice that had power to shake for a moment his strong will; but he felt the truth of D'Azeglio's teaching: 'Your kingly duty overrides all others,' and he listened silently, uncomplainingly, to her reproaches, but never yielded. Even while he was watching over her last hours she implored him pathetically to be true to the traditions and faith of his fathers.

The queen-mother breathed her last two days after the signing of the treaty, that is, January 12. Her broken-hearted son had to suppress his tears, and present a calm front to the poor young wife, whose sufferings now left her no hope of recovery. Her husband attended her continually, never leaving her except to visit his brother, and for the last five days and nights he never closed his eyes. Those who saw the haggard, grief-stricken face of the poor king in those sad days felt the deepest commiseration for him. All his Piedmontese subjects declare that he was deeply attached to his wife, and that her death was a terrible blow to him. This we may believe, because we have it on the evidence of men who were no courtiers, and whose testimony cannot be doubted. But it is also true that his connection with the Countess Mirafiore was the cause of bitter sorrow to Queen Adelaide. And who can tell what remorse was mingled with his grief, when the royal mourner thought of his motherless little ones, as he bent over the couch of his dying wife, and met the gaze of the sad loving eyes which sought his continually?[1]

The queen consort expired on January 20, just eight days after the queen dowager. Her death was an irreparable loss, for such a wife and mother as Adelaide must have made her influence felt alike in the family and the court.

One invalid was all that now remained to the unhappy king,—his gallant brother, sinking rapidly day by day, while he still hoped to lead his brave soldiers to the war, and obliterate the memories of 1849. 'I shall be better next week,' the poor consumptive would say; but every

---

[1] 'Egli aveva assistito, del continuo, i suoi ammalati, che si consolavano nel trovarselo vicino; ma più di tutti la moglie, la quale, affranta dai patimenti, volgeva intorno lo sguardo a quando a quando, per fissare colui ch' ella chiamava "mio buon Vittorio."'—GHIRON.

week found him worse. On the day that the troops marched out of Turin they came by the palace, and the duke was carried to the window to look out at them. As they disappeared from his gaze, he sighed as if his heart would break; it seemed as if his last hope was gone. He died on February 10, exactly a month after the signing of the treaty. Next day, the king issued a public announcement of his loss.

Grief comes upon grief, misfortune upon misfortune. My loved brother, he who was my companion in the battle-field, a perpetual comfort and aid to me in deeds and in counsel; he who, over and above the tie of blood, was bound to me by the most powerful affection of a warm reciprocal friendship, is no more! He breathed his last sigh yesterday evening, a little after ten. With a lacerated heart I announce to you this my new grief, which will be profoundly felt, I am certain, by all the nation, who in the Duke of Genoa not only admired the prince of high aims and indomitable valour, but saw also the splendid example of every virtue.

Ferdinand, Duke of Genoa, was born in 1822, and was just two years younger than Victor. He had a good intellect, a kind heart, and a chivalrous spirit. To say he was brave would be superfluous praise in treating of a Prince of Savoy; but the duke was an able as well as a gallant soldier; and if Victor merited the title, which his people proudly cede him, of 'First Soldier of Italy,' Ferdinand, they assert, ought to be called the second. In 1848 he was invited to the throne of Sicily, on condition that he should be called by his second name, Albert, his first, Ferdinand, being too hateful to the islanders by reason of the Bourbon kings who had borne it.

The affection and esteem which Victor Emmanuel felt for the duke, and which made him thank Providence for having given him such a rare brother, were fully reciprocated by him, and if he had been spared he would have been a great consolation to the king in his hour of trial. But a cruel fate swept his house clean of all its grown members at one swoop, leaving him alone in his sorrow; while the clergy, loudly proclaiming that the judgment of heaven had descended on the wicked king for his persecution of the Church, hissed at him that he was accursed, and tried every secret art to terrify his afflicted soul.

These denunciations were quickly drowned in a roar of popular indignation, and execrations on the priests who dared to insult the sovereign's grief; for now the hearts of king and people beat in unison, and his sorrow was theirs. The citizens beset the palace day and night with inquiries for the health of the royal family; and inside, men of all shades of opinion met with tears in their eyes, drawn together by a common calamity. All Turin, all Piedmont, was in the greatest affliction, and by every evidence which it is possible at such a moment to show, made the royal mourner feel that he had his people's truest sympathy.

The king had ordered that each of the soldiers who had escorted the queen's body to Superga should receive 200 francs. They took it, but only to spend in purchasing two magnificent garlands to lay upon her tomb, and that of the queen-mother—saying that they were more than rewarded by the honour. Loyalty in Piedmont must have been a sincere and high-wrought sentiment when it could make common soldiers feel as delicately and act as gracefully as high-bred gentlemen.

The good Archbishop of Genoa, Monsignor Charvaz, hastened to Turin to lend what consolation an old friend and pastor might, and his presence was much needed; for to feel himself cut off from the Church at such a moment was agony to Victor Emmanuel. Cavour, so potent in mundane matters, had no spell to charm away his master's grief, or quiet his disturbed conscience. He wanted a minister of religion to speak gentle words of faith, and charity, and love, to soothe his wounded spirit. 'They tell me,' said he, in a voice broken by sobs, 'that God has struck me with a judgment, and has torn from me my mother, my wife, and my brother, because I consented to those laws, and they threaten me with greater punishments. But do they not know,' he added, 'that a sovereign who wishes to secure his own happiness in the other world ought to labour for the happiness of his people on this earth?'

D'Azeglio says:—

I found him thinner by half than he had been. His waistcoat, which used to be tight, I could put my hand in, and still it hung loose on him. But, with the exception of a couple of days, he attended to affairs, and signed documents, saying to me these noble words, 'I am king; it is my duty!' Certainly he appears fifteen years older. However, the stuff, physical and moral, is strong, and I have no fear.

CHAPTER IX.

RATTAZZI'S LAW.—CRIMEAN WAR.—VISIT TO PARIS AND LONDON. A.D. 1855.

DURING the illness of the two queens and the Duke of Genoa the king was not only harassed by the question of the Anglo-French alliance, but by the still more difficult one concerning the redistribution of Church property in Piedmont. The wealth of the bishops and monastic communities was enormously out of proportion with the resources of the country, while the inferior clergy were sunk in poverty, and had to be partly supported by the state. There were 2,540 parishes with only an income of 20*l.* per annum, and the assistance rendered to them by the state, with other ecclesiastical expenses which it could not afford, amounted to 200,000*l.* The Church owned at this time more than a tenth part of the landed property of the country, and had amassed untold wealth by other means.

The arrogance and intolerance displayed by the bishops in their bitter opposition to every attempt at reform, and the absolute refusal of the Pope to sanction any readjustment of ecclesiastical property, roused the Sardinian Government to take decisive measures to strip the prelates of some of their power and privileges. The extreme Liberals were for confiscating all Church property and paying the clergy a salary, but Cavour chose a medium course. Whenever a see fell vacant he reduced the number of superfluous bishops by withholding presentation, which was the right of the government. Meanwhile his colleague Rattazzi, Minister of Grace and Justice, introduced the famous bill for the suppression of a certain number of religious houses, and other changes in ecclesiastical affairs, which struck the old-fashioned folk called *Codini* with horror, and roused the fiercest opposition on the part of the clergy. It was impious; it was sacrilegious, it was everything that was wicked; nothing but destruction could come to the country which permitted such disastrous laws to pass.

The bill was under discussion when the terrible calamities which befel the king interrupted the sittings, and gave occasion to the clergy to point out that Providence had manifestly blighted the House of Savoy for its sins against the Church. The government could not shut the mouths of the disaffected clergy without laying itself open to the charge of persecution; and the clergy left nothing undone to stir up a religious fanaticism among the people. The king, stunned and prostrated mentally and physically by the cruel trials he had passed through, shrank from a conflict between Church and State, and was disposed to compromise matters when the bishops offered to make up the necessary sum to pay the parish clergy if the Rattazzi Bill were withdrawn.

On April 14 the king and court went to Alessandria to pass in review the 25,000 troops, about to set out for the seat of war, and to give them new banners. All the soldier awoke within him at the sight of his brave army, always so loyal and devoted to their king, and he longed to be free to lay down the sceptre and resume the sword once more. 'Ah, General,' he said to La Marmora, with a profound sigh, 'happy you! You go to fight soldiers; I remain to fight monks and nuns!'

The ministers of France and England had accompanied the Sardinian court to Alessandria to assist at the presentation of banners, and they were much pleased with the aspect of the men.

Order of the Day.

Officers, Non-commissioned Officers, and Soldiers!—A war founded on justice, on which the tranquillity of Europe and the fate of our country depends, calls you to the East. You shall see distant lands where the Cross of Savoy is not unknown; you shall see brave people and armies whose fame fills the world. Let their example stimulate you to show to all that the valour of your fathers has not decreased. On former occasions I have conducted you to the field of honour; and I remember with pride how I shared with you the dangers and fatigues of war. To-day I am grieved to separate from you for a time; but I shall follow you in thought everywhere, and that will be a happy day on which I shall be permitted to join you once more.

Soldiers! here are your colours! They were generously unfurled by the magnanimous Charles Albert, and they will help to remind you in a distant country of eight centuries of noble traditions. Defend them! Bring them back crowned with new glory, and your sacrifices shall be blessed by present and future generations.

From the soul-stirring prospect of military glory, which was the only thing that could have roused him from his unhappy state at that moment, Victor Emmanuel turned to the hateful contest with monks and nuns. His soul sickened at the ignoble warfare, and when the Bishop of Casalmonferrato, in the name of the episcopacy of Piedmont, made the offer in the Senate of a large sum for payment of clerical dues, the king wished to accept it. This brought on a ministerial crisis. While it lasted the king consulted not only the most eminent and able of his own subjects, but the ministers of France and England. All agreed that he ought to recall Cavour; and so he turned again to the *Bestia Nera*, as the fanatics called the great reformer, and reinstated him in power. The Senate resumed the discussion on the suppression of monasteries, etc., and after long debates agreed to the Rattazzi Bill with modifications, which the Chamber of Deputies accepted, and, the royal sanction being given, it became law.

'We shall always count it one of the proudest acts of our political career,' said Cavour, 'that we knew how to sacrifice every personal consideration for what we considered a sacred duty.'

Many were the friendships lost and bitter enmities incurred by him and the king in their daring determination to pass this measure. The relentless animosity of a numerous and influential class, finding themselves suddenly despoiled of their ancient privileges and a great portion of their wealth, Victor Emmanuel was made to feel to the utmost. They had tried to work upon his feelings and his conscience by reminding him of his dead mother's wishes, and when he was proof against all their subtle attempts to conquer his reason, they slandered and calumniated him without scruple on the points where he was most sensitive. Victor Emmanuel, besides having a great reverence for the Church, entertained such a personal regard and esteem for Pio Nono as made the struggle doubly painful to him. When the accident happened at St. Agnes' Church near Rome, from which the Pope escaped unhurt, the king wrote him a cordial letter of congratulation. This was in April, before the obnoxious bill was passed, and Pius replied courteously to the missive.

The ministry was recomposed, General Durando being Minister of War, Signor Rattazzi of the Interior, Count Cibrario, an able and devoted servant of the Crown, particularly dear to Victor Emmanuel, Minister of Foreign Affairs, while Count Cavour, President of the Council, also took charge of the finances.

This question settled—if it could be called settled while such a storm of clerical indignation was raging throughout the country—Victor Emmanuel turned his longing eyes towards the Crimea, where the allied armies were suffering from the ravages of cholera. He desired to share their hardships and dangers, but his people would not consent; so he had to content himself with the joyful news of the victory won by the allies at the Tchernaya, August 16, 1855, in which his Piedmontese comported themselves most valiantly, and La Marmora proved himself one of the ablest generals in Europe. Queen Victoria and the Emperor Napoleon sent warm congratulations to the King of Sardinia, and he thrilled with exultant pride, while all Italy rejoiced. He was just then doing the honours of Turin to a succession of royal guests—the Prince of Portugal, afterwards his son-in law, and the son and daughter of the good King Leopold of Belgium, for whom he had a great respect.

Late in the autumn the king, returning from the chase tired and heated, and having to cross a river to arrive at his *castello*, with his usual impatience refused to wait for the boat which should have carried him over, and plunged with his horse into the icy water. Violent fever, accompanied by racking pains in his bones, was the natural consequence of this imprudence. Great alarm was felt for several days, and Cavour was in a state of intense anxiety, not on public grounds alone, but also because, like everyone who shared the counsels of the genial, warm-hearted Victor, he had become personally attached to him. He watched his convalescence with joy; and, partly for the king's sake and partly for political motives, he begged him to accept the invitation to visit his august allies, Victoria and Napoleon. It was desirable to draw the bonds of friendship closer by personal intercourse; and also to contradict the slanders which the clerical party were circulating in England and France.

At first Cavour thought it better not to accompany his master, as it might give too political a character to the visit. But afterwards he was persuaded that he might profit by the occasion to let his English friends know more particularly the state of affairs in Italy.

He made it a condition that Massimo d'Azeglio should accompany them, 'his presence being necessary to prove to the world that we are not infected by the revolutionary stain.' Cavour and Azeglio had quarrelled; but they immolated all ill-will on the altar of patriotism. A reconciliation took place, and mutual esteem soon ripened into a firm friendship, which was only dissolved by death.

Before setting out on the journey, the Legislative Assembly was opened, November 12. It was the first time the king had opened Parliament since his domestic afflictions, and though nearly a year had elapsed, the memories awakened by the ceremony had an agitating effect on him. The Prince of Carignano now stood beside the throne in the place of his brother, while the gallery where his wife and mother were wont to sit was vacant. His voice trembled a little when he first began to speak, but he conquered the weakness as he went on.

The King's Speech.

Gentlemen Senators, Gentlemen Deputies,—The year that is almost finished has been for my heart a period of cruel trials. They were alleviated by seeing the tears of the whole nation associated with the mourning of my house, and in the midst of my sorrows God sustained me to fulfil my duty.

I turn my glance to the great struggle which for two years has raged in the East. I did not hesitate to unite my arms to that party which combats for the cause of justice, civilisation, and the independence of nations. I was urged to it by the desire to share in the triumph of those principles which we are propagating, the generous instincts of the Subalpine people, and the traditions of my family. Our soldiers, uniting with the valiant armies of France, England, and Turkey, seconded by the zeal and activity of our fleet, have shared perils and glories with them, and increased the ancient fame of this warlike country.

May God crown their united efforts with greater success, and render possible a lasting peace securing to each nation its legitimate rights.

The expenses of the war will render necessary a fresh recourse to the public credit. The scarcity of the harvests, the renewed scourge of cholera, united with other unexpected contingencies, have diminished the public revenues. If, contrary to the desire of my heart, necessity compels us to ask fresh sacrifices of the nation, my government will seek by every means to render these imposts as light as possible. It will project a law for the more equal distribution of taxes, so that they will not press so heavily on the poorer classes.

Other laws to improve the political administration and economy of the State, the courts of justice, and public instruction, shall be proposed for your consideration.

Gentlemen Senators, Gentlemen Deputies,—The arduous mission which is confided to you, you will prosecute so as to give proofs of that prudence and laboriousness, of that constant affection for the interests of the country, for which you have been distinguished. We shall thus continue the noble example of a king and a nation bound by the indissoluble ties of love and confidence, in joy as in grief, being always in accord in maintaining the two great bases of public happiness—order and liberty.'

The king was received on his first appearance with the warmest demonstrations of affection, and was loudly applauded at the conclusion of his speech. He was touched and gratified by these demonstrations; for Victor, not pretending to be superior to popular praise, always acknowledged himself proud of the devotion of his subjects. 'How could my uncle,' he once said, speaking of the Grand Duke of Tuscany, 'by his own doing, sacrifice the affections of his people? If I reigned not over a little state like Piedmont, but an empire vast as America, and I was obliged to do what he has done, to preserve the little throne of Tuscany, I would not hesitate a moment, I would renounce empire.'

On November 30 the king started from Turin. At Lyons, Cavour and Azeglio awaited him. The latter humorously describes how they drove side by side in the same carriage for public edification, like rivals shaking hands on the stage. Victor Emmanuel was well received in Paris, and the emperor and empress vied with each other in the most delicate attentions. The arms of the Sabaud family were emblazoned on the Sèvres china, and everything destined for his use. On the table of his *salon* was a portfolio of drawings, representing all the glorious feats of arms of the Piedmontese in 1848. This delicate flattery was not confined to the monarch alone. D'Azeglio found in his room four of his own beautiful pictures, for which the galleries and royal palaces had been searched. Cavour may be supposed to have had his own peculiar vanity, though not so patent as that of the soldier-king and the noble artist; and without doubt his French hosts knew how to tickle it in some graceful, subtle way—at which he may have smiled, but must have been pleased.

The sovereigns parted with the warmest expressions of personal regard on both sides; and before saying adieu the emperor asked the momentous question, which must have set Victor's brain throbbing, ' Que peut-on faire pour l'Italie?'

The Honest King's welcome in England, if not so ingenious in complimentary devices, was beyond all doubt as hearty and sincere. He was just the sort of man the English nation delights to honour. The people love a hero, particularly a hero who has fought for some oppressed nationality, and when that hero who defended his nation's rights was himself a sovereign who rejected the despotic power which his neighbours wanted to thrust upon him, resting his authority on the devotion of his subjects—their enthusiasm knew no bounds. There was something, too, in the admiration and sympathy which Victor Emmanuel and his minister always openly expressed for England, pointing to it as an example of the splendid effects of constitutional monarchy. 'The Times' spoke of the illustrious guest as 'a prince gallant in war, wise in council, constant in adversity, tried above the common lot in domestic as well as political life, and under every aspect worthy of the cordial sympathy of the English people.'

The Queen and Prince Consort were not less warm than the nation in the welcome they gave him. D'Azeglio, in his charming letters, describes the interesting visit, and says they were entertained with feudal magnificence. Queen Victoria bestowed the Order of the Garter on her illustrious namesake, whom she treated as 'an old friend;' and the visitors were enchanted with everything English, except the climate, which in mid-winter did not make a favourable impression. The Italians made their entry into the metropolis in a bitter north wind. 'In full dress in an open carriage, with no mantle to protect me, I suffered the agonies of the *inferno* with neuralgia in my face,' says Azeglio. King Victor was much too hardy a hunter to be ruffled by a north wind, and he enjoyed everything, particularly the reviews, for the English troops filled him with admiration. The City of London gave a grand banquet at the Guildhall in honour of the royal guest, where he was received with the warmest demonstrations ever accorded to a foreign prince. King Victor did not speak English, and he preferred to reply to the Lord Mayor's address in his own language rather than French.

My Lord Mayor,—I warmly thank the Lord Mayor and the aldermen and the *comune* of the City of London for the courteous felicitations that they have presented me with on the occasion of my visit to Queen Victoria and the English nation.

The welcome I have met in this ancient home of constitutional liberty—of which this address is a confirmation—is a proof of the sympathy inspired by the policy I have followed till now, and in which I intend to persevere.

The close alliance between the two most powerful

nations of the earth, which I am now visiting, is an honour to the wisdom of the sovereigns who rule them not less than to the character of the peoples. They have learned to substitute a profitable friendship for an ancient rivalry, and this alliance will contribute to the triumph of civilisation.

In spite of the misfortunes that have weighed on the beginning of my reign, I also have entered into this alliance, because the House of Savoy believes it to be always its duty to unsheathe the sword in the cause of justice and independence; and if I bring to my allies the forces of a small kingdom, I bring at least the strength of a loyalty which no one has ever doubted, supported by the valour of an army which always follows faithfully the banner of their king. We cannot lay down our arms till we have obtained an honourable and lasting peace; and with the aid of Providence this will be arrived at by seeking to reconcile the true rights and just desires of every nation.

I thank you for the good wishes which you have offered me to-day for my future and that of my kingdom. But while you speak to me of the future, I am happy instead to speak to you of the present, and I congratulate you on the high position England occupies as due to the free and noble character of the nation, and to the virtues of your queen.

On December 11, Turin welcomed the return of her beloved king with clamorous applause—all the warmer because he was so highly appreciated in other countries.

CHAPTER X.

THE CONGRESS.—THE PEACE. A.D. 1856.

THE fall of Sebastopol early in the year 1856 ended the winter's campaign, and an armistice was concluded between the belligerents. In order to take part in a conference to consider the future plan of action for the allies, General Alfonso La Marmora was recalled from the Crimea. The king was delighted to see his old friend who had so well represented him at the war, and expressed the greatest regret for his brother, General Alessandro La Marmora—famous as the founder of the Bersaglieri—who had died of cholera in the Crimea.

The Congress was to meet in February at Paris, and every state was to be represented by two plenipotentiaries. The King of Sardinia wished to send as first plenipotentiary Cavaliere Massimo d'Azeglio; but he objected, saying that he disliked the office, hated courts, was no diplomatist, and in short would not go unless it were an absolute obligation. Count Cavour hated the office equally, because he heard that as Austria had proposed the peace, and was pressing it upon Russia, she would have a powerful voice in the Congress, and Piedmont would look small.

'What is the use of our going to the Congress to be treated like children?' said he. But the king overcame his reluctance, and he wrote to the Marquis Villamarina, who was to be the second plenipotentiary:—

> I have not hesitated, in spite of the innumerable affairs that claim my attention in Turin, in spite of my excessive repugnance to play the diplomat—I have not hesitated to announce to the king that I am ready to start for the Congress, and I pray you to join me in this ungrateful mission.

To tell how bravely he struggled to maintain the dignity of his country against the Austrian schemes to humiliate her, belongs to Cavour's life; but it reflects glory on the reign of Victor Emmanuel, and should not be altogether unnoticed. Cavour's large-hearted patriotism was not confined to the narrow limits of Piedmontese territory, but embraced all Italy. Piedmont was naturally his first care, for she was the centre and seat of independent thought and action. But all Italy was his country; he had one great end in his life for which he laboured incessantly, indefatigably—and that was

Italian unity. He now seized the opportunity of the Congress to make the wrongs of Italy fully known to all Europe. He had previously written a letter to the emperor in which he had fully answered his question, 'What can we do for Italy?', concluding thus:—

> The emperor can render immense service to Italy—firstly, by inducing Austria to do justice to Piedmont and maintain her engagements; secondly, by obtaining from her a mitigation of the régime that weighs upon Lombardy and Venetia; in the third place, by forcing the King of Naples not to scandalise civilised Europe by a deportment contrary to all the principles of justice and equity; in the fourth place, by re-establishing an equilibrium in Italy such as was settled at the Treaty of Vienna, that is to say, rendering possible the removal of the Austrians from the Legations and the Romagna, by placing those provinces under a secular prince, or procuring them the benefit of a laic and independent administration.

Cavour had the warm sympathy of the English plenipotentiaries, Lords Clarendon and Cowley, and also that of the Buonaparte family. He put himself in friendly relations with the Russian envoys, though Russia and Piedmont had long been on bad terms and lately were open enemies; in short, he left nothing undone to win sympathy for his country, and gain a hearing for her woes; but other questions had to be first decided. The Congress was drawing to a close, and Cavour had found no opportunity to introduce the state of Italy. Austria had been careful to circulate the idea that it was a land of lawless revolutionists; and after the Congress was ended, she would resume her tyranny in the provinces under her rule, and her aggressions against Piedmont, if the question were allowed to sink into oblivion. Outside the Congress the representatives of England and France, in answer to Count Cavour's importunities, invited him to make known his views on the state of Italy, and he drew up a memorial and laid it before these two powers. At last with much difficulty he obtained the emperor's consent to bring the Italian question before the Congress. The particulars of that conference were not made known, but a letter written by the Tuscan minister at Paris will give an idea of what a lively discussion it was.

[Strictly private.]   Paris : April 15, 1856.

In the preceding despatch I had the honour to announce to your Excellency that the Sardic plenipotentiaries were finally allowed to discourse in the Congress on Italian affairs. To the particulars contained in that report I may now add the following :—The motion of the Sardic plenipotentiaries took place on the twentieth supplementary sitting, that is, on April 8. Signor Cavour, having drawn a very ugly picture of the general condition of our peninsula, touched upon the delicate theme of the presence of foreign troops in the pontifical States and in the ducal States ; and endeavoured to show that by means of proper reforms the discontent might be removed, and the country guaranteed against the immense danger of the increasing activity of the revolutionists. He took pains to show that in the Papal States, as in the ducal, there was no want of elements to constitute a force of their own sufficient to maintain order ; and in support of his argument he cited with words of high praise the example of Tuscany, and on the management of our troops he dwelt with much eulogium.

As to the state of the Two Sicilies, Count Cavour, without dissimulation, spoke in the hardest terms, picturing it in the most repulsive colours. He spoke in the same terms of the condition of the Lombardo-Venetian kingdom, and hinted at the necessity of some reforms more in accordance with the requirements of the present age. . . .

Lords Clarendon and Cowley supported strongly the motion of Count Cavour, and passed in review the leading points treated of by the Sardic plenipotentiaries. It was at this point that Lord Clarendon questioned Count Buol in a very warm manner on the intentions of the Cabinet of Vienna with regard to Italy; and Count Buol replied more warmly in a manner to take away all hope that Austria was disposed to enter line upon that ground. The discussion assumed a very grave aspect. Clarendon, piqued by the bare, peremptory reply of Buol, said, 'If your intention is really to make no promise, nor enter into any engagement towards Italy, it amounts to throwing down the gauntlet to Liberal Europe, which will not fail to take it up. The question will then be decided by means the most vigorous and energetic. It is a great mistake for you to believe that *our* forces are exhausted.' It was Clarendon who, talking of the Pontifical States, was bold enough to say that the government of the Pope was *une honte pour l'Europe*. This, which the English plenipotentiary said in a moment of passion, excited the Count Buol, and he replied with great vivacity.

I have reason to believe that the Premier of King Victor Emmanuel is satisfied to be able to say to the Piedmontese Parliament that he has thought of Italy, that his motion has been listened to with favour by the ministers of England and France: and has awakened the sympathy of Europe. I know that the Count Walewski is occupied in trying to reproduce this stormy discussion in the best aspect, and to eliminate from it all traces of the thorns and thistles, the invectives and resentments of the sitting.

'Milord,' said Cavour to Lord Clarendon, coming out of the Congress, 'you see that diplomacy will do nothing for us; it is therefore necessary to think of other means, at least as far as regards Naples.'

He paid a visit to Lord Clarendon subsequently, and briefly stated the case thus:—

That which has passed in the Congress proves two things: first, that Austria is decided to persist in her system of oppression and violence towards Italy;

secondly, that the forces of diplomacy are impotent to modify that system. The consequences for Piedmont will be dreadful. With the irritation on our side, and the arrogance of Austria on the other, there are but two alternatives to take: reconcile ourselves to Austria and the Pope, or prepare to declare war at the Court of Vienna in a future not far distant. If the first part is preferable, I must on my return to Turin advise my king to call to power the friends of Austria and the Pope. If the second hypothesis is best, my friends and I will not shrink from preparing for a terrible war—a war to the death.

Lord Clarendon replied that he believed it was inevitable, but for the present it was best not to speak of it.

'Milord,' urged Cavour, earnestly, 'I have given proofs of my moderation and prudence; and I believe that in politics it is necessary to be excessively reserved in words and very decided in action. There are positions in which there is less peril in a bold course than a very prudent one. La Marmora thinks with me that before long we shall be able to make war, and you will have to aid us.'

'Certainly, if you are in serious embarrassment you may count on our aid,' replied the English plenipotentiary. Doubtless in speaking thus he meant to defend Piedmont from overt acts of aggression, and did not contemplate taking part in a national war of redemption; but this last was plainly what Cavour meant, as he had dwelt more on the general state of Italy, and Lombardy, and Venetia in particular, than the grievances of Piedmont against Austria.

In spite of the fact that the emperor still held back, and told the Sardic minister to go to London and talk to Lord Palmerston before he would give him a decided answer, while the English premier gave him to understand that they would be disposed to defend Piedmont only, not Italy, against Austria—Cavour felt that he had advanced the national cause not a little by openly declaring his country's wrongs before Europe. For the first time Europe was informed officially—not by a conspirator or revolutionist, but by the minister of a king of one of the most ancient dynasties of Europe—that there existed an *Italian* question, and that means ought to be adopted to remove the cause of the disturbance which constantly threatened the peace of the continent.

The treaty of peace was signed on March 30, after which had followed the discussion on Italian affairs.

On April 29 the Sardic minister returned to Turin, well pleased with himself as having done his country good service, and sure of a cordial reception from his king, whom he had kept informed of the minutest particulars of the Congress. He hastened to the palace immediately on his arrival to salute the king and give him the latest news. Victor Emmanuel embraced him, then caught both his hands and shook them repeatedly with a warmth of look and manner which spoke his thanks better than words. He immediately bestowed on him the Order of the Santissima Annunziata.

By June all the Sardinian troops were returned from the Crimea, that is, all that survived—about 4,000 had perished from cholera or in the field—and were received in Turin with enthusiastic applause. On the 16th the king held a grand review in the Piazza d'Armi—a solemn ceremony initiated by thanksgiving for the safe return of the army *in patria*. It was a very imposing spectacle in itself, and the emotions it excited made it more interesting. The king, accompanied by the English, French, and Turkish ambassadors and a brilliant staff, entered the Piazza, round which rose an amphitheatre of seats filled with spectators, and in the midst an altar where the bishop and clergy stood performing the service. The king listened to the prayers on horseback, looking, says his biographer, 'like the statue of his glorious ancestor, Emanuele Filiberto.' The service ended, Victor Emmanuel passed down the lines, amidst the ardent acclamations of the soldiers, who cried *Viva il Rè!* while the spectators added, *Viva l'esercito!*

Viva La Marmora! The gallant general, who rode side by side with the king, was overcome with emotion when he thought of his brave soldiers sleeping in the Crimea, and among them his own brother. When the king had made the round of the Piazza he addressed the troops:—

Officers, Sub-officers and Soldiers!—Hardly a year has passed since I saluted you in sorrow, because I could not be your companion in this memorable undertaking. I meet you again with joy, and tell you you have deserved well of your country. You have responded worthily to my expectations, to the hopes of the country, and to the confidence of our powerful allies, who to-day give you a solemn testimony of it.

Firm in the calamity that afflicted a portion of you, dauntless in war, well-ordered always, you have increased the fame and influence of this elect part of Italy. I retake the banners that I consigned to you, and which you have brought back to me victorious from the East. I shall preserve them as a record of your fatigues, and as a sure pledge that when the honour and the interests of the nation oblige me to return them, they will again be defended by you on the field of battle with equal courage, and covered with new glories.

The king's address was received with immense enthusiasm on the part of both citizens and soldiers. The proceedings terminated by the king distributing the medals for military valour,—his own and those sent by Queen Victoria and the Emperor for the men specially distinguished in the Piedmontese army. All Italy was full of admiration and congratulation for the gallant little army of Piedmont which had so well maintained the national honour; and in spite of the jealous watchfulness of the governments, they subscribed —Lombards, Venetians, Tuscans, Romans, Neapolitans —a sum to provide 100 cannons for the fortress of Alessandria.

The king promoted Alfonso La Marmora to the

highest rank, and loaded him with honours; but he did not wish the general to resume his place in the Cabinet, because on some points they differed strongly. Cavour, however, persuaded the king that the uncompromising soldier's services were necessary, and he yielded. 'The king loves and esteems you sincerely,' wrote the count to his friend. And La Marmora loved and esteemed Victor Emmanuel; nevertheless, they often disagreed.

'Now that you have resumed office,' said the king, 'I hope you will do as I wish.'

'Sire, I will do my duty, now as always,' was the proud reply. It was no idle boast. La Marmora's character commands even more admiration than his great talents—talents which are rarely found united with so much simplicity, modesty, and self-abnegation.

CHAPTER XI.

CONTINUED DISAGREEMENTS WITH AUSTRIA.—MACHINATIONS OF THE CLERICALS AND SECTARIES. A.D. 1857–58.

TIME had not mitigated the burning sense of wrong which Piedmont felt towards Austria as the implacable enemy of her liberties; nor the fear and hatred which Austria felt towards Piedmont as the head-centre of revolutionary doctrine subversive of her power in the peninsula. These hostile sentiments had settled into a chronic irritation, which at times broke out in fierce diplomatic conflicts. Victor Emmanuel suffered from this suppressed rage against Austria more perhaps than any man in his kingdom. After the treaty of peace in 1849, he had tried hard to conquer it, and accept his fate with a good grace. For a few years a semblance of amicable relations was kept up, though they never exceeded the coldest courtesy. When the Archduke Albert of Austria expressed a desire to see his sister, the Queen of Sardinia, he was not invited to Turin for the purpose.

Victor Emmanuel did not wish to entertain his obnoxious relative with false compliments; all he would do was to permit his wife to meet her brother on Lombard territory. With the queen's death every tie was severed, and Victor felt free to pursue the policy his inclination dictated, that inclination being uncompromising enmity towards Austria, as long as an Austrian soldier remained on Italian soil.

It is idle to deny that his soul was filled with this ambition of driving the foreigner out of Italy, from the day he ascended the throne. Of course his ministers did not avow it in diplomatic language, but *he* never concealed his wishes. 'They said Italy should have been my father's, and Italy shall be mine,' he said at the time of the Crimean War. We must remember this was after the Italian princes had all betrayed the national cause and united themselves with Austria. He kept alive and concentrated in himself the hopes of the national party; Lombards, Romans, Neapolitans, all agreed that the young King of Sardinia was the only man in Italy who could ever work out the redemption of their common country. This was reason enough to make him hated and feared by Austria, whose great aim was to prove Italy, what Prince Metternich said she was, a mere 'geographical expression.'

'The King of Sardinia,' wrote a Neapolitan minister to the Court of Vienna, 'only waits a favourable moment to put himself at the head of a revolutionary movement throughout Italy.'

So far they did him no wrong, for that was really his intention. But they did slander him and his government when they persisted in trying to convince Europe that the king and his ministers organised and fomented conspiracies against the governments of other States; that political assassinations and all lawless deeds had their origin among the most well-ordered, well-conducted, loyal people in the peninsula, as the Piedmontese undoubtedly were. Nothing could be more contrary to Victor Emmanuel's policy and that of his great minister, than lawless violence, and secret conspiracies. His object was to *detach* the cause of Italy from Mazzinianism, and unite it in his own person with constitutional monarchy. It was absurd to suppose that the representative of an old hereditary sovereignty, like Victor Emmanuel, could be a revolutionist in the sense they said he was, to imagine that the head of the Savoy dynasty could think and act like a political adventurer who had no family name to sustain, a demagogue who had no position or character to lose. But the Austrian press, which once attacked Pio Nono as a demon of revolution, could not be expected to make nice distinctions with regard to Victor Emmanuel's Liberalism. He was opposed to Austrian rule in Italy, and that was enough to make those writers represent the King of Sardinia as a sort of brigand chief, who, though he maintained a savage discipline in his own State, recognised no international obligations and kept no faith with neighbouring princes. These calumnies were partly believed till the Crimean war brought Piedmont into notice, and made her people and king better known throughout Europe. Cavour's agitation of the Italian question at the Congress of Paris did much to enlighten the world, while it provoked the rulers of Austria beyond description. Renewed accusations and recriminations followed. The king's government was not remiss in replying that the disorders complained of had their origin in the bad system of administration pursued in the Italian principalities. The King of Naples and the dukes followed in the wake of Austria, and laid at the door of Victor Emmanuel every political offence perpetrated in their dominions.

> The king [writes Cavour in one of his notes] repels every insinuation tending to generate the belief that he disturbs abroad, by means direct or indirect, that peace, that tranquillity, which he knows how to maintain constantly in his own state. It is not by the reasonable and temperate exercise of moderate liberty that disorders and insurrections are born. The history of Piedmont during these late years proves it clearly. The

grand-ducal government knows by experience in how many circumstances Sardinia has efficaciously co-operated to impede disturbances, internal and external. . . . The king knows what international obligations mean, and fulfils them scrupulously.

Again, he says, in reply to an opposition member,—

We have always followed a frank, loyal policy without duplicity, and so long as we shall be at peace with other potentates we will not employ revolutionary means, nor ever seek to excite tumults or rebellions in their states.

If we had proposed to ourselves such an aim as the honourable Brofferio hinted ; if we had intended to send ships to aid revolutionary movements, before doing it we would have declared war. As to Naples, it is with pain that I reply to the hon. Brofferio. He has spoken of a very melancholy fact, the blowing up of a magazine of a ship of war, involving the loss of many lives—a horrid deed. He has spoken in a manner to lead one to believe that this act was the work of the Italian party. I deny the assertion boldly in the interest of Italy. No, gentlemen, these acts cannot be placed to the account of the national Italian party. They are the isolated acts of some deluded wretch, who may merit compassion, but must be stigmatised by all wise men ; and above all, by those who have at heart the honour and interest of Italy.

In the month of February, while Victor Emmanuel and Cavour were fighting these battles on Italian ground, a heavy misfortune from without came upon them, which both felt deeply. It was the defection of their best ally, in whom they trusted most, who had never misjudged them ; whose soldiers, only last year, had mingled their blood on the battle-field with that of the Piedmontese ; who had welcomed King Victor and his ministers with the warmest hospitality and most eager demonstrations of sympathy that could be imagined. Suspicions of the

French Emperor's fidelity had induced the British Government to form an alliance with Austria, not without a protest from the more generous-minded portion of the nation. 'L'Italia era la vittima immolata sull' altare di tale riconciliazione,' says an Italian historian. In the month of February the Neapolitan ambassador at London wrote to his king—strictly private—as follows :—

> The English Government, firmly bound as it is at present to Austria, will not admit of a change of dynasty in the Two Sicilies. It has abandoned the protection of revolution in Italy, and renounced the idea of the independence of Sicily. Lord Clarendon assures me of this as a *gentleman*.

The word *gentleman*, italicised, is in English.[1]

This alliance was a heavy blow to the Italian cause. Even without the material aid which Lord Clarendon had led Count Cavour to expect at the termination of the Crimean War, the moral support of such a power as England was felt to be very important. It is true that the British Government undertook to make Austria behave better for the future ; and some amelioration of the condition of the Lombardo-Venetian provinces was due undoubtedly to English influence. An amnesty was granted to the banished Lombards, who had for the most part taken refuge in Piedmont, their confiscated property was restored, and the enlightened and benignant Archduke Maximilian sent as viceroy to conciliate the discontented inhabitants.

With these liberal measures towards Lombardy-Venice, Austrian fury against Piedmont raged more violently than ever ; and the most virulent attacks on the government appeared in the official gazette of Milan—attacks which Cavour never failed to answer with a proud defiance. To him the sudden clemency of the Vienna Government was only an artifice to win over the Lombards to the side of Austria in case of another war with Piedmont. That such a war was imminent he could no

---

[1] Archives of Foreign Affairs in Naples. See *Camillo Cavour, Documents Edited and Unedited.*

longer doubt, as great military preparations were constantly going forward near the frontier. At last diplomatic relations were broken off between the two countries. On March 22 the Austrian ambassador took his leave of the King of Sardinia, putting the affairs of his legation in the hands of the Prussian minister. The same day an order was sent to the Sardic ambassador to quit Vienna, and leave *his* affairs in the hands of the French legation.

In order further to conciliate his Italian subjects, the Emperor Francis Joseph made a tour through the provinces; but his welcome was strictly official; he was received with chilling coldness everywhere. On the very day he entered the Lombard capital the official gazette of Turin announced that Milan was about to present a testimonial of esteem and regard to the Piedmontese army.

'The decisive moment approaches,' said Victor Emmanuel solemnly to Cavour. But though' they knew it to be inevitable, they did not wish to precipitate it too soon. The difficulties which the Piedmontese Government laboured under were aggravated by another insurrectionary attempt of Mazzini, who, as usual, rushed forward to complicate still more the already too complicated state of affairs. This conspiracy being hatched at Genoa furnished the friends of despotic power with an argument against the Sardinian Government, and involved it in a tedious dispute with Naples, which lasted nearly a year.

The loss of the English alliance was somewhat compensated for in the increasing friendship of the Czar of Russia. Two of his brothers visited Victor Emmanuel at Turin, and brought him their sovereign's warmest assurances of regard. His mother, the widow of the late Emperor Nicholas, came to pass the winter at Nice, where the king visited her twice, and bestowed such delicate attentions upon her—she being in feeble health—that she declared him to be the most gallant prince in Europe; and before returning home in spring she paid a visit to Turin to thank him for his hospitality.

The King of Saxony was another royal guest whom Victor Emmanuel received during that winter. He was pleased to have an opportunity of showing a German prince how well ordered and contented his subjects were, and what progress they were daily making in civilised arts. Wherever a railway was to be opened or a foundation-stone laid, the king was sure to be there to applaud and encourage the workers in their undertaking.

On August 30 Victor Emmanuel went to Chambéry to inaugurate the opening of the Mont Cenis pass, and the following day he went to place the first stone of a bridge across the Rhone. He was received very warmly by the Savoyards; and amongst other deputations that waited on him was one composed of a number of noble ladies who had a petition to present. They were received with great courtesy, which gave them hope that their petition would not be rejected. It prayed his majesty to revoke the decree which had been issued a short time before, by the Minister of Public Instruction, to close the School of the Sacred Heart in Chambéry, because the sisters refused to obey the law which required teachers to have a diploma.

The king's gallantry did not carry him so far. He frankly replied:—

'I should be happy to do your ladyships any pleasure possible. But you must know that as a constitutional sovereign I must be the first to set an example of respect for the laws, and I cannot interfere.'

'And where shall we have our daughters educated in future?' asked one of the petitioners.

'I can tell you where they will find instructors far superior to the *suore*. Educate your girls yourselves,' said the king with a low bow to the deputation.

The ladies, baffled by the complimentary refusal, retired without further remonstrance.

Towards the end of the year 1857, the Parliament, now four years old, was dissolved. The general election which took place in November was seized upon as a grand occasion for the reactionary party to put their machinery in motion. In their efforts to overturn the Liberal government, the clergy did not scruple to make common cause secretly with the Mazzinian faction; and between the 'clericals' and the 'sectaries' the moderate government stood in a precarious position. Cavour writes despondingly at this time:—

> Public affairs hold me in very great suspense. Abandoned by England, having in front of us Austria, malevolent and hostile, obliged to struggle against Rome and the other Italian princes—you can imagine how difficult our position is. . . . In spite of all, I am not quite discouraged, because I believe that the country is with us.

The elections, however, went against him, and it needed all his extraordinary ability to hold the ground he had gained so hardly, inch by inch, the last seven years. But the patience and perseverance of this great man were inexhaustible, and the king's courage and resolution indomitable.

In the king's speech at the opening of Parliament, he alluded briefly to 'the interruption of friendly intercourse with a neighbouring state,' without offering any explanation on the subject, or expressing any hope of a better understanding in the future. The fact was he did not hope it, and feeling that war was inevitable, he did not choose to give utterance to any diplomatic regrets on the subject. Victor Emmanuel's speeches from the throne are stamped with the sincerity of his own character; though they were of course the composition of his ministers, he was particular to read them with care, so that nothing should be put into his mouth, as coming personally from him, of which he did not approve; and he often required an alteration or insertion of a phrase, and often added a paragraph.

'The ministerial responsibility covers me, I know,' he often said, 'but still I must think of my own conscience.'

Yet he was rarely at variance with his ministers; for

if his objection to any measure was not perfectly just and reasonable, he was open to conviction, and ready to acknowledge himself wrong. Once the Minister of Public Instruction, Lanza, had a difference with the king on the subject of two nominations, which he had made in the colleges, of foreign professors—the Committee of Public Instruction having preferred two Piedmontese. The king sided with the committee, and refused to sign when presented with the nomination. Lanza respectfully argued the case, and put before the sovereign the bad policy and illiberality of not employing men of high ability, no matter whence they came; but as these men were Italians they were their own countrymen, and entitled to be regarded as Victor Emmanuel's subjects, since they entertained the same aspirations after national independence. The king, convinced, took up his pen and signed, thanking his minister with a warm shake of the hand for the frankness with which he had spoken.

At the end of this year, just a few days before the opening of Parliament, an illustrious senator, the Count Siccardi, died, leaving a grateful memory behind him of the services he had rendered his country, in carrying the anti-clerical laws in the face of such terrible difficulties.

The year 1858 opened inauspiciously by a criminal attempt, which threatened utter ruin to the Italian cause by estranging the power most disposed to befriend it. A young Italian, Felice Orsini, who had suffered much from Austrian oppression, and had been bred in the unwholesome air of secret societies, where he imbibed the pernicious doctrine of the justifiableness of tyrannicide—tried to destroy the French emperor on his way to the theatre, by the explosion of a sort of bomb, popularly called an 'infernal machine.' Fortunately the plot failed. Orsini and his two confederates were arrested and tried. It turned out that they had been in England just before, where they had planned the murderous attempt. England was then open to precisely the same charge as Piedmont had been with regard to the conspiracies conceived in Genoa by Mazzini. Free countries naturally become the refuge of political exiles; they come without any encouragement on the part of the rulers, for they are not desirable subjects. But as long as they respect the laws of the state, they are permitted to live in peace, and go away when they like; and it is impossible for the government to be responsible for what projects they may design in the country, and perpetrate when they get out of it. Despotic rulers, however, always look with suspicion on neighbouring countries which enjoy more liberty than their subjects. And so the French emperor hurled the same reproaches at his late ally, as Austria had done at Piedmont. He called England 'a den of assassins.' British journals replied by reminding him of the *coup d'état*, and informing him that 'England loathed an assassin, whether killer of thousands or killer of one.' This was unkind, as the offence had been condoned when he was taken into the alliance, in consideration of his general good conduct after its perpetration, and the promise of future good faith and uprightness. But the fact was, that though he had won the queen's confidence and affection, the English nation never put perfect trust in him, and of late there had been a suspicion that the star of his destiny was moving in a northerly direction, and likely to stand still over the British Isles. So the indignation felt against him was general throughout the whole kingdom. Napoleon III. in his outcry against conspiracies seemed to have utterly forgotten the hospitality that England had once extended to him, a political exile, much addicted to conspiracy; and that he had gained the throne by a conspiracy even more culpable than Orsini's, bad as it was. His appeal to all the powers, however, called attention to the subject, and it was found that the secret societies were gaining ground to an alarming extent. The English Government sent information to the King of Sardinia that *his* life was also threatened by the fanatical republicans, inspired by Orsini's example. Even in the city of Turin an article in one of the journals appeared apologising for the deed.

Victor Emmanuel and his advisers were deeply distressed by the unfortunate event. It seemed as if some perverse fate were trying to circumvent every effort to regenerate Italy. In order to neutralise the effect of Orsini's attempt on the mind of the emperor, Victor Emmanuel wrote him a long private letter, putting the case clearly before him, and earnestly entreating him not to condemn or abandon the nation for the misdeeds of a few fanatics. Cavour writes to a friend in profound melancholy at the prospect before him.

> The present time is full of difficulties and dangers; they augment daily. There is no longer any restraint on the fury of the sectaries, and their perversity increases the strength of the reaction, which becomes every day more threatening. In the midst of these opposite perils, what are the Liberals to do? If they divide they are lost, and with them falls the cause of Italian liberty and independence. We shall stand in the breach imperturbable and resolute; but fall we must, unless our friends group themselves round us to aid in our defence against the assaults that come from right and left.

A bill was introduced into the Piedmontese Parliament to define the offence of 'apologising for regicide,' and to punish more effectually the crime of conspiracy.

Orsini's death redeemed his life, and proved him to be one of those disinterested enthusiasts, whose fine nature had been warped by bad example and teaching. Penitent for his crime, he wrote a touching letter to the emperor, not asking for grace for himself, which he did not desire,—but humbly entreating aid for his beloved Italy. This letter was forwarded to Cavour, who had it published, with a few words of introduction from himself, pointing the moral.

The king requested Cavour to address a letter to the Papal Government, begging them to cease inundating the country with discontented subjects of the Holy See, and pointing out that the system of banishing every suspected person was most pernicious to the Roman

States, and to Italy at large. 'Keep them at home; punish them if necessary, but keep them at home,' was, in brief, the burden of the missive.

> This system of expulsion from their own state (writes Cavour)—exercised on so large a scale by the Pontifical Government, that in our state alone there are one hundred subjects of the Holy See—cannot but have dreadful consequences. The man exiled on suspicion, or because his conduct is not so good as it ought to be, is not always corrupt, or affiliated indissolubly with revolutionary factions. Kept in his own country under surveillance, or punished if necessary, he might mend his ways, or at least not become dangerous. But irritated by illegal measures, sent into exile, constrained to live outside respectable society, often without the means of subsistence, he necessarily puts himself in relation with the fomenters of revolution. It is then easy for them to seduce him and bind him to their society. The exile, in short, becomes a sectary—often a very dangerous sectary.[1] Hence one can say, with reason, that the system followed by the Pontifical Government is calculated to swell the army of revolutionists. . . . To the measures adopted by the Holy See is to be attributed the extraordinary vitality of the Mazzinian party.

On March 14, which was the king's birthday, and also that of his eldest son Humbert, now fourteen, he conferred upon the prince the rank of captain in an infantry regiment, because he wished 'to attach him to the army whose perils and glories he should one day share, when the honour of the country required it.'

---

[1] In Italian, *settario* means simply member of a secret society, or sect, as they call it.

CHAPTER XII.

'J'ATTENDS MON ASTRE.' A.D. 1858-9.

VICTOR EMMANUEL and Camillo Cavour, by a happy union of diplomatic ability, courage, and prudence,—not only lived down the slanderous attacks of their enemies, but turned the tables on them, and showed clearly to all Europe that while Piedmont was peaceful, contented, and loyal, all the other States of Italy were a prey to violent disorders, the result of gross misgovernment,—more especially the Two Sicilies and the States of the Church.' We have not space here to dwell on the sufferings of the inhabitants of the kingdom of Naples and the Roman States; but their condition presented a picture to excite indignation and pity.[1]

The Austrian provinces, hitherto much oppressed, now enjoyed a respite under the mild rule of the Archduke Maximilian. But this change of policy on the part of the conquerors did not mitigate one iota the sentiment of hostility which the natives felt towards them. No amount of conciliation could now win their hearts. They had suffered too much in the past; the iron had entered into their soul. And though Maximilian was personally popular, the firm resolve to banish the House of Hapsburg from Italian soil was stronger than ever in the hearts of the Lombards and Venetians. There was something noble in the indifference they showed to the material advantages offered them by the ruling race, and in the proud cold bearing with which they received the conciliations of a most amiable and fascinating prince, whose winning qualities had power to disarm hostility in the breasts of the most inveterate enemies of his house. Maximilian admired and respected their pride, and when he became an in-

---

[1] See *I Casi di Napoli* (Massari); Gladstone's *Prisons of Naples*; *La Vita di Pio Nono*; *Correspondenze di Panizzi*; *Ricordanze della Mia Vita*, da Settembrini.

dependent sovereign, eagerly sought the friendship of the Italian king, with whom he kept up the best relations to the end of his brief unhappy reign. This generous, just, and noble-minded prince deserved a better fate than that which his injudicious friend, Napoleon III., allotted to him as Emperor of Mexico.

Many illustrious exiles, who by no means came under the denomination of the *sectaries* and *conspirators* condemned by Count Cavour, had fled from the oppressed principalities, and received an hospitable welcome in the Sardinian states. These had seen the folly of partial and local revolutions, without proper guidance and discipline. They desired nothing more than a just amount of liberty under a constitutional monarchy, such as Piedmont enjoyed, but such as their sovereigns, they knew by experience, would never grant. They desired the next revolutionary movement to be an uprising of all Italy to expel the foreigner and his satraps, and this movement to be led by a native prince. So they had come to centre all their hopes of regeneration on the one honest king in the peninsula, whose example seemed all the brighter because of the darkness by which he was surrounded.

These exiles had beset King Victor from the time he came to the throne with passionate appeals for help for their afflicted countries. Almost all the books written on the subject of Italian nationality, and narratives of the revolutions, were dedicated to him, or to the memory of his father. If he ventured to congratulate himself on the improving state of his kingdom and the contentment of his subjects, they did not fail to remind him that there were others of his Italian countrymen, who felt as loyally towards him, still groaning under an oppressive foreign yoke. All this made a deep impression on his mind, stirred all his generous sympathies, and kept constantly alive in his soul the noble ambition which his father had bequeathed to him of accomplishing national emancipation. The decisive moment approached which Victor Emmanuel felt could no longer be postponed. It was now three years since, at the close of the

Crimean War, Napoleon III. had asked that momentous question which thrilled his listener's heart, *Que peut-on faire pour l'Italie?* And nothing had been done, nor attempted.

Victor Emmanuel thought that it was time to represent to his ally that if he desired to do something for Italy, and take away the cause of a continual disturbance of the peace of Europe, the time had arrived. In obedience to a secret invitation, Count Cavour met the Emperor Napoleon, on July 20, at Plombières. The business was kept strictly private between the king and himself, so that no one knew the purport of the meeting till the end of the year. The result of that interview was calculated to raise Victor Emmanuel's hopes and fill his soul with glorious anticipations. In spite of the secrecy enjoined by his minister, he was heard to say in confidence, 'Next year I shall be King of Italy, or plain M. de Savoie.' Reviewing the troops in the Piazza d'Armi, the king, in speaking to a colonel, gave expression to some 'bellicose' words, which, being repeated and exaggerated, caused great disturbance in the diplomatic world, and brought down severe rebukes upon him. A few careless words to one of his own officers at a review, were criticised in the journals as a 'speech.' Indignation articles, even in France, were written upon the subject; and it was said that the unrestrained ambition of the Sardinian king, supported by his turbulent minister, threatened Europe with the calamities of war. Cavour, who had to act as a cork, bottling down the patriotic ardour of his king, entreated his majesty not to make such warlike speeches in public or private, since the eyes of Europe were jealously watching his every word and movement. But though he reproached his imprudence, no one admired the fiery spirit, which he alone knew how to rein in, more than Cavour himself.

Towards the end of the year 1858 another visit from the royal family of Russia showed increasing esteem and cordiality on their part. The Grand Duke Constantine and his wife were such enthusiastic admirers of Victor Emmanuel and his state, that a Russian noble said they had become quite *Piedmontese*. The princess said to Cavour, 'In Russia we are proud to have such a friend as your king.'

The auspicious year 1859 opened with brighter prospects than the last. It was just ten years since Charles Albert had made up his mind to embark on that last fatal venture of his life which brought his country to the verge of destruction. *J'attends mon astre*, was the motto he had chosen; and unlucky as had been that star for him, his son still waited in the sure and certain hope that it would rise all glorious one day and reward his faith and patience. It had taken all those ten years for Victor Emmanuel, by constant strenuous effort, to recover the prestige lost in the campaign of 1849. But he had done it; and now that the ten years' armistice—which Count Balbo had called the Peace of Milan—was about to expire, he stood on the threshold of the new year, impatient for the moment when he might unsheathe the sword and wash out the memory of Novara.

The Parliament was to be opened January 10, and the king and his ministers were much exercised over the royal speech for a fortnight before it was to be delivered. Victor Emmanuel was disposed to throw down the gauntlet without further delay; he could not give utterance to language calculated to mislead the public. Cavour said they were not yet prepared for war, and it would be giving the enemy an unfair advantage to announce their intentions so soon. 'Then, if I cannot speak clearly, better say nothing,' said the king; and the minister had much trouble in convincing him that he must say *something*. Piedmont—all Italy—expected to hear the voice of the king, and must not be disappointed. 'We will say all we can,' said Cavour. 'We must try and reconcile prudence with candour.'

'Well, then,' said Victor, at last yielding, as he generally did, to Cavour's convincing arguments, 'I will speak; but I wish the speech to be brief.' This all-important composition, which was to unite brevity and clearness, prudence and boldness, frankness and reticence —which was to give comfort and hope to the Italians, but not to give open offence to Austria—was found to be a very difficult task, and was not completed till the day before the opening of Parliament.

On New Year's day, the king, according to custom, received a number of deputations who came to wish him the compliments of the season. First there was the diplomatic body; and in conversing with them Victor Emmanuel was reserved and cautious, as he had promised Count Cavour he would be. It was some time since diplomatic relations with Austria had been broken, so he was not under the necessity of receiving a representative of that much-hated power. The new French ambassador was Prince La Tour d'Auvergne, who was struck with the king's good sense and dignity. '*J'admire l'élévation d'esprit avec laquelle le roi Victor cause des affaires,*' he said to Signor Massari coming out from the reception. With the senators and deputies he also behaved admirably. But the magistrates unfortunately spoke of the important events of the past year, which drew from the king the remark that the year they were entering on might bear still more important ones. As soon as the deputation was gone he was seized with remorse; and when Cavour entered the room, he came to meet him with a smile of compunction, saying,

'Forgive me, I have done it!'

'How, and with whom, your majesty?' asked the Count in some anxiety.

'In speaking to the magistrates.'

'The magistrates!' said Cavour, with his good-humoured laugh. 'The most peaceable people in the world! How did you do it?'

'Forgive me,' said the king again. 'I followed your advice as long as it was possible; but I really could not keep in any longer.'

Cavour's exquisite sense of humour was highly tickled at the incorrigibility of his royal pupil, and we can imagine him laughing till he had to take off his gold spectacles and wipe them, while the king joined heartily in the laugh against himself. The glimpses we get of the intercourse between Victor Emmanuel and his illustrious minister convey the idea of perfect confidence, friendship and sympathy; though they sometimes had sharp disputes on public questions.

Cabinet councils were held on January 8th and 9th in preparation for the opening of Parliament on the 10th, but still the speech of the Crown was unfinished, because it was so difficult to be bold and frank as the king required, and at the same time cautious and ambiguous as prudence dictated. The speech was in point of fact written out in a manner to satisfy the king, but the ministers still hesitated as to the advisability of allowing him to deliver it exactly as it was worded. The last paragraph, dealing with the Austrian difficulty, held the pith of the discourse. It had been sent for approbation to the Emperor, but he, finding it too strong, suggested the famous passage,—'While we respect treaties, we are not insensible to the cry of anguish (*grido di dolore*) which comes up to us from many parts of Italy,'—which pleased the king and was adopted.[1]

The royal speech was brief, but it contained that which satisfied the king, ministers, Parliament, and nation. It became a memorable historic utterance, for the famous *grido di dolore* set all Italy on fire, and hastened the inevitable breach with Austria. The king was up at daybreak on the morning of the 10th, reading over the speech, and making some trifling alterations. Then he read it aloud to Count Cavour, to see that his tones gave the proper signification to the words. He had, unfortunately, a sore throat, and he said, laughing with his usual jocularity, 'I am afraid that with this confounded sore throat the first tenor will not sing his part well.'

As he ascended the stairs of the Palazzo Madama a deputation of senators came to meet him, according to custom; and to one he was particularly fond of, he said with a happy smile, 'Dear Cibrario,

---

[1] The origin of the *grido di dolore* has been kept a secret by Signor Massari till his recent publication of La Marmora's life.

you shall hear nice things!' The Chamber presented an unusually festive appearance, and was crowded to excess. Nothing was known of the policy for the coming year, and everyone was impatient to hear the royal utterance, seeming to expect something more than an ordinary 'king's speech,' a mere rehearsal of facts already well known to the public. His majesty took his seat on the throne amid loud applause; but when he opened the paper he was about to read, there was a sudden profound silence; all awaited with eager impatience the words about to fall from his lips. He held his audience in suspense another minute, while he swept the assembly with a flashing eye which revealed the excitement of his mind.

Gentlemen Senators, Gentlemen Deputies,—The new Legislature, inaugurated a year ago, has not disappointed the hopes of the country nor my expectations. By means of an enlightened and loyal concord we have been enabled to surmount the difficulties that beset our policy external and internal, thus rendering more solid those broad principles of nationality and of progress on which our liberal institutions repose. Following on the same road this new year, you will be able to accomplish improvements in the various branches of the legislation and of the public administration. In the past session there were presented to you various projects for amending the administration of justice. Resuming the interrupted examination, I trust that in this you will be able to provide for the re-ordering of the magistracy, the courts of assizes, and the court of procedure. You shall be called again to deliberate on the reform of the administration of the communes and of the provinces. The lively interest that the subject awakes will be an incitement to dedicate to it your special care.

There shall be proposed to you some modifications of the laws of the National Guard. In order to preserve the basis of this noble institution intact, and render it more efficacious at all times, it is necessary

THE EFFECT OF THE SPEECH. 137

to introduce some improvements suggested by experience.

The commercial crisis from which our country has not been exempt, and the calamity which repeatedly strikes our principal industry, diminishes the income of the State, and prevents us for the present realising the hope of equalising the expenses with the public revenues. That will not prevent you—in the examination of the future balance-sheet—from trying to reconcile the needs of the State with the principles of a severe economy.

Gentlemen Senators, Gentlemen Deputies,—The horizon in which the new year rises is not quite serene. That notwithstanding, you will apply yourselves with your usual alacrity to your parliamentary labours. Strengthened by the experiences of the past, we will go resolutely forward to meet the future. This future will be happy, if we repose our policy on justice, on the love of liberty and of country.

Our country, small in territory, has acquired credit in the councils of Europe, because she is great in the idea she represents, in the sympathy that she inspires. This situation is not exempt from perils, for, *while we respect treaties, we are not insensible to the cry of anguish that comes up to us from many parts of Italy.* Strong in concord, confident in our good right, we await with prudence and resolution the decrees of Divine Providence.

To appreciate the thrilling effect produced by this discourse, we must remember that it was quite new to the audience. They had not been behind the scenes 'assisting' at the composition of it, nor known how that *grido di dolore*, which went straight to their hearts, had been the suggestion of the Emperor. And though the king read the speech which everyone knew had been prepared for him, there was a fire and animation in his look and tone as he delivered it, which made it seem the spontaneous expression of feeling which rushed from the heart to the lips of the royal speaker. The scene in the assembly must be described in the vivid language of an Italian eye-witness [1] :—

At every period the speech was interrupted by clamorous applause, and cries of '*Viva il Rè!*' But when he came to the words, *grido di dolore*, there was an enthusiasm quite indescribable. Senators, deputies, spectators, all sprang to their feet with a bound, and broke into passionate acclamations. The ministers of France, Russia, Prussia, and England were utterly astonished and carried away by the marvellous spectacle. The face of the ambassador of Naples was covered with a gloomy pallor. We poor exiles did not even attempt to wipe away the tears that flowed copiously, unrestrainedly from our eyes, as we frantically clapped our hands in applause of that king who had remembered our sorrows, who had promised us a country. Before the victories, the plébiscites, and the annexations conferred on him the crown of Italy, he reigned in our hearts; he was our king!

Before the day was done the speech was repeated by thousands of lips; it passed like an electric shock from one end of the peninsula to the other. It was quoted by hundreds of writers and speakers, both friends and enemies, with the passionate comments which their respective feelings dictated.

The comments of the *Codini*, condensed, read somewhat in this style: 'Threatening language of the Sardinian king; boundless ambition, unscrupulous as to means; nothing sacred that blocks his way; ready to plunge Europe into a bloody war to gratify insatiable desire for dynastic aggrandisement,' etc., etc.

The *Liberali*, on the other hand, with rapturous applause, spoke their gratitude to the honest king and daring soldier, who had lent an ear to their cry of anguish. He had spoken like a patriot prince, whose Italian heart was still the same as when he led the for-

---

[1] Massari, author of a *Life of Gioberti*, a *Life of Cavour*, a *Life of Victor Emmanuel*, a *Life of La Marmora*.

lorn hope of Piedmont against the Austrian guns at Novara. Ten years of patient endurance had not changed his sentiments; he was still theirs—Italy's—the champion of their liberties, the first soldier of Italian independence. Under the banner of such a leader, who would not be proud to enrol himself? *Viva Vittorio*, the gallant, the loyal, and the true! *Viva Casa Savoya!* —these and like expressions were heard on all sides.

They prepared themselves for war; the young men in the different States collected all the little wealth that they might without exciting the suspicion of their governments, and quietly took their way northwards to be ready at a moment's notice. Amongst these were nobles of the highest rank, some nephews of cardinals, and one nephew of the prime minister of Tuscany. Every town sent its contribution of a gallant little band to the national war, which was expected even sooner than it actually broke out.

Victor Emmanuel had to pay a good price for the alliance of the French Emperor. Two sacrifices he had to make which wounded his heart deeply, and which nothing but the cause of Italy, which absolutely depended on those sacrifices, would have induced him to accomplish. The Bonaparte family desiring much to connect themselves with the ancient dynasties of Europe, a marriage was proposed between the emperor's cousin, Prince Napoleon Jerome, and Clotilde, the eldest child of Victor Emmanuel, then not much past fifteen years. The princess was a bright girl, with a mind matured beyond her years, full of maternal care for her brothers and sister, and devotedly attached to her father, who loved her tenderly. The first mention of the marriage the king met with a repugnance which could not be overcome. To separate his child at so tender an age from all family ties, and give her to a man who had more than twice her years, was an idea which he could not entertain. But the statesmen returned again and again to the subject, and he was given to understand that this matrimony must be a condition of the French alliance. The king consulted the opinion of all the men he most esteemed, and laid the whole matter before them. They admired the strength of his paternal affection, but naturally thought more of the national welfare than the happiness of the princess; and expected that a king should sacrifice personal feelings for the public good. At last Victor Emmanuel, with a heavy heart, said to his minister, 'You have convinced me of the political reasons which render this marriage useful and necessary to our cause. I yield to your arguments, but I make a great sacrifice in so doing. My consent is subject to the condition that my daughter gives hers freely.'

It was not in the nature of things that a young girl should receive this proposal with a good grace. Her father would not urge her, but Cavour was there, who knew how to play upon the finest chords of the human heart with the most skilful and delicate touch. The princess was convinced that, to be worthy of the noble race from which she sprung, she must sacrifice herself for the honour of that house, the love of her father, the redemption of her country. She was Victor Emmanuel's daughter—with all his generous pride of race and love of country—and she consented. Cavour, wily diplomatist as he was, had a warm heart, and when he related the scene to a friend, and described the noble bearing of the young girl, his eyes were filled with tears. 'I have the hope that my good daughter will be happy,' said the king, trying to persuade himself that the marriage would turn out well. The ceremony took place on January 29, and the wedded couple set out for France at once. The bride was accompanied by ladies of the Sardinian court, and the king went as far as Genoa, to see them embark. It was a bitter moment to Victor Emmanuel; the princess could hardly tear herself from her father's arms, and he broke down utterly in saying the last farewell.

Among the wedding presents which the king bestowed on the day of the marriage, was a very handsome ring which he gave to Count Cavour. 'Your majesty knows I have no wife—nor will I ever take one,' observed the minister, apropos of rings.

'*La sua sposa è la Patria.* I know it,' replied the king gracefully.

The other sacrifice which Victor Emmanuel was called upon to make was the cession of Nice and Savoy to France, in return for her aid in helping to liberate North Italy 'from the Alps to the Adriatic,' as the emperor expressed it. It was a bitter trial to him to have to surrender the cradle of his race, from which his dynasty took its title; but nothing should be allowed to stand in the way of national independence. The treaty of alliance was signed January 18, by Prince Napoleon and General Neil on the part of France, and Count Cavour and General La Marmora on the part of Sardinia. It was kept strictly secret, as the emperor bound himself to aid the king only in case of Austria being the aggressor. Victor Emmanuel's patience was at its last ebb; Austria had the power of tormenting him in a thousand ways without absolutely invading his dominions. But still his allies preached patience to him. '*Il faut attendre, sire,*' said General Neil. '*J'attends depuis dix ans, Général,*' was the brief but pregnant reply.

The marriage of the Princess Clotilde following close on the warlike speech of the king had a significance which the diplomatists were quick to understand. Austria had already made military preparations on a large scale; Piedmont now did likewise. The volunteers from all parts of Italy hastened to the Subalpine capital; and the prince of volunteers, Giuseppe Garibaldi, put his sword at the command of the Sardinian king, whose born subject he was, though he had earned his great military renown in the service of republics in divers parts of the world. All minor differences of opinion were at that moment forgotten by every sincere lover of his country. Lombardy and Venetia, particularly, were in a state of wild excitement; the youth of every class in those provinces flocked in great numbers to the standard of Victor Emmanuel. Ladies of rank gave their money, jewellery, and articles of luxury; poor women made a sacrifice of their every comfort to aid the national cause; all encouraged and animated their male relatives to join the Sardinian army. And it was marvellous to see how quickly, at the first scent of war, the luxurious, pleasure-loving nobles left their palaces, villas, horses, and carriages a prey to Austrian greed, and betook themselves with cheerful alacrity to the life of privation and hardship which is the lot of an Italian soldier.

CHAPTER XIII.

THE FIRST SOLDIER OF ITALIAN INDEPENDENCE.
A.D. 1859.

NOTWITHSTANDING all the preparations for war on the part of the belligerents, each equally eager to attack the other, four months elapsed before the first gun was fired. These months were consumed in vain but strenuous efforts on the part of England, Prussia, and Russia to accommodate matters peacefully. Towards the end of January the Austrian minister, Count Buol, sent a despatch to the London ambassador, in which he tried to prove that the King of Sardinia was responsible for all the discontent and disorder of the peninsula; and proposing that the great powers should unite to make Piedmont modify her institutions. The indignation of Victor Emmanuel when he heard of this attempt to undermine him, knew no bounds. It was like bearding a lion in his den to hint at meddling with the constitution of his state. Piedmont at least was his, and should enjoy that freedom for which he and his father had fought, and shed their subjects' blood. Sooner than surrender it, they would die at the foot of their Alps, or 'all go to America.'

Cavour, however, was a match for Count Buol. In reply to a question of Lord Derby as to what was the best expedient to pacify Italy and improve her state, he sent a memorandum, which was an able indictment against Austria for her unjust usurpations in Italy, and a rehearsal of all the efforts made by her to annihilate the independence of the Italian principalities, and showed that she desired to have Piedmont, like the rest, absolutely subject to her despotic will. He turned the tables upon Austria completely, accusing her of being the cause—the sole cause—of all the ills of the unhappy country. He demonstrated clearly that the only way to save Italy from continually recurring revolutions was to grant a home government to Lombardy and Venetia, to oblige the other states to have a constitutional form, and to preclude the possibility of Austrian intervention.

In another despatch to the young Marquis d'Azeglio —nephew of Massimo—who was Piedmontese ambassador in London, Cavour said that he admitted the liberty of Piedmont was a continual danger to Austria; but Austria, having violated conditions in substance and in spirit, had now come to encircle Piedmont with a cordon of iron, watching for a convenient opportunity to uproot her liberal institutions. Could and ought Piedmont to await with stupid resignation the accomplishment of such an end?

On this Austria cleverly retreated a little, confessing that reforms were needed in the principalities, and that she had already initiated them in Lombardy-Venice; and intimating that she was willing to be further guided by the advice of England.

A European congress for the adjustment of Italian affairs was then proposed; and Austria put in motion every influence to induce the great powers to insist on Sardinia disarming before it took place. The first article of the Austrian declarations for the consideration of the Congress was: 'To examine what would be the best means to lead Sardinia back to the fulfilment of her international duties, and to take measures to avoid a return of the present complications.' The other governments tried to induce Piedmont to disarm for the sake of peace, and urged France to use her influence with her ally for the same end.

The Piedmontese government listened to these counsels as a man would to a friend who advised him in a kindly manner to commit suicide. Disarm! they said, while Austria, who had first prepared for war, was armed to the teeth! Impossible, utterly impossible. The great powers, though friendly for the most part towards Italy, were bent on maintaining peace at any price. France, though bound by secret treaty to Piedmont, dare not stir unless Austria made some fresh aggressive movement. Friends and enemies all seemed united to crush the independence of poor little Piedmont. But her brave king and his incomparable minister held their heads erect, while diplomatic notes were flying in every direction, piling difficulties on difficulties.

The next Austrian move was to get the governments to consent to exclude Piedmont, as a secondary power, from the Congress.

Count Cavour's reply to this notification was full of deep indignation at the injustice of his late allies, who could forget what they owed to a state which four years before had lost 4,000 men and spent 50,000,000 francs, to maintain European equilibrium. He added that, since Piedmont must have no part in the Congress, she would hold herself free to take such measures as she thought best to maintain her rights. By way of ceding something, Austria proposed that both countries should keep an armed force near the frontier ready for 'accidental aggressions.' Piedmont, at the earnest request of England, promised that if no fresh Austrian troops were sent into Italy, King Victor would not call out the reserves, nor hold the standing army in the defensive position it had occupied during the last three months. Fresh obstacles and difficulties and bushels of notes followed.

England at last notified to the government of Turin that she had obtained the consent of the other powers that a Sardic plenipotentiary should be admitted to the Congress, 'but to treat only of the question of disarmament.' Count Cavour replied, rejecting the concession, as humiliating to his king and his country. He was worn out with the diplomatic war, and in March went to pay a visit to the emperor to try and bring matters to a conclusion.

Before returning to Turin he made a tour through Switzerland and Germany. He was received very well in Prussia; and everywhere as he passed on his journey he met with demonstrations of sympathy. He writes to a colleague : 'Austria, thank God, by her bad faith, has alienated all the continent from her.' The Turin people met their illustrious fellow-citizen at the railway with a grand demonstration, and nearly pulled him out of the carriage in the excitement of their feelings, and joy at seeing his broad, smiling face again amongst them. They followed him with loud applause to his palace, and he had to come out on the balcony to thank the people before they dispersed.

Next morning the hero of this ovation was describing it to the king in glowing colours—for he was not afraid of making him jealous—when his majesty interrupted him, laughing :—

'My dear Count, you need not tell me. I know all about it better than you do. When you were on the balcony I was in the street, lost in the crowd, shouting *Viva Cavour*! with the rest.'

There is a charming touch of nature in this little incident, which gives one an idea of what a pleasant king to serve was this appreciative warm-hearted Victor, who was not afraid of derogating from his royal dignity by sometimes mingling with his people as one of them, and entering into their feelings. He used often to go about in disguise, not only in the mountain districts, where he was comparatively unknown, but even in Turin. A gentleman encountering him one evening in the street, asked him to let him light his cigar with his, and in offering the desired courtesy the king came near enough to be recognised by his surprised interlocutor. In the days of his youth he had suffered so much boredom from the rigid etiquette of his father's court, that he was all the more inclined to disregard it when he became king.[1]

Count Cavour returned from his trip with renewed vigour for the contest which was not yet ended. England, bent on maintaining peace, made another effort with France to induce her to insist on a simultaneous disarmament; and at the same time used her influence so strongly with the other powers as to make them admit a Sardic plenipotentiary, *on equal grounds*, at the Congress.

This proposition the emperor could hardly object to, so he telegraphed to Turin his advice to accept. Cavour did not reply immediately, because of secret information he had received as to the warlike intentions of Austria. He waited, and, as he had been led to expect, on April 23, 1859, the Austrian ultimatum reached Turin: immediate disarmament or war, with three days to decide.

It was a relief to both king and minister. The quarrel had passed from the jurisdiction of diplomacy to the arbitrament of the sword, and the soldier-king buckled on his armour with a feeling of solemn satisfaction. He had 'awaited his star,' and now it rose, beckoning him on to glory. The Parliament decreed that the troops were to be put in motion immediately for the frontier of Lombardy, and that the supreme command should be confided to their valiant and beloved sovereign. While the Parliament was applauding Cavour's speech, the Austrian plenipotentiaries empowered to receive the reply of the Sardinian government arrived. They were answered by the martial

---

[1] One little incident will serve to show the severe restraint under which the Savoy princes were held in those days. Weary of ceremony and state, Prince Victor, one evening, soon after his marriage, conceived the bold design of taking his wife for a walk alone, like a simple citizen. The Princess Adelaide, doubtless, thought it a pleasing adventure to elude the vigilance of maids of honour and gentlemen-in-waiting, and escape from the palace on her husband's arm. The young people were recognised of course, and the scandalised courtiers hastened to tell the king that the Duke of Savoy and his bride were seen promenading in the city, on foot, and unattended! The prince was severely rebuked for the offence, and ordered not to leave the palace for some days.

aspect of the city, even before official response could be communicated. Prince Carignano was nominated regent in the king's absence, and when Victor Emmanuel put his signature to the document, he threw down the pen with a sigh of relief, saying, 'Now I shall sign nothing more!' He made his will, and gave minute instructions to those who remained in charge of affairs at home, as to what should be done in the event of his fall.

Royal Proclamation to the People of the Kingdom.

Austria assails us with a powerful army, which, while simulating a desire for peace, she had collected for our injury in the unhappy provinces subject to her domination.

Not being able to endure the example of our civilised institutions, nor wishing to submit to the judgment of a European congress on the evils and dangers she has caused in Italy, she now violates the promise given to Great Britain, and makes a law of honour a cause for war.

Jealous custodian of our common patrimony of honour and glory, I take up my sword again, confiding the state to the rule of my beloved cousin Prince Eugenio (Carignano).

With my soldiers, the valiant soldiers of the Emperor Napoleon III., my generous ally, will fight the battles of liberty and justice.

People of Italy! Austria assails Piedmont because I have maintained the cause of our common country in the councils of Europe,—because I was not insensible to your cries of anguish. Thus, she violently breaks now the treaties which she never has respected.

So to-day the right of the nation is complete, and I can, with a free conscience, fulfil the vow I made on the tomb of my parent, by taking up arms to defend my throne, the liberties of my people, the honour of the Italian name. I fight for the right of the whole nation.

We confide in God and in our concord; we confide in the valour of the Italian soldiers, in the alliance of the noble French nation; we confide in the justice of public opinion.

I have no other ambition than to be the first soldier of Italian Independence. Viva l'Italia!

VICTOR EMMANUEL.

Order of the Day.

Soldiers!—Austria, who at our confines concentrates armies and threatens to invade our territories, because here liberty is united with order; because not force, but harmony and affection between sovereign and people, rule the state; because here has been heard the cry of anguish from oppressed Italy;—Austria dares to intimate to us, armed only on the defensive, that we must lay down our arms, and put ourselves at her mercy. The outrageous proposal should have a suitable response. I have replied to it with scorn.

Soldiers!—I give you this announcement, sure that you will make it yours, this insult to your king and country. The announcement that I make is, war. To arms, then, soldiers! You will find yourselves in front of an enemy who is not new. But if he is valiant and well-disciplined, you need not fear the comparison. You can boast the days of Goito, Pastrengo, Santa Lucia, Sommacampagna—ay, even Custoza itself—where only four brigades fought for three days against five different bodies of troops.

I shall be your leader. In former times I have seen most of you in the fervour of battle, when I fought by the side of my magnanimous father, and I admired and felt proud of your valour. You, I am sure, will know how to preserve and increase the fame of those days. You shall have with you the intrepid French soldiers, conquerors in so many great battles,—who were your companions at the Tchernaya, and whom Napoleon III., always ready to defend a just cause, sends to our aid.

March, then, confident of victory, and wreathe your banner with fresh laurels—that banner with its three colours, under which the chosen youth of all Italy ranges itself, indicates to you that yours is the task of accomplishing Italian Independence. This just and sacred enterprise shall be our cry of war.

VICTOR EMMANUEL.

Turin, April 27, 1859.

The day before his departure from the capital the king called Count Nigra, minister of the household, to give him his instructions. 'Signor Nigra,' he said, 'we are near great events, and we must prepare for every eventuality. I confide to your care all that is most dear to me—my children. I know I leave them with another self.'

'Your majesty may go in peace. I will be answerable for all' was the reply.

'Here is my testament,' pursued the king. 'If I should be killed, open it, and see that my will is executed. I will try to bar the road to Turin, but if I should not succeed, and the enemy advances, remove my family to a place of safety, and follow scrupulously what I tell you. In the Gallery of Arms you will find four Austrian banners taken by our soldiers in the war of 1848, and deposited there by my father. They are the trophies of his glory, and I wish to preserve them. If need be, abandon everything else—valuables, jewels, archives, collections—all contained in my palace,—but save the banners. Let me but find my children and them safe, the rest does not matter.'

Next morning, before marching, a solemn service was held in the Duomo, which was crowded with excited citizens, more bent on admiring the spectacle of the warrior king kneeling before the altar, asking Heaven's blessing on his enterprise, than on attending to their own particular devotions. He departed at the head of his troops amidst enthusiastic acclamations, and fervent blessings and prayers for his safety and success. So was he received in every village through which he passed till he reached the great fortress of Alessandria, where the troops were concentrating. The ten years of peace had not diminished Victor Emmanuel's military ardour, though they had brought him more experience and heavier responsibilities. His devotion to the cause of Italy was as warm as when on the field of Novara he had fiercely sworn, '*Italia sarà!*' The enthusiasm which filled his soul imparted a dignity and grandeur to his bearing, and—his homely features notwithstanding—made him look all a king.

'It was fine,' says Bersezio, 'to see him ride up the ranks of his soldiers, or in the midst of his people as he acknowledged with dignity their enthusiastic *evvivas*; but finest when in the heat of battle he flung himself with impetuous valour upon the enemy.'

It was not only his own subjects and soldiers who were stirred into enthusiasm at the sight of the hero-king. A French officer who saw him for the first time on his arrival at Alessandria thus writes:—

> A great noise was raised; we heard the tramp of horses and cries of enthusiasm. Certainly some great man must be coming! In fact, in a minute after I saw enter under the portico of the palace, King Victor Emmanuel. I recognised his countenance by the rugged features, such as one sees at any humble fireside. There was that eye, ardent yet soft, which darted a straight, bold glance over a provokingly aggressive pair of moustaches. I leave it to others to cite this prince or that, named in the pages of history. But henceforth from to-day I will think that a king on horseback in a moment of danger is a sight to make the heart beat. Lamartine has said, 'Horses are the pedestals of princes.' . . . Whatever happens, I shall never forget King Victor Emmanuel as I first saw him, on horseback, with his sabre by his side, breathing freely and joyously the warrior air of Alessandria, as an atmosphere suited for his lungs. Other memories as well as mine will preserve this image, and in the minds of the people an image is a judgment.

General La Marmora, knowing the king's rash spirit, ventured to remonstrate with him about exposing himself to danger, and Victor, unlike himself, answered rudely, that if the general felt afraid he might keep in the background. This was an outburst of temper, caused by the worry he had been subject to, since war had been declared, on the duty of taking care of himself. La Marmora and other friends persuaded a senator, Plezza, who was royal commissioner at Alessandria, to remonstrate with him in the name of all. 'Say to those gentlemen,' replied the king, 'that in a few days I must send to death who knows how many thousand men. I have not the courage to send them to meet death if I do not act so as to let them see that the cause is such as deserves that we ought all to meet it if need be, and that I myself am ready to do so.' This reply of the king, being repeated from mouth to mouth, had a powerful and inspiriting effect on the soldiers.

At San Salvador the Sardinian army was in danger of being surrounded by the enemy; a sort of panic seized the men, and Victor Emmanuel, acting under the advice of some of his officers, had decided to make a retrograde movement. La Marmora, hearing this, forced his way into the royal chamber in spite of orders that no one was to be admitted, and protested vehemently against a retreat. Angry words were exchanged, and the general wound up by saying that if the army retreated he would not, as he would rather fall into the enemy's hands than be the scorn of Frenchmen. In consequence of this the king delayed the departure of the troops, and next day the panic passed, when news arrived that the French were coming to their assistance. Victor Emmanuel then behaved like himself, and penned an affectionate and apologetic letter to his general, thanking him for his timely opposition.

On May 13 the French Emperor landed at Genoa, whither the king went to meet him. The French troops were greeted with great warmth in all the towns through which they passed. The Piedmontese people fêted them and bestowed presents on them just as they did on their own men; and the two armies fraternised most satisfactorily.

Between the sovereigns also a warm friendship sprang up, which there is every reason to believe was sincere on both sides. Napoleon III. was capable of a faithful and lasting friendship, and had a wonderful knack of winning the regard of those who had intimate intercourse with him, as we can see in the 'Life of the Prince Consort,' where the queen describes with charming simplicity his growing influence on her and her husband. Victor Emmanuel felt the emperor's fascination, and quickly grew to like him personally, while on public grounds he experienced the strongest sentiments of gratitude for the aid he was rendering to his country when all other sovereigns refused to help her. It was not in Victor Emmanuel's nature to inquire if the emperor were or were not guided by selfish, ambitious motives; enough for him that he befriended Italy in her distress; and the memory of that service never could be obliterated from his mind, though his patience was often sorely tried by the conduct of his 'generous ally.'

CHAPTER XIV.

'ITALY SHALL BE FREE FROM THE ALPS TO THE ADRIATIC!' A.D. 1859.

MEANTIME the Austrians, assembled in great force on the frontier, at the first intimation of war crossed the Ticino and began to devastate the Sardinian territory. The king's troops were commanded to flood the country in order to impede the enemy's advance on the capital. In this work the peasant-farmers took an active part, eagerly assisting the soldiers in the destruction of their own crops. It was a great sacrifice for the poor people, but in that moment of exalted enthusiasm they were ready to sacrifice not only their harvest but their lives, for *la patria*.

THE FIRST VICTORY.

It was a happy thought this of inundating the country; for the enemy began to advance rapidly into the interior, and for several days Turin was threatened with an attack. The government was in the hands of the Prince of Carignano, who, aided by the energetic services of the citizens, and those old nobles who had not gone to the seat of war, made haste to put the city in a state of defence. The king was in great anxiety, and kept up a constant correspondence with the capital till the danger was passed. The courage and quiet resolution displayed by the whole population of Turin was very gratifying to Victor Emmanuel, who expressed his feelings in a letter to the old General de Sonnaz, who was in command of all the forces that could be mustered together for the defence of the city.

> Your Excellency,—The noble, patriotic, and valiant conduct that you have displayed in these past days when the capital was threatened by a raid from the enemy, during which time you collected together such forces as were available, and enrolled them with the division of cavalry,—I appreciated so highly that I experienced a lively desire to express to your excellency my great satisfaction and earnest thanks. This bold act, spontaneous as it was, is a new proof of that constant devotion to the throne of which my father and I have had so many evidences in times past; and another gem added to the brilliant services which entitle your excellency to my particular goodwill, and to the esteem and gratitude of the country and army.
>
> To-day, since the peril which menaced the capital is passed, your excellency can resume the command of the military division of Turin, and I will rest in the firm confidence that if there should arise any grave trouble, the country and the king may count on the arm and the heart of your excellency—a heart and an arm which never grow old.
>
> VICTOR EMMANUEL.
>
> Occimiano, May 18, 1859.

For some time before the war, the great body of

volunteers had been put under the command of General
Garibaldi. They had taken the field before the royal
troops, and in several encounters with the enemy on the
Po, had come off victorious—a fact which greatly cheered
the spirits of the Piedmontese.

On May 20, at Montebello, took place the first encounter of the allied armies with the Austrian, and so
far as it went it was a brilliant success. On May 30th,
that is, the eleventh anniversary of Goito, where Victor
Emmanuel first distinguished himself, there was fought
a more important battle. At Palestro the Austrians
had collected strong forces to oppose the passage of the
Piedmontese across the Sesia. General Cialdini attacked
them with great energy at one point, and General
Fanti at another, while the king, who directed the
movements of all, seeing his men swept down rapidly
by the terrible Austrian fire, led on a third division,
passed the bridge with overwhelming impetus, and assailed Palestro with a fury before which the enemy
had to give way. On receiving fresh succours the
Austrians returned to the combat, and twice drove the
Piedmontese back, but twice had to yield in their turn.
In all the three different points the Austrians were
ultimately forced to retreat, and the Italians remained
in possession of the position.

Royal Proclamation.

Soldiers!—Our first battle signalises our first victory.
Your heroic courage, the admirable order of your
lines, the daring and sagacity of your leaders, have
triumphed to-day at Palestro, Vinzaglio, and Casalino.
The enemy, repeatedly attacked, after an obstinate
defence, abandoned the strong positions into your
hands. This campaign could not open under happier
auspices. The triumph of to-day is a pledge that
future victories are reserved for the glory of your
king, and the fame of the valiant Piedmontese army.
Soldiers, your exultant country expresses through
me her gratitude, and, proud of your battles, she adds

to her story the names of her heroic sons, who for the second time on the memorable day of May 30 have successfully and valiantly combated for her.

VICTOR EMMANUEL.

The Austrians, knowing the importance of the village of Palestro, returned at daybreak next morning with all the fresh forces they could collect to try to retake it. As Victor Emmanuel, armed for the affray, was about to leap to the saddle, he paused one moment to send a line to his dear Cavour—

'You must be pleased with the news of yesterday evening. I am mounting my horse. This evening you shall receive other good news.'

The Austrians, wishing to regain the positions lost the day before, took the offensive, and fought with a desperate resolve to gain the day; the Italians, with an equally desperate tenacity, were resolved to cede those valuable posts only with their lives.

It was an obstinate and bloody battle. The Italians, fighting furiously and falling in great numbers, were almost surrounded and overwhelmed, when the Zouaves came to the rescue and, with a dauntless bravery, threw themselves on the enemy and made themselves masters of the cannons. Inspirited by the help of their gallant allies, the Italians renewed the attack with great vigour, all the more courageously that just then Victor Emmanuel, 'plunged in the battery's smoke,' was seen galloping to the front, sword in hand, waving on Italians and French to the defence of a bridge. The sight of their king inspired the Piedmontese with fresh ardour; and the Zouaves, with the cry of *Vive l'Empereur*, threw themselves precipitately along with them upon the enemy, and a furious contest ensued, in which the day for a long time remained doubtful.

The Zouaves were lost in admiration of Victor Emmanuel's gallantry. He was the first of Zouaves, they said, for 'he would listen to no reason.' The French standard-bearer fell at his feet, struck by two balls; and he rushed on into the thickest fire, deaf to the remonstrances of the Zouaves, who entreated him to withdraw a little in the background. The idea of thinking of his own life at such a moment was out of the question for Victor Emmanuel; but the 'First Soldier of Italian Independence' ought to have remembered that he was necessary to the cause for which he fought, and ought not to have so recklessly thrown himself into the jaws of death. At one dreadful moment he was almost cut off from his followers and surrounded by the enemy. 'In that instant,' says the narrator, 'from thousands of breasts there rose a cry of terror; the Zouaves, the staff officers, the Bersaglieri, all with horror in their faces, threw themselves like a thunderbolt on the enemy; like lightning they encircled the king, and saved his precious life and liberty.' 'Are you afraid I shall throw you into the shade?' he said, in reply to their remonstrances. 'Do not fear; there is glory enough for all.'

The day was won, the king was safe, and the joy of the Sardinian army can be better imagined than described—a joy in which the Zouaves heartily shared, making the field ring with shouts of *Vive le Roi*! Henceforth he was their peculiar hero; that evening they elected him their corporal, and carried to his headquarters the pieces of cannon taken from the enemy.

The king sent back the cannon with the following letter to Colonel de Chabron:—

From Headquarters, Torrione, June 1, 1859.

Monsieur le Colonel,—The emperor in placing at my orders the third regiment of Zouaves, has given me a precious proof of his friendship. I thought that I could not better welcome this choice troop than by furnishing an occasion to aid in a new exploit those who in the fields of battle in Africa and the Crimea have rendered so redoubtable the name of Zouaves.

The irresistible impetus with which your regiment, Monsieur le Colonel, rushed yesterday to the attack, excited all my admiration. To throw themselves upon the enemy at the bayonet's point, and possess themselves of a battery, while braving the fire of the *mitraille*, was the affair only of some moments. You ought to be proud to command such soldiers, and they ought to be happy to obey a chief like you.

I appreciate highly the thought which induced the Zouaves to bring to my head-quarters the pieces of artillery taken from the Austrians, and I pray you to thank them for me. I hasten to send this fine trophy to his majesty the emperor, to whom I have already made known the incomparable bravery with which your regiment fought yesterday at Palestro, and sustained my extreme right.

I shall always be very glad to see the third regiment of Zouaves fight beside my soldiers, and gather new laurels on the fields of battle which await us.

Will you, Monsieur le Colonel, make known these sentiments to your Zouaves?

VICTOR EMMANUEL.

The Zouaves having elected the King of Sardinia to be their corporal, the emperor said smiling, 'Now that you belong to my army I have a right to reprove you for your imprudence yesterday. If that happens again I will put you under arrest.'

On the evening of the 31st Victor Emmanuel addressed a proclamation to his own troops, and despatched 'the other good news' which in the morning he had boldly promised Cavour.

To the Sardinian Army.

Soldiers!—To-day a new and splendid feat of arms has been signalised by a new victory. The enemy assailed us vigorously in the positions of Palestro. They conveyed heavy forces against our right, in order to impede the conjunction of ours with the troops of Marshal Canrobert.

It was a supreme moment. Our ranks were far inferior to the adversary; but there stood in front of the attacking party the valorous troop of the fourth division, led by General Cialdini, and the incomparable third regiment of Zouaves, who, working in conjunction with the Sardic army, contributed powerfully to the victory. It was a murderous fight, but at the end the allied troops repulsed the enemy, having inflicted upon him serious losses, including a general and many officers. We have about 1,000 Austrian prisoners. Eight cannon were taken at the bayonet's point—five by the Zouaves, three by our men.

At the same time that the battle of Palestro was taking place, General Fanti, with equally happy success, repulsed with the troops of the second division another attack directed by the Austrians upon Confienza.

His majesty the emperor, on visiting the battle-field, expressed his heartfelt congratulations, and appreciates the immense advantage of this day.

Soldiers! Persevere in these your sublime efforts, and I feel certain that heaven will crown the work so courageously initiated.

VICTOR EMMANUEL.

From Headquarters at Torrione, May 31, 1859.

This order of the day, in Victor Emmanuel's own style, gives briefly a fair idea of the day's doings, only his own exploits are necessarily omitted.

While recording the triumph of the Piedmontese army, it would be unjust to withhold the tribute of praise from those exiles who, before Garibaldi's volunteer army was organised, had abandoned home and country, and gone to aid their Sardinian brothers in their struggle for liberty. There were no braver nor more devoted men in the army than these poor 'foreigners,' as they were then called; and many touching anecdotes are told of how willingly they died, praying for their country, and blessing 'the champion of their liberty,' as he walked over the field, taking cognisance of his losses, and giving orders for the care of the wounded.

It must always be a melancholy moment to a general when, the excitement and exultation of victory passed, he begins to count the costs, and sees so many of his brave followers laid low; and Victor Emmanuel, whose emotional nature was quickly touched, felt depressed by the spectacle. In the course of his mournful walk he came to where a young Roman lay, with the life-blood slowly ebbing from his side. At the sight of the king his eye brightened, and he said to the companion who supported him,—

'Raise my head; let me look at him again. My leader, my hero, my king!'

Victor Emmanuel approached, and the volunteer exclaimed, 'God preserve you, saviour of Italy. For the sake of this blood, for the glory of your throne, for the memory of your martyred father, I conjure you to make our country free!'

The king, deeply moved, bent over the dying volunteer, placed his hand on his, and with tears in his eyes gave once more the oft-repeated promise to liberate Italy if life were spared to him.[1]

On June 3, the allied armies arrived at Novara, the painful memories of which were fast being obliterated by the exultation of the present successes. On the 4th the great and decisive battle of Magenta was fought and won by the allied armies, and placed Lombardy at the feet of the Sardinian king.[2]

Two days after this victory Victor Emmanuel received the deputation which came in the name of the whole population of the state to offer their fealty to him, and beg to be united to Piedmont. As a confir-

---

[1] Bersezio.

[2] There was a little incident of this battle which we recollect being reported by some newspaper correspondents at the time, though we have never met with it anywhere since, which is interesting and significant. Among the Austrian dead there was found a youth, 'whose musket had never been loaded,' and on him were papers declaring that he, a Venetian, had been forced to serve, but he never would fire on his countrymen, and only desired to be killed by them. The Italians took off the hated white uniform and buried him with their own dead, 'that his spirit might have rest.' This is the origin of Mrs. Browning's poem *The Forced Recruit.*

mation of the union, the king immediately appointed some noble Lombards to offices of state.

On June 8, four days after the battle of Magenta, the allies made a triumphal entry into Milan, and went straight to the magnificent cathedral, to return thanks in a solemn service. While they were thus engaged came the news of another success gained by the French troops at Melegnano, so that the campaign was one unbroken series of victories from beginning to end; and as for the allied armies, so also it was for the volunteers under Garibaldi, who, being a perfect master of irregular warfare, harassed the enemy in such a way as to contribute not a little to the successful issue of the campaign.

Royal Proclamation.

People of Lombardy!—The victory of the liberating army brings me among you. Your national rights restored, your votes will confirm your union with my kingdom, which is founded on the guarantees of a civilised life. The temporary form of government which I establish to-day is required by the necessity of war. When assured of independence, men's minds will acquire the coolness and strength necessary to prepare the foundation of a liberal and lasting *régime*.

The Subalpines have made, and still make, great sacrifices for the common country. Our army, which welcomes in its ranks many valiant volunteers of other Italian provinces, has already given splendid proofs of its courage, combating victoriously for the national cause. The Emperor of the French, our generous ally, worthy of the name and genius of Napoleon, putting himself at the head of the heroic army of that great nation, wishes *to liberate Italy from the Alps to the Adriatic.* In a rivalry of sacrifices you will second these magnanimous proposals on the fields of battle, you will show yourselves worthy of the destinies to which Italy is now called after so many centuries of suffering.

VICTOR EMMANUEL.

June 9, 1859.

The Lombards welcomed back their dear exiles with frantic joy, and passionate demonstrations of gratitude to the liberator so long prayed for, who was now in very truth their king, for the Austrians, everywhere beaten, had retired beyond the Mincio into the Venetian provinces. It was in the Lombard capital, after so many brilliant feats on the part of both leaders, that Victor Emmanuel and Garibaldi first met.

The king had always felt interested in the strange romantic career of the poor fisherman's son, who had been described by the Papal and Bourbon adherents—trembling in '48 at the sight of the *Camicia rossa*—as a bloodthirsty anarchist, a communist, an antichrist, in fact; and whose story, divested of this warm colouring, was not such as to recommend him particularly to the favour of an hereditary monarch. He was a republican Italian, and a cosmopolitan defender of peoples' rights in every land. With those in authority he had earned a reputation somewhat like that of the Irishman who on landing in America asked, 'Is there any government established in this country? Because, if there is, I'm agin' it.'

Garibaldi had hitherto found himself pretty well *against* every government where he happened to sojourn: that was the fault of the governments, of course; but nevertheless it made him be dreaded by order-loving people, who thought a little tyranny preferable to continual revolutions.

The daring courage, the childlike simplicity, the originality of this strange man, whose soul seemed cast in the mould of ancient days, won the admiration of a kindred spirit, singularly free from the prejudices of his class—one who could value a man for his own worth apart from all accessories of rank or position. It was flattering to a king like Victor, the voluntary homage of this wild republican; and it was flattering to the great volunteer, the tone of brotherly equality with which the head of an ancient dynasty received him. The meeting between the two heroes at Milan was most cordial, full of mutual congratulations and expressions of esteem. The king fastened the gold medal for military valour on the breast of the valiant general, who was proud to receive it from his hands, not because he was a king, but because he was a patriot and a hero.

But Lombardy had not seen the last of that obnoxious individual popularly known as *lo Straniero*. It was not to be expected that a great military power, with vast resources at her command, would relinquish those rich provinces to her old hereditary foe without a desperate struggle. Hastily collecting troops in those provinces still subject to her sway, she returned to the combat with renewed vigour. So secretly, speedily, and cleverly was the move executed, that the Austrian army was in front of the allies before they had dreamed of a renewal of the contest. But both French and Sards were equal to the occasion; and on June 24 was fought the double battle of Solferino and San Martino, which was the crowning glory of this glorious campaign. The French call this day 'Solferino,' but the Italians like to speak of it as 'San Martino,' that being the name of the hill from which the Sardinian king and his soldiers dislodged the Austrians, after a prolonged and bloody combat, which lasted from early morning till seven o'clock in the evening. During all this time the king was in the saddle, directing the movements of the troops over the extensive battle ground, and with four divisions under his immediate command he opposed a greatly superior force, fighting his way from Lonato to San Martino to the aid of General Mollard, whom he knew to be hard pressed by the enemy in that position. 'By his able dispositions,' writes a Frenchman, 'by the magic effect of his presence, by the impetus with which he knows so well how to inspire his soldiers, his troops were able to accomplish prodigies, displaying an inexhaustible tenacity in resistance as well as in attack.'

The Austrians under the command of General Benedek encountered General Mollard at San Martino early in the morning. The Italian general, knowing the importance of this position, was resolved to hold it at any cost. San Martino is a high hill, the precipitous sides of which were protected by little forts, and it commanded all the roads between Solferino and the Lago di Garda. After a hard struggle, the Austrians, being superior in numbers, forced the Piedmontese from the height and pursued them into the plain. The king having in the meantime sent them succours, they returned to the combat, climbed the hill of San Martino once more, under a furious fire, and drove the enemy from the position at the point of the bayonet. But in that attack the Piedmontese ranks had been terribly thinned, and again the enemy, with an overwhelming effort, forced them from the height. Meantime an officer from the king arrived to say he was hastening to their assistance. 'Our allies are winning a great battle at Solferino; it is the wish of the king that his soldiers should win one at San Martino,' said the aide-de-camp. 'Say to the king that his orders shall be executed,' was the proud reply of General Mollard.

Before noon Victor Emmanuel had sent a message to the French commander, Marshal Hilliers, 'who was winning a great victory at Solferino.' The mountain sides were so bestrewed with wounded that the king's messenger had to lead his horse to avoid trampling on them. He found the French commander in possession of the field and the enemy retreating. The marshal spoke slightingly of the Piedmontese slowness in advancing, and said,—

'*Vous n'avez pas encore appris à marcher comme nous.*' The Sardinian replied that some of their troops had been called to support the emperor in the plain, and that those that remained under the king's command had a vastly superior force to combat. The marshal looked at his watch and said, 'It is one o'clock. I hope that by evening your army will have arrived at Pozzolengo.'

Pozzolengo was two miles from Lonato; and before reaching it, it was necessary for Victor Emmanuel to overpower the forces that opposed him there, and then go to the defence of San Martino, which was the all-important post that must be conquered finally before proceeding to Pozzolengo. When his aide-de-camp returned and told him what the French general had said, he was somewhat piqued. It was not quite just to reproach him with 'slowness' under the circumstances. He despatched a messenger to La Marmora—about three-quarters of an hour's ride—saying, 'Go immediately to La Marmora, tell him that I order him to take the command of Durando's division, with half of Fanti's, and to hasten to San Martino; say at the same time that I am sending orders to Mollard and Cucchiari to attack it in front at half-past four, while La Marmora at the same time will attack it at the side. San Martino *shall* be ours—we will go to Pozzolengo this evening!'

The orders of the king were punctually obeyed; against the appointed hour he himself was there with his own followers ready to lead the attack at the other side.

'My sons,' said he, 'we must take San Martino, or the enemy will make us do San Martino.' San Martino was the day on which the people of that country always removed from one house to another; hence removing came to be called *doing San Martino.* The king's bad pun was received with loud cheers. They took San Martino after a desperate resistance, and Victor Emmanuel, according to his promise, arrived at Pozzolengo late in the evening. When Marshal Hilliers was complimenting the king on his day's work, he took care to let him know that he had heard his remark about the slowness of his 'march.' Victor Emmanuel did not wait to repose himself before expressing his warm thanks to the army which had so nobly sustained him throughout the day.

Royal Proclamation.

Soldiers!—In two months of war from the invasion of the banks of the Sesia and of the Po, you have advanced from victory to victory to the banks of the Garda and the Mincio. In the glorious path you have traversed in company with our generous and powerful ally, you have given the most splendid proofs of discipline and heroism.

The nation is proud of you. Italy counts among your ranks her best sons, applauds your merit, and from your actions draws happy auguries for her future destinies. To-day you have won another great victory; you have poured out your blood unsparingly, conquering an enemy great in numbers and protected by the strongest positions.

In the day, now famous, of Solferino and San Martino, you fought from the break of day till the close of night, led on by your intrepid officers, and repulsed the repeated assaults of the enemy, forcing him to re-cross the Mincio; leaving in your hands, on the field of battle, men, arms, and cannon. On their part, the French army obtained equally great results, equal glory, giving new proof of that incomparable valour that for centuries has called the admiration of the world on their heroic ranks.

Victory has cost us heavy sacrifices; but by that noble blood so freely shed for the holiest of causes Europe will learn that Italy is worthy of a seat amongst the nations.

Soldiers!—In the preceding battles I had often occasion to signalise the names of many of you in the order of the day. Now I bring to the order of the day the whole army.

VICTOR EMMANUEL.

From Headquarters, Rivoltella, June 25, 1859.

This was the last battle of the campaign, which was strangely and unaccountably cut short by the emperor's resolution to advance no further than the Mincio. Forgetful of his promise to liberate Italy 'from the Alps to the Adriatic,' he left poor Venice still in the clutches of the Austrian eagle, and led his army homewards.

CHAPTER XV.

THE PEACE OF VILLAFRANCA, A.D. 1859.

It was not to be expected that the inhabitants of the states of Central Italy could sit still while the Sardinians and Lombards were carrying on a successful war for the expulsion of the foreigner. Tuscany rose against the grand-duke, demanding a Constitution. He ordered the troops to fire on the people from the battlements of the Forte di Belvedere. The officers replied that they dare not give such an order, as the men would refuse to shoot down their fellow-citizens. 'And what will become of us?' asked the crown prince, indignantly.

'Grant the Constitution,' was the ready answer of the ministers. The grand-duke asked time to deliberate, retired to a villa, and from thence took his departure, escorted to the frontier by the carabinieri, to protect him from insult—an unnecessary precaution; the courteous Tuscans saluted him respectfully as he passed, too glad to be rid of him without bloodshed. He hoped to return, as in 1849, with an Austrian army at his back—but this time he miscalculated. The Duke of Modena and the Duchess of Parma fled precipitately; with the duchies rose also the Pontifical States—the provinces of Bologna, Ferrara, Umbria, the Marches—all joined in the national cry of *Viva l'Italia! Viva Vittorio Emanuele!* In fact, all the inhabitants of Central Italy loudly proclaimed their determination to be free—and none more resolutely than the subjects of Pio Nono. After the battle of Magenta deputations from the provinces arrived in Turin, entreating a union with North Italy. Cavour, not being able to give any answer that would satisfy the deputations, sent them to the camp to speak to the king himself. They arrived the day before Solferino, and were immediately admitted to the royal presence. The Piedmontese headquarters were at Calcinate, where the king had taken up his abode in a poor little country house. They found him standing by the window, with one hand on his sword-hilt, and the other resting on a writing table, where he had just laid a letter from the holy father, more disagreeable than usual, as was natural under the circumstances.

The Marquis Pepoli read the address from the provinces, and then added some words of his own earnestly urging the king not to leave them without a government, and begging him to accept provisionally a military dictatorship. Victor listened in thoughtful silence, and then told the gentlemen to thank the populations they represented; begged them still to put confidence in him, even though he could not now accept their offer; protested that he was ready to surrender himself utterly for the accomplishment of the great end they had in view; Italy should be 'made' beyond all doubt, but it was necessary to wait. He was afraid 'diplomacy' would throw serious obstacles in the way of a dictatorship.

'The Pope gives me much annoyance, and I cannot do as I should like,' he added, showing the letter he had lately received. He then directed them to lay the case before the French Emperor; and they received from him the advice to arm themselves 'to the teeth,' and wait what might turn up. Finally, Cavour was summoned to the camp. Something must be done immediately; the papal troops had entered the town of Perugia, overcome the citizens with great slaughter, and committed disgraceful atrocities. The other insurgent cities wanted the protection of some sort of governing body, while putting themselves in a state of defence. Cavour's advice was not to assume the title of Dictator nor Protector, but simply to send royal commissioners to Bologna with the sole object of maintaining order, and organising military forces in the surrounding provinces. Governors in the king's name had been sent to the principalities of Tuscany, Parma, and Modena; but dealing with the papal territories was a more delicate matter. Victor Emmanuel was already under the censures of the church, and he was now threatened with excommunication in its extremest rigour. The governor chosen for the Bolognese province was Pio Nono's old favourite, Massimo Azeglio. 'Am I to go to Bologna to do the anti-Pope?' said he, smiling, when he received the king's command. On the very day that it was officially announced that the commissioner was about to take temporary charge of the Romagnian provinces, the Pope's allocution arrived, breathing the fiercest anathemas against the king and his government if they carried out their impious intentions. 'Atrocious deeds like those of Perugia, and threats like those of the allocution,' wrote Sir James Hudson, 'ought to persuade the sincerest Catholics of the approaching fall of the temporal power of the Popes.'

Ferdinand II. of Naples had died on May 22, a few minutes after receiving the news of the battle of Montebello. The old tyrant's last moments were embittered by the victory of 'the Sardo,' whom he had always hated, as representing the principles of religious and civil freedom, which his soul abhorred. At the beginning of the struggle with Austria the Savoy family had no designs on the other kingdoms of Italy. Both Charles Albert and Victor Emmanuel had again and again offered to form a federation with the other Italian princes for the expulsion of the foreigner,—in which case they would have contented themselves with the annexation of Lombardy and Venetia to the kingdom of Sardinia. But the other princes steadfastly refusing this alliance, breaking their promises of granting reforms, and above all maintaining their position altogether by the aid of Austria, and acting under her control,—they had gradually come to see no way for the redemption of Italy but a complete overthrow of the principalities. Personal and dynastic ambition was doubtless blended with patriotic fervour in the soul of Victor Emmanuel; but it was an ambition which the Italians themselves excited and commended to the last degree. The crown of Sicily had been offered in 1848 to the younger son of Charles Albert and refused, after which many conciliatory embassies from Sardinia had been sent to Ferdinand, as also to Leopold and Pius, entreating them to reform their respective governments,—but all in vain.

Now that the old king was dead, Victor Emmanuel, with that generosity which was his most striking characteristic, resolved to bury all the offences and insults of the past ten years in his grave, and offer his frank and cordial alliance to the son of his old enemy. He did not do this without the concurrence of Poerio, and the other noble Neapolitan exiles, who, like him, thought it a duty, for the sake of peace, to smother personal animosity. But the Bourbon pride and obstinacy, like that of the Stuarts, blinded them to their danger. Francis II. declined the honour of an alliance with the liberator of Italy,—unfortunately for himself, but happily for his country.

The Emperor Napoleon having promised and proclaimed that Italy should be free from the Alps to the Adriatic, and having had one unbroken series of victories from the Sesia to the Mincio, it was natural to expect that he would carry his conquering arms into Venetia, and finish the work he had undertaken. But all of a sudden this unaccountable man was taken with a panic —some say it was the spectacle of Solferino the day after the battle which struck him with horror; others that the empress had informed him of the growing jealousy of Prussia after every victory which threatened to have serious consequences, and of the displeasure of the Russian government at the expulsion of the dukes, who had taken refuge in the dominions of the Czar and asked his protection. Be this as it may, he was resolved to turn back from the enterprise. And he demanded an armistice from the Austrians, as if he had been the beaten party. Victor Emmanuel, it may be imagined, did all that man could do to dissuade him from throwing away the fruits of their united victories. It was all in vain; the man of fate would move no further, and Victor, with a heavy heart, resigned himself. '*Povera Italia!*' he exclaimed mournfully, then added, 'Whatever shall be your majesty's decision, I shall always feel grateful for what you have done for Italian independence, and you may count on me as a friend.'

The Marshal Vaillant ventured to remonstrate with the emperor. 'Sire,' said he, 'an armistice means peace.'

'That is nothing to you,' was the polite rejoinder.

'Sire,' said the undaunted marshal, 'you have promised to make Italy free from the Alps to the Adriatic.

'*Je vous répète, maréchal, cela ne vous regarde pas.*'

The armistice was concluded, and the preliminaries of peace arranged, July 8. The Emperors of Austria and France had settled that the banished princes were to be restored without violence, that Piedmont was to be left in possession of Lombardy, and that the Pope was to be persuaded to make some reforms in his government. The grief of the disputed provinces, when they heard of the proposed peace, was indescribable. No calamity that war had brought could cause such bitter anguish as the Italians, especially the Romagnuoli, then felt. They had borne oppression so long, they had suffered so much for their sympathy with their northern countrymen, they had contributed their money and their blood to the national cause, and now, in the moment of victory, they were abandoned to the tender mercies of their ecclesiastical rulers,—after having laid their homage at the foot of the throne of Sardinia. It was a cruel case, and Victor Emmanuel would have sacrificed some years of his life to be able to fulfil their wishes. But he had no choice; to make war alone and unaided would have been madness.

The news of the armistice struck Cavour like a thunderbolt. He did not see things from the emperor's point of view, and peace under such circumstances seemed like insanity or treachery. It would be difficult to imagine how he felt without knowing how entirely he had made every other consideration in life subservient to the cause which now seemed wantonly ruined.

The world [says his biographer] will ever remain ignorant of the immense labour and fatigue of mind that Count

Cavour passed through in those days [preceding the war]. But history in its justice will relate how in the midst of such a boiling over of violent passions, of mortal hatreds, of generous excitement, of storms and worries indescribable, he remained imperturbably serene, calculating the current events, knowing how with extraordinary acuteness of mind to master men and things, to hit the best opportunity for action; and though he held in the hollow of his hand the fomenting revolution, never did he once depart from the course of patient moderation, which alone could save the Italian question from becoming lacerated by the claws of the Austrian eagle, in that last and most difficult period of the negotiations.

But once the note was sounded for bold and strong measures, the patriotic spirit of Camillo Cavour shared largely the enthusiasm, the just resentment, of his nation. Let us look at his work. At one and the same time he was President of the Council, Minister of Foreign Affairs, Minister of War, Minister of the Interior. He had a bed placed in the apartments of the War Ministry, and during the nights he walked in his dressing-gown from one department to another, giving directions as to police regulations, diplomatic correspondence and preparations for war, inflaming everyone by his example of laboriousness and patriotism.[1]

His herculean labours did not affect his health, for he had great courage, hope, and patience to support him; and as the news of each successive victory reached Turin, hope became certainty. What his sensations were when the news of the armistice reached him may be imagined. The heavy responsibility of having urged the king and nation into a fruitless war weighed upon him, mingled with the fierce indignation which he felt towards his false ally, for such he considered Napoleon. He set out for the camp, hoping, as the preliminaries were not yet signed, he might still stop

[1] Bianchi.

the proceedings. He had an interview with the emperor which proved ineffectual in changing his resolution. His destiny had carried him to the Mincio, but it refused to move further in an easterly or southerly direction.

Cavour's passions, though habitually concealed under an imperturbable serenity and *sang froid*, were profound and strong, and they were now stirred to their depths. For the first and only time in his public career he allowed them to master him, completely obscuring his usually clear, unerring judgment. He had generally acted as a check on the fiery impulsiveness of the king, but now they seemed to have changed characters. Victor Emmanuel, calm and resigned, was listening to a French officer reading the preliminaries of the treaty in the presence of La Marmora and three other witnesses, when the count entered. White with anger, which he made no effort to suppress, he stormed against the emperor, and upbraided the king with his complaisance. He said he ought to refuse to accept Lombardy, and withdraw the Piedmontese army into his own proper territory. The king argued against this extreme measure, saying he was pledged to the Lombards, and it would be unjust and unfaithful to abandon them. But Cavour would not admit of any compromise. The interview was long and painful; and though the king maintained a dignified calm throughout, he was deeply offended.

> The vehemence of Count Cavour's language attested the excitement of his soul [says Massari]. All the more painful and keenly felt was the struggle between the king and minister, because both desired intensely to arrive at the same end, to secure the destinies of Italy. General La Marmora, always ready for every good work, conquered his own grief, and tried to calm the generous ire of Count Cavour, and put an end to the king's distress.

The count returned to Turin almost broken-hearted. ' In the space of three days he had grown older by many years.' The day the peace was signed at Villafranca Cavour sent in his resignation, and all his colleagues with him. Paleocapa, the blind Venetian minister, wept. 'My blindness is no longer a grief to me, since I can no longer hope to revisit my beloved Venice,' he said.

It must not be supposed that the king did not feel as much as his ministers the sudden termination of the war; but for once he seemed to see a little farther into the future than the astute Cavour, and did not utterly despair. His trouble was aggravated by his quarrel with the count, which threw on him the whole responsibility of accepting a very unpopular peace. The treaty was signed July 12, Victor Emmanuel, by the advice of the emperor, putting in these words: '*J'accepte pour ce qui me concerne*,' meaning that he accepted Lombardy, but had nothing to say to the question of the duchies or the Romagna, which left him free for future action. He issued a farewell address to the Lombards, couched in the affectionate terms of a sovereign to his own subjects, renewing his pledge to protect them, and telling them to confide in their king.

Victor Emmanuel entered the Subalpine capital in company with the Emperor Napoleon. The joy of seeing their beloved king safely returned was damped by the depression of spirits consequent on the peace. Yet a certain warmth of greeting to the foreign sovereign gratitude demanded. He had done much for them, and doubtless had his reasons for not doing more. The king had accepted the peace, and he would not have done it if it could have been avoided. The Turin people, reasoning thus, behaved very well and decorously on the occasion of the emperor's visit. The day after his return the king received Sir James Hudson in a private audience. He had always regarded him as a personal friend, and it was a relief to open his mind, and confide all his troubles to such an intelligent sympathiser as the English minister, who had shown that he had the interests of Italy at heart.

The Cavour ministry only held office till their successors were appointed. Their chief was nursing his wrath to keep it warm; and the king was full of indignation against him for the disrespectful manner in which he had deported himself in their last interview, when in wanting to force his rash counsels upon him he had forgotten what was due to his personal dignity. But without Cavour, Victor Emmanuel felt deprived of his right arm. He had some difficulty in forming a new ministry, but finally Signor Rattazzi undertook the conduct of affairs, with the aid of Generals La Marmora and Dabormida, all honourable men and true, but the three of them could not make one Cavour. The new ministry began by a timid retrograde movement. Orders were issued to all the royal commissioners governing the insurgent provinces of Central Italy to leave their posts and return to Turin.

'But these patriots understood,' says Signor Ghiron, 'that it would be grateful to the king to disobey these orders, and that it would expose the country to the gravest perils to abandon them,' so they remained. Cavour never would have put his government in such a position as to issue orders which ought to be disobeyed. Massimo d'Azeglio, who was at Bologna with 11,000 men under his command, to keep the peace of the surrounding provinces, positively refused to stir.

'I thought,' he wrote to his wife, 'that the king would not wish to dishonour himself and me by leaving those provinces in a state of anarchy, and I disobeyed. Instead of moving the troops to Turin, I sent 9000 to the frontier of Romagna to defend the people who had been confided to me from the Swiss of Perugia. I invested my powers in Colonel Fallicon, my head staff officer, and I left all at their posts, the government in full authority; so there has been no disorder, and I came on the fifth day to Turin to tell the king to put me under a council of war. The king said I had done rightly, and that there must have been some mistake in the order.'

The Roman legations and the duchies, when they heard of the peace, sent deputations to Turin; the king received them kindly, and tried to soothe their excited feelings by renewed promises of future help.

'What do they think of me in Tuscany?' he asked of the secretary of the provisional government in Florence.

'We confide always in the loyal protection of your majesty.'

'I am glad of it,' he replied. 'I could not have any peace if I thought you could doubt me for a moment, or imagine that I, for my own interests, had abandoned the brave people who had put their trust in me.'

The Marquis Pepoli, who had been the head of the deputation from the Emilian provinces, to pray for annexation with North Italy, immediately on hearing of the peace hastened to Turin and asked an audience of the king. The particulars of that interview the marquis himself related to a mournful assembly in Bologna, January 23, 1878.

> The Peace of Villafranca struck us all with horror. We lost every hope, for we feared a fresh intervention, and we had neither soldiers nor money to offer any efficacious opposition to the violence of the foreigner. It was then that the provisional government sent me to Turin to speak directly to the king. In fact, as soon as I arrived in that city, Victor Emmanuel granted me an audience. I explained frankly, without reticence, our doubts, our fears, our urgent needs. The king replied benignly, 'You have not the faith that saves. Why do you doubt me? Do you believe that I would have put my signature to the Peace of Villafranca without a formal promise that any fresh intervention would not be allowed?'
>
> Seeing that I was not yet quite easy, he added, —
>
> 'If after my words the Bolognese still doubt, tell them, in my name, that if the Austrians should again invade the sacred soil of *la Patria*, I will abdicate like my father, and come to fight in the ranks of the Romagnuoli volunteers.'
>
> 'I believe your majesty's words,' I broke forth; 'but how shall we be able to provide for our wants, without money and without credit?'

'My government cannot come to your aid, for the diplomatic reasons which you know too well,' said the king. 'The House of Savoy is poor, therefore I cannot offer you the material aid you require. One thing only can I give—my signature. With that, try to provide necessaries, and arm yourselves for the day of battle.'

So saying, he wrote on a sheet of paper and handed it to me, with a kind look. I bathed the august hand with tears; and if I lived for a hundred years, never can I forget, as an Italian, as a citizen, that most noble act.

The Lombards at this time, to show their devotion to their new sovereign, celebrated the tenth anniversary of the death of the late King Charles Albert by a religious service in his honour held in the cathedral of Milan. His grateful son wrote to the podestà as follows:—

My dear Count Belgiojoso.—The testimony of pious mourning offered by the people of Milan, July 28, to the memory of my father's great soul, moved my heart deeply. The Milanese associating themselves thus spontaneously with the domestic mourning of their king, shows that the bond that unites them to me is a bond of love, and gives me deep satisfaction. Their honouring in this unusual way the memory of Charles Albert, signifies that years and changing circumstances have not diminished their reverence and gratitude to the initiator of their independence, and in the name of Italy I thank them.

Although I had no need of any fresh proof of the affection and loyalty of my Milanese, it was at the same time so consoling to me, that I feel the need of showing them how I have understood them. The honourable podestà, by making himself interpreter of my sentiments with his fellow-citizens, will fulfil one of my dearest wishes.

VICTOR EMMANUEL.

Turin, July 31, 1859.

CHAPTER XVI.

THE VOTE OF THE ITALIAN PEOPLE. A.D. 1859.

CAVOUR'S wrath calmed down after a time, and he began to see things in a clearer light; but he was still resolved to remain in retirement. In the autumn he wrote to a friend as follows :—

> I am full of faith in the future triumph of the cause for which I have struggled so long, and to it I am always ready to consecrate what life and strength I still possess; but I am fully persuaded that my participation in politics at this moment would be damaging to my country. Her destinies have been put back again into the hands of diplomacy. Now I am in bad odour with the diplomatists; my resignation is very grateful to them, and its effect will be such as to render them more favourable to the unhappy populations of Central Italy.

In August the king visited Lombardy privately; the final treaty of peace not being yet signed, it would not have been good taste to do so officially. During this visit to Milan he expressed a desire to see Manzoni, and was told that he was ailing. Then Victor declared he would go to see him in his own home, but Manzoni would not permit this, and hastened to pay his respects to the king as soon as he was able. Victor Emmanuel received the author of *I Promessi Sposi* with such marks of regard and profound respect as quite overwhelmed the modest poet. He was agreeably surprised to find the king, who thought and spoke either in Piedmontese or French, express himself so well in Tuscan; and found him more cultivated and appreciative than he had expected. Here is the judgment of the gifted and pious Lombard on his new sovereign :—

> I see in the character of the king the intervention of

Providence. He is exactly the sovereign that circumstances require to accomplish the resurrection of Italy. He has rectitude, courage, incorruptible honesty, and disinterestedness: he seeks not glory or fortune for himself, but for his country. He is so simple, never caring to appear great, that he does not meet the admiration of those who seek to find in princes and heroes theatrical actions and grandiloquent words. He is natural because he is true, and this makes his enemies say that he is wanting in regal majesty. To found Italian unity he has risked his throne and his life.

We have heard some English persons criticise Victor Emmanuel's manners just in the way Manzoni describes; but 'to found Italian unity,' they should remember, something more was needed than a drawing-room exquisite; and there are a great many elegant gentlemen who would 'look' the character of king as far as state ceremonies were concerned much better than he, but who would have cut a poor figure under circumstances in which he made a brilliant one. The Italians might well overlook the defects of their unconventional sovereign, who knew how so well to defend their rights and his own dignity when occasion required.

The Peace of Villafranca was referred to a conference held at Zurich for formal settlement. It began its sittings early in August and lasted till November. Great difficulties arose on the question as to what was to be done with the dispossessed princes. The Emperor of France had promised the King of Sardinia that no foreign intervention should take place. How then were they to be restored? The provinces were in arms, protesting vehemently against the return of their former rulers, declaring their right to decide their own destinies, and persisting in offering the sovereignty to Victor Emmanuel. It was not to be expected that *he* would take any part in the restoration of the banished dukes.

'The negotiators of the Peace of Villafranca,' says Massari, 'seemed to think that they had only to declare that Leopold of Lorraine should go to Florence, Francis D'Este to Modena, the Duchess de Bourbon to Parma, and the Pope's legates to Bologna, Ferrara, Forli, and Ravenna. But the inhabitants had quite different views on the subject.'

Baron Ricasoli in Florence, and the famous Farini (whose *Stato Romano* we have several times referred to) in Modena, took the lead in maintaining the liberty they had won. An Assembly was convoked of representatives of all the provinces; and in this general Parliament, which was conducted with the utmost order and moderation, it was resolved that they should be citizens of the kingdom of Italy, subjects of Victor Emmanuel.

Meantime, while the inhabitants of Central Italy were sending deputations to Turin, and declaring loudly in their assemblies that they would have no other sovereign than the hero of San Martino, the Austrian rulers and the dispossessed princes were making a fearful outcry about the usurpations of the Sardic king, and trying every art to detach the French emperor from his alliance. In fact, Napoleon was worked upon so strongly that he sent envoys to the provisional governments of the duchies to stop any further demonstrations in favour of Victor Emmanuel, and to himself he sent a special ambassador, the Count de Reiset, for whom he knew the king had a great esteem, to persuade him not to receive the offer of the dominions in question.

Victor explained frankly to the count that he did not regard the matter merely as a question of enlarging his dominions. It was the spontaneous desire of the populations of those provinces that they should be united to his kingdom, and though he felt for the embarrassment of his ally, he could not bring himself to disappoint the confidence that those peoples had reposed in him after the warm sympathy they had shown for him and his government, and the piteous tenacity with which they now clung to him for protection.

In fact, the king gave the Florence deputation, which arrived on September 3, a very cordial reception. The Count Ugolino della Gherardesca read the address offering the throne of Tuscany to Victor Emmanuel in the name of all its inhabitants.

Victor Emmanuel's reply to the Tuscans.

I am profoundly grateful for the vote of the Tuscan Assembly of which you are the interpreters to me. I thank you for it, and with me my people thank you.

I receive this vote as a solemn manifestation of the will of the Tuscan people that, in putting an end, in that land which is the mother of modern civilisation, to the last vestiges of foreign domination, they desire to contribute to the construction of a strong realm, and place Italy in a position to be able to provide for her own independence.

The Tuscan Assembly has of course understood that all Italy is involved in her fate, and that the fulfilment of this vote cannot be effected but by means of the negotiations which are taking place for the re-arrangement of Italian affairs.

Strengthened by the right your vote confers on me, I will second your desire, and uphold the cause of Tuscany before those powers in which the Assembly, with much good sense, places its hopes; and above all with the generous Emperor of the French, who has done so much for the Italian nation. Europe will not refuse, I hope, to exercise towards Tuscany that work of reparation which under less favourable circumstances she has exercised for Greece, Belgium, and the principalities of Moldavia and Wallachia.

Wonderful example of temperateness and concord, gentlemen, your noble country has given in these times. And to those virtues which the school of misfortune has already taught to Italy, you will add, I feel sure, that which overcomes the most arduous trials and assures the triumph of just enterprises—perseverance.

There was a court dinner in the evening. The king was most affable to all the representatives of the Tuscan cities, particularly to Count Ugolino della Gherardesca, who sat at his right, and with whom he jested about his classic name, saying he thought all the family of Ugolino had perished in the tower of Pisa.

Close upon the Tuscan deputation came those of Modena and Parma together, with equally warm protestations of devotion, and were received with the same honours.

The king replied in similar terms to those he had used to the Tuscans, but in the last two paragraphs he expressed himself somewhat more decidedly as to the *right* of the Italian people to choose their own government.

> Confide, gentlemen, in the sense of Europe; confide in the efficacious protection of the Emperor Napoleon, who led the legions of France to fight victoriously for the redemption of Italy. Europe has already recognised the right of other peoples to provide for their own safety by the choice of a government which will guard their liberty and independence. She will not be, I hope, less just nor less generous to these Italian provinces, who ask nothing more than to be governed by a moderate national monarchy; and which are already united by geographical position, common race and interests.
>
> I do not say to you, persevere and unite in this undertaking. The vote which your Assemblies have renewed, and the valiant soldiers whom in the day of battle you sent in such numbers to my standard, render testimony that the peoples of Modena and Parma have a strength of purpose and virtue which they have proved and sealed with their blood. I may well congratulate you on the order and moderation of which you have given such a splendid example. You also have demonstrated to Europe that the Italians know how to govern themselves, and that they are worthy to be citizens of a free nation.

Among the Parma deputation was the musical composer Verdi, who has always been distinguished for his patriotic sentiments.

The last deputation, and the most difficult to deal with, was that from the provinces of Romagna. The king felt no less kindly and gratefully to those brave people, who had suffered as much if not more than the others for his sake, or the sake of the principle he represented. But unhappily they were the subjects of the Pontiff; and there was great risk at such a critical moment of rousing religious susceptibilities and bringing down upon him the pious indignation of the Catholic powers. He was already under the censures of the Church because he had taken upon himself to direct the provisional governments of the insurgent cities. The king received the deputation from the Pontifical States at the royal villa of Monza, near Milan.

Victor Emmanuel's reply to the Romagnuoli.

I am grateful for the votes of the people of the Romagna, of which you, gentlemen, are the interpreters to me. As a Catholic prince I shall preserve in every event a profound and unalterable reverence towards the Supreme Head of the Church. As an Italian prince I must remember that, Europe having recognised and proclaimed that the conditions of your country require prompt and efficacious remedies, I have contracted towards it solemn obligations.

Meantime I receive your votes, and strong in the right they confer upon me, I will maintain your cause before the great powers. Confide in their sense and justice, confide in the generous sentiments of the emperor, who will try to complete the great work of reparation to which he has already placed his hand so powerfully, and which has assured him the gratitude of all Italy.

The moderation which has guided your movements in the most painful moments of uncertainty, shows undoubtedly that the mere hope of national rule in the Romagna is enough to quiet civil discords.

Accept my thanks, gentlemen. When in the days of the national struggle you sent me numerous volunteers, who displayed so much valour under my banner, you understood that Piedmont did not fight for herself alone, but for our common country. Now preserving unanimity of will and maintaining public order, you will fulfil that duty which is most grateful to my heart, and that which will best assure your future. Europe will understand that it is a common duty, as it is a common interest, to close the era of Italian insurrections by procuring the accomplishment of your legitimate desires.

In spite of what Victor Emmanuel considered his prudent and temperate bearing, great indignation was felt by the Catholic powers, and the Emperor of the French was attacked for encouraging this ambitious usurper in his iniquitous and sacrilegious designs. And those whose sympathies were not Catholic preferred the conservation of the established order of things, even when the *régime* was acknowledged to be bad, lest a worse might be the result of any change. One nation there was which understood and appreciated the grand design of the Sardinian king, and befriended him as far as moral support went in the councils of Europe. And though the British Government never allowed its sympathy for liberty to carry it into a war, a great number of Englishmen felt strongly for Italy in her struggle for freedom and civilisation, and subscribed largely for the aid of the volunteers.

Baron Ricasoli of Florence, and Signor Farini of Modena, as heads of the provisional governments, sent envoys to all the courts of Europe to enlighten public opinion on the Italian question, and contradict the false reports set afloat by the dispossessed princes and the papal party. The most perfect order reigned in the duchies and in the legations; the inhabitants felt that they were on their trial before Europe, and they wished to show that they were fit to be citizens of a free nation. Ricasoli was made Dictator of Tuscany, and

Farini of the Emilian Provinces, and under the government of these able and patriotic men matters went on so as to leave nothing to be desired. The world stood in admiration and amaze at the spectacle of such perfect self-control, order, and tranquillity as Central Italy presented under circumstances calculated to excite all the fiercest passions of an ill-educated, hot-blooded, impulsive race, with one exception. No act of revenge, no insults nor outrages towards priests or agents of the late governments stained the record of that bloodless revolution during the six months of suspense in which their destiny hung in the balance. It is one of the brightest pages in the reign of Victor Emmanuel, and reflects more honour on the Italian nation than the glorious victories of which they are so justly proud.

The suspense was too much for Garibaldi: patient waiting was not the *forte* of the gallant volunteer. He had been actively organising troops all this time, and now he prepared to make a descent upon the provinces on the Adriatic coast called the Marches. It was one of those critical moments when one false move would ruin the whole cause. The Sardinian Government was much alarmed, and counselled the king to summon Garibaldi to his presence and lay his commands upon him not to proceed with his design. The general obeyed the royal summons, and in a private interview Victor explained his policy and the strong reasons he had for wishing the papal frontier to be respected while awaiting the judgment of Europe.

Garibaldi was no respecter of kings, as such, but he loved and admired the man who had made himself champion of Italian independence. At this time Victor Emmanuel's influence over the gallant volunteer was greater than that of the republican party, and he laid down his arms at his request. Pity he was not always so amenable!

Time passed on, and the Treaty of Villafranca was put into effect by the king's government—that part of it at least 'which concerned him;' but the fate of Central Italy still hung in a state of painful suspense.

It was a difficult position for the provisional governments, having for many months to hold in check the passions of a people excited to the last degree between hope and despair. But Victor Emmanuel had said, 'Be patient, be moderate; confide in the justice of Europe and my devotion to your cause;' and so they waited. Meantime they desired as an additional tie to the House of Savoy, that they might have the king's cousin, the Prince of Carignano, as viceroy. Victor Emmanuel could not bring himself to refuse the request, though it was thought imprudent to grant it.

In the month of November the idea of a European Congress, which had been for some time ventilated, became a decided thing, and all the powers began to nominate their plenipotentiaries. When the question came up as to who was to represent Sardinia, there was but one opinion on the subject. Camillo Cavour was the name that rose to every tongue, not only in Italy but in every country that had a regard for the interests of that unfortunate peninsula. Lord John Russell declared that a Congress to consider the Italian question would be impossible without Cavour. The count was beginning to get tired of his inactive life, and he was quite willing to take up the burden which in a moment of inconsiderate passion he had cast off; but the king was not so willing to recall him to office. He was deeply offended by the way in which he had deported himself in their last interview, and he could not at once get over it. But after a brief struggle, his nobler self conquered; he put aside personal resentment so far as to allow Count Cavour to be nominated first Sardinian plenipotentiary for the Congress; and with him was associated Cavaliere Luigi Desambrois, then minister at Paris.

CHAPTER XVII.

THE ROBBER KING. A.D. 1860.

THE evening of New Year's day 1860, the king was at the theatre, and being in conversation with some gentleman of the court on public affairs, the subject of the Congress came up. 'Our cause is in good hands,' said the king, who knew that Cavour was near and overheard his words. 'It is confided to a very gifted advocate.' He glanced at the count with a smile, who bowed profoundly as he returned the smile. But notwithstanding this exchange of courtesies they were not reconciled. Cavour had consented to attend the Congress, but he was at variance with the ministers then in power, though both Rattazzi and La Marmora had been his personal friends; he was in favour of a more vigorous action in the national questions, and he thought they were timid and hesitating at a moment which called for a bold and resolute policy. The king's plenipotentiary had to put himself in accord with the king's ministers before he was called to attend the Congress; but notwithstanding prolonged discussions no conclusion was arrived at, to Victor Emmanuel's great vexation. Fresh complications arose every day, fresh disagreements in the cabinet, and a ministerial crisis was expected. The king, more and more annoyed, begged his ministers to try to come to some sort of understanding. He felt he was drifting, in spite of himself, towards the painful necessity of calling Cavour to the head of affairs. He had consented to his representing Sardinia at the Congress, but he felt a great repugnance to replacing him in his old position as President of the Council. There was a struggle going on in Victor Emmanuel's soul which kept him in a state of painful perplexity. An accidental circumstance brought matters to a crisis.

Cavour, weary of disputing with the cabinet, resolved to retire for a while to his country seat of Leri. Before starting he paid a visit to his friend Sir James Hudson, and while in the house of the English minister, a gentleman sought him in haste with a message from the ministry, begging that he would send in writing his last conditions, to see if they could come to an understanding. Time was short, and to hasten matters Sir James Hudson seated himself at a table and said he would write from the count's dictation. The condition on which Cavour expressed himself willing to attend the Congress was that Parliament should be dissolved in the month of March. (It was then January 16.) The ministers were not disposed towards a general election, and one of them in reading the letter recognised the English hand of Sir James Hudson. General La Marmora, offended at what he considered the interference of a foreign diplomatist in the internal affairs of the state, thereupon sent in his resignation. The king was ill in bed, but he did not allow a moment's time to be lost. When he had made up his mind on the right course to pursue he acted with promptitude and decision. An officer was sent in hot haste to Palazzo Cavour with orders to bring the count back with him immediately. He was just stepping into his carriage to go to the station when the royal messenger caught him. The king received him coldly, as if the memory of the Villafranca interview had come to his mind.

Cavour's anger was passed; perhaps he felt he had been wrong, if not in his advice, in his manner of giving it, and that some concession was due to the king who had sacrificed his pride in sending for him; he remembered the close tie which had bound them together for seven years, labouring heart and soul for one common object; and he made the *amende*, which at once restored him to the old confidential footing he occupied before the war. 'Do what you think best in everything,' said the king; 'the responsibility of whatever happens will be yours.'

In five days Cavour had composed a new cabinet to his own taste. The Minister of War was General Fanti, who had commanded the army of the league in Central Italy; which meant that it was the policy of the government to annex those provinces. The gifted Count Mamiani, who had taken a prominent part in public affairs in 1848, and was a subject of the Pope, was made Minister of Public Instruction; this too was not without a certain signification. There was joy in the disputed provinces when Cavour returned to power, and there was bitter vexation in the ranks of the *Codini*. The Chambers were dissolved; and Massimo d'Azeglio was called once more from his retirement on Lago Maggiore and sent as governor to Milan. In the month of February the king visited Lombardy in royal pomp, accompanied by Count Cavour and all the diplomatic body. The reception he met with was enthusiastic in the extreme. It is said that many Austrian officers were there *incognito* to judge with their own eyes how the population felt on the subject of the change.

The longer the central states remained under a provisional government, openly directed by the cabinet of Turin, the more difficult was the task of restoring the exiled princes. It was now seven months since the dukes had fled, and no power seemed to think it a duty to reseat them on the thrones they had justly forfeited. The idea of the Congress had been abandoned; and as nothing seemed likely to be done by Europe with regard to Italian affairs, the government of Victor Emmanuel thought it was time to put an end to the state of uncertainty, which, if further prolonged, might be dangerous.

The greatest difficulty was not about the duchies, but the Legations. The late subjects of the Pope were more resolute in maintaining the liberty they had just acquired, and more devoted to the dynasty of Savoy than the Tuscans, and naturally so, for the government from which they had violently wrenched themselves was much worse in every respect than that of the Lorraine family. Macaulay says it is not possible to be 'a good man and a bad king,' but if ever that paradox existed it was in the person of Pius IX., whose private character was so excellent, so lovable, and whose government was beyond all question atrocious. The state of affairs was much aggravated by the presence in the Pontifical

States of bands of foreign mercenaries collected from all Catholic countries, who acted like a blister on the irritated and excited state of the public mind. Victor Emmanuel and his government thought it was time to take the initiative in settling the affairs of Central Italy, before some disturbance should give excuse for a fresh foreign intervention. It was evident that the Pope could not govern by himself without some foreign support, and the Sardic Government was of opinion that this foreign support should be superseded by Italian arms.

Victor Emmanuel to Pius IX.

Most Blessed Father,—With your venerated autograph of December 3 last year, your holiness enjoins me to sustain before the Congress the rights of the Holy See. I must thank your holiness for the sentiments which counselled you to address yourself to me in these circumstances, and I should not have delayed doing what you requested had the Congress met. I had expected that the meeting of the plenipotentiaries, then definitely decided, would respond in a more adequate manner than I could on the grave subject treated of in the letter which you did me the honour to address to me.

Your holiness, invoking my aid in recovering the Legations, appears to lay to my charge what has taken place in that part of Italy. Before confirming so severe a censure, I respectfully entreat your holiness to weigh the following facts and considerations.

A devoted son of the Church, descended, as you know, from a most religious race, I have always nourished a sense of sincere attachment, of veneration and respect, towards Holy Church and its august head. It never was, and it is not my intention to fail in my duties as a Catholic prince, or to curtail as far as in me lies, those rights and that authority which the Holy See exercises on earth by Divine commission from heaven. But *I* also have sacred duties to fulfil, before God and man, towards my country and towards the people whom Divine

Providence has confided to my government. I have always sought to reconcile the duties of a Catholic prince with those of an independent sovereign of a free and civilised nation, both in the internal rule of my states and in my foreign policy.

Italy has been for many years torn by movements which all aim at the same object, the recovery of her independence. In those events my magnanimous father took an important part, and, *following the impulse given from the Vatican*, attempted to redeem our country from the domination of the foreigner. In accepting this policy, I do not believe I am putting myself in opposition to the divine will, which cannot certainly be that nations should be divided between oppressors and oppressed.

As an Italian prince I wished to liberate Italy, and for that purpose I thought it my duty to welcome for the national war the concourse of all the populations of the peninsula. The Legations, for long years oppressed by foreign soldiers, rose in arms as soon as these were withdrawn. They proffered me at once the dictatorship and their assistance in the war. I who had done nothing to raise the insurrection, refused the dictatorship from respect for the Holy See; but I accepted their assistance in the war of independence, because that was the sacred duty of all Italians. And when the presence of a daring leader was near putting in peril the peace of the provinces occupied by your holiness's troops, I used my influence to withdraw him from those provinces. Those people remained perfectly free from any outside influence, contrary to the advice of the most powerful and generous friend Italy ever had.[1] They asked with extraordinary spontaneousness and unanimity to be annexed to my kingdom. Their desire was not acceded to. Nevertheless these people, who had formerly given such signs of discontent and caused continual apprehension to the court of Rome, have governed themselves for many

---

[1] Napoleon III.

months in the most praiseworthy manner. They have provided for public affairs, for personal security, for the maintenance of order, for the guardianship of religion. It is a fact well known, and I have taken care to verify it, that in the Legations now the ministers of religion are protected and treated with respect, and the temples of God more frequented than formerly.

Be these things as they may, there is a general conviction that your holiness cannot recover these provinces unless by the force of arms, and foreign arms.

This your holiness cannot desire. Your generous soul, your evangelical charity, would shrink from shedding Christian blood to recover a province which, whatever be the issue of war, would remain morally lost to the government of the Church. The interests of religion do not require it.

These are dangerous times. It is not for me, a devoted son of the Church, to indicate the safest way to restore quiet to our country, and to re-establish on a solid basis the prestige and authority of the Holy See in Italy. At the same time I believe it my duty to lay before your holiness an idea of which I am fully convinced. It is this: that taking into consideration the necessity of the times: the increasing force of the principle of nationality: the irresistible impulse which impels the peoples of Italy to unite and order themselves in conformity with the model adopted by all civilised nations—an impulse which I believe demands my frank and loyal concurrence—such a state of things might be established not only in the Romagna but also in the Marches and Umbria, as would reserve to the Church its high dominion and assure to the Supreme Pontiff a glorious post at the head of the Italian nation; while giving the people of those provinces a share in the benefits that a kingdom, strong and highly national, secures to the greater part of Central Italy.

I hope that your holiness will take into benign consideration these reflections, dictated by a soul sincerely devoted to you: and that with your usual goodness you will accord me your holy benediction.

VICTOR EMMANUEL.

Turin, February 6, 1860.

This letter speaks for itself, and gives an admirable compendium of the story of the revolution from a Liberal standpoint. It expresses, only in more measured language, what all the Liberal party were saying, preaching, and writing, just as the Pope's reply in his encyclical letter, which we have not space for here, expresses what the Clerical party were saying, preaching, and writing. The utterances of the rival sovereigns, both honourable men, may be taken as an example of what human evidence is worth. But in reading these contradictory epistles, it is right to remember that Victor Emmanuel never lent his authority to any sort of false dealing or duplicity, that he was a man to inform himself accurately on such questions, and was, in fact, in a position to learn the truth easily; while the Pope was very old, and growing feeble in mind as well as body, shut up in his palace, and surrounded only by one class, whose interest it was to blind him as to facts, and incite him against the Nationalists; and that this party, who alone had the ear of the Pope, defend the practice of 'pious frauds,' and do not hesitate to make false statements, if the end to be gained is a meritorious one. Would they be likely to consider it a sin to blacken the character of an impious people or government who wanted to rob the patrimony of St. Peter?

The good Pope probably believed what he wrote, when he stated that in the provinces revolted from his rule all sorts of immorality had increased, and the most violent disorders prevailed. But nothing could be further from the truth. The fact was that those people never were so well-behaved and well-ordered as during the period when their fate was hanging in uncertainty. The reason is easy to understand; their souls were filled with the ennobling enthusiasm for national existence, which while it lasted absorbed all baser passions; they felt that 'the eyes of Europe were upon them,' and it behoved them, as Victor Emmanuel had said, to show themselves worthy to be citizens of a free nation.

The Pope had answered the king's proposition in his encyclical, which was a long indictment against him and his government; but he was too courteous a gentleman not to reply by an autograph letter to that of his majesty. There was a grace and refinement—a something, that the Italians call *poesia*—about Pio Nono, which gave him a great charm. In the moment of his deep distress, for such it undoubtedly was, when a cardinal announced the fact of the annexation, saying, 'The provinces of the Romagna no longer belong to your holiness, but to the King of Sardinia,' he replied with a playful irony, 'When did those provinces ever belong to me?'

Pius IX. to Victor Emmanuel.

Your Majesty,—The idea which your majesty has thought well to lay before me is not wise, and certainly not worthy of a Catholic king, and a prince of the House of Savoy. My reply is already given to the press in the encyclical to the Catholic episcopacy, which you can easily read.

All else I have to say is that I am deeply afflicted, not for myself, but for the unhappy state of your majesty's soul, finding you unmoved by past censures, or by the fear of those still greater ones that must fall upon you when you have consummated the sacrilegious act which you and yours intend to put into execution.

With all my heart I pray the Lord to enlighten you with His grace, that you may recognise and weep for the scandals given, and the serious evils brought by your co-operation upon this poor Italy.

Pius PP. IX.

From the Vatican, February 14, 1860.

This letter called for no answer in words, inasmuch as it put all compromise out of the question. It was then that Victor Emmanuel consummated what the

Ultramontanes call the great crime of his life, and what the Italian nation calls the most glorious achievement in modern history. Undaunted by the 'heavier censures' than those already promulgated, with which he was threatened, within a month from the receipt of the Pope's reply, he and his unholy minister had carried into effect their sacrilegious intentions. Once more the question was put to the vote in the popular assemblies, and once more the populations of Central Italy declared unanimously for annexation with free North Italy. So, after the prolonged trial of their faith and loyalty, they were at last received into 'the Italian family,' to their indescribable joy. Having accomplished the work of spoliation, the robber king once more addressed himself to the Pontiff, thinking perhaps that the march of events, which he could not control, would convince him of the necessity of going along with the age to a certain extent.

Victor Emmanuel to Pius IX.

Most Blessed Father,—The events that have been accomplished in the provinces of the Romagna impose upon me the duty of explaining to your holiness with respectful frankness the reasons for my conduct.

Ten continuous years of foreign occupation in the Romagna, while it brought grave offence and injury to the independence of Italy, have not been able to give order to society, repose to the population, or authority to the government. The moment the foreign occupation ceased, the government fell, without one arm to support or re-establish it. When left a prey to themselves, the people of the Romagna, hitherto held to be ungovernable, showed by a conduct which won the applause of Europe how easy it would be to introduce among them the order and discipline, civil and military, by which other civilised peoples are ruled. But the uncertainty of their precarious state—already too prolonged—was a danger to Italy and to Europe.

The hope of a European Congress before which

the question of Central Italy was to have been brought being abandoned, no other solution seemed possible than that of putting once more to the populations the question of their future destinies.

The universal vote for annexation to the constitutional monarchy of Piedmont was reconfirmed with such solemnity that I had to accept it definitely for the sake of the peace and the welfare of Italy. And for the same end of peace I am always disposed to render homage to the high sovereignty of the Apostolic See.

As a Catholic prince I do not feel that I offend against the immutable principles of that religion which with filial and unalterable devotion I glory to profess. But the changes now made regard the political interests of the nation, the order, moral and civil, of society,—regard the independence of Italy, for which my father lost his crown, and for which I should be ready to lose my life.

The difficulties of the present day overturn territorial dominions around us in a manner which the force of events has rendered necessary. To the necessity of the time all principalities have been obliged to yield, and the Holy See itself had to recognise it in ancient and modern days.

In such modifications of the sovereignty, justice and the civil reasons of state prescribe that every care should be taken to reconcile ancient rights with the new order of things; and it is for this that, confiding in the benevolence and good sense of your holiness, I pray you to facilitate the work for my government, which on its side will neglect no precaution, no effort, to arrive at the desired end. If your holiness receives with benignity the present opening of negotiations, my government, ready to render homage to the high sovereignty of the Holy See, will also be disposed to supply in equal measure the diminution of its revenues, and to provide for the security and independence of the Pontiff.

Such are my sincere intentions, and such I believe the wishes of Europe. And now that I have candidly opened my mind to your holiness, I await your deliberations with the hope that, by means of the goodwill of governments, a satisfactory understanding may be arrived at, reposing on the agreement of the princes and on the contentment of the peoples, which will give a stable foundation to the relations of the two states.

From the gentleness of the Father of the faithful I promise myself a benevolent reception which will give hope of extinguishing civil discord, pacify exasperated spirits, and relieve all of the grave responsibility of the evils that might arise from contrary counsels.

In this expectant confidence, I ask with reverence the Apostolic benediction.

VICTOR EMMANUEL.

Turin, March 20, 1860.

Six days after this letter was written the bull of excommunication was issued. Pio Nono cursed Victor Emmanuel, and with him his councillors, soldiers, and subjects, old and new, were all thrown out of the Catholic Church without further ceremony, as abandoned and incorrigible sinners. This was Pio's answer as Pope to the king's appeal for a reconciliation; but even when breathing anathemas he did not seem to be actuated by a personal animus, and he never withheld the courtesy of an autographic reply to Victor's letters. It is curious to observe in their correspondence how persistently the excommunicated monarch, after laying bare with the utmost unreserve his plans of spoliation, asks the Apostolic benediction; and it is also curious and noteworthy to see that the irate Pontiff indirectly responds at the end of each letter to the demand by promising to *pray for him*. The Pope's letters have the merit of being briefer than those of the king, but we must remember that Victor Emmanuel said all he wanted to say to the Pope himself, while Pio Nono made Christendom ring with encyclicals, allocutions, and addresses of appalling length and wordiness.

Pius IX. to Victor Emmanuel.

Your Majesty,—The events that have taken place in some of the States of the Church impose on your majesty the duty, as you write me, of giving me an account of your conduct in relation to them. I might stop to combat certain assertions contained in your letter, and tell you, for example, that the foreign occupation in the Legations was for some time confined to Bologna, which never formed part of the Romagna. I might tell you that the supposed universal suffrage was imposed, not spontaneous (I abstain from asking your majesty's opinion of universal suffrage, and also from giving mine). I might tell you that the Pontifical troops were impeded from re-establishing the legitimate government in the insurgent provinces, for reasons well known to your majesty. These and other things I might tell you *à propos*. But that which above all imposes on me the duty of not accepting your majesty's plans, is the steady increase of immorality in those provinces, and the insults offered to religion and to her ministers, for which reason, even if I were not bound to hold intact the patrimony of the Church, by a solemn oath which hinders me from opening negotiations to diminish its extent, I should still find myself obliged to reject every project, in order not to stain my conscience by an acquiescence that would lead me indirectly to sanction and participate in those disorders, and help to justify an unjust and violent spoliation. For the rest I not only cannot give a benevolent reception to the projects of your majesty, but instead I protest against the usurpation that you have carried out, to the harm of the State and the Church; and I leave on your majesty's conscience, and that of every other co-operator in the spoliation, the fatal consequences that may follow. I am persuaded that your majesty, on reading again, with a mind calmer, less prejudiced, and better informed as to facts, the letter you have addressed me, will find there many things to repent.

I pray the Lord to give you those blessings of which, in your present difficult circumstances, you have most need.

Pius PP. IX.

From the Vatican, April 2, 1860.

This dignified and gentlemanly letter must command the sympathy and respect of everyone who looks only at the present trying position of the venerable Pontiff, forgetful of his antecedents. However narrow his views and his sympathies, he was acting according to the dictates of his conscience, and contrary to his worldly interests, for he knew well he had no power to withstand the overwhelming impetus of the national will. But the Romans could not forgive his apostasy in 1848. Had he never been a liberal reformer, and not broken his faith, solemnly plighted to the Italian cause, on which he had repeatedly called God's blessing; had he not abandoned his country in the extreme hour of her agonising struggle with the invader of her liberties; had he not been borne back to his capital by foreign arms, and held on the throne by grinding oppression; then, indeed, his subjects could not but have admired the firmness, courage, and fidelity to principle, however mistaken, which dictated this reply. But was the oath, they asked, not to diminish the patrimony of St. Peter, already diminished without his consent, more sacred than the pledge given to the national leaders and the Roman people? Undoubtedly the Pope considered it so, and thought moreover that the general deportment of the Roman people in 1848—which was far from blameless—justified his abandonment of the Liberal cause.

Pio Nono was convinced that he was doing his duty, and sacrificing himself to a most sacred obligation, by holding to the Church. Victor Emmanuel was as strongly and firmly convinced that he had a grand mission on this earth, which was to liberate and unite Italy in one state; and he was fully persuaded that it was a sacred and bounden duty for him to accomplish that work. Each felt that on the triumph of his principles depended the happiness and well-being of his country, and nothing but evil could follow on the success of his adversary. So the Italian question became a duel between the head of the Church and the head of the State.

The excommunication, once such a terrible punishment, did not hurt Victor Emmanuel in the least, unless in a sentimental way. There were patriotic priests, and bishops too, in Piedmont, who stood by their king, and administered the rites of the Church to him and his family. Nevertheless, his feelings were deeply hurt by the Pope's hostility, and he desired intensely to be reconciled to him. With an extraordinary perseverance he continued to write private and confidential letters, laying his views before him, and trying by every argument to convince him that political freedom did not mean any offence or injury to religion; protesting that he was ready to make any compromise or sacrifice his holiness might demand, short of giving up his darling scheme of uniting Italy. The Pontiff's sovereignty should be guaranteed, his revenues secured; in fact there should be no difference in his position, except that Italian instead of foreign arms should surround and protect the Holy See, and the tricolour united with the Pontifical colours, as in 1848, should float on the Capitol.

'The Pope will never abdicate,' said a friend to Cavour, as he was propounding his theory of 'a free Church in a free State.' 'We do not ask so much; a tacit renunciation would be enough. And do you believe there is really anything to abdicate? Do you think that temporal power still exists?' asked the count, who maintained that the Pope would be more free and have more authority under Italian than French protection.

Victor Emmanuel's efforts to win upon the native gentleness of Pius IX., and rekindle in him a little spark of the old patriotic fire, proved fruitless; to every proposition he replied with the unvarying *Non possumus* which has become famous.

In the month of March the two dictators of Central Italy betook themselves to Turin to present the documents of the plébiscite, and lay down their authority at the feet of the constitutional monarch. To the addresses delivered by these gentlemen the king replied in equally complimentary terms.

Carlo Luigi Farini, Dictator of Emilia, to Victor Emmanuel.

Sire,—I have the honour to place in your hands the legal documents of the universal suffrage of the populations of the Emilia. Your majesty, who pitifully heard their *cry of anguish*, will welcome benignantly this pledge of faith and gratitude. Their legitimate wishes fulfilled, these populations, O sire, will have no other desire than that of deserving well of your majesty and of Italy, emulating in civil and military virtues the other peoples of your monarchy.

Baron Ricasoli, in the name of Tuscany, spoke to the same effect, but at more length.

Victor Emmanuel's Reply to Farini.

The manifestation of the national will, of which you bring me authentic testimony, is so universal and spontaneous that it re-confirms before Europe, in a different state of things and at a different time, the vote formerly expressed by the Assemblies of Emilia. Such signal manifestations put a seal to the proofs of order, of perseverance, of love of country, of political wisdom, which in a few months have won for those people the sympathy and esteem of all the civilised world. I accept their solemn vote, and henceforth I will glory to call them my people.

In uniting to the constitutional monarchy of Piedmont, and making equal to her, other provinces—not only the states of Parma and Modena, but also the

Romagna — which already, of their own accord, had separated themselves from the Pontifical rule, I do not mean to lessen my devotion to the venerable head of the Church—a devotion which has been, and always will be, warm in my heart. As a Catholic and Italian prince I am always ready to defend that independence necessary to his supreme ministry, to contribute to the splendour of his court, and to render homage to his high sovereignty. The Parliament is about to unite. It will receive in its bosom the representatives of Central Italy with those of Piedmont and Lombardy, thus consolidating the new kingdom, and giving a larger prospect of assured liberty and independence.

To Baron Bettino Ricasoli, Dictator of Tuscany.

The homage that you bring me in fulfilment of the solemn vote already manifested by the Assembly in which was collected the flower of the Tuscan population, crowns that series of invincible propositions, of generous works, which make Tuscany deserve the affection of every Italian and the applause of all civilised peoples.

I accept this vote, which after many months of trial is now strengthened by the unanimity of popular suffrage, and I glory to be able to call the Tuscans also my people.

Associating her lot with that of my kingdom, Tuscany does not renounce her glorious traditions, but continues and increases them, making them common with other noble provinces of Italy. The Parliament in which the representatives of Tuscany shall sit beside those of Piedmont, Lombardy, and the Emilia, will, I am certain, inform all its laws with the fruitful principle of liberty, which will assure to Tuscany the benefits of self-government without weakening, but rather strengthening, that intimate communion of efforts and of will that is the most efficacious guarantee of the prosperity and independence of our country.

The ex-dictators received the order of the SS. Annunziata; Baron Ricasoli was made Governor of Tuscany, and Farini, Minister of the Interior.

Victor Emmanuel to the People of Central Italy.

Your desire is satisfied: you are united with my other peoples in one sole monarchy; your concord and perseverance have deserved this reward. Great benefit is this for our country and for civilisation: but in order that it may bear good fruit it is necessary to persevere in the virtue of which you have given such a wonderful example; and above all must be cultivated the firm readiness to make sacrifices, without which great enterprises are ill-accomplished and badly secured.

I place in you that faith which, not in vain, you have placed in me. The condition which binds us indissolubly is, honour towards our common country, and universal civilisation. I have not in the past had any other ambition than to hazard my life for the independence of Italy, and to give the people an example of loyalty which, restoring the public *morale*, united with liberty, should give a solid foundation to the state. I have now the ambition to procure to myself and to my family, from the people just united, that devoted affection for which the Subalpines are celebrated; I am ambitious to fortify the Italians in those noble sentiments by which is formed the strong temperament of peoples who know how to bear adversity and prepare for good fortune.

VICTOR EMMANUEL.

Turin, March 25, 1860.

The elections took place on the same day, amidst great excitement, and ovations for those who had been most active in the work of uniting the provinces. Count Cavour was elected in no less than eight constituencies, Farini and Ricasoli in several. All the most gifted and distinguished men in Italy were sent to that Parliament in Turin, and were received by the Subalpines with an enthusiastic and brotherly welcome; and the robber king congratulated himself and his accomplices on the great work of spoliation successfully accomplished.

CHAPTER XVIII.

KING OF ELEVEN MILLION SUBJECTS. A.D. 1860.

VICTOR EMMANUEL was now at the head of a kingdom containing about eleven million inhabitants, as the emperor had calculated in a conversation with the Sardic ambassador before the annexations, to which he was a consenting party, had been effected. It was a glorious triumph to be made ruler of those provinces which had forced themselves, so to speak, into his kingdom—to gain the jurisdiction of which not a drop of blood had been shed; and no man could enjoy more thoroughly such a triumph than King Victor. But there is no rose without a thorn. The price had to be paid for French aid in the recovery of Lombardy and the tacit consent of the emperor to the annexation of the Central Provinces. Victor Emmanuel had already sacrificed his daughter on the altar of Italian independence; she, filled with the enthusiasm of her family, like Jephtha's daughter, surrendered herself willingly; nevertheless the sacrifice wrung the paternal heart.

And now the second instalment of the debt to his 'august and generous ally' had to be rendered in the cession of Nice and Savoy—the latter the dearest province of all his kingdom—the cradle of his race. Besides his personal feelings, which were very strong on the subject, England—who had openly approved of the annexation of the duchies, and had been very kind and encouraging with regard to the encroachments on the patrimony of the Church—did not like this proposition of taking a slice off Italy and putting it on to France; and Victor always liked to be on good terms with England. On the other hand, France had given active and efficient aid to the national cause, when England had withheld hers. He undoubtedly owed a great debt to the emperor, who represented to him that the enlargement of the frontier was necessary to persuade Frenchmen that there was nothing to be feared from the increasing power of the Sardinian king. This was true enough, for there was a great dread in France of a powerful rival kingdom growing up at her door. M. Thiers and others spoke strongly against Italian unity, and warned the country to beware of the insatiable ambition of 'the Wolf of Savoy.' Distinguished Italians sojourning in France, who had an opportunity of judging of the state of feeling, urged Cavour to assent, saying that if the treaty were not signed they would lose all French sympathy and friendship. Cavour wanted to save the provinces by putting the case to arbitration and paying a large sum, but he found it was impossible; and all he and the king could do was to stipulate for the people the right of giving their opinion. The emperor could not object to a plébiscite; so Victor Emmanuel was able to say to the deputations who waited on him with affectionate reproaches, that the question should be decided by their votes. It was hard to tell his faithful subjects, who had been so devoted to him and his dynasty, that they must transfer their allegiance to another sovereign, and that he *wished* them to do so. He did it, however, saying that, though he felt the separation to be a terrible sacrifice, he knew they would be equally prosperous when united to France; he hoped they would be good subjects to the emperor, but he begged them not to forget the old country, as he never could forget the proofs they had given of devotion to him and to the national cause.

On March 24 the treaty was signed, and at the same time the king issued an address to the inhabitants of Nice and Savoy, trying to reconcile them to the change by reminding them of the affinity of race, language, and customs between them and the French. Unwillingly the Savoyards gave their consent to be disunited from the mother country; but the transfer was effected without any serious disturbance, in spite of the passionate protests of a few fiery spirits like Garibaldi. Nice was the birthplace of the great volunteer, and his grief and indignation knew no bounds when he learned that it had been transferred to a foreign rule.

The Parliament was opened on April 2 with unusual pomp. The representatives of the new states, the most distinguished men of Southern and Central Italy, mingled with the Sardinian and Lombard senators and deputies in taking the oath of allegiance. It was a roll-call of illustrious names, among which were Manzoni, Capponi, Ricasoli, Farini, Mamiani, Poerio. Great enthusiasm prevailed, and loud acclamations followed the swearing-in of the new members. Then a profound silence followed, and the king delivered his speech, every paragraph of which was received with applause, with one exception.

The King's Speech.

Gentlemen Senators,—Gentlemen Deputies,—The last time I opened Parliament, when Italy was sunk in sorrows, and the state menaced by great danger, faith in Divine justice comforted me, and augured well for our destinies. In a very brief space of time an invasion was repelled, Lombardy liberated by the glorious achievements of the army, Central Italy freed by the marvellous merit of her people; and to-day I have here assembled around me the representatives of the rights and of the hopes of the nation. For so much good fortune we are debtors to a magnanimous ally, to the valour of his and our soldiers, to the self-abnegation of the volunteers, to the persevering harmony of all the peoples; and let us render to God the merit of it all, for, without superhuman aid, such enterprises, memorable in present and future generations, are not accomplished.

In gratitude to France, for the good of Italy, to consolidate the union between two nations that have a common origin, principles, and destinies—and finding it necessary to make some sacrifice—I have made that which has cost my heart dear. Subject to the vote of the people, the approbation of Parliament, and the consent of Switzerland with regard to the guarantees of international rights, I have made a treaty for the reunion of Savoy and Nice to France.

Here the royal speaker's voice grew thick, and he could hardly finish the sentence. He paused a minute or two before he resumed in his usual firm sonorous accents.

Many difficulties we have yet to overcome, but, sustained by public opinion and the love of my people, I shall not allow the least of their rights or liberties to be injured. Though firm as my fathers were in the dogmas of the Catholic Church, and reverence for its Supreme Head, should the ecclesiastical authorities adopt spiritual arms for temporal interests, I, with a safe conscience, and reposing in the traditions of my fathers, will find strength to maintain entire civil liberty and my authority,—of which I owe account only to God and my people.

The provinces of the Emilia have had an administration in conformity with that of the older provinces; but with regard to Tuscany, which has had laws of its own, a particular temporary provision is necessary.

The shortness of the time and the rapidity of events have prevented the preparation of the laws which must give stability and strength to the new state. In the first period of this legislature you will only have to discuss the most urgent questions. My ministers will then prepare, with due consultation, the designs on which you must deliberate in the second period.

Founded on the *Statuto*, the unity, political, military, and financial, the uniformity of laws, civil and penal, and the progressive administrative liberty of the province and the commune, will renew in the Italian people that vigorous and brilliant life which in other forms of European civilisation was produced by the self-government of the municipalities, but which in the present day is rejected by the constitution of a strong state and the genius of the nation.

Gentlemen Senators,—Gentlemen Deputies,—In turning our attention to the new ordering of affairs, not seeking in old parties other than the memory of the services rendered to the common cause, we invite all sincere opinions to a noble emulation that we may attain the grand end of the well-being of the people and the greatness of the country. It is no longer the Italy of the Romans, nor that of the Middle Ages ; it must no longer be the battle-field of ambitious foreigners, but it must be rather the Italy of the Italians.

On April 15 the king embarked at Genoa and landed at Leghorn, in order to make a tour through his new dominions. He was welcomed with indescribable enthusiasm in all the towns through which he passed ; and beautiful Florence was decorated for his reception with the exquisite taste which distinguishes her inhabitants. Triumphal arches in imitation of antique marble, festooned with evergreens, were erected at the ends of the streets, the whole fronts of the houses were draped in flowers, the pavements were carpeted with laurels and bays, the tricolour floated from every window and housetop, and the passage from the railway station to the Palazzo Vecchio was one continual shout of applause.

'Why such frantic joy?' asked a distinguished foreigner of a lad who was clapping his hands and cheering vociferously at the sight of his new sovereign.

'We are Eleven Million Italians!' was the reply. Mamiani, who accompanied the king on his tour, thus describes the effect :—

> I believe that rarely if ever has there been recorded in the history of any people such an entry of a prince into a newly annexed province as that of our king ;

and I who have been many times witness of the enthusiasm feel quite incapable of giving an account of it. In the chief cities where he passed he excited an ardour, an intoxication of pure universal joy, to which no pen and no style can do justice. I will only say that at his presence there arose from the thickly-packed and enthusiastic multitude, a thunder of applause that never ceased, and that resounded high above all other noises of carriages, of bells, of artillery, which were completely extinguished and drowned. Over the king and around him fell incessantly, continually, the loveliest flowers, like thick rain. At every step there were festoons, arches, triumphs, national banners by the thousand, arras, damasks, rich pavilions, pictures, emblems, inscriptions,—everywhere a jubilee passionate, intense, interminable. How many triumphs of Cæsars, how many coronations of kings, what act of taking possession by great monarch, captain, or conqueror, has ever called forth such ovations? I believe none. For no king ever brought with him like this all the great social and political good—liberty, independence, means of defence, personal dignity, the right of self-government.

Victor Emmanuel found all the men of letters devoted to him, because his was the only state in Italy in which education and intellectual life were encouraged and fostered. 'I am only a soldier,' he used to say, modestly; but he knew how to appreciate talent of every sort. We have seen what Gioberti and Manzoni thought of him; and on his arrival in the Tuscan capital, Gino Capponi was amongst the first to welcome the new sovereign. Victor Emmanuel, grasping the hand of the venerable historian, said: 'I rejoice to press the hand of the first citizen of Florence.' There came also the octogenarian poet, Niccolini, though hardly able to support himself on his feet, happy to behold, and once before he died, the deliverer in whom he had taught his countrymen to trust. He presented the king with his *National Poems* and *Arnold da Brescia*, and read an address to him. There was something touching and beautiful in the enthusiasm of the old poet, trembling on the brink of the grave, and Victor was profoundly moved by it. The beauty of the language we cannot render; we can but hope to convey the sentiments expressed in that address.

G. B. Niccolini to Victor Emmanuel.

I come, O sire, although bowed down by years and ill-health, I come with infirm step and with unutterable emotion which renders me almost mute, to revere in you the liberty-loving monarch, the stupendous example to the world of loyalty, the first soldier of the war of Italian independence, the elect of the people, the desire, the joy of all Italy. And if it be permitted to me, O sire, I come to express the joy of my soul, to tell you that when I wrote, more than thirty years ago, these poor lines,—

> Qui necessario estimo un Rè possente.
> Sia di quel Rè scettro la spada, e l' elmo
> La sua corona ; le divise voglie
> A concordia riduca, a Italia sani
> Le servili ferite e la ricrei,—

I did not dare to hope for a fate so benignant as to see, before closing these eyes for ever to the sweet light of Italy, my most ardent desire for you fulfilled.

Still, if I have ever desired that my humble words might carry power with them, I had it in my soul last year, when, with the assistance of a young friend, almost a son in my affections, I gave to the light one of the books which with a frank and reverent love I now offer you,—a book which recommends to all the Italians whom fortune permits to elect a worthy prince, that they should use every effort to unite themselves under your constitutional and heroic sceptre.

While Victor Emmanuel was on this tour, taking possession of the newly annexed provinces amidst the indescribable joy of the 'Eleven Million Italians,' far other scenes were going on in Sicily, the inhabitants of that unhappy island, unable longer to support the Bourbon rule, having risen in a formidable rebellion which the royal troops found it impossible to crush.

CHAPTER XIX.

THE REVOLUTION OF NAPLES. A.D. 1860.

IN the latter part of the year 1859 and the beginning of 1860, the kingdom of Naples had become the seat of secret intrigues set on foot by the court of Vienna, in which Cardinal Antonelli, the widow of Ferdinand II., and the young King Francis took an active part. A continual correspondence was kept up between Vienna, Rome, and Naples on the subject of the restoration of the old *régime* in Italy. The conspiracy was already on foot when Victor Emmanuel was frankly offering his alliance to Francis, begging him to make himself *Italian*. 'I do not understand what is meant by Italian independence,' said Francis, 'I only recognise the independence of Naples.'

The Count of Syracuse, brother of the late king, who had been banished and despoiled of his property for marrying an English lady, and other offences against the traditions of his house, now made earnest appeals to his nephew to save the family from everlasting infamy before it was too late: but Francis was deaf to all entreaty, and the Count of Syracuse finally washed his hands of him, and threw himself into the arms of the national party.

In spite of the great caution observed, the astuteness of Count Cavour was able to discover the existence of the conspiracy alluded to, all the secrets of which have never transpired, though enough proofs have come to light to reveal the fact that Antonelli was the leading spirit, as the following notes to the Neapolitan Government will show:

> Albano, Oct. 9, 1859. [Most private].
>
> I return this moment from an audience with the Holy Father at Castillo. H. H. has conceded the authorisation of the eventual passage of our troops through the Roman territory on the line parallel to the Tronto. Mons. Bernardi will go this evening to tell Card. Antonelli. The Holy Father desires this agreement to remain strictly secret.
>
> DE MARTINO.

> Jan. 6, 1860.
>
> The Austrian ambassador labours strenuously to push the Holy Father to the most extreme resolutions. A Catholic League, he says, can alone save the Pontificate and society.
>
> DE MARTINO.

To form this league an earnest appeal was made to Spain, as the most Catholic power; but the minister, O'Donnell, firmly refused his sanction to engaging in a war against Italy, 'because of the unpopularity' which would attach to it.

Meantime it was noted by the Piedmontese Government that Neapolitan troops were being concentrated in the Abruzzi, and that foreign volunteers, collected from all countries, were pouring into the Pontifical States. The intrigues we have mentioned were known to the King of Sardinia and his minister, but not to the public, when Garibaldi was allowed to equip two vessels and convey his followers to the aid of the Sicilian insurgents. That the government shut its eyes to the proceedings of the volunteer chief there is no manner of doubt now, though at the time, and even afterwards, it was a subject of dispute, for Cavour with a masterly dissimulation neither denied nor affirmed his complicity in the undertaking. When Francis II. not only rejected Victor Emmanuel's offer of friendship, but engaged in a secret conspiracy for the overthrow of his power and the destruction of Italian independence, it became clear to the Turin Government that only a deadly war could settle the long-standing quarrel with the Bourbon, and nothing prevented their declaring it but the disapprobation of the great powers, and the shifting, inconsistent policy of their French ally.

It was not to be expected that the news of the insurrection in Palermo (April 6) should be received with anything but pleasure, or that the Sardinian Government would throw any impediment in the way of the volunteers going to the aid of the Sicilians. Garibaldi, who always held himself a free agent, and bound to any government only so long as his opinions and theirs coincided, had pledged himself to the southern nationalists in February, and in pursuance of that promise now prepared to take command of the rebel army in Sicily.

The Turin Government threw no obstacle in his way; they even adroitly put arms and ammunition within his reach: while the authorities at Genoa allowed him to sail under their eyes without molesting him. A Sardinian fleet set out in a southerly direction at the same time, the Admiral Persano having received a note from the prime minister to the following effect:—

'Signor Conte, try to navigate between Garibaldi and the Neapolitan cruisers. I hope you understand me.'

To which the daring sailor replied:—

'Signor Conte, I believe I understand you; if I am mistaken, you can send me to prison.'

This was something more than 'winking at' the volunteer expedition, and the suspicions of the diplomatic world were aroused. Indignation was freely expressed by most of the great powers; and the Neapolitan minister described Garibaldi's descent on Sicily as 'an act of savage piracy perpetrated on a friendly state.' Angry notes poured in from Vienna, Berlin, and St. Petersburg to the court of Turin. The brave Garibaldians, 'the flower of the Italian youth,' as Cavour called them, were variously described in the complimentary terms of 'a horde of pirates,' 'desperadoes,' 'bandits,' 'dregs of the human race,' etc. The

Vienna Government ordered a fleet from Trieste to take its way to the South Mediterranean to protect Naples ; the Czar declared that he would do the same only for the material position which Russia occupied, and directed his minister to telegraph to Turin his profound indignation, demanding the punishment of the authorities at Genoa, and inquiring if the filibustering Captain Garibaldi still wore the uniform of his Sardic majesty? The English naval officers at Genoa looked on encouragingly, if they did not aid in the embarkation of the Italian volunteers: and their conduct was also described as *infâme*.

Cavour bore this cross-fire of diplomatic batteries directed against him with wonderful courage and calmness, and ably defended himself and his ministry from attacks on every side. Why, he asked, should Sardinia throw herself in the way of an enterprise against an incorrigible government? What right had the world to expect that she was bound to hinder Garibaldi's disembarkation in Sicily? If the Irish and Austrian volunteers could overrun Italy in order to form a Pope's Brigade, without let or hindrance, the Government of Turin could not, without divorcing itself from the national cause, forbid the Ligurian cruisers to carry Italian men to render that aid to the Sicilians which brothers in distress have a right to expect from brothers. And if Giuseppe Garibaldi had raised the standard of popular war, and the flower of Italian youth were enlisted in his troop, the monarchy could not without destroying the foundation of its strength, wrest the arms from the hands of those gallant volunteers. It would be to throw Italy into complete anarchy. In short, Victor Emmanuel and his government were pledged to the national cause, and they did not mean to stultify themselves by taking part with the enemies of that cause.

It needed all Cavour's bold spirit and subtle Italian intellect to carry his sovereign and country through the breakers that stormed round them at this period. So well had he concealed the secret encouragement he had given to the volunteers, that he had to bear the bitterest reproaches and upbraidings for his supine indifference to the sufferings of his fellow-countrymen in the south. He was even accused by the Mazzinians of opposing and thwarting the leader of the expedition. While he was being vilified by the republicans, reproached by the royalists, and stormed at by the diplomatists, he listened with that sublime serenity of soul which carried him through one of the most trying of political careers to a glorious *finale*, and said nothing but what was absolutely necessary in reply to the great powers. Victor Emmanuel went hand in hand with him in his daring policy: and the news of Garibaldi's unbroken series of victories in Sicily filled them both with hope and joy.

To Signor La Farina at Palermo.

Turin, June 19, 1860.

I have received your letters of the 12th and 14th, and I will preserve them as historic documents... Persano will give you all the aid he can without compromising our banner. It would be a great matter if Garibaldi could pass into Calabria. Here things do not go badly. The diplomatists do not molest us too much. Russia made a fearful hubbub—Prussia less. The Parliament has much sense. I await your letters with impatience.

CAVOUR.

The diplomatists did not allow him much respite however. Garibaldi's increasing successes in Sicily alarmed the Bourbon government for Naples; and special envoys were despatched to London and Paris to invoke the aid of those powers to protect the Neapolitan coast against the 'filibusters.' France proposed a truce with Garibaldi for six months; Victor Emmanuel's government would only consent to interfere with the volunteer movement on condition of the absolute approval of England—which they knew would not be given. Not only did England positively refuse to intervene, but she protested against France doing so.

Count Cavour then wrote a statement of facts to Lord Palmerston and Lord Russell, to further strengthen the national cause; and also exhorted the Marquis d'Azeglio to use all his influence in England on behalf of the Sicilians.

The infamous government of Naples, and the horrible sufferings of political prisoners, had become generally known after the escape of Poerio and his companions, and had excited sentiments of indignation and pity in the British Isles, where so many miserable exiles had found refuge in former times, before liberal Piedmont opened an asylum for them. These banished ones were the flower of the population. In 1853, Charles Dickens, visiting Naples after many years, records the following dialogue in his correspondence:—

'I knew a very remarkable gentleman when I was last here,' I said to a Neapolitan marchese who came to see me the night I arrived: 'a very remarkable gentleman, who had never been out of his own country, but was perfectly acquainted with English literature, and had taught himself to speak English in that wonderful manner that no one would have known that he was a foreigner. I am very anxious to see him, but I forget his name.' He named him, and his face fell directly. 'Dead?' said I. 'In exile.' 'Ah, dear me!' I said, 'I have looked forward to seeing him more than anyone in this country.' 'What would you have?' said the marquis in a low voice. 'He was a remarkable man—full of knowledge, full of spirit, full of generosity. Where should he be but in exile? Where could he be?'

That word *exile* is a mournful sound in all countries and all languages; but in Italian it is pregnant with a bitter anguish which northerns, however well they love their country, cannot fully understand. An Italian prefers to live at home in poverty rather than enjoy wealth and luxury abroad—and to banish him from his native place is like tearing his heartstrings out by the roots.

In historical questions the evidence of a romancist is not admissible; but a good novel will be read by thousands who do not care to examine historical evidence; and so the romancist wields a mighty power over the sympathies of his fellow-men. *Uncle Tom's Cabin* excited the indignation of the whole world against Negro slavery; and Giovanni Ruffini's exquisite story, *Doctor Antonio*, in which he depicted so feelingly and truthfully the wrongs of his country, did no small service to the Italian cause. The sympathies of the English nation were now entirely with the revolution; subscriptions were collected in aid of the Sicilian rebels and the volunteer army; and the great pirate himself became the idol of young English enthusiasm to an extraordinary degree, considering that he was a total stranger. When Englishmen felt so strongly on the subject, what must have been the feelings of young Italians when this last great struggle for nationality was going on!

A frenzied enthusiasm took possession of the population; young men of all classes left their employments and their studies, and hastened to take part in the great work of Italian redemption. The *camicia rossa* was the most glorious of uniforms; Garibaldi was a matchless hero, to whom the history of ancient or modern times presented no equal; he was a Cincinnatus, a Belisarius, a Washington, a Kosciusko, all in one. In fact the gallant chief, all unconsciously on his part, began to rival the soldier-king in the affections of the nation. Victor Emmanuel, so far from being jealous, felt nothing but intense pleasure in all this feverish enthusiasm, in which he shared as warmly as any one of the volunteers. His only trouble was that he could not show his sympathy more openly; but Cavour as usual restrained him. The count could bear, for the sake of the cause he had at heart, to be misunderstood by the public, and blamed for checking the king's generous impulses; but he wished to set himself right with Garibaldi, for whom he had a great admiration, and many kind messages he sent him through Admiral Persano.

'Assure General Garibaldi,' he writes, 'that not less than he do I desire to complete the great enterprise; in order to succeed it is indispensable that we work in concert, at the same time adopting different means.'

Again:—

Turin, July 13.

Signor Ammiraglio,—This moment I received your letter, for which I thank you. Declare formally in my name to General Garibaldi that it is a solemn falsehood that there exist other secret treaties; and that the rumours of the cession of Genoa or Sardinia are set on foot by the arts of our common enemies.

CAVOUR.

Turin, July 28.

Most esteemed Admiral,—I received your letters on the 23rd and 24th. I am rejoiced by the victory of Milazo, which honours the Italian arms, and must help to persuade Europe that the Italians are now determined to sacrifice life itself to recover liberty and country. I pray you to give my sincere and warm congratulations to General Garibaldi, etc.

CAVOUR.

CHAPTER XX.

KING OF ITALY.

MEANTIME the Papal Government had been collecting mercenaries from all parts of the world, and the Pope invited General Lamoricière to take the command of his heterogeneous army. This general had been one of the French commanders at the siege of Rome in 1848, when he had uttered the never-to-be-forgiven, never-to-be-forgotten words: *Les Italiens ne se battent pas.* That was before he had measured swords with the Italians in Rome, after which he had reason to change his opinion, though it is not recorded that he retracted it. No injury that his arms had inflicted on the suffering city was remembered half so bitterly as this insult. He now set out on his second crusade, declaring that he was ready to unsheathe his sword against this modern *Islamism*—an expression which excited great indignation in Piedmont. 'This brave General Lamoricière,' said Victor Emmanuel, with a scornful laugh, 'baptises us for Turks, and transforms the Sabaud cross into a crescent. He may learn yet that we are the true crusaders.'

Just at this time the Count of Syracuse, finding all remonstrances with his nephew hopeless, took refuge with the King of Sardinia. The adhesion of this middle-aged Bourbon, so closely allied to the throne of Naples, was a significant fact, and Victor Emmanuel gave him a cordial welcome.

Francis II., after some months' fighting, and vain appeals for help to other powers, finding it impossible to stem the tide of war, began slowly to take in the idea that the spirit of nationality was something too powerful for him to combat, and that, to save his throne from wreck, the only chance was an appeal to Victor Emmanuel. It was too late. The idea of Italian unity had progressed with giant strides since the Sardic envoy had been dismissed from the court of Naples with a rejection of the proffered alliance. Even if Victor Emmanuel had willed to restore the Bourbon power, he could not have done it now with the victorious Sicilians and volunteers ready to cross the Strait of Messina. The Neapolitan plenipotentiaries were received with due courtesy, and a dinner given in their honour; but they were made to understand that the day of compromise was passed; Italian unity must be accomplished.

Nevertheless, Victor Emmanuel wrote privately to Garibaldi, asking him to content himself with Sicily for the present, and not cross to the mainland. But Garibaldi had independent ideas of serving his king and country. He entered Calabria as soon as circumstances permitted, swept across the country like an avalanche, driving the Bourbon troops before him everywhere, and took possession of the capital, from whence the king had fled.

Some sort of governing head was necessary for the order of the kingdom thus set at liberty, and Garibaldi was elected Dictator. Very soon serious differences arose between the Government of Turin and the dictator. Garibaldi thought it better for the national interests to hold Naples unannexed till Rome was also liberated, and the volunteers might then present all Italy, united, to Victor Emmanuel. He asked the king's consent to a two years' dictatorship, and demanded at the same time the dismissal of Cavour from office.

The minister became seriously alarmed; not for himself—his position was too well-assured for any fear of that:—but the growing power and popularity of the general threatened to take the national cause out of the legitimate hands of the monarchy, and put it into those of the republican party, with whom Garibaldi had old and strong ties. Cavour resolved to appeal to Parliament, and let the representatives of the nation decide the question. They voted for immediate annexation. The question was, would the erratic chief who had conquered the kingdom of Naples with a band of volunteers, submit to the decision of Parliament? It is true that his war-cry had been *Vittorio Emanuele e l' Italia!* but there were many Mazzinians at Naples, and Cavour feared that he might be strongly influenced by them. He never for a moment accused him of personal ambition, for he knew how to read the human heart much better than the hero of Milazo.

'I count largely,' writes Cavour, 'on Garibaldi's loyal spirit, generous instincts, and the great affection he nourishes for the king.'

That he nourished an antipathy for him, Camillo Cavour, he also knew well, and deeply regretted it; but Garibaldi's attacks could not move his generous rival to the smallest resentment.

The critical moment had now arrived when the royal army must take the lead in the national struggle, or remain in a secondary position to the volunteers. The inhabitants of Umbria and the Marches did not cease to implore King Victor to give them that liberty which he had bestowed on the other provinces subject to the Pope's rule; and now the presence of the foreign army under General Lamoricière excited them to the last degree,—while Garibaldi was preparing to march to their aid. Nothing but prompt action on the part of the government could save Italy from anarchy. The emperor was acquainted with the intention of the court of Turin, and replied with the simple words—*Faites vite*.[1] In truth they did not waste time, the Sardinian army being already on its way to the Marches when the powers were informed of the fact. The memorandum to the ambassadors contained these significant words, which were a sufficient apology for the hasty and unexpected irruption into the Pontifical States:—

'If we do not arrive on the Volturno before Garibaldi arrives at Cattolica, the monarchy is lost,—Italy remains a prey to revolution.' It was the solemn duty of the king to lead the national movement. The people were resolved to be free, and if Victor Emmanuel would not be their head, they would find one more dangerous to the peace of Europe; therefore it behoved him and his government to take the guidance of the revolution into their own hands, so that they might conduct it the more speedily to a peaceful termination, and establish an order of things that would prevent a recurrence of these troubles.

Order of the Day.

Soldiers!—You enter the Marches and Umbria to restore civil order in the desolated cities, and to give liberty to the people to express their own wishes. You will not have to combat powerful armies, but to liberate unhappy Italian provinces from companies of foreign adventurers. You do not go to avenge the insults offered to me and to Italy, but to prevent popular hatreds from breaking out into vengeance on bad rulers. You will teach them the pardon of offences, and show an example of Christian tolerance

---

[1] Though the *faites vite* has been contradicted and denied, there is good reason to believe it true.

to those who stupidly compared to *Islamism* the love of the Italian country.

In peace with all the great powers, and far from giving any provocation, I wish to remove from Central Italy a continual cause of turbulence and discord. I will respect the seat of the Head of the Church, to whom I am always ready to give, in accord with the allied and friendly powers, all those guarantees of independence and security, which his blind councillors have in vain promised him from the fanaticism of a malignant faction, conspiring against my authority and the liberties of the nation.

Soldiers!—They accuse me of ambition. Yes, I have one ambition; it is to restore the principles of moral order in Italy, to preserve Europe from the continual perils of revolution and war.

VICTOR EMMANUEL.
Cavour.
Farini.

September 11, 1860.

General Cialdini met the papal troops at Castelfidardo, where he won a complete victory. Ancona soon fell into his hands, and some thousands of prisoners surrendered themselves, with the general. The foreign mercenaries being utterly overcome, the citizens received the conquering army with joy and gratitude.

All this time the Pope never lost heart; he was full of faith in the ultimate triumph of his arms, and said to General Lamoricière before he went to battle that he was absolutely certain that God would 'convert his enemies or destroy them.' The necessity of destroying them was painful to the kind-hearted Pope, who would have much preferred their conversion. But since they were not moved by all the censures and anathemas of the Church, it was plain they were incorrigible. The robber king's proclamation to the army, in which he spoke of the *Papalini* as 'a malignant faction, conspiring against his authority and the liberties of the nation,' showed that his majesty's soul was in a very bad state; he had never before expressed himself so strongly, so bitterly, against the ecclesiastical government. But irritated and indignant as he was, he was careful to prevent his soldiers avenging the insults that had been heaped upon him and the national cause. He gave the strictest orders to the commanding officers—and, after the fall of the papal power, to his representatives in hose provinces—to be moderate and patient with the *Clericali*, and to treat the prisoners with the same consideration as the royal troops.

The governors of the newly-acquired states were men of distinguished ability and high character. The Marquis Pepoli was sent to Umbria, Signor Valerio to the Marches, and the Marquis Gualterio to the province of Perugia. The present Pope, Leo XIII., was then Bishop of Perugia, and his good sense and moderation formed a contrast to the conduct of the other bishops. He not only did not embarrass the government by useless opposition, but he assisted in maintaining order in his diocese, though he had not, nor has he now, any sympathy with liberalism.

Cavour had tried in vain to persuade the great powers that the sudden descent on the Papal States was a necessity to save society from anarchy; all except England, who gave her open approval, expressed themselves greatly shocked by the audacious proceeding; Prussia, Russia, Austria, and even France, recalled their ambassadors. The Eldest Son of the Church could not openly approve of the spoliation of the holy father, though he had said 'strike quickly' when consulted on the subject, and his representative, M. Talleyrand, took a cordial leave of the great 'spoliator,' heartily wishing him success in all his undertakings.

It was easier to disapprove of what was done than to find a remedy for the ills of the distracted Peninsula. No foreign intervention nor European congress had ever yet hit upon a means of establishing order, peace, or anything approaching contentment in the population. Now all Victor Emmanuel asked, all the Italians asked of Europe, was to *let them alone*—leave them to work out their own redemption as best they might.

The king had tried all peaceful means to reconcile ecclesiastical pretensions with the liberties and rights of his subjects and the spirit of nationality. His moderate counsels had been rejected, his propositions of compromise treated with scorn. While he had been trying to come to terms with the papal government, they had been secretly conspiring against him and flooding the country with foreign soldiery. It was time to put an end to this dangerous state of things, even in the interest of the Pope, who would have fared much worse at the hands of the threatened republic than under the gentle and tolerant rule of the Savoy prince. Cavour and the king were agreed to strike boldly, and they conquered.

'We are misunderstood by the other nations,' said the minister, 'but the time will come when they will judge us with more equity.'

'Courage!' replied the king, who assumed the part of comforter when Cavour was depressed, 'let us do our duty and go forward.'

Towards the end of September the king paid a visit to the newly-acquired provinces, and was received at Ancona amidst a perfect ovation on the part of the soldiers, the citizens, and the peasantry, who hailed him as Liberator of Italy.

Order of the Day.

Soldiers!—I am pleased with you because you have proved yourselves worthy of Italy. By your arms you have conquered the enemy, and by your conduct the calumniators of the Italian name. The vanquished ones whom we shall set free will speak of you and of Italy to foreign peoples. They will have learned that God rewards those who serve him with justice and charity; not those who oppress the peoples and trample on the rights of nations.

A strong Italian monarchy must be founded on liberty; by order and concord the people will aid us; and the national army will add fresh lustre to the glory that for eight centuries has shone on the cross of Savoy.

Soldiers, I take the command. It costs me too much not to be first in moments of danger.

VICTOR EMMANUEL.

Ancona, October 4, 1860.

To the Marines.

Soldiers of the Navy!—You have deserved well of me and of your country. Your exploits under the walls of Ancona are worthy of the heirs of the glories of Pisa, of Venice, and of Genoa.

Soldiers, the nation beholds you with pride—your king thanks you. Great is the destiny of the Italian navy.

VICTOR EMMANUEL.

Victor Emmanuel was proud of the behaviour of his soldiers, and he had every right to be. The valour of the Sardinian troops and their enthusiastic devotion to their king was already well known; but the discipline, order, gentleness, and moderation with which they deported themselves in the hour of victory towards the enemies who had come from all parts of Europe to try to crush their independence at the moment when it seemed within their grasp, was beyond all praise. The Sardinian army, now mixed with so many other national elements, we must henceforth call the *Italian* army.

The king had been particular to impress on his representatives in the provinces the duty of being strictly just and moderate, so as not to give the Clericals any reason to complain. Nevertheless they did complain: and in sermons and journals sent forth loud cries of persecution. Signor Valerio, royal commissioner in the Marches, was much disturbed by the unjust attacks upon him, and he complained to the king of the tone of the Clerical press.

'Dear Valerio,' said his royal master, 'if I am content with you, is it not enough? And are you quite sure you do not push forward too rapidly? We must be patient and moderate.'

But all the clergy were not opposed to Victor Emmanuel. When at Ancona he paid a visit to the Holy House of Loreto, and greatly edified the community by his reverential bearing. The canons invited the royal visitor to lunch, and he accepted. Subsequently he went to visit the Jesuits' college, converted into a temporary hospital after the battle of Castelfidardo. Victor Emmanuel's tenderness for the sick soldiers had done much to endear him to the army. He was a constant visitor to the hospitals, cheering the invalids by his kind encouraging words, by presents of cigars, and various little favours—the value of which chiefly consisted in the fact that they came directly from the royal hand. Many anecdotes the volunteers tell of his *bonhomie*, his gentleness, his sympathy for suffering. His genial presence brought light and animation to the pale faces of the sick and wounded soldiers.

'Your wound is slight?' asked the king of a youth whose bright smiling face attracted him. 'Not very, your majesty,' was the reply, as he lifted from under the covering a bandaged stump. He was promised promotion. Those whose families were in bad circumstances had money given them. When the king came to a poor fellow whose head was all bandaged up he asked, 'Are you wounded severely?'

'Your majesty, I have lost my eyes,' replied the patient. The king bent his head sadly. No money nor promotion could heal such a wound as this; but he made the young man feel his sympathy. Inquiring about his family, he learned that he had a mother who was very dear to him: and Victor Emmanuel took a medal off his own breast and put it into the hand of the blind soldier with a kindly pressure, telling him to send it to his mother as a proof of how well he had served his country.

After the battle of Castelfidardo the wounded prisoners of the Pope's army were housed with the royal troops, so that the king, in visiting his own soldiers, was obliged to pass by the beds of his enemies. Some of them saluted him courteously, and spoke to him in French; all looked at him with much curiosity, with the exception of a Belgian, who covered his face with the sheet to shut out the hateful sight of the sacrilegious monster. The king returned the salutations, and replied affably to any question or remark addressed to him by the prisoners.

'What handsome people!' he said on coming out of the hospital. 'What a pity that they will fight against us when we are at peace with their countries.' The officers of Lamoricière's army were almost all French, and most of the men Irish. As soon as their wounds permitted, they, with their general, were put on board the ship *Conte di Cavour*, and conveyed to Marseilles.

Meantime Garibaldi, after some hesitation, and a hard contest with his evil advisers, allowed his nobler nature to conquer, and submitted to the decision of what we may now call the National Parliament, since it embraced representatives of all the states of Italy except Naples. The king marched southwards to take possession of that kingdom, and before starting he issued a proclamation *To the People of South Italy*, which was a *résumé* of the history of his reign from the day of Novara to the present time, with an explanation of his policy and the motives which had guided him. As it is a lengthy address, and deals with facts already recorded here, it is not necessary to transcribe it. We give the concluding paragraph:—

> People of South Italy,—My troops advance among you to maintain order; I do not come to impose my will upon you, but to see that yours is respected. You will be able to manifest it freely. That Providence which protects just causes will guide the vote which you will place upon the urn. Whatever be the gravity of the events which may arise, I await tranquilly the judgment of civilised Europe and of history, because I have the consciousness of having fulfilled my duty as king and as an Italian. In Europe my

policy perhaps will not be without effect in helping to reconcile the progress of the people with the stability of the monarchy. In Italy I know that I close the era of revolutions.

VICTOR EMMANUEL.

Given in Ancona, October 9, 1860.

As a proof that some of the priests were national in their sympathies, it is recorded that on October 15, before the plébiscite, in a church in Abruzzo, there was a solemn service held for the salvation of 'our king Victor Emmanuel,' in which many ecclesiastics took part. The people of the Abruzzi were passionately desirous of annexation, and petitions with thousands of signatures were sent to Ancona, begging an immediate plébiscite. The king was pleased with this, for he said it would show the powers that he had good reason for passing the Tronto. 'Italy must be made by us, or it runs the risk of being unmade for ever,' he said to Dr. Tommasi, a Neapolitan who took an active part in the revolution. 'Garibaldi is a hero, but he does not know how to combat the difficulties of the situation. We alone can meet them.'[1]

The king journeyed southward with two Neapolitan gentlemen attached to his staff, Dr. Tommasi and Signor Devincenzi, that they might supply him with useful information about the state of the country. A deputation of distinguished Neapolitans met him as soon as he crossed the frontier, begging of him to hasten to the capital, as his presence was much needed to calm the agitation and uneasiness of the inhabitants. He made the whole tour of the country on horseback, starting at daybreak every morning after partaking of a cup of coffee and a roll, and never halting till late in the evening when he dined at some country house or inn. After dinner he occupied himself in reading and replying to the numerous letters and telegrams which

[1] Garibaldi, as soon as Victor Emmanuel arrived in Ancona, wrote to him to say his presence in Naples was desirable.

followed him—mostly from Count Cavour—and rarely retired to rest before two o'clock; but he was always ready again at dawn for the day's journey. At the close of one such day, when the king and his followers had ridden through a heavy rain for many hours, Dr. Tommasi, not being acquainted with his new sovereign's habits, remarked that his majesty must be fatigued. 'I,' said Victor with a frown, 'I am never tired.' During this journey the king talked freely to his new subjects, and showed much intelligent curiosity about the kingdom of Naples. He was astonished at the want of proper roads through the country, and he could hardly believe some things that he was told about the scarcity of schools and teachers.

'I cannot understand,' said the citizen-king, 'how even a despotic sovereign should wish to abase the civil condition of his own state. But where the light of liberty does not illuminate a government it is blind.' He talked a great deal about the political prisoners, particularly Poerio, and asked Devincenzi to tell him all about him. Ferdinand had offered him (Poerio) liberty, if he would ask pardon, and the prisoner replied, 'Not I, but the king, ought to ask pardon. He has destroyed the constitution he had sworn to defend, he has oppressed his fellow-citizens. I will never bow to what I think wrong.'

'Bravo, bravo!' cried Victor, enthusiastically, 'those are the sort of men that I like.' Then after discussing the Neapolitan character, he said, 'It seems to me that among you there is no medium; you are either very good or very bad, either a Poerio or——'

He did not finish the sentence, but it is easy to supply the ellipsis by the next question:—

'Have you ever known Ferdinand II.?'

'Yes, sire.'

'And was he the monster that so many say?'

Devincenzi replied by narrating some facts about the late king.

'Perhaps,' suggested Victor Emmanuel, 'he was under the influence of the Jesuits, and that want of spirit was the cause of some of his errors. You must know that it took all my strength to resist them, and without a character of iron I could not have succeeded. But what a struggle I had.'

The conversation one day turned upon England, where Signor Devincenzi had lived; and Victor showed himself very anxious to know how he was regarded in that country.

Sir James Hudson often assured him of the good-will of his compatriots. 'But,' said the king, 'he is attached to our cause, and his opinion may be biassed by friendship.'

When Signor Devincenzi told him that it was true that he was really much esteemed by the English people, he replied,—

'I am very glad. I have a great respect for the English nation, and I desire that my Italians may deserve the reputation the English enjoy.'

It came quite natural to Victor to call them 'my Italians;' he had long regarded them as his; for, as Signor Massari had said, 'Before the victories and the plébiscites had given him the crown of Italy, he was our king, he reigned in our hearts;' and now he felt he was in truth no longer the Sardic, but the Italian king.

One bright morning as the king, at the head of his troops, and surrounded by his generals, set out for the day's ride, he saw another body of horsemen approaching, which proved to be the Red Shirts, with their gallant chief in the midst, come to lay down the dictatorship at the feet of his constitutional sovereign. Garibaldi's picturesque figure, with the grey mantle flung over the red shirt, his auburn locks blowing in the wintry breeze, was easily distinguishable by the keen eyes of Victor Emmanuel. The two leaders rode quickly forward, and when near enough to salute, Garibaldi reined up his horse, and said in an agitated voice, 'King of Italy!'

'I thank you,' was the simple response of *il Rè galantuomo*. They clasped hands and stood looking at each other in eloquent silence, the black eyes and the blue flashing forth mutual congratulations, while the royal troops and Garibaldians, mingling together fraternally, rent the air with joyous acclamations. *Viva Vittorio, Rè d'Italia! Viva Garibaldi! Viva l'Italia!* were the cries echoed again and again over the country.

Alas for the instability of human friendship! Who that had seen Victor and Garibaldi riding

———hand in hand,
'Neath the blue sky of their regenerate land

on that happy day, could have guessed that the future held in store for them such dark ones as Aspromonte and Mentana?

On November 7 Victor Emmanuel made a triumphal entry into Naples, amidst the wildest demonstrations of popular enthusiasm. Deputations of citizens of all classes struggled with each other to have the first word from the king, to give him the first welcome, and express their gratitude and affection.

'I have hastened my coming,' said he to a friend, 'to save the country from a civil war.'

'Your majesty's name exercises a perfect fascination on General Garibaldi,' said Pisanelli.

'I know it,' replied the king. 'I never for a moment doubted Garibaldi's great soul; but I have good reason to suspect many who are about him, and who might exercise a fascination upon him even more potent than mine, because nearer.'

The king and the dictator drove through Naples in the same carriage, amid the frantic plaudits of the populace, who almost went mad with the excitement of having two such heroes to fête at the same time.

Then Garibaldi, refusing all the honours and emoluments which his grateful sovereign wished to bestow, went his way, still a poor soldier of fortune, to his lonely Isle of Caprera.

CHAPTER XXI.

BY THE GRACE OF GOD AND THE WILL OF THE NATION. A.D. 1861.

DURING the last days of December, Victor Emmanuel was on his homeward journey from the southern provinces and he arrived in Turin just two days before the expiration of the eventful year of 1860. As in the central provinces and in Naples, so in Sicily, he had travelled through the country on horseback, and made himself acquainted with that land of brigands as far as it was possible in a hasty tour. It would but weary the reader with vain repetitions to recite all the ovations that greeted him in every town, all the graceful demonstrations of loyalty and gratitude which his presence called forth. Enough to say that his journey was like the triumphal march of a hero who had saved his country from destruction and covered her with glory. Dearly as he loved popularity, his soul must have been satiated with plaudits before he found repose and quiet in his palace at Turin, with his own faithful but less demonstrative Subalpines round him.

On the first day of the new year Farini, Viceroy of Naples, resigned office because of a domestic affliction, and the Prince of Carignano was appointed in his stead. A royal proclamation to the Neapolitans said:—

> I do not know how to give you a better proof of my affection than in sending you my beloved cousin Prince Eugenio, to whom I am accustomed in my absence to confide the administration of the monarchy.

Naples, however, was not quite free from the Bourbons. Gaeta still held out, though besieged by Cialdini and Menabrea; and the fortresses of Messina and Civitella were still in possession of the adherents of the fallen dynasty. The French fleet hovered about under the pretence of protecting the coast. Negotiations on the subject were carried on briskly between Paris and Turin, and finally the fleet sailed off. Gaeta fell into the hands of the Italians; the other fortresses soon followed, and the conquest of the Two Sicilies was complete. Then France, still pretending, withdrew her ambassador from the court of Turin, while England loudly proclaimed her approbation of Victor Emmanuel's proceedings, and was warm in admiration of the good sense and moderation with which the Italians had carried out so great a revolution. This moral support, at a moment when diplomacy was looking askance at him from every other side, was a source of much gratification to Victor Emmanuel, and he felt sincerely grateful for it.

The great events of the past year, in which the kingdom of Sardinia had swelled into the kingdom of Italy, rendered another general election necessary. The new Parliament was opened on February 18 with unusual pomp. The representatives of the lately annexed provinces, mostly men of distinction, who had taken an active part in the recent events, were loudly cheered when taking the oath of allegiance. The king's speech was received with uproarious applause, particularly by the southern members.

The King's Speech.

Gentlemen Senators,—Gentlemen Deputies,—Almost entirely free and united, by the wonderful aid of Divine Providence, the willing agreement of the peoples, and by the splendid valour of the army, Italy now confides in your virtue and your wisdom. To you it belongs to give her common and stable institutions. While assigning the largest amount of administrative liberty to those peoples who have had different customs and laws, you will take care that the political unity sighed after for so many ages shall not be curtailed. The opinion of civilised people is propitious to us; the just and liberal princes who preside in the councils of Europe are propitious to us; Italy will become for Europe an efficacious instrument of universal civilisation. The Emperor of the French, while holding firm the maxim of non-intervention—to us a great gain—has thought proper to recall his ambassador. If this is a matter of regret, it cannot alter our gratitude to him, nor our faith in his attachment to the Italian cause. France and Italy, who have a common origin, traditions, and customs, were united on the fields of Magenta and Solferino by a bond which is indissoluble.

The government and people of England—that ancient land of freedom—strongly affirm our right to be the arbiters of our own destinies; and they have been lavish of kind offices, the grateful memory of which shall never perish.

To the loyal and illustrious prince who has lately ascended the throne of Prussia, I sent an envoy, as a mark of honour to him and sympathy for the noble German nation, which I hope will be more and more persuaded that Italy, constituted in its natural unity, does not offend either the rights or the interests of other nations.

Gentlemen Senators —Gentlemen Deputies,—I feel certain that you will hasten to present to my government the means of completing the armaments by land and sea, so that the kingdom of Italy, placed in a condition not to fear attack, shall repose more easily in the consciousness of her strength on a reasonable prudence. On other occasions my words sounded bold; but there is a time to dare and a time to wait. Devoted to Italy, I have never hesitated to place in jeopardy my life and my crown when her interests required it; but no one has a right to risk the life and the destinies of a nation.

After many signal victories the Italian army, always increasing in fame, obtained a new title to glory, by taking one of the most formidable fortresses in the country. The thought consoles me that *there* was for ever closed the lamentable series of our civil conflicts. The navy has shown in the waters of Ancona and Gaeta that there still survive in Italy the mariners of Pisa, of Genoa, and of Venice.

A band of gallant youths, led by a captain whose name resounds through the most distant lands, have proved that neither servitude nor prolonged misfortunes, have been able to unnerve the Italian people.

These facts have inspired the nation with great confidence in its destinies. I am glad to make known to the first Parliament of Italy the joy which, as a soldier and a king, I feel in my heart.

The first thing the Parliament had to do was to proclaim the kingdom of Italy. In a cabinet council the king declared his desire to be called Victor Emmanuel II., not wishing to put the slight upon his worthy predecessor and godfather, of seeming to ignore his existence in assuming the title of First. The council made no objection. Indeed there was no fear of a confusion of names in the history of the Savoy dynasty; Victor Emmanuel II. of Sardinia would be always known as first King of Italy. Secondly, the king said, that as he had done everything that he had accomplished by and with the Italians, and, as he firmly believed, with the approval and help of Providence, he wished to be proclaimed in these terms:—

VITTORIO EMANUELE II., PER GRAZIA DI DIO E PER VOLONTÀ DELLA NAZIONE, RÈ D'ITALIA.

Parliament approving, the proclamation was made in accordance with the king's wishes.

After the great changes which had taken place in the state, Cavour thought well to send in his resignation. There was probably, along with other motives for the step, some difference between the king and the minister at this juncture. Victor's fiery temper and Cavour's love of power—what Brofferio called his *prepotente* character—led to an occasional collision, which, however, was never allowed to bear serious consequences. While the crisis lasted the king consulted the most eminent of his new subjects, Farini, Ricasoli, Poerio, and all were of one opinion that Cavour was the right man in the right place. Brofferio says that he also was consulted, and advised the recall of his great adversary. One day Poerio presented himself to the king, who exclaimed laughing, 'I know what you are going to say; you are come to again advise me to send for Cavour.' Cavour was recalled, of course, and soon formed the ministry of the kingdom of Italy, in which he introduced some natives of the newly annexed provinces.

In all this joy, excitement, and triumph in the attainment of Italian unity, the painful fact remained that it was not quite accomplished. In the reunion of 'the Italian family' the most illustrious member was still left out in the cold, though earnestly begging for admittance. Everyone felt that without Rome as capital the work of redemption, of unity, was incomplete. The question was taken up and hotly discussed by the new Parliament while in the first flush of national pride. Cavour made one of his most masterly and telling speeches on the subject, which produced a powerful effect, and enchanted the king. He said, 'I consider myself bound to proclaim in the most solemn manner before the nation the necessity of having Rome for the capital of Italy, for without Rome for the capital Italy cannot be constituted.' The Parliament and the nation felt with him, but they were not willing, like him, to temporise and wait. The very name of Rome had a magic sound in it which fired the souls of the Italians into a frenzied enthusiasm.

> One must be Italian [says the Spaniard Castelar, in his *Old and New Italy*], one must feel southern blood in one's veins, must have been educated in this glorious history, under the painted wings of classic poetry, to

comprehend all the influences that Rome exercises over the Italian mind. Those who wished to make Italy a monarchy, and afterwards denied her the capital which is hers by nature, did but construct a headless body.

Cavour was resolved to have Rome for the capital, and that at no distant day. He was even then opening negotiations with the Emperor Napoleon on the subject, for without the concurrence of France he would not take any action in the matter, and there is little doubt that the question would have been brought to a speedy solution if he had been spared another year to put the finishing stroke to his great work. But Garibaldi, and the extreme party whom he represented, did not want to work in accord with France; the Roman difficulty, they thought, should be solved not by diplomacy, but by the sword. The cession of Nice and Savoy was still fresh in the memory of the general, and in a debate on the condition of the army in Naples, he bitterly attacked the premier, winding up by saying, 'Never will I extend my hand to those who have made me a foreigner in Italy.'

Count Cavour was deeply wounded. He rose to reply with a visible emotion, which by a great effort he conquered, defending himself with splendid eloquence and powerful reasoning, but with calmness and dignity, an absence of all personal resentment, that won the sympathy of all. It was one of his finest speeches; alas! that it should have been one of his last.

> I know [said he] that between me and the honourable General Garibaldi there exists a fact which divides us two like an abyss. I believed that I fulfilled a painful duty—the most painful that I ever accomplished in my life—in counselling the king, and proposing to Parliament, to approve the cession of Nice and Savoy to France. By the grief that I then experienced I can understand that which the honourable General Garibaldi must have felt, and if he cannot forgive me this act I will not bear him any grudge for it.

Remembering how soon that eloquent voice was to be hushed in the silence of the tomb, it is pleasant to be able to record that the general, at the earnest request of the king, sought a friendly explanation with Cavour, and offered that stainless palm of his,

> Horny with grasp of the familiar hilt,

to the great statesman whom he so imperfectly understood and so often wronged.

Meantime the new kingdom was threatened with an interdict, the last and most extreme punishment with which an offending prince and people can be visited by the Pontiff. The Pope had exhausted himself in protests, censures, and anathemas; his ammunition was almost spent; there only remained this great gun to let off; it might miss fire and fall harmless like the others, still the fear of it might have some effect. But no, Victor Emmanuel was only becoming more hardened by familiarity with cursings. One of his ministers warned him that an interdict could not take effect in his state unless the document were put into the hands of the sovereign. 'If that is the case,' replied the king, 'you may be content. Whenever I see a priest who looks as if he wanted to speak to me, I will put my hands in my pockets, and never take them out till he is gone.'

The Piedmontese were wont to celebrate as a great festival the anniversary of the *Statuto* granted by Carlo Alberto in 1848, and now this fête, coming round just after the proclamation of the kingdom of Italy, was made the occasion of universal rejoicing. The king desired new banners to be presented to the army, and General Fanti read in his name this address.

> Officers, Sub-officers, and Soldiers!—Thirteen years have passed away since my august father, crossing the Ticino to carry on the war of national independence, consigned to you the tricolour banner with the cross of Savoy, with the words *The destinies of Italy are maturing*. Under that banner you won brilliant victories, arresting for a time our adverse fortune. But

force of virtue and constancy of purpose made it wave freshly, gloriously, in distant regions by the side of the insignia of the most powerful armies in Europe.

Afterwards re-treading the fields of Lombardy, recalling the memory of Goito and Pastrengo, you gathered splendid laurels in company with the illustrious French eagle. A new and glorious light shone then on the entire peninsula. The people of Italy, uniting themselves round the flag of national independence, accomplished deeds that their remote descendants will remember with gratitude and love. To-day the destinies of Italy are mature.

Soldiers, to you I consign the new banners in the name of redeemed Italy. On their borders are emblazoned the names of the battles fought. To your courage I confide these emblems of loyalty and honour, on which the shield of my family, glorious for eight centuries of valour, is engrafted with the symbol of national redemption. VICTOR EMMANUEL.

Turin, June 2, 1861.

CHAPTER XXII.

DEATH OF CAMILLO BENSO CAVOUR. A.D. 1861.

COUNT CAVOUR laboured continually to convince the Catholic states that the temporal power of the papacy was incompatible with national unity and liberty, that it was an anachronism which must give way before modern progress, and that the holy father would enjoy a more exalted position, more real authority, if he were rid of the embarrassment of it. The Italian Government, he said, was slandered by those who represented that they wanted to overturn Catholicism; on the contrary, they wished to make it more respected, more respectable, than it had been for long ages. In taking possession of Rome they would contract a lasting peace between the Church and civilisation.

All history proved, he said in one of his speeches, that nothing but a miserable and corrupt despotism could result from the union of the spiritual and civil authority in the same hands. That the State and the Church should be separated was desirable as much in the interest of the one as the other. The authority of the Pope, the independence of the Church, would be much better assured by the free consent of twenty-six million of Italians than by the presence of a body of mercenaries gathered round the Vatican, or even by a valorous and friendly, but still a foreign army.

> It remains [said he] to convince the Pontiff that the Church can be independent, while losing the temporal power. But we will present ourselves to him, and say, 'Holy Father, the temporal power is no longer for you a guarantee of independence. Renounce it, and we will give you that liberty which you have in vain for three centuries demanded from all the great Catholic powers—that liberty which you have sought to drag from them in small portions by means of concordats, for which, O Holy Father, you were constrained in return to concede privileges—and worse than privileges—to concede the use of spiritual arms to temporal powers, in order that they might grant you a little liberty. Well, that which you have never been able to obtain from those powers who boast themselves to be your allies and your devoted sons, we come to offer you in all its fulness; we are ready to proclaim in Italy this great principle, Free Church in Free State.'

These were Cavour's sincere convictions. He was a Catholic as Victor Emmanuel was; that is, he believed in the Church itself, apart from the priesthood. In the heat of the combat with Rome, remembering the fate of Santa Rosa, he had made a compact with a liberal priest that in case of sudden illness he should come to him, no matter where he was, to administer the sacraments.

In these last two months of his life, Cavour worked more assiduously, more devotedly than ever, pressing on the emperor and on the papal government a solution of the Roman question as though he felt his time was short and the great labour of his life would be still unfinished if Rome were left outside the kingdom of Italy. The king shared his anxiety, and they spent hours together every day, conducting diplomatic correspondence on the one all-absorbing theme. They felt that there could be no union, concord, or peace till that question was finally settled. Rome was the head-centre of the machinations of the retrograde party (*Codini*), and Francis de Bourbon had taken up his abode there, and was pursuing his favourite amusement of conspiracy. It transpired at this time that in some of the Neapolitan provinces brigandage, which was on the increase, and threatened to overturn all law and order, was, in a measure, due to his influence. King Victor then wrote angrily to Paris, 'Tell the Emperor to put an end to this torment of Francis II. at Rome!'

Giovane Italia was growing daily more rampant, and making its cry of *Rome the capital of Italy!* more loudly heard: while the Romans, intensely excited by the great events around them, threatened to rise continually. Amongst their most ardent sympathisers was Garibaldi, who kept his king and government in constant trepidation because of his utter contempt for diplomacy. Cavour so ably urged upon the emperor the pressing necessity of a speedy arrangement, that Napoleon had all but given the order for the evacuation of the Roman territory by the French troops, on condition that the Italians should undertake to protect the papal frontier in their stead. Nor was the great statesman's reasoning quite without effect on Pius IX. and his advisers, who at this time seemed disposed to consider the subject more calmly than they had hitherto done. In short, there were then great hopes of a speedy and satisfactory conclusion to the question which, if prolonged, threatened the peace of Italy and of Europe.

'When once I see the king enthroned in the Capitol,'

said the count, 'I will retire to Leri to plant cabbages, tend my vines, and repose myself for the rest of my life.'

But meantime he allowed himself no repose; and it was noted by his friends that during the debates of those last days of May, Cavour had become irritable and excitable, and did not display his usual tolerance of contradiction. On the 29th he returned from the Chamber after speaking, very much agitated, and in the night was taken ill with violent pains, and fits of fever.

The physicians held out little hope from the first, the disease being of a virulent nature, and the nation awaited the catastrophe in grief-stricken silence. The evening before the death, the king, restless and unhappy, went himself to the Palazzo Cavour, and ascending by a private stair (as he often did), entered the sick chamber unannounced. The patient was lying in a drowsy state with his eyes closed, and those in attendance maintained a respectful silence while the king stood for some minutes looking down at him with an emotion too deep for words. At last Farini leaned over him and whispered, 'The king is here.' Cavour opened his eyes; the light of his glorious intellect was almost spent, but he recognised the king and put out his feeble hand. 'Ah, *Maestà*!' he said, and murmured some faint words of farewell. Victor Emmanuel, with tears in his eyes, bent down and kissed him, and departed with a heavy heart.

Next morning, June 6, he received the news of the death: and though he expected it, it was still a shock to learn that the heart and brain that beat and thought only for Italy and for him, were cold and senseless. 'Better for Italy if it were I who had died!' sobbed the poor king in the privacy of his own apartments, where he gave way unrestrainedly to his grief for his own and his country's loss. But in public he held the calm and dignified language which became his position. While gratefully acknowledging all Cavour had been to him, and mourning for him with undisguised sorrow, he let the world know that he could stand alone, and that he meant not to deviate one iota from the bold policy on which he had entered.

The grief of all Italy was equal to that of the king. Every patriotic Italian felt that he had lost a personal friend in the great statesman, and feared for the consequences of his sudden demise at such a critical moment. Massimo Azeglio wrote from his retirement on Lago Maggiore to Farini :—

> Thanks, dear friend, for your letter, though it made me weep afresh like a child.. Poor Cavour! It is only now I know how much I loved him. The last two days have seemed like a frightful dream to me. I am no longer good for anything, but I have prayed to heaven for our country, and a gleam of comfort has come to me. If God *will* He *can* save Italy even without Cavour.

But it was the opinion of many that without Cavour nothing short of a miraculous interposition of Providence could save Italy.

The king, who felt he never could bestow enough honour on the memory of his illustrious minister, wanted to bury him with the royal family in Superga, but was prevented by the count's will, which provided that he should be laid in the vault of the Cavour family.

Count Cavour's reputation had spread to foreign lands, and all the friendly nations sent special envoys to Italy with condolences and testimonies of sympathy for the misfortune which had befallen the country. The Emperor Napoleon wrote an affectionate letter to Victor Emmanuel, and sent an ambassador, which was his first recognition of the kingdom of Italy. There was a grace in choosing the time, when the king was in trouble 'for the loss of the man who had most powerfully contributed to the regeneration of his country.'

Camillo Cavour had cherished the dream that, Rome won and his king crowned in the Campidoglio, he would retire to repose himself under his olives at Leri and give up political life. But such a peaceful old age was not for him. He was cut down with his armour on, in the heat of the combat, almost in the moment of victory, and like a true soldier breathed his last sigh with the battle cry of his party on his lips. '*Frate*,' he said, pressing the hand of his confessor, a few minutes before he expired, '*Frate, libera Chiesa in libero Stato!*'

CHAPTER XXIII.

ITALY WITHOUT CAVOUR. A.D. 1862–3.

THE new ministry was formed by Baron Ricasoli. Victor Emmanuel turned to his state duties with a feeling of loneliness and a sense of increased responsibility. Henceforth he gave more personal attention to foreign affairs, dictated correspondence, and wrote much. From a number of notes written in his own hand, for the use of an envoy at Paris, we quote one or two.

> I desire that the person that the emperor sends here to represent him, be one who knows how to reconcile in an amicable manner the interests of two countries so closely allied.
>
> I desire that the emperor should be reassured as to the state of the army, which every day is increasing in strength on the basis of the ancient Piedmontese army; and that he should not believe the erroneous reports which have been communicated to him. My wish is to *Italianise* Piedmont, and *Piedmontise* the army.
>
> I have in no respect changed my way of thinking on the Roman question. It is a matter of time. I am not ambitious to go there now, nor for some time. I am aware that at present France cannot do otherwise than she is doing; and I am firm in my idea that the question of Venice should precede that of Rome.

Victor Emmanuel to Count Ponza di San Martino.

Dear Count,—I thank you for the various letters you have written me, and still more for your work. The affairs of the government of the Neapolitan provinces go well, and I am sure, with your activity and capacity, they will continue to improve.

The death of Count Cavour is a grievous fact, and I feel it deeply; but that mournful event shall not arrest for one moment the onward march of our political life. I see the future before me clear as a mirror, and nothing can daunt me. I wish strength and courage to the present ministry, for grave trials are still in store for us; but if God gives me life we shall pass through them fearless and uninjured. The recognition of France will be an accomplished fact within this month. It is not well to push the Roman question; I delay it as much as possible, feeling sure that that of Venice ought to precede it, and I am firm on this point.

Dear Count, remember me sometimes, and remain always firm in the faith, as I am: the future is ours. I press your hand.   Your affectionate,
VICTOR EMMANUEL.

Turin, June 15, 1861.

In the month of July, Russia and Prussia followed the example of England and France, and acknowledged Italian unity. At the same time the young King of Portugal sent an ambassador extraordinary to ask the hand of Victor Emmanuel's youngest daughter, Maria Pia, and to present his portrait to the king. The offer was received favourably; in fact, Victor Emmanuel, who knew Don Louis personally and liked the Braganza family, desired the alliance very much. In the course of three months the marriage was officially announced, and there were great rejoicings on the occasion, and congratulatory addresses innumerable. The senators and deputies who came in the name of the legislative bodies to present an address, Victor Emmanuel invited to enter his daughter's reception-room, and speak their farewell compliments personally,—that she might carry away a livelier impression of the affections she left behind her. The young princess was moved to tears, and in thanking the deputation said she would never forget the land of her fathers. The king accompanied her to Genoa, where he consigned her to the charge of the Portuguese ambassadors. The last hour before parting the father and daughter spent alone with each other, and when they reappeared the eyes of both were red with weeping. Maria Pia was Victor Emmanuel's youngest child, and god-daughter of Pio Nono.

The most striking want—at least, the one that travellers suffered most from—in the Pontifical States, was the absence of railway communication, all the Popes before Pio Nono's time having had a strong prejudice against steam-engines; while even he gave only a tardy and reluctant sanction to the dangerous innovation. Long after other civilised states enjoyed the advantages of locomotives, the Pope's subjects still jogged over mountain and moor in carriages,—the tedium of the journey being frequently enlivened by encounters with brigands; and it was the custom for a gentleman when starting on a trip of thirty or forty miles, to make his will and confession, like a soldier preparing for battle.

Under the new *régime* this want of railway communication was being gradually supplied; and in the November of 1861, the line between Bologna and Ancona being complete, Victor Emmanuel went to open it with an imposing ceremony. The king was greeted with great warmth all along the line. When the train ran parallel to the road great crowds were assembled who waved their hats and cheered vociferously, crying *Viva Vittorio Emanuele in Campidoglio!* The king said to his ministers—'Yet there are people in Europe who think when I speak of the necessity of settling the Roman question, that it is my caprice or ambition. If they heard those cries they would be persuaded of the just desires of the people, and that it is a necessity for the tranquillity of Italy and the peace of Europe.'

At the end of this year the Crown Prince of Sweden, now the reigning sovereign, visited the King of Italy, and they became fast friends. Baron Ricasoli only held office about nine months; not feeling equal to the difficulties he had to encounter, he resigned in March 1862, and Signor Rattazzi was empowered to form a new ministry. Naples was still tormented by brigands, and consequently in a disturbed state. The ministers thought the king's presence there would have a good effect: and in fact it had a very powerful one on the excitable Neapolitans, who all united in the warmest demonstrations of affection for him. While there, his son-in-law, the Prince Napoleon, came in state to visit him in the emperor's name, and there was a great nautical fête in the Bay of Naples on the occasion.

TELEGRAM.

The King of Italy to the Emperor of the French.

I have just now visited the fleet which you have sent to meet me in this port. This act on your part of kindness for me personally, and sympathy for the Italian cause, has touched me deeply, and I thank you for it. It is a long time, sire, since I have felt such happy emotion as this day. The order that reigns in these southern provinces, and the warm testimonies of affection I receive on all sides, reply triumphantly to the calumnies of our enemies; and will convince Europe, I hope, that the idea of Italian unity rests upon a solid basis, and is profoundly engraven on the hearts of all Italians.

Accept the assurance of my sincere and unalterable friendship.

Naples, May 3.

All things were going smoothly in foreign affairs, but the Rattazzi ministry were getting into difficulties at home. The volunteer troops had become a source of serious embarrassment to the government; their position having in fact been the immediate cause of the quarrel between Garibaldi and Cavour. Cavour knew Garibaldi was a great power, and might become a dangerous one; so he met the general's explanations and demands in a conciliatory spirit, promising to do what he could for the volunteers,—Garibaldi in his turn promising not to thwart or contradict the ministerial policy. The count's sudden death had left things still in an unsettled state, and the difficulties went on increasing. It was found disagreeable and dangerous to have two standing armies under separate heads and a separate discipline, and it was proposed to amalgamate the Garibaldians with the royal troops. Endless disagreements arose out of this question, and the king, who was excessively worried about it, begged his councillors to arrange matters delicately, so as not to wound the susceptibilities of the gallant volunteers, nor offend their illustrious chief.

As soon as this question was in a manner accommodated, a more serious one arose. The central provinces lost all patience in waiting so long for a peaceful solution of the Roman question. The leaders of the Young Italy party became more warlike in their language, and excited the peasantry to riotous proceedings, which the government had to put down forcibly, and this disagreeable fact helped to make the Rattazzi ministry unpopular.

Garibaldi's name had been used as an incentive to those disturbances, and now the hot-headed general embarked for Sicily, to take the command of a troop who were bound for the Eternal City, resolved to cut with the sword the gordian knot of the Roman question. The government used energetic measures to maintain its dignity, and not allow an irregular warfare to be carried on without its sanction. The times were difficult, no doubt, and the ministry had a hard road to tread, but Cavour had gone through more critical times and had known how to make use of Garibaldi's enthusiasm, to hold the seething revolution in check, without appearing to do so, and to avert civil discords when they seemed inevitable. 'If Cavour had lived, we should have been in Rome within six months,' said the king a short time after the death. It is not improbable that he would have brought the Roman question to a conclusion before the year was out, and so 'taken the wind out of the sails' of the republicans, prevented all the troubles that the unsettled state of affairs occasioned, and thus have spared Victor Emmanuel the inexpressible pain of opposing his soldiers to the volunteers. Acknowledging the impossibility of guessing what contingencies might have arisen, as far as one can judge by probabilities, it is safe to say that if the great minister had survived another year or so the history of Victor Emmanuel's reign would not have been blotted by the name of Aspromonte.

Royal Proclamation.

Italians,—In the moment in which Europe has rendered homage to the sense of the nation, and recognised its rights, it grieves my heart to see inexperienced and deluded youths forget their duty, their gratitude to our best allies, making the name of Rome a signal of war—that name to which are turned all our united efforts and thoughts.

Faithful to the *Statuto* to which I have sworn, I have held high the banner of Italy, made sacred by the blood and glorious by the valour of my people. No one follows this banner who violates the laws, and who injures the liberties and safety of the country, making himself judge of her destinies.

Italians! be on your guard against a blamable impatience and imprudent agitations. When the hour comes for the accomplishment of the great work, the voice of your king will make itself heard among you. Every appeal that is not his, is an appeal to rebellion, to civil war. The responsibility of it, and the rigour of the laws, will fall upon those who do not hearken to my words. King by the choice of the nation, I know my duties. I must preserve the integrity and

the dignity of the crown and of Parliament, if I am to have the right to ask of all Europe justice for Italy.
VICTOR EMMANUEL.
Turin, August 3, 1862.

It was in vain. The Garibaldians were already in the field, and having crossed from Sicily, were marching through Calabria with ever-increasing forces and the cry of 'Rome or death' on their lips. Victor Emmanuel had now no choice left him but to put down rebellion by force of arms. General Cialdini's painful duty it was to lead the royal troops on this occasion. He encountered the Garibaldians at Aspromonte, in Calabria, and a fight ensued in which the volunteers were of course defeated, and their officers arrested. Garibaldi, with a ball in his foot, from the effects of which he has never recovered, was carried a state prisoner to Piedmont, where the best surgeons in the kingdom were sent to his aid; but all their efforts to relieve him only inflicted more intense agony on the sufferer, and it was a year before the lead was extracted from the wound.

This unhappy episode was a bitter grief to Victor Emmanuel. It was his pride that he was the free choice of the Italian people, that he had never drawn his sword but against the enemies of his country, and though the Garibaldians were all in the wrong, still they were his subjects, and the thought that Italian blood should have been shed by his soldiers afflicted him deeply. Above all he felt the misfortune of the gallant chief, who had done so much for the Italian cause, and for whom he had such a warm regard. But there was no help for it. The national existence was at stake if he allowed his authority to be defied by this ill-advised volunteer movement.[1]

Aspromonte gave a final blow to the Rattazzi ministry. Never very popular, it was utterly shaken by the reaction in favour of Garibaldi. Now that the danger was passed, and the untamable old lion *hors de*

---

[1] It is only just to remember in Garibaldi's excuse that he was misled by the vacillating policy of the Rattazzi ministry, which, it is now clear, played fast and loose with him.

combat, his rash inconsiderateness, his violation of the laws, were overlooked, and only his past glorious services remembered. There were fierce debates on the subject, and the ministry found it expedient to send in their resignation, suggesting a dissolution of Parliament. The king did not approve of the dissolution, and preferred to accept the resignation of the Rattazzi cabinet. After a good deal of worry and consultation, the king decided to call Luigi Carlo Farini to office. The name of this enlightened and liberal statesman, who had ruled the Emilian provinces as dictator so ably during the interregnum, was a guarantee for a good administration. Unhappily his health obliged him to retire very soon from public life, and he was succeeded by Minghetti. On the whole this first year without Cavour had been a very trying one to Victor Emmanuel.

In the beginning of 1863 the Minghetti ministry turned their attention to the financial affairs of the state. Several bills relative to taxation were laid before the Parliament, and permission asked to contract a loan. When authority had been granted by both Houses, the king thus expressed his gratification.

Victor Emmanuel to Signor Minghetti.

Dear Minghetti,—I thank you again for your work with regard to the loan, in my own name and that of the nation. May the accomplishment of this act be the forerunner of great events, and conduct us to the completion of Italian glory. You know how this glory has been the dream of my whole life—how it comprises all my aspirations. Firm in the faith, with a fearless and tranquil heart, I await it—and we shall attain it.

As soon as I return to Turin I shall send for you. Meantime I press your hand with all my heart.

Your most affectionate
VICTOR EMMANUEL.

The Parliament met on May 23. The speech from the throne did not contain any remarkable statement. We transcribe the opening paragraphs :—

Gentlemen Senators,—Gentlemen Deputies,—In opening this new session as King of Italy, I am glad to thank you for so much work done during the past two years. You confirmed the right of the nation to its complete unity. This right I shall maintain inviolable. The parliamentary labours were hardly begun when Providence snatched from us the illustrious man who was my able coadjutor in the arduous enterprise of our regeneration. This grief was mine, and equal to mine was the grief of all Italy for our loss.

The marriage of my daughter with the young King of Portugal, while strengthening a beneficial alliance between two free states, has shown me, now as always, that the joys of my house are shared by the nation.

These two paragraphs were composed by Victor Emmanuel and written in his own hand. Signor Minghetti has preserved the speech as a precious relic of his *Gran Rè*.

Meantime the Roman question remained in abeyance—to the great detriment of the nation, for it kept Central and Southern Italy in a state of fermentation which the government could not long hold in check. The Bourbon intrigues at Rome, encouraging brigandage in the Two Sicilies, destroyed all security of life and property, and impeded foreigners from visiting the country. The Emperor of the French, occupying the false position of champion of Italian independence and protector of the temporal power of the Pope, would not do anything, nor let the Italian Government do anything, towards settling the momentous question.

Just at this time an incident occurred which came near exhausting Victor Emmanuel's patience and causing a rupture with France. Four ruffians having committed 'deeds of violence, blood, and rapine,' in Naples, escaped to Rome, where they found a safe asylum, and from thence went on board a French vessel at Civitavecchia, bound for Marseilles. The Prefect of Genoa,

Marquis Gualterio, being aware of this, conceived the bold idea of seizing these felons on his own responsibility. In so doing he knew he was violating a treaty, and he expected to be disowned by his own government and dismissed. There was a great outcry made about the insult to the French flag, and the emperor's government demanded the restitution of the 'passengers.' A long diplomatic controversy ensued, and had to be settled finally by a personal correspondence between the sovereigns. The criminals were surrendered to the Italian Government, the king promising to deal mercifully with them.

In this year a bill for the suppression of more religious houses was brought in by Signor Pisanelli. When the minister carried it to the king for his approval he said with a sigh—'This law will entangle the skein still more, and will bring upon me a fresh quarrel with all the monks and nuns of the kingdom. Well, I will reply to their complaints that I am sorry to give them pain, but I am, above all considerations, a constitutional sovereign.'

He was never tired of reminding himself that he was a constitutional sovereign, and must set an example of obedience to the laws, as if he felt it necessary thus to check his naturally imperious will. If for a moment he seemed to have forgotten the fact, and felt like one of his despotic ancestors—but this happened rarely—he quickly called himself up, and with a frank, dignified humility, acknowledged that he was wrong.

Once when the king was on a tour in the provinces, an eminent citizen asked grace for a servant sentenced to hard labour for defaming her mistress. The king, without thinking, immediately promised that the sentence should be remitted; but on referring the matter to the Minister of Grace and Justice he found that he refused to admit that the case was a proper one for the exercise of the royal clemency. The king was deeply mortified, but he replied without resentment,—

'Very well, *Signor Ministro*, you are doing your duty, and I cannot complain. But if you could have found a way to save "goat and cabbage," I should have been glad. As it is, I will not try to escape the pain that I have merited for having once only since I have practised this profession (he always spoke of his kingship as a profession) forgotten that I am, that I ought to be, and wish to be, a constitutional king.'

One day Pisanelli complained of the republican writers who accused the king of ambition.

'Very well,' replied Victor with a merry twinkle in his eye, 'I will punish those gentlemen.'

'How?' asked the minister.

'When we have got to Rome and I have ascended into the Campidoglio, I will take off my hat and say, "Gentlemen, you have believed me to be an ambitious man; I am not such. *Viva la Repubblica!*"'

Years after, when Victor Emmanuel was in possession of Rome, this Signor Pisanelli appeared at a court dinner without his decorations, having forgotten them at Naples. It did not escape the king's notice, who after dinner asked him if he had become republican? The minister wittily reminded him of what he had said in Turin—that when once in Rome he would proclaim a republic—and said that naturally he would follow the example of his king. 'But you ought to remember,' said Victor laughing, 'that I said that by proclaiming the republic I would punish the republicans. You will not deny me the right of grace; and this time it is a grace much more just than many you have made me sign, as the penalty would strike the few guilty and the many innocent.'

This year Victor Emmanuel travelled a good deal through the central provinces, to the great delight of his new subjects, to whom he was still a curiosity—a liberal king who mixed freely and fearlessly among the people being a thing hitherto unknown in that part of the peninsula. When in Tuscany he paid a visit to the ex-dictator, Ricasoli, at his Castle of Brolio, near Siena; and to commemorate the event, the baron ordered a large painting representing his majesty's entrance.

In November he went, accompanied by his ministers and a large following, to open the railway line between

Pescara and Foggia. The crowds that followed him blocked up all the thoroughfares and rendered the passage from the palace to the church impassable; the horses had to stop again and again, while the enthusiastic populace surrounded the royal carriage with uproarious *evvivas*. At last the king got out and walked to the church in the midst of the people, followed by his train. The foreign ambassadors who were present thought this was rather an imprudent act, considering that the country was still infested by Bourbon outlaws and brigands; but Victor Emmanuel knew no fear. For more than eight centuries the princes of Savoy had confronted every conceivable danger that man may meet, but the dagger of an assassin had never been raised against them in their own country. Emmanuel Philibert was once near being shot, but it was during the war in Flanders, and the author of the attempt was a lawless German count. Not even in times of revolution, when regicide was considered by the Italian sectaries a most heroic deed, did any of them turn their hands against the life of the Savoy princes. So the first liberal king, the emancipator and uniter of Italy, who realised all that they had been dreaming of for ages—felt he had no reason to fear assassination. And surely his son, who in his brief reign of twelve months has given so many proofs of his fitness and capacity to perpetuate his father's work, who has in no way fallen short of his duty, but in all things shown himself a worthy successor of *il Rè galantuomo*, ought to have as little reason to fear it. Yet they have tried to murder him, the assassin protesting, Brutus-like, that he had the greatest respect and veneration for *Humbert*, but that he conceived it to be his duty to kill the *king*. Alas for the fate of kings! Even were Humbert not the brave, honest, patriotic man he is, one would have thought that gratitude to his father's memory would suffice to protect him from insult and injury. And if the son of Victor Emmanuel is not safe from murderous attempts, what crowned head may repose in peace? But though this atrocious crime has revealed the painful fact that young Italy has not yet shaken off her old curse of lawless societies, it has also given occasion for the nation at large to show her loyalty and devotion to the House of Savoy by demonstrations of affection the strength and passion of which could not be believed by those who did not witness it. The most vivid descriptions would seem cold when compared to the reality of the feeling which shook society from one end of the peninsula to the other, when the news of the attempt was made known. It called forth some of the noblest instincts of human nature and the finest traits in the Italian character, and on this account we hardly think the king himself can regret the circumstance which has shown him how deeply rooted in the heart of the nation is her affection for him and his family. The republicans or internationalists, after all, are but a few thousand at most, while twenty-five million Italians loudly proclaim their devotion to the monarchy.

The seeds which for forty years Mazzini had sown broadcast over Italy, and which Garibaldi has done much to foster, are still bearing fruit, but let us hope the noxious plants may soon be uprooted from the soil. If young Italians would study Azeglio's writings, and shut their ears to the wild utterances of the hero of Caprera, it would be well for them individually, and for the state of which they form a part.

We owe an apology to our readers for this digression; but it is impossible to remain an indifferent spectator of the enthusiasm the event alluded to has called forth, impossible not to sympathize with the indignation and the joy of the nation at such a moment, and almost involuntarily our pen has run into the all-absorbing theme of the hour.

CHAPTER XXIV.

THE SEAT OF GOVERNMENT TRANSFERRED TO FLORENCE. A.D. 1864-5.

THE Roman question, daily increasing the embarrassments and dangers of the state, still dragged on; and Victor Emmanuel, who had his eye on Venice all the time, having a fixed impression that if it could be recovered he would find less difficulty in getting rid of the foreign occupation in Rome, now adopted energetic measures to bring about a settlement of this Venetian question, urging the English Government to use its influence with Austria to induce her to accept some compromise and surrender the Italian province peaceably. The Archduke Maximilian, Emperor of Mexico, favoured the idea of Italian unity, and wished the matter to be arranged amicably between his relations and the King of Italy.

Meantime the Italian Government continued to invite the French to withdraw their forces from the Roman States, and leave the Pope face to face with his own subjects without the aid of foreign bayonets. This the emperor, fearing to offend the papal party, could not make up his mind to do. But to make the road to Rome easier for the Italians, he proposed a transfer of the capital from Turin to some more southern town, Florence or Naples—he did not care which. The French minister, M. Drouyn de Lhuys, said:—

> Of course in the end you will go to Rome. But it is important that between our evacuation and your going there, such an interval of time and such a series of events should elapse as to prevent people establishing any connection between the two facts; France must not have any responsibility.

The suggestion was adopted by the Italian ministry.

PROPOSED REMOVAL OF THE CAPITAL.

When Signor Minghetti first broke to the king the subject of changing the seat of government, and making Florence or Naples a stepping-stone to Rome, he was quite overwhelmed, and pleaded, even with tears, for his native city to be spared such a cruel sacrifice as long as the Roman question remained unsettled.

> You know I am a true Turinese [he said], and no one can understand what a wrench it is to my heart to think I must one day abandon this city, where I have so many affections, where there is such a feeling of fidelity to my family, where the bones of my fathers and all my dear ones repose. However (he added), if we cannot do otherwise, I will make even this sacrifice for Italy.

This idea preyed on Victor Emmanuel's mind and made him very melancholy. A few days after, he met at a railway station a Neapolitan gentleman who was a favourite with him.

'Dear Tommasi, I am glad to see you,' he said. 'In a short time you will hear news of a great event.' 'What event, sire?' asked the doctor. The king did not answer, but continued with emotion, 'I have decided; when the interest of Italy is involved, I do not wish to have any remorse. It grieves me to the depth of my soul, but I will consent.' 'Your majesty, I do not understand.' But Victor Emmanuel, with a wave of his hand, stepped into the carriage without answering.

La Marmora was called into the cabinet, and after much discussion by letter and a visit to Paris declined to approve of the proposal of the French government—for the reason that he did not like the Italians, after the evacuation of the French, to be bound to protect the papal frontier from all aggression. The Marquis Pepoli, who was intimate with the emperor, had just returned from Paris, and the king asked him if he thought it possible to remain in Turin without renouncing the advantages of the convention with France. When he replied in the negative Victor Emmanuel burst into tears. 'Since the cession of

Savoy and Nice,' he said, 'no public event has cost me such bitter regret. If I were not persuaded that this sacrifice is necessary to the unity of Italy I would refuse.'

The king accepted the conditions, which provided that the French were to evacuate Rome in two years, and fixed on Florence as the residence of the court. The convention was then agreed to and signed. The ministers were touched by the king's sorrow; and Visconti Venosta said to a friend:—

> It is a most ungrateful office that I have to perform in bringing a great sorrow upon the city of Turin—had it not been for which, instead of being minister of the King of Italy, I should still be suffering under a foreign rule.

The minister had not exaggerated the effect of this change upon Turin. The wildest consternation, the most passionate grief, reigned in the city. The more ignorant part of the populace, who could not understand the state reasons for the sacrifice of Turin after all she had done for the Italian cause, made riotous demonstrations against the government; while the better class of citizens broke into bitter lamentations and complaints of the cruel ingratitude with which they were treated. The ministry had to resign on September 24; and the king sent for La Marmora. The general, who was travelling in Switzerland when he received the royal summons, hastened home, and though he had disapproved of the convention, he generously consented to assume the difficult and ungrateful office of premier.

The new ministry set themselves to examine the unpopular convention which had driven their predecessors out of office, but it being already signed there seemed no remedy. The king said, 'I have signed the convention; I must maintain it; *I will* maintain it. I believe it is for the good of Italy.'

The single-minded, chivalrous La Marmora stood loyally by the king in his trouble. 'The king's signature is there—that is enough,' he said, in the Chamber. After long and painful discussions the convention was approved by a large majority in both houses.

On New Year's day 1865, the city deputations who waited on the king were received by him with unusual warmth, and he hoped the inhabitants of his beloved native city would continue worthy of their old reputation for devotion to their common country. The fury against the government had calmed down during the three months since the change of ministry; but great depression and melancholy prevailed, and there were not wanting demagogues to take advantage of it, to stir up the Mazzinian element to make a demonstration against the king. On the occasion of a court ball, January 31, the populace crowded round the palace, shouting, and hissing, and even throwing stones to impede the entrance of the guests. The king in deep indignation set out immediately for Florence, accompanied by La Marmora.

All Italy cried shame on the populace of Turin, and tried to atone for the outrage by extraordinary marks of devotion. Crowds waited at every station along the line, cheering and applauding vociferously; but it was nothing to the reception the king met in Florence, which welcomed him with redoubled warmth because he had chosen that city for his capital. All the most distinguished men hastened to offer their homage, and among them Gino Capponi, for whom the king had a great admiration, and on whom he bestowed the order of the SS. Annunziata. But all this applause could not heal the wound inflicted by the Turinese. A storm of fierce emotions was raging in his heart, and he could not long keep up the farce of smiling, bowing, and looking happy when he was miserable. He hastily left Florence and retired to the Villa San Rossore, near Pisa.

The day after the seditious demonstration above mentioned, Turin awoke to a sense of shame for the disgraceful performance. It is true that it was only the mob, and for the most part boys, who had taken part in the outrage; but the respectable portion of the community were conscious of having encouraged a spirit of discontent, and expressed themselves bitterly on the subject of the removal of the capital—so that they now felt the whole city was involved in the disgrace. All the other towns raised a cry of indignation at the disloyal demonstration, and Turin felt crushed under the displeasure of the king and the nation. The nobility and the municipality, wishing to set matters right, conceived the idea of presenting an address to the king, deploring the insult and expressing their devotion to his person and throne. When this address was signed by many thousand names, they humbly solicited an audience, which the irate monarch, still sulking in his little hermitage by the sea, disdainfully refused to grant. The minister, Signor Lanza, and the Prince of Carignano, earnestly pleaded the cause of the offending city, and Victor Emmanuel's fierce but short-lived anger gave way before the evidences of repentance which it displayed.

The Marquis Rorà, Syndic of Turin, read the address, which completely melted Victor's soft heart. His full pardon was given in a few frank and generous words, which he could hardly pronounce for the emotion that choked his utterance. It was noticed that after this day Victor Emmanuel was no longer gloomy and taciturn. He recovered his usual cheerful gaiety of manners. But his heart was in Turin; he longed to be back to see the old familiar streets, palaces, and gardens, where his life had been spent, and to receive the affectionate greeting of the citizens. On February 23 he returned to the Subalpine capital, and was welcomed with transports of joy by all classes, without a dissentient voice.

To meet the expenses of the change of capital and other requirements of the state, the Minister of Finance, Sella, found it necessary to resort to fresh taxation. Previous to laying the matter before Parliament, and asking the nation for new sacrifices, he said to the king, that it would be well that an example of disinterestedness should be given by the highest person in the state.

Whereupon the king, without a word, surrendered a fifth part (three million francs) of his civil list.

Such acts as this, carefully recorded by the Liberals, are as carefully suppressed by the Clericals. Not even in conversation do they ever let slip a single kind or generous action, of all the many that Victor Emmanuel did in public and private; but they dwell with gusto on his faults, and exaggerate them. These faults the Liberals on the other hand regard as spots on the sun, not worthy of notice, and accordingly as a general rule do not notice them. The whitest swan and the blackest crow could not be more diverse than the two pictures we are called upon to contemplate under the heading, 'Victor Emmanuel.' Let us take, for example, a few sentences at random from the first publications at our hand.

Clerical:—He left behind him a bad name, an impoverished nation, and an example which the world must condemn. In public affairs he was an utterly unscrupulous man; in private he was bold, haughty, full of passion, and wholly given over to licentiousness, etc.

Liberal:—What a great monarch was Victor Emmanuel! What a fine noble life was his! How full of sublime teaching for kings and for peoples! All agree, in death as in life, to honour the name of the first King of Italy—the greatest, best, and most glorious king she may ever see—the model patriot, etc., etc.

When the story of Victor Emmanuel has grown dim through time, the future historian will be puzzled to choose between the conflicting records of the extreme parties. But we have no hesitation in saying even the most extravagant partisans of the king are more honest and truthful than his detractors; and there are always some just-minded, moderate men who do not allow their feelings to bias their judgment, and who frankly acknowledge that their hero was not perfect, though he had a hundred claims on their affection and gratitude.

Just at this time Victor Emmanuel was pleased to receive a courteous letter from the holy father asking him to send some confidential person to Rome to consult about the nomination to certain vacant bishoprics; but the king's envoy and the Pope did not come to an understanding, and the negotiations were broken off.

In this year Spain, the only European power which had not yet acknowledged the kingdom of Italy, sent an ambassador to the court of Victor Emmanuel. Queen Isabella was always the implacable foe of liberty, and had hitherto given great encouragement to the Ultramontane party, so that it was a triumph to see this last enemy succumb under the pressure of popular opinion.

Before opening the new Parliament in Florence the king paid a visit to Naples, then suffering terribly from the ravages of cholera, to give relief to the afflicted people, and comfort and encourage them by his presence, as his custom was on such occasions.

On November 18, 1865, the first Parliament was opened in Florence.

The King's Speech.

Gentlemen Senators,—Gentlemen Deputies,—When in that generous city which has guarded the destinies of Italy in her new-born fortunes, I inaugurated these parliamentary sittings, my words were ever full of encouragement and hope, constantly justified by the feats that followed. With a soul full of the same confidence to-day I see you united round me in this noble seat of illustrious memories. Here also, intent on the full vindication of our right to self-government, we shall conquer every obstacle.

On closing the last legislature, in deference to the Head of the Church, and with the desire of satisfying the religious scruples of the majority, the government welcomed a proposal for negotiations with the Pontifical See; but they were obliged to break them off when they thought the conditions would be derogatory to the rights of the crown and the nation. The fulness of time and the inevitable force of events will solve the question between the kingdom of Italy and the papacy. On us meantime it is incumbent to observe faithfully the convention of September 15, which France will in the established time carry into complete effect. The virtue of waiting is to-day rendered more easy to Italy than it was in the past, for since I last addressed Parliament its condition has been improving.

In the progress of our work we are comforted by the sympathy of all civilised peoples. By community of interests and by the tie of gratitude we are bound in a close accord with France. We are in good relations with most of the other states of Europe, and with the governments of the two Americas. A vast field was opened to commerce by the advantageous treaties concluded with England, Holland, Denmark, Switzerland; as already with France, Sweden, Belgium, Turkey, and Persia. Spain a short time ago recognised the kingdom of Italy. Bavaria and Saxony have manifested the same desire which Germany and Prussia have already put into effect. The ties between the Latin race and the noble Germanic peoples thus strengthened will enable the Italians to entwine with theirs their interests and aspirations, and help to extinguish obsolete prejudices and rancours. In this manner Italy, taking her place among the great states of Europe, will contribute to the triumph of justice and liberty.

At home our policy has already produced wonderful effects. In the course of a few years—in the administration, in the laws, in codes, in public works, in the army—results have been obtained for which in other countries they have laboured for generations or have gone through deplorable intestine struggles. That so many difficulties are overcome, augurs well for the future.

My ministers will present drafts of laws to completely systematise the legislative unification of the kingdom of Italy, to redeem from ignorance the poorer classes, to improve the condition of credit, and to push forward more energetically the public works. Other laws you will amend as experience and opportunity counsel. The great difficulty is to repair the unbalanced state of the finances without taking from the nation its strength of arms by land and sea. I am grieved beyond measure that an unavoidable necessity obliges us to ask from my people new sacrifices. But I am certain their public spirit will not fail you, gentlemen; I have had too many guarantees of it in the privations they have already sustained with such wonderful constancy. But I desire you to divide the taxes in the most equitable and least burdensome manner possible, reducing the public expenses to the narrowest limits.

The Italian people ought to divest themselves of all the remains of the past which stand in the way of the full development of their new life. You will have to deliberate upon the separation of the Church and State, and the suppression of religious corporations. Proceeding in this manner the insidious practices of enemies, or the spite of fortune, will not destroy our work. A great change is going forward among the peoples of Europe. The future is in the hands of God. If in the accomplishment of the destinies of Italy, fresh trials should arise, I feel certain that her valiant sons would press around me once more. Where the moral force of civilisation prevails, the mature judgment of the nation will not fail to profit by it.

Gentlemen Senators,—Gentlemen Deputies,—In order that the rights and the honour of Italy may remain inviolate, it is necessary to advance frankly on the road of our national policy. Certain of your concurrence, confident in the affection of the people and the valour of the army, I will not shrink from this most noble undertaking which we must transmit complete to future generations.

CHAPTER XXV.

THE FINAL EXPULSION OF THE FOREIGNER.
A.D. 1866.

EARLY in the new year Victor Emmanuel lost his third son, Odone or Otto, Duke of Monferrat, and his dear old friend Cavaliero Massimo d'Azeglio. The death of the poor deformed prince could hardly be called a misfortune for himself, as he was a constant sufferer. But his bright intelligence and gentle disposition had endeared him to his family, and his robust and soldierly brothers treated him with affectionate consideration. The compassionate tenderness the afflicted boy inspired in his father may be imagined from the following anecdote. When in Rome King Victor drove almost every afternoon on the Pincian Hill. At the entrance there stood a hunchbacked boy, for whom he always had a pile of coppers wrapped in a paper. One of the gentlemen in waiting made inquiries about the youth, and told the king that he was quite undeserving of his bounty. 'Che vuole?' was the reply. 'He reminds me of Odone, and I cannot pass him by.'

Though Massimo d'Azeglio had long retired from public life, he was still dear to Victor Emmanuel as the brave, disinterested, and noble-hearted man who had sacrificed every personal regard when he consented to take office in the first miserable year of his reign, sharing his grief, his humiliation, his unpopularity, supporting and sustaining him in the noble part he chose to act of *Rè galantuomo*. Victor Emmanuel felt strongly the fascination of his versatile genius; and in the inscription on the monument which he helped to erect to his memory, he calls him his 'friend.' The readiness with which the great artist and author would assume an office of state when required, and then step down into comparative poverty, living by his brush, is a charming trait in his attractive character. No pecuniary reward would he take on his retirement. Victor Emmanuel wanted to bestow on him the Order of the SS. Annunziata, but he declined with the smiling remark that it was not meet for the king's cousin to sell pictures. The readers of his correspondence will remember that at the time of the Peace of Milan the Emperor of Austria offered him the Order of St. Etienne, and he replied that if the emperor really wished to show to him some mark of benevolence, let him give him the pardon of the Lombards who had been excluded from the amnesty.

The king was not in Turin when D'Azeglio's hopeless state was made known, but the Prince of Carignano visited him the day he died, and his last words to him were, 'Remember me, and that I have always been a devoted and affectionate servant of the House of Savoy.'

All through the past year Victor Emmanuel had been trying to wring Venetia out of the grasp of Austria, in a peaceable manner, if possible, but if that were not possible he was resolved to resort to arms once more. His speech in November plainly pointed to war as more than a probability; and, Austria firmly refusing to surrender her possessions, both parties prepared for another struggle. Foreign domination once established in a country is an incubus difficult to shake off. In Italy the monster called *lo Straniero* died hard, clinging convulsively to his victim and sapping the life-blood from her veins with his expiring breath. Lombardy had been won and lost, and won again, with a generous prodigality of the noblest blood in the country; and now the Italian soil must drink once more the warm libation from Italian hearts before *la Patria* could be completely redeemed and united.

The quarrel between Austria and Prussia was growing all this time, and Italy proposed an alliance defensive and offensive with the latter power. The ministry had become unpopular because of the corn-grinding tax, which to the present day has never ceased to be a source of discontent, and Sella, the Minister of Finance, author of the obnoxious bill, sent in his resignation, and all his colleagues with him. The king was greatly annoyed by the defeat of the government at this critical juncture. La Marmora, who had his entire confidence, was empowered to form a new ministry. The general had some difficulty in getting a Minister of Finance, but a politician was at last found bold enough to undertake the unenviable duty of directing the monetary affairs of the new kingdom. La Marmora remained President of the Council and Minister for Foreign Affairs; General Pettinengo was called to the War Department, and he accepted office simply to please the king. The distinguished and patriotic young general, Giuseppe Govone, was sent to Berlin to treat of the alliance. He fulfilled the office with tact and ability, and the treaty was concluded April 8, 1866.

When this fact became known, Austria, on the brink of war with Prussia, began to think that she must rid herself in some way of the worry of the Italians on her southern frontier, in order to be free to combat her powerful northern enemy. The cabinet of Vienna did not apply directly to the cabinet of Florence, but to that arbiter of the destinies of nations, Napoleon III., proposing to cede Venetia on condition that the Italian government should detach itself from the Prussian alliance. It was a strong temptation; to recover the long-disputed provinces without the risks and expenses of war would have restored the minister to the popularity he had lost in the matter of the convention with France. But La Marmora was proof against all such temptations. He would brave popular rage, but he would not fail in the smallest particular in any of his engagements. In order to leave his sovereign free to exercise the royal prerogative, he sent in his resignation, which Victor Emmanuel, being entirely of his mind, refused to accept.

After an ineffectual attempt to accommodate matters by a congress, war was declared against Austria, on June 20, 1866, and La Marmora, having appointed Ricasoli as his deputy at the head of the council, led the army northwards. The Italians, though grumbling against the ministry because of the recently imposed tax, received the announcement of war with unmeasured applause. The day before the battle is always one of pleasing excitement and enthusiasm; the day after, when the costs come to be counted, one of mourning. Victor Emmanuel appointed his cousin regent, and carried his sons along with him to the seat of war. At sunrise the king passed through the streets of Florence, amidst loud acclamations, good wishes, and blessings, to the railway station, where he embraced Baron Ricasoli, saying, 'I commend our country to you.'

The ardent applause which greeted the king was in answer to one of his fiery proclamations issued the day before, explaining the reasons of the war, which were—the inveterate hostility of Austria to Italian liberty, her refusal of a pacific settlement of the quarrel by means of a congress, and her threatening attitude on the Italian frontier, which was a continual source of disturbance and inquietude to his state. He thanked his people and army for the ready response they had given to his call; expressed a strong conviction that the justice of their cause would be recognised by public opinion, and concluded thus:—

> Italians,—I commit the government of the state to my most beloved cousin Prince Eugenio, and I take up again the sword of Goito, Pastrengo, Palestro, and San Martino. I feel in my heart a conviction that this time I shall completely fulfil the vow I made on the tomb of my magnanimous parent. I will be once more the first soldier of Italian independence. *Viva l'Italia!*
>
> Given from Florence, June 20, 1866.
>
> VICTOR EMMANUEL.
Ricasoli.

To the National Guards.

> Officers, Sub-officers, and Militia of the National Guards,—I commit the sovereign authority to my beloved cousin Prince Eugenio, and I turn again to fight the last supreme battles for the liberty and inde-

pendence of Italy. While the forces of land and sea will vindicate the nation's rights against the threats and provocations of Austria, you will maintain her well ordered and tranquil, because in obeying the laws she will strengthen her liberties and prepare herself for the glorious future that awaits her. You have constituted this kingdom by your votes: preserve it intact by your discipline and your citizen arms. To you I commit, in full confidence, the guardianship of public order, and calmly I go where the voice of Italy calls me.
VICTOR EMMANUEL.

Victor Emmanuel to Napoleon III.

Sire and Brother,—I announce to your majesty that, faithful to the convention made with Prussia, I have this morning sent a declaration of war to Austria. My army, which confronts the enemy, counts over 250,000 active men. I have a reserve of 50,000, and very soon I may have another as good. I start to-morrow to assume the command of the army. My heart is joyous and full of confidence in the future.

I thank your majesty for all that you have done for us, and I pray you not to forget us, and me in particular, who am your majesty's good brother,
VICTOR EMMANUEL.

The emperor replied that in the interests of his country he had resolved on maintaining a strict neutrality; but he would never cease to pray for the happiness of his 'good brother' and the independence of Italy.

Order of the Day.

Officers, Sub-officers, and Soldiers,—Austria arming on the frontier challenges you to new battles. In my own name, in the name of the nation, I call you to arms. This cry of war shall be as heretofore a cry of joy to you. Whatever be your duty I will not tell it you, because I am satisfied that you know it. Confiding in the justice of our cause, strong in the right, by our arms we must accomplish our unity.

I assume to-day the command of the army, to fulfil the duty which awaits me and you, to liberate the people of Venetia who have long groaned under an iron yoke. You shall conquer, and your name shall be blessed by present and future generations.

VICTOR EMMANUEL.

Victor Emmanuel's happy prognostications were not this time destined to be fulfilled. The forces of Austria were led by the able and experienced commander the Archduke Albert, who had distinguished himself at Novara. On the ill-omened field of Custoza, where the Italians had been defeated in 1849, the opposing armies met; and both being in good condition, well disciplined and brave, there was fought a prolonged and bloody battle, in which the Italians were worsted, but not routed. They valiantly maintained their positions, and though their losses were heavy, those they inflicted on the enemy were also severe.

On July 20 the Italian navy suffered an overwhelming defeat at Lissa in the Adriatic, and these two great misfortunes plunged Victor Emmanuel into the deepest grief. He felt disabled from continuing the war: all the sacrifice of life had been in vain: national unity was as far off as ever. He had deported himself with his usual gallantry at Custoza; and the young princes, for the first time in action, had shown a spirit worthy of their father. Amedeo was slightly wounded; and this gave an opportunity for the generals to protest against the reckless exposure of lives so precious to the state. General Cialdini said the thought that at any moment they might be deprived of all the royal family, had weighed heavily upon his mind. The king combated the idea for his sons as well as himself. He said he did not expose himself from mere recklessness, but from a sense of duty, to inspire his men with more courage and show them that he considered the cause worth fighting for, worth dying for, if need be. 'I appreciate this anxiety about the lives of the princes,' he said, 'but my sons are soldiers and must fight. If we princes of Savoy remained at home at ease while our soldiers fought for us, we should end like the Bourbons of Naples.'

Meantime the Prussian arms were everywhere victorious over Austria, and about ten days after the battle of Custoza it was announced in the *Moniteur* that Austria had asked the Emperor Napoleon's mediation, offering to cede him Venice, and that he was making over that province to the King of Italy. Italy could not accept it without the consent of her ally Prussia; and while negotiations were going forward on the subject, the brief seven weeks' campaign was brought to a conclusion by the great victory of Sadowa, and on July 26 the preliminaries of peace were signed by the Austrian and Prussian plenipotentiaries.

Though defeated by the Prussians, the Austrians had been victorious in two encounters with the Italians, and these reverses, coming after such sanguine expectations, having sunk the country in gloom and misery, the national misfortune had to be accounted for by imputing mismanagement to the government. The king, finding his army very much diminished, and hemmed in between the Austrian forces, the Po and the Adige, began to see the necessity of an immediate armistice. But to take upon himself the responsibility of concluding an armistice, so sure to be unpopular, would be rash. He despatched General Menabrea to Florence to explain the desperate state of things at the seat of war, and ask the approval of the government to what was an unavoidable step. To wait for a reply might be dangerous; and the king and General La Marmora opened negotiations with the Austrians at once, resolved to disregard every consideration but what was best for the country.

It was then that La Marmora, with that high-souled loyalty which always distinguished him, resolved to throw himself between the king and the nation. A constitutional sovereign must not be permitted by his minister to do anything that would bring upon him the odium of his people. 'I take the whole responsibility, whatever may happen,' said he.

'This is too much, dear La Marmora,' replied Victor Emmanuel, pressing both his hands with emotion; 'I must have my share.'

The king and the general sustained each other in their patriotic resolution to conclude an armistice. 'They will accuse us of having betrayed the country,' said Victor, 'but we will sacrifice even our reputation to preserve the army, and with it the nation.'

The government approved of the armistice. Venice was restored to Italy by the Emperor of France, with the approval of Prussia. There was a sting in the thought that it was not wrung from the talons of the Austrian eagle by the valour of Italian arms, but by the force of diplomacy; still it was a delightful fact that Venice was free, with the tricolour waving on St. Mark's. The Italian soil was delivered from foreign occupation; the never-to-be-forgotten cry, *Fuori lo Straniero!* which had resounded so long throughout the peninsula, was to be heard no more.

During the period of the armistice, before the treaty of peace was signed, there was an interlude which diverted the public interest from the late disasters in the form of an insurrection in Sicily, which was quickly suppressed by General Cadorna, who had with him the sympathy of the respectable portion of the community. It was conducted by those lawless adventurers who had been hitherto accustomed to live as they pleased, and prey upon their neighbours, and consequently disliked the new order of things, as tending to do away with their privileges. This movement was the last expiring effort of the Bourbons to restore their dynasty in Italy.

As soon as the treaty was signed at Vienna, October 2, the Venetian Assemblies unanimously elected Victor Emmanuel with acclamations, and begged for immediate annexation to the kingdom of Italy. On November 4, in the city of Turin, Victor Emmanuel received the deputation which came to proffer him the homage of the inhabitants of Venetia; and not only did the citizens greet them with demonstrations of joy, but visitors from all parts of the Peninsula were assembled to welcome them, as brothers long separated by a cruel fate, at last reunited to the Italian family. The exiled Venetians wept for joy to think they should see again their dear native city. The king, in bestowing the Order of the SS. Annunziata upon Generals Cialdini and Menabrea, also decorated the breast of the blind Venetian, Paleocapa, who had resigned with the Cavour cabinet, disgusted with the peace of Villafranca, but who was now full of joy at the thought of breathing his native air once more.

Victor Emmanuel was radiant with happiness. Who will blame him if in that moment he forgot Custoza and Lissa, and thought only that the labour of his life was accomplished, that the vow he made on his father's tomb, so often renewed, was at last fulfilled; that the foreigner was finally expelled from Italian soil, and he was no longer required to hate anybody? With him, the hackneyed phrase, 'This is the happiest moment of my life,' was no mere figure of speech, for he had never used it before in any public address.

Victor Emmanuel's Reply to the Venetians.

Gentlemen,—This is the most beautiful day of my life. It is now nineteen years since my father proclaimed from this city the war of national independence. To-day, his birthday, you, gentlemen, bring me the manifestation of the popular will of the Venetian provinces, which we now unite to the great Italian country (*patria Italiana*), declaring as an accomplished fact the desire of my august parent. You confirm by this solemn act that which Venetia did in 1848, and which she maintained with such admirable constancy and self-abnegation. Let me here pay a tribute to those brave men who with their blood, and with sacrifices of every sort, kept undiminished faith to their country and to her destinies. With this day shall disappear from the Peninsula every vestige of foreign domination.¹ Italy is made, if not completed; it now rests with the Italians to make her great and prosperous.

Gentlemen, the Iron Crown is also restored in this solemn day to Italy. But above this crown I place that which to me is dearer—the crown of my people's love.

On November 7 Victor Emmanuel made a solemn entry into the most beautiful, and, after Rome, the most interesting city of the Italian peninsula. To tell how he was received would only be to repeat what already has been said about similar entries into the other capitals. Enough to say that 'the Bride of the Sea' gave him a welcome in no way inferior to that of the sister cities. While here he had the pleasure of meeting and entertaining the firm friend of Italian independence, Lord Russell. At the same dinner, which was composed of a curious conglomeration of guests, was the Austrian General Moring, and the Cardinal Trevisanato, Patriarch of Venice.

After visiting several towns of Venetia the king returned to Florence on November 21.

Hot upon the settlement of the Venetian question, came the discussion of that of Rome, which after the evacuation of the French troops seemed more complicated than ever. The Catholic powers were now anxious to accommodate the quarrel between Italy and the Pope, and they offered to guarantee him his income and his independence if he would reconcile himself to the national will. But Pius IX. was immovable in his determination to oppose it to the last.

It was proposed that the Eternal City, and the little Pontifical State around it, should be guaranteed to the Pope and protected by the Italian Government. But to this arrangement the Italians never would consent, for without Rome the unification of Italy was incomplete. As for the Romans they had a thousand reasons

---

[1] The French, in fulfilment of the convention of September 1864, were evacuating Rome.

for opposing such an arrangement. The bare consideration of the idea by their more fortunate countrymen outside the sacred limits of the Church's State, would seem cruel ingratitude after all they had suffered for the national cause. In the midst of this agitation and diplomatic discussions on the Roman question, Parliament was opened, to receive for the first time the Venetian deputies, who took their oaths and seats in the midst of that pleasing excitement which always followed the annexation of a new province; and King Victor spoke in that tone of congratulation which was natural to a man who, if he did not 'swallow a province a day,' as a Milanese soldier once said, had within the last seven years absorbed seven principalities.[1]

The speech from the throne is so long that we will only give the opening paragraph and that one which refers to Rome.

The King's Speech, December 15, 1866.

Gentlemen Senators,—Gentlemen Deputies,—The country is free at last from every foreign domination. My soul exults in telling it to the representatives of 25,000,000 Italians. The nation had faith in me, I had faith in the nation. This great event crowning our common efforts, gives new vigour to the work of civilisation and renders more secure the political equilibrium of Europe.

. . . . . .

The French Government, faithful to the obligations it assumed in the convention of September 1864, has withdrawn her military forces from Rome. On its part the Italian Government, maintaining its engagements,

---

[1] King Victor related the following anecdote to his ministers one day: 'In 1861 I was holding a review on the Piazza d'Armi in Milan. Opposite me was a regiment, the soldiers of which held their eyes fixed on mine, as discipline prescribes. Two of them, without moving their heads, held the following dialogue, which, though spoken in a low voice, I overheard, for, as you may have perceived. gentlemen, I have excellent hearing. "Look at our king, is he not fine and fat?" "That he is, but considering that he eats a province a day, what wonder that he should be fine and fat?"'

has respected, and will respect, the Pontifical territory.

The good understanding with the Emperor of the French, to whom we are bound by the ties of friendship and gratitude, the moderation of the Romans, the wisdom of the Pontiff, the religious sentiment and right judgment of the Italian people, will all contribute to reconcile Catholic interests and national aspirations, which are being mixed up confusedly in the agitations at Rome.

Reverential towards the religion of our fathers, which is also the religion of the greater part of the Italians, I render homage at the same time to the principles of liberty that inform our institutions, which, applied with sincerity and breadth of judgment, will help to remove the old causes of difference between the Church and State. These our provisions, reassuring Catholic consciences, will, I hope, assist in the fulfilment of my desire, that the Supreme Pontiff should remain independent at Rome.

General Pettinengo having resigned his post as Minister of War, in the belief that the king was dissatisfied with him, Victor wrote as follows :—

Victor Emmanuel to General Pettinengo.

I am vexed to see in a letter from you, directed to the Count Verasis, that you imagine that I am ill-disposed towards you. If such were the case, I must very soon have forgotten the many services rendered by you to the State, the special merit of having accepted, solely to oblige me, the portfolio of War in difficult times, and finally the zeal which you showed for the army when it was put on a war footing. If some things have not gone as I desired, I certainly did not mean to blame you, dear general; I attributed it rather to an old system, which has need of modifications.

Ingratitude is, for the most part, the reward of those who labour for the public good. I also have had hard experience of this for a long time; and, less fortunate than you, I cannot yet ask my dismissal. These lines I hope will be sufficient to prove to you, dearest general, that you preserve always the esteem and the friendship of

Your most affectionate
VITTORIO EMANUELE.

CHAPTER XXVI.

THE KING AND POPE.—FINANCIAL DIFFICULTIES.—MARRIAGE OF PRINCE AMEDEO. A.D. 1867.

THE French army being withdrawn from Rome, the Pope had no other defenders than his foreign mercenaries; his little state was hemmed round on all the land sides by the possessions of the robber king, who had undertaken to defend him against foreign aggression and protect him in the exercise of his spiritual authority. As temporal sovereign he was tottering on his throne; his subjects were thoroughly disaffected, and in that ancient seat of priestly power which once ruled Christendom, the Pope could not now command the willing obedience of other than his Swiss guards and ecclesiastics. Not daring to trust himself without the protection of a large military force, he again raised a foreign legion, to take the place of the French troops. This proceeding irritated the Romans more than ever; and instead of practising that patience which the king recommended, they lost all hope in diplomacy, and took to their old expedient of conspiracy.

'The internal tempest which rages in Rome,' writes Castelar, 'is at once perceptible to the stranger. There are 400 persons now in prison for political offences. A priest of high position, and an intimate friend of the Pope, assures me that there are in Rome now 70,000 Garibaldians. A state which scarcely contains

600,000 souls keeps a standing army of 20,000. These 20,000 are men of different nations, languages, and customs.'

Meantime it was necessary for the court of Florence and that of Rome to hold some communication with reference to ecclesiastical preferments. A dispute arose about the Archbishopric of Milan, the Pope not approving of the king's nomination, and *vice versâ*. At last the matter was amicably settled to the satisfaction of all parties. Several letters were exchanged between the heads of the Church and State on these ecclesiastical matters. The Pope's missives, when not treating of the political questions of the day, were courteous and not unfriendly; and he was heard to say at this time that he preferred dealing with Victor Emmanuel than with the Bourbons of Naples or Leopold of Tuscany.

Victor Emmanuel's communications, it is needless to say, always breathed a profound reverence for the Head of the Church, as such; and as it was in this character he now approached him, the correspondence between the two illustrious rivals merged into a kindlier tone than one would have believed possible between the excommunicated monarch and the offended Pontiff. The correspondence was of a private nature; but Victor Emmanuel communicated the general contents to his confidential advisers. Pio Nono in one of his letters explained why he could not recognise nor bless Victor as 'King of Italy,' though in his own person, and in his quality of King of Sardinia, he did so willingly.

The king, in speaking of this letter, said:—

I replied to the following effect:— I have often read in books approved of by the Roman Church, that the Almighty sometimes avails himself of a king to castigate a pope, or a pope to castigate a king. If your holiness cannot recognise nor bless the King of Italy, as such, you can at least bless in him the instrument of which Divine Providence avails himself for ends beyond our penetration.

Meantime the question of the separation of the Church and State, and the readjustment of ecclesiastical property, was before Parliament, and the government being defeated with a motion of censure, resolved to appeal to the country in a general election.

The king's speech on opening the new Parliament, March 22, will give a general idea of the state of affairs. The nation was now on the verge of bankruptcy, and nothing but the secularisation of Church property could save its credit.

The King's Speech.

Gentlemen Senators,—Gentlemen Deputies,—For the good of Italy, which has confided her destinies to me, I esteemed it well that the representation of the country should calm itself at the sources of national suffrage. I hope that it has there derived a consciousness of the grave necessities of the country, and the strength to provide for them.

We have had the time for bold propositions and daring enterprises. I met them confident in the sanctity of the cause which God had called me to defend. The nation replied eagerly to my voice. With harmony and persevering labour we acquired independence and we maintain liberty.

But now that her existence is assured, Italy requires that we do not, in intemperate rivalries, lose the vigour of mind and soul which is necessary to give her wise and stable laws; so that, in peace and tranquillity, those elements of prosperity which Providence bestows so largely, may have time to fructify. The nation expects that Parliament and government will undertake resolutely this work of reparation. The people love and prize institutions in proportion to the benefits they bring them. It is necessary to show that our institutions satisfy the noblest aspirations of efficiency and national dignity, while at the same time affording a guarantee for the good order of the state and the well-being of the population, that in them their faith in the liberty which is the honour and the strength of our constitution may not be diminished.

For the attainment of this object my government will present for your deliberation a complete scheme for the improvement of the administration, which will strengthen at the same time both liberty and authority.

. . . . . .

The necessities and engagements of the state hinder me for the present from lightening as I could wish the heavy imposts which weigh upon my people. But a legitimate liquidation of the ecclesiastical assets, a severe economy in the expenses, a diligent application of the new laws, an austere morality maintained in all parts of the public administration, will operate so that the taxes may become less burdensome. Only the prompt discussion and efficacious execution of the proposed reforms can restore our credit and remove the necessity of new taxes. To-day the question of the finances is for Italy not only a question of supreme interest, but also a question of honour and of national dignity. I doubt not the Parliament will turn all its attention to solve it.

On solemn occasions we have promised to Europe that when once we were complete in our entity as a nation, she would find in us a power given to civilisation, to order, and to peace. It now rests with us to maintain that promise, and to respond to the hopes that we have taught her to conceive of us.

Gentlemen Senators,—Gentlemen Deputies,—The honour, the welfare, and the future of Italy are in your hands. If it was a glory to have, with so many sacrifices, conducted to fulfilment the work of our independence, and impressed on the nation the movement and vigour of life, it will be no less glory to set her in order within, to make her sure of herself, respected, prosperous and strong.

Another ministerial crisis followed on the opening

of Parliament. Baron Ricasoli resigned, and Signor Rattazzi was called to form a new ministry.

In the April of this year died, comparatively young, Baron Carlo Poerio, to the great grief of the king and the nation. Poerio was the Silvio Pellico of Naples; he had suffered indescribable martyrdom in the prisons, in the galleys, in exile; but so far from making a merit of this, he shrank with a painful modesty from any mention of his trials. His simple, beautiful character had won the admiration of Victor Emmanuel, who had conceived for him an immense regard, and felt his death as a national misfortune.

On May 30, Victor Emmanuel's second son, Amedeo, Duke of Aosta, married Maria Vittoria, daughter of Prince Pozzo della Cisterna,—the head of a rich and very ancient Piedmontese family, devoted to the national cause. The prince was not much past twenty-one, but his youth was full of promise which his manhood has since fulfilled. As ruler of the most disordered country in Europe, his firmness, courage, and rectitude of purpose were acknowledged even by those who rejected his authority. The bitterest enemies of monarchy find it difficult to pick a hole in the character of Amedeo of Savoy—save only that he has a slight dash of the superstition of his fathers. The bride was in every way worthy of the noble prince who had chosen her, and the marriage was—for a royal marriage—a wonderfully happy one. The princess being Italian made this matrimony particularly acceptable to the nation, and there were great rejoicings and demonstrations of loyalty on the occasion.

CHAPTER XXVII.

MENTANA. A.D. 1867.

MEANTIME things were going from bad to worse in Rome. The hatred between the governing and the governed was becoming fiercer and more uncontrollable. The Inquisition was at work to discover treason as well as heresy, seditious acts and words were punished with extreme rigour, the sentences passed being in many cases unjust; the soldiers of the foreign legion were insolent and overbearing, and the patience of the Romans was quite exhausted. The immense number of ecclesiastics congregated in the capital and filling every office of the state, and the close connection which many of them had with the old nobility, made the clerical party still formidable, supported as it was by a strong military force. Nevertheless, the citizens resolved to appeal to arms once more, though many of their most daring spirits were in prison, in the galleys, or in exile.

The liberator, who had listened to the 'cry of anguish' from the provinces, seemed deaf to all their entreaties, and preached patience to them while the rest of Italy was congratulating herself on being 'made.' So they turned their hopes to the rash but generous chief who had made so many hopeless efforts to aid them in the past. During the five years that had elapsed since Aspromonte, Garibaldi had lived in retirement in Caprera, nursing his wound and brooding over the disjointed state of the world, which he was firmly convinced would never be set right till all the priests were exterminated. This hostility to the clergy endeared him to the Romans; and almost all the popular songs of this time had the *Camicia Rossa* for a hero. They asked him where did he hide himself when the voice of Italy called him: why did he not take his flight to the Capitol, where the bones of Brutus and Cassius summoned him? Was he afflicted, suffering, depressed? Then he was all the more dear to them for those very reasons; the scorn of the Moderates only made him the greater—

> Ed Aspromonte farti non possa
> Meno magnanimo, Camicia Rossa !

He responded to the call, and took the field once more, with the old cry of 'Rome or death!'—magic words, which drew hundreds of ardent young enthusiasts into the ranks of his veteran band of volunteers, ready at the bidding of their chief to undertake any desperate enterprise.

The clerical party in Rome, knowing the disaffection that reigned in the city, and dreading the approach of the Garibaldians, made an outcry which was echoed by the Ultramontanes in France—all declaring that the Italian Government was false to the convention of 1864. The cry of the papal party frightened the vacillating emperor into ordering a large body of troops to embark for Civitavecchia to protect the Pontifical States.

Victor Emmanuel found himself in a most embarrassing position. Saving only the first year of his reign he never had passed through such a difficult and trying one—with regard to public affairs—as this year of 1867.

All the complications of the Roman question were becoming more intricate. He was pledged to protect the papal frontier, but not to occupy the territory with his troops. And now that it was about to be invaded by Italian volunteers, in defiance of the king's government, how was he to fulfil his compact without sending troops across the frontier? Fearful agitation reigned, not only in the capital, but throughout Italy, the sympathy of the whole nation being with the Romans and the Garibaldians. The king's sympathies there is no doubt were with them also. It was hard for him, feeling as he did, to act the unpopular part which diplomacy dictated and the interest of the country demanded. To make matters worse, the ministry was in a critical position; in fact no ministry had had any stability since the convention of 1864, and consequently great care and responsibility fell upon the king. Orders were given to use severe repressive measures with the volunteers; Garibaldi was arrested, and, at his own request, carried to Caprera, where he was kept in honourable confinement. Victor Emmanuel could not bear to subject the general to harsh treatment, for he was still suffering from the effects of his wound at Aspromonte; and the memory of that day was bitter to the king.

Garibaldi's body might be imprisoned at Caprera, but, like old John Brown,

> His soul went marching on.

The fire which he had fanned into a flame could not be quenched. It increased in fury when the news arrived that a French army was embarking at Toulon to re-occupy the Roman State; and a civil war, or war with France, seemed imminent. At this unhappy moment the Rattazzi ministry, unable to cope with such overwhelming difficulties, resigned. The king called in General Cialdini; but to compose a ministry at such a crisis of public affairs was no easy matter. Many days passed before anything was decided with regard to the constitution of the new cabinet. The volunteers gathering strength and determination, approached the Roman frontier. The king and the country had often felt Cavour's loss, but never more than at this terrible juncture, when Victor Emmanuel stood alone, trying to guide the tempest-tossed ship of state from foundering on the rocks which threatened her with destruction. His Neapolitan biographer, in speaking of this period, says:—

> I have already had occasion to note, but the repetition is not superfluous, the rare acumen with which Victor Emmanuel solved the most delicate constitutional questions, and in the most difficult moments knew how to draw himself out of an imbroglio by wise, and in every way unexceptionable resolutions. That would be a title to merited praise even in a king of

England, descended in a long line from constitutional princes, because they have drunk in and been penetrated with the teaching which is derived from constant observance of the traditions of Parliament. But it excites marvel in a king like Victor Emmanuel, the first of his race to exercise the prerogative, lofty but at the same time most delicate, of a constitutional sovereign. It is an example unique in history.

General Cialdini failing to construct a ministry, General Menabrea hastily collected together a few devoted adherents of the throne, who, like the king, were ready to sacrifice their popularity to save the country from imminent danger. Strong measures were taken to maintain public order. The royal troops were ordered to guard the papal frontier, hoping to check the Garibaldian movement and induce the volunteers to unite themselves with the regular army.

Royal Proclamation.

Italians!—Bands of volunteers, excited and seduced by the work of a faction, without authority from me or my government, have violated the frontier of the state. The respect due equally by all citizens to the laws and international conditions sanctioned by the Parliament and by me, establishes in these grave circumstances an inexorable obligation of honour. Europe knows that the banner raised in the neighbouring lands, on which was written the destruction of the supreme spiritual authority of the Head of the Catholic religion, is not mine. This attempt places the common country in grave peril, and imposes on me the imperious duty of saving the honour of the nation, by not allowing to be confounded in one two causes absolutely distinct—two objects totally diverse.

Italy must be secured against the dangers that may come. Europe must be convinced that Italy, faithful to her engagements, does not wish to be, and will not be, a disturber of the public order. War with our allies would be a fratricidal war between two armies which have fought for the same cause.

I am the depository of the right of declaring peace or war for the nation, and I cannot tolerate the usurpation of it. I trust therefore that the voice of reason will be listened to, and that the Italian citizens who are violating that right will quickly place themselves in the ranks of our troops. The perils and the disorders which this ill-advised project may create among us ought to be forsworn by them, who should maintain firmly the authority of the government and the inviolability of the laws.

The honour of the country is in my hands, and the confidence that the nation had in me in her days of mourning shall not be disappointed. When the excitement has calmed down and public order is fully re-established, then my government, in agreement with that of France, and according to the vote of Parliament, will try sincerely by every loyal effort to find a solution which will put a termination to the grave and important question of the Romans.

Italians!—I have and always will put confidence in your sense, as you have done in the affection of your king for this great country, which, thanks to our common sacrifices, we have at last placed upon the roll of nations, and which we ought to transmit to our sons honoured and entire.

VICTOR EMMANUEL.

Florence, October 27, 1867.

Meantime negotiations were being carried on with the French Government to impede the disembarkation of the troops at Civitavecchia. General La Marmora was despatched in hot haste to remonstrate with the emperor, and tell him, if he did not want to see the young nation sunk in a bloody revolution, to refrain from interference. The Marquis Pepoli being then in the French capital, also had an interview with Napoleon III., and communicated the result to the king, who telegraphed a reply to the following effect:—

To the Marquis Pepoli, Paris.

Received your report. I thank you. The government, desiring to make known to the Emperor of the French the new condition of the country, which is alarming, sends La Marmora. You will go to the emperor to-day or to-morrow. Tell him on my word, that, in case of the French disembarkation, we should occupy part of the Pontifical territory, this occupation shall not be political; and I pledge myself that no complication or misadventure shall happen between the French and us in pursuance of the orders that I have given; tell him that I find it impossible to act otherwise because of the great excitement of the country. Turin is already rising, and Naples threatens to do so; I am to call troops to arms, because Parliament, which had taken them from us, is not now able to repress the disturbances.

Entreat the emperor to believe in my good faith and friendship for him, but ask him to consider my position. Tell him if the Garibaldian bands are repulsed (by the papal troops) we will disarm them.

Let the emperor tell me immediately where we can hold a congress. I think Savona a convenient place; and the sooner it is done the better for both of us. Write me something by telegraph, and then start at once and come to me with the latest news. I have need of you here; your presence is necessary in these difficult moments.

VICTOR EMMANUEL.

Oct. 30; hour 3.45.

This telegram, the composition of which shows that it was written in great haste and agitation, will give a faint idea of the distress and anxiety which the king suffered at this period. 'Do not think of me,' he said to his ministers; 'think only of saving Italy by any measures possible. Do what you esteem best; I will bear the consequences.'

In spite of the ill-regulated zeal of the volunteers and their disobedience to his authority, Victor Emmanuel had a great tenderness for those misguided youths; and he had earnestly hoped that his proclamation would have recalled them to a sense of their duty as citizens and subjects. In the hope of winning them over to join the ranks of the royal army, the Italian troops were ordered to cross the papal frontier.

This precaution was interpreted in a hostile sense by the Pontifical authorities, who loudly proclaimed that the King of Italy had violated the convention. It was well for them, however, that Victor Emmanuel stood between them and the seething fury of the nation at that moment; if he had slackened the reins of government and let the storm take its course, guided by the republican leaders, history would have had a different story to tell than the defeat of the volunteers at Mentana. Whoever has read Garibaldi's book, *The Rule of the Monk*, will be able to form an idea of how the clergy were regarded by the Republican party, and the fate that would have been allotted to the dignitaries of the Church had they come into power. Happily for humanity and civilisation, a wise, firm, and tolerant prince was at the head of the state, who, in order to maintain his treaty in the spirit, sacrificed the letter.

But matters had gone too far with the Romans and their sympathisers outside to admit of a peaceable termination. Menotti Garibaldi, at the head of the volunteers, had entered the State of the Church, and the inhabitants rose as one man to welcome them and join their ranks. In each town their forces were augmented; they passed through the country defeating the papal troops everywhere, and marched on the Eternal City. It had been pre-arranged that the conspirators in the city were to admit the invading forces by the gate of St. Paul; but the government having discovered a great quantity of firearms concealed near this gate, the plot miscarried. The rebels, surprised, made a desperate resistance, but were overcome and cut down with great havoc; those outside, attempting an entrance, also fell victims to the well-armed and well-disciplined Swiss Guards. The leader of the rebel band was the brother of the late prime minister of Italy, Cairoli, who won so much renown, in November last, by saving his king's life almost with the sacrifice of his own. Young Cairoli fell mortally wounded, and expired crying, *Viva Roma!* Deeds of great brutality were afterwards committed by the papal soldiers, but were disowned by the government when they came to be publicly known.

The Roman Consulta, or senate, presented a petition to the Pope, signed by 12,000 citizens, entreating him to call Victor Emmanuel's army to Rome, as the only means of restoring order and peace. But that was the last course which Pius would have thought of adopting.

Meantime Garibaldi, having escaped from Caprera, took the field once more, and met with a decided success at Monterotundo, a few miles from Rome, 800 prisoners remaining in his hands. At the head of 3,000 men he reached Mentana, where he encountered the French army, which the emperor had sent to defend the temporal power. Superior in numbers, in discipline, and in arms, the French made fearful havoc in the ranks of the volunteers, who fell under the deadly fire of the *chassepots* like grass before the scythe.

At this moment Pepoli arrived from Paris, and found the king almost broken-hearted, brooding over the thought of all the generous young blood which ensanguined the field of Mentana. He agreed to recall his troops from the papal territory, so as to give no one an excuse for saying he violated the convention. Who will blame him if at that moment his heart was full of bitterness towards his 'august ally,' who had all but ruined at the last moment the work of his lifetime?

He directed the marquis to write a letter to the emperor. When Pepoli had written it he gave it to the king to read, who exclaimed, 'How is this? you have said nothing about the *chassepots*. Ah, those *chassepots* have mortally wounded my heart as father and as king. I feel as if the balls had torn my flesh here,' and he put his hand to his breast. 'It is one of the greatest griefs that I have ever known in all my life.'

The marquis having supplied the omission, handed the letter again to the king, and observed the tears rolling down his cheeks as he murmured '*Poveri giovani*' (poor youths).

The Marquis Pepoli to the Emperor of the French.

Sire,—The king's government, in recalling the Italian troops from Roman territory, has rendered a service, in my opinion, not only to Italy, but to the cause of liberty in Europe, avoiding fatal complications and a civil war. It finds itself, however, in a dubious and grievous position with regard to the country. It finds itself accused of having ceded to foreign pressure, which is the worst and most cruel accusation which can be brought against a government. It is necessary that it should be reinforced, if it is to govern the country with a firm hand, if it is to vindicate the principle of offended authority, if it is, without going beyond the laws, to find in the laws themselves the remedy for the evils that torment Italy.

Your majesty will effectively contribute to this by removing even the appearance of an alliance with the Clerical party, which would be, I will not say fatal to Italy, but most fatal to France, and the Napoleonic dynasty.

I dare to hope that your majesty will not hesitate to do this, because if the need of satisfying the national susceptibilities, and the obligation of respecting your own word, counselled you to refuse every demand to suspend the expedition to Rome, the same reasons do not exist to-day to make you refuse to recall your army. No; the permanence of the French banner at Rome would not be a pledge to the national honour, but to the ireful vengeance of the reactionary party. I dare affirm that the return of the French expedition would be saluted by all liberal Europe with joy, and that an immense majority of the French people would applaud it.

Believe me, your majesty, it is best to break with a

party which dreams of commencing the restoration at Rome and finishing it at Paris. Do not league yourself with the Legitimist clericals. Your majesty can, if you will, be the head of the Liberal party in Europe, of that party which has the future in its hands, which will regenerate the world, in spite of the efforts of the feudal party. It is your majesty's mission to finish once for all with the old world; you ought to have the glory of uniting religion and liberty. You have made the word of France respected; you can, if you will, reconquer lost ground, complete the work initiated, and be the Charlemagne of liberty in Europe.

Pardon, sire, if I have spoken with my customary frankness. But Italy to-day, after the withdrawal of her own troops, has a right to ask justice from Europe. If your majesty follows a liberal policy in Rome, the benefits of it will react on the internal policy of France.

The late events have suffocated every remembrance of gratitude in the heart of Italy. It is no longer in the power of the government to maintain the alliance with France. The *chassepot* gun at Mentana has given it a mortal blow.

But this alliance is not contemptible, sire; it is an alliance more safe and effective than that of the Clerical party. Your majesty can, if you will, without offending the dignity of your nation, revivify it and make it fruitful.

GIOACHINO PEPOLI.

Florence, Nov. 6, 1867.

But while Victor Emmanuel wept the fate of the brave youths who fell at Mentana, he had to vindicate his outraged authority by punishing those who survived. The leaders of the movement were arrested, and the arch-offender, Garibaldi, was conducted to the fortress of Varignano a close prisoner. He was cheered enthusiastically at Spezia, and at every place where he was seen. He was once more the hero of the day, and Victor Emmanuel was under a cloud. After order had been restored somewhat, Garibaldi, whose health was much broken, asked and obtained the royal pardon, and was once more conducted to Caprera.

Certainly, between the Garibaldians, and the reactionists, and the French emperor, Victor Emmanuel did not lie on a bed of roses. He had been forced to act a part most repugnant to his feelings, which placed him in a false position towards his subjects and involved him in unmerited unpopularity. Between two evils he had chosen the least, resolved to do his duty at any personal cost; but the trial was great. 'I have the honour of bearing the title of king, and sometimes I find it very heavy,' Victor Emmanuel once wrote in a private letter; and we can well believe it. To constitute a vast kingdom out of a number of small states long divided, to 'make' a nation, as he expressed it, out of such elements as went to compose the 'geographical expression' known as Italy, involved a herculean labour which few men would have had the strength and perseverance to conduct to a *finale*, and which could not possibly be accomplished without many difficulties and trials. We can imagine him sometimes, weary of the fitful fever of his existence, looking with envy at a sovereign like Queen Victoria, calmly reposing on the broad and solid foundations of an old hereditary and constitutional monarchy.

The ministry, as the Marquis Pepoli had said, was in a dubious and painful position. The Chambers were reopened on December 1, when the Roman question was put under discussion and gave occasion to passionate debates. One deputy proposed a resolution to approve the conduct of the government, expressing regrets that the friendly relations with France had suffered, and declaring in explicit terms that Italy had a moral right to Rome. The resolution was rejected by a majority of two. 'In the majority there were deputies of the extreme right who would not agree to the affirmation of Italy's right to Rome; deputies of the left, who would not express regrets for the altered relations with France; deputies of the centre, who were irritated by the offensive words pronounced with regard to Italy in the French rostrum; and those deputies who habitually oppose any ministry whatever.' The ministry resigned, and the king accepted their resignation, but immediately empowered General Menabrea to form a new cabinet.

At the time of the ministerial crisis there arrived in Florence a distinguished traveller on his way to Rome— an English statesman for whom Victor Emmanuel had a profound respect. Lord Clarendon was an old acquaintance; and the king talked freely to him of his difficulties and perplexities, and asked him to be the bearer of a message to the Pontiff. He begged him to assure his holiness of his affection, which no political dissension had power to change; to lay before him the true state of affairs, and to say that the longer the policy of resistance lasted, seeking support from foreign interventions, the more painful would be the inevitable end. Lord Clarendon delivered the message. 'They are strange people, these Italians, pretending to unite Italy without my aid,' said the Pope. Lord Clarendon suggested that his holiness might aid in the process by sending his blessing to the King of Italy. But Pius was still obdurate. He said he did not trust in foreign interventions, but in some miracle of Providence. 'Providence has worked miracles, your holiness, during the last ten years, but all in favour of Italy,' was the prompt reply of the Englishman.

CHAPTER XXVIII.

MARRIAGE OF THE CROWN PRINCE.—ANECDOTES OF VICTOR EMMANUEL'S CHARITY.—SPANISH REVOLUTION. A.D. 1868.

HUMBERT, Prince of Piedmont, was now in his twenty-fourth year, an unusually long time for a crown prince to be permitted to live in single blessedness. His younger brother was already provided with a wife, and that he had escaped matrimony so long was owing to a fatal accident which had carried off the young archduchess who had been fixed upon as a suitable match to strengthen the growing friendship between the Houses of Savoy and Hapsburg. When a decent time had elapsed after this misfortune, the king ordered his prime minister to find him a bride for the prince.

'*Voglio assolutamente ch' Ella mi trovi una sposa per Umberto.*'

General Menabrea promptly replied that she was already found; there was only wanting the will of his majesty and the consent of the prince. It was the daughter of the Duke of Genoa, the Princess Margherita, whom he had fixed upon as the future Queen of Italy. The king had not thought of his niece in this light; so he asked the general to tell him about the qualities of the princess, and what had suggested the idea to him. Menabrea related anecdotes illustrative of her noble disposition, strength of character, delicacy of feeling, and dilated on the advantage of securing this flower of womanhood to the House of Savoy and the Italian nation, before she was snatched up by the Prince of Roumania, who was about to offer her his hand.

The king listened with increasing satisfaction, and then, striking the table with his fist, as he often did when he was excited, exclaimed—' Bravo! from all that you have related I recognise in her the Savoy blood. Now that you have told me so many nice things about my niece, I will go and assure myself of it personally.'

He set out for Turin immediately, and arrived unexpectedly at the palace of the Duchess of Genoa. In private conversation with the princess he fully satisfied himself that all he had heard of her goodness was true, and henceforth he took her to his heart as a daughter.

The Duke of Genoa died young, leaving his two children, Margherita and Tommaso to the guardianship of their mother, and their uncle the king, with injunctions that they should be educated *in patria*; he had great faith in early impressions, and he wished his children to love their country as he and his brother did. Margherita was now a lovely girl of eighteen, delicately fair, with eyes of a deeper hue than usually accompany a blonde complexion, and a smile of bewitching sweetness. That smile is always ready in answer to the loyal and affectionate greetings of the people; whether it be gay or sad, and we have seen it both, it goes straight to the hearts of the Italians, and stirs a sentiment of respectful admiration in the foreign spectator. Margherita's excellent qualities, winning sweetness of character, and personal grace, have endeared her to the nation in an extraordinary degree, particularly since her husband came to the throne. As princess she was beloved, as queen she is absolutely adored.

It is probable that the proposition of marriage with Umberto was agreeable to the princess; the Savoy family entertain a high opinion of one another, and no doubt she liked her kinsman better than the Prince of Roumania, a foreigner whom she had never seen. Umberto readily gave his consent. Princes must marry whether they like it or not, and this being the case, where could he find so desirable a bride as his fair cousin? So the marriage was quickly arranged.

Prince Umberto had, like his father, early earned for himself the reputation of a gay character. But Victor Emmanuel's kingly virtues and genial pleasant ways made people overlook and excuse the faults from which princes are so rarely exempt, while Umberto, being as yet untried in public life, had no title to the gratitude or forbearance of the nation. His manners moreover were not conciliatory; being of a reserved and undemonstrative nature, he had no aptitude for exchanging the small attentions which the Italians call *moine*, and which go a long way in winning their affections. Consequently he was popular only so far as that he was his father's son and a Savoy prince, and that he had proved himself a true soldier in the campaign of 1866. But this was enough to call forth great rejoicings on the occasion of his marriage, and to sustain the hope that when the time came to act, he would prove himself a worthy successor of the great founder of Italian independence. That hope has been justified. Umberto has shown himself a man of excellent sense, tact, and good feeling; and he has gradually and quietly grown into the heart of the nation, where he now reigns supreme.

Victor Emmanuel was very fond of his heir. 'I know Umberto,' he said once; 'he is an excellent youth; he has good sense and a good heart; he will do well.' One of his ministers relates the following anecdote. Returning from Milan, where he had had an interview with the prince, he repeated the conversation to the king in all its particulars, even to some expressions of affection which the young man had used in speaking of his father. The king listened with pleased attention. Just then a letter was handed to him which proved to be from his son. When he had read it he turned to the minister with visible emotion, and said—'You are right. I wish you to read this letter; you will see how Umberto writes to me. In my family no one knows how to feign, much less when they are but twenty years old. You are right in what you tell me.'

Subsequent events have proved how unfeigned, how profound, was Umberto's affection for his father, and it is satisfactory to know that they understood one another.

The marriage was celebrated at Turin with great pomp, in presence of all the royal family. There came from Paris the Prince Napoleon and Princess Clotilde, as well as Queen Pia of Portugal, and Prince Frederic of Prussia; between the latter of whom and the Savoy family a great intimacy sprang up.

The civil marriage was gone through on April 28, and the religious ceremony the following day in the cathedral, the Bishop of Savona officiating. On this occasion the king instituted a new order of knighthood, called *La Corona d' Italia*. The bride and bridegroom made a tour of all the principal cities in Italy, Rome of course excepted. But the Roman ladies, notwithstanding their mourning for the sad events of the preceding autumn, presented an address and a magnificent garland to the princess.

THE KING'S CLEMENCY AND CHARITY.

The Roman question kept up a constant atmosphere of political agitation, but the king and the government tried to calm the excited state of men's minds by turning the attention of Parliament to more prosaic subjects, such as public instruction, assimilating the laws of the different states of the kingdom, and other like questions.

The king was not opposed to capital punishments in theory, but he was always disposed to seize upon any extenuating circumstance to commute a capital sentence. In this year there was in the ministry a Signor Filippo, keeper of the seals, whom Victor Emmanuel liked very much, and christened 'the mild minister.' He had, however, repeatedly opposed the royal desire to extend a pardon to different criminals. 'How is it,' asked the king one day, 'that you who are so gentle to the appeals of others always exercise towards me the greatest severity?' 'Your majesty must be aware that they turn to the king as a last extreme, that is, when they have failed in every attempt with the ministers.' 'Yes, I understand,' replied the king. 'I fear I am in the position of a physician of the first order, who is generally called in when the case is desperate, the patient at the end of life, and it is next to impossible to save him. I do not complain of you; on the contrary, I commend you for doing your duty. I wish justice to be done, and grace extended only to those who merit it.'

The king's character, however, was so well known that he was beset by such petitions continually, and it often cost him an effort to reject them. He made no effort, however, to resist the appeals for pecuniary help from those in distress. To such his heart and purse were ever open; and his charities were done in such an unostentatious, unsystematic way that the world can never form any just estimate of all he did. Of the many anecdotes we have heard illustrative of his kindliness and liberality during his six years' residence in Florence, we take two or three.

One day the king came home from a walk very much disturbed, and sent for the President of the Council.

'I have met a poor mutilated soldier who was wounded at San Martino,' he said; 'he is not able to work, and he is starving, because they have never given him a pension. Speak to the Minister of War immediately about it. I wish the wrong done to this poor fellow to be remedied without delay.' But he did not wait for the War Office to set matters right. He sent the crippled soldier a considerable sum from his private purse.

One day, as the king was driving out of the palace court, a poor old woman trying to offer him a petition, fell, and the carriage was near passing over her. In answer to his inquiries if she were injured, his attendants assured him that she was not. 'But the carriage almost ran over her,' said the king; 'she must have been dreadfully frightened, and she ought to have some compensation.' Next day a royal messenger arrived at the poor habitation of the old woman with the sum of one hundred francs. 'Oh, what a lucky fall!' she exclaimed when the notes were handed out to her; 'what a blessed fall!'

A short time ago a lady who resides in Florence related to us the following little incident. A woman who was employed in the *pension* where she was staying had a son called out for military service, which she thought a great hardship. One day she came home in good spirits, and entering the apartment of the lady showed her some pieces of gold. The lady asked her where she had got it. 'From the king's own hand. I have come from the Palazzo Pitti,' was the reply.

'Impossible! You never would have been admitted to his presence.'

'No; but I waited at the gate till he was coming out, and I told him they had taken my son for a soldier, and asked him to release him. "My good woman," says he, "I can do nothing for you; they have taken my *two* sons to be soldiers, and I cannot release them." Then he put the gold in my hand, saying, "Mind; do not come back any more."'

The royal carriage was just driving up to the door of the theatre one evening, when two shabbily dressed women, who had been lying in wait, hastily approached. One of them drew something from under her cloak, and a large heavy object came into the carriage, striking the king in the face and knocking off his hat. It proved to be a hard square cushion, embroidered with beads and gold braid. Victor was very angry. He entered the theatre carrying the offending cushion in his hand. The first person he met was Signor Fausto—who tells the story—just at the door of the royal box. He was crimson in the face, partly from a sense of outraged majesty and partly, perhaps, from the hard and crushing properties of the gorgeous cushion.

'Go,' said he, 'and see who is that madwoman who has permitted herself the liberty of throwing this in my face.' The gentleman hastened to obey, and found the unfortunate delinquent trembling outside the door, expecting some terrible sentence. She was a poor actress, employed in the humblest position in the theatre. She had no treasonable nor offensive intention towards his majesty; the sofa-pillow was meant as a present. Meantime the story had spread, and the head of the police had come to examine the mysterious cushion, to see if it contained an Orsini bomb, or anything dangerous and explosive. When Fausto returned to the royal box he explained that the cushion was simply meant as a gift. 'Well, then,' said Victor, holding it disdainfully by the tassel, 'take it to her and say I have no need or use for such an article.'

As he was handing it to a servant, a note fastened to one of the tassels caught his eye; he opened and looked at it, and then read it to the gentlemen present. The petitioner prayed his majesty to deign to accept this humble offering from 'the poor mother of a family overcome by financial difficulties.' 'Ah, the usual moral,' said the king, nodding his head with a smile. His good humour was restored.

Next evening, his majesty being again at the theatre, he called Signor Fausto to his box.

'What has become of the famous lady of the cushion?' he asked.

'The poor creature has been dismissed by the manager,' was the reply.

'Ah, I am sorry for that. Go to him in my name, and ask him to pardon her,' said the king. Then turning to one of his gentlemen he said—'Take her 250 francs, and tell her never to throw anything in my face again—at least not without warning me first.'

In this year took place the Spanish revolution, and Queen Isabella, the implacable enemy of civil and religious liberty, was chased from the throne and country. She was the last of European sovereigns to recognise the kingdom of Italy, and when pressed to do so had sent as her representative one who had been a courtier of the King of Naples and a professed enemy of Italian unity. The downfall of another Bourbon could not be otherwise than pleasing to Victor Emmanuel, who very soon opened friendly relations with the provisional government established by the leaders of the revolution. Marshal Prim's admiration of Victor Emmanuel suggested the idea of offering the throne of Spain to a prince of the House of Savoy. The subject was ventilated in Spain and Italy some time before the proposition was actually made. The king was not averse to it. To restore order to Spain was a dangerous and difficult enterprise, but if one of his family succeeded in the task, it would open up immense advantages to Italy and the Liberal cause; and for the prince who accomplished the regeneration of that unfortunate country it would win immortal honour.

CHAPTER XXIX.

BIRTH OF AMEDEO'S SON.—DANGEROUS ILLNESS OF THE KING.—BIRTH OF UMBERTO'S SON. A.D. 1869.

MEANTIME the young prince against whose peace the statesmen of Spain and Italy were plotting, still happy in his liberty, was just rejoicing over the birth of a little son, which took place on January 15. It was Victor Emmanuel's first Italian-born grandson, and he was delighted beyond measure. He hastened to Genoa, where the Duke and Duchess of Aosta were staying when the happy event took place, baptized him by the name of his most illustrious ancestor, Emanuele Filiberto, and bestowed upon him the title of Duke of Puglia. Congratulatory addresses poured in on the king and the prince from all parts of the country, and the Genoese made great demonstrations of loyalty on the occasion. The king's thanks were conveyed in a letter the stilted style of which plainly shows that it was not written by himself.

Victor Emmanuel to the Syndic of Genoa.

Illustrissimo Signor Sindaco della città di Genova,—The new testimony of attachment which we have received from our good city of Genoa, on the occasion of the birth of our grandson, the Duke of Puglia—of which your lordship was the interpreter to our beloved son, the Duke of Aosta—has been very pleasing to us. It is not new to us, however, the affection of our Genoese for our person and for our house, the most solemn testimony of which we considered to be your valid co-operation, which never failed us, in the grand undertaking of the reconstruction of the nation, to which we dedicated our life. You were examples of patriotism in the hard struggles and sacrifices of the days of battle, and now you are examples to the Italians in the laboriousness of your industries and your commerce. If Italy will follow this impulse and this example, which speaks encouragingly in the multiplicity of your dockyards and your workshops, she may pursue her path in safety to reach those destinies to which the records of your fathers point. As they carried gloriously and puissantly the banner of St. George, so you and your sons shall bear, we are certain, gloriously and puissantly the banner of Italy.

VICTOR EMMANUEL.

On his return from Genoa the king made a tour in the south of Italy. In the spring he received visits from several members of the royal family of Russia, and some distinguished Austrians, among whom was General Moring, who had arranged the treaty of peace. Victor Emmanuel won golden opinions among his old enemies when they came to know him personally.

'Your sovereign is a true king,' said one of the Austrian visitors on this occasion to General Menabrea.

The Empress of the French, on her way to the East, touched at Venice, and the King of Italy with four of his ministers hastened to the City of the Lagunes to give her a hospitable reception. Later there came from the opening of the Suez Canal the Austrian minister, Count de Beust, to visit the king, at the request of the emperor. Victor made him a knight of the SS. Annunziata.

The moment the Austrians were well 'over the border,' within the natural confines of their own state, and the treaty signed that was to keep them there, Victor Emmanuel's heart began to expand towards the Hapsburg family, with which he had been closely allied by marriage, though national and dynastic hatreds had held them divided so many years. Now that his vow was fulfilled, it was easy for him to bury every bitter remembrance of the past and offer a cordial friendship to his old hereditary foe, who could not doubt the sincerity of that friendship, seeing that he had been so sincere an enemy. The emperor responded warmly to his advances, and the kindly feeling grew rapidly, so that there was a project of a matrimonial alliance between the two houses, which, however, was blasted by death.

No one would have suspected that there was any lurking tenderness in Victor Emmanuel's heart towards the House of Austria from the year 1848 to 1866, during which period he seemed to be in a chronic state of fiery indignation against it. Yet according to his own confession after peace was made, he had suffered much from this state of things, and it was an immense joy to him to be reconciled to those enemies whom he had never been able to forget were still his relations.

In the November of this year the king was in his Villa San Rossore, near Pisa, when he was seized by a malignant fever—the same which had twice before threatened his life. It was confidently believed that his constitution must succumb to this third attack; and he was reduced to such a low state that he gave himself up, and made all arrangements in expectation of a speedy dissolution. It was on this occasion that Victor Emmanuel, doubtless under clerical pressure, went through the religious ceremony of marriage with Rosina, Countess Mirafiore, by whom he had two children, then grown up. The popular version of the transaction which is generally recounted to foreigners is as follows.

The king feeling death approaching called a priest, who having heard the confession of the royal penitent, refused him absolution till he would promise to restore the property robbed from the Church. Whereupon the king replied that he had not sent for his reverence to discuss political questions, which were the work of the Parliament and nation, but to administer ghostly advice to a dying man. Then the baffled priest attacked the monarch in his vulnerable point. 'You have here with you a woman who is not your wife.'

'*Peccavi*,' said the king; 'in that you have a right to dictate to me; what ought I to do?'

'Marry her,' said the priest.

'Bring her here,' was the penitent's prompt reply.

And the matrimony was accordingly solemnised at the bedside of the dying king by the priest, whose malicious object it was to create dissensions in the royal family.

Like most popular stories, this dramatic version of the transaction is not strictly correct; nor is it to be supposed probable that the public could be exactly informed as to the words that passed between a priest and penitent on a matter so entirely personal as the one in question. We will now quote the account of the scene given by Massari, whom we consider the most trustworthy writer on all matters relating to Victor Emmanuel's private life. He was intimate with the king, his ministers, and the officers of his court, and would naturally have informed himself of all that had passed— or, at least, all that concerned the public to know:—

> Conscious of his great danger, he with perfect calmness manifested his last wishes, and made all the arrangements which he considered suitable. He celebrated in religious form his marriage with the Countess Mirafiore; and wishing to receive the comforts of religion, desired expressly that a priest should be called. He, having received the confession of the dying king, said:— 'I cannot give your majesty absolution if you do not first make a solemn retractation of all the acts effected during your reign against the rights of Holy Church.' And he presented a paper with the formula made out, ready for the king's signature. In that supreme and terrible moment, Victor Emmanuel's fortitude and sense of dignity did not fail him. He replied serenely and resolutely:—'I am a Christian and Catholic, and I die such. If I have done wrong to anyone I repent of it sincerely, and I ask pardon of God. But the signature you ask of me is a political act, and in my quality of constitutional sovereign I cannot execute such an act without the consent of my responsible advisers. Go then into the next room; there you will find the president of the council of ministers; talk to him,—he will answer you.'
>
> The priest went out, and found in the next room

General Menabrea, to whom he related what had passed,—excusing himself for his conduct by saying that he was acting in accordance with orders received from Cardinal Corsi, of Pisa. The general did not hesitate a moment about his reply. The absolution must be given immediately; any further insistance to obtain a retractation would be an act of violence to the conscience of the dying; and he reminded the priest that violence of that sort—especially when exercised towards the sovereign—was punishable by law. The priest had already committed a crime, which if he did not repair, he, the minister, would immediately give orders to the *carabinieri* to arrest him, to the end that justice should be done for the patent offence to the majesty of the sovereign and the laws of the state. The priest submitted to the just and severe rebuke, re-entered the king's room and gave him absolution. Victor Emmanuel had preserved throughout the utmost calmness and *sang froid*; but now he experienced such a lively emotion that it brought on a salutary crisis.

The king himself, however, told General Menabrea that he owed his recovery to a glass of port wine which his valet gave him when all hope was over,—and that immediately on swallowing it he felt life coming back to him. It is not improbable that the sudden revulsion of feeling aided the salutary effect of the wine.

This Cardinal Corsi, by whose command the priest had refused the king absolution, was a most violent and uncompromising *papalino*. When the king went to hear service in the cathedral of Pisa one day, with all his court and a following of citizens which numbered some thousands, he found the great entrance closed against him. Some one proposed forcing the door, and the indignant people only wanted the slightest assent to give expression to their feelings by some overt act against the priestly authority. But the king, seeing a side door open, said smiling, 'Let us pass in here, my friends; it is the narrow way that leads to paradise.'

Very soon after the same thing happened at Bologna. The king, on visiting the Duomo, was received by one or two inferior clergy at a side entrance. Great indignation was expressed by the citizens, so much so that the bishop was somewhat alarmed, and came to apologise to the king, excusing his absence on the plea of illness. The king replied :—'You were quite right not to inconvenience yourself, my lord. I do not go to church to visit priests, but to worship God.'

The year 1869 had opened with the birth of a prince, and towards the close of it another little Sabaud made his *début*. This last, being heir to the throne of Italy, would have made a great noise on his entrance into the world, if his grandfather had not been at that moment hanging between life and death. On November 11 the Princess Margherita gave birth to a son who was christened Vittorio Emanuele, with the title of Prince of Naples, where he was born. This event prevented Prince Umberto from being with his father at the time of his illness, and the crisis was passed before he learned how great the danger had been.

At the end of this year negotiations were opened for a triple alliance between France, Austria, and Italy, but without any result, because the French emperor would not consent to the withdrawal of the troops from Rome, and Victor made that condition a *sine quâ non* for the Italian alliance. This prolonged occupation, in defiance of the wishes of the Romans and the nation at large, as well as those of the king, kept up the bitter memories of the *chassepots* of Mentana, and well-nigh obliterated all feeling of gratitude for the aid Napoleon had given in the liberation of Lombardy.

A new Parliament was convoked in November, and the king, for the first time in his reign, refused to open it in person, making his recent illness the excuse; but the real reason was a deep chagrin at not being able to announce anything definite about the Roman question. Another ministerial crisis followed the opening of the Chambers, and Signor Lanza was called to the head of affairs.

CHAPTER XXX.

FRANCO-PRUSSIAN WAR. A.D. 1870.

'A Roma ci siamo e ci resteremo.'

TOWARDS the end of the year 1869 Pius IX. called the famous Ecumenical Council which was to promulgate the doctrine of his infallibility; and in the beginning of the new year the fathers of the Church came from all parts of the Christian world to the Eternal City. The government resolved to abstain from any interference in ecclesiastical matters and to afford every facility to the bishops to pass through Italian territory on their way to Rome, so long as no offence was given to the civil power. On this occasion Victor Emmanuel appealed to the Liberal bishops who stopped to visit him in Florence, to use their influence for the sake of the country's peace and in the interests of religion, to end the strife between Church and State. They did make an effort to bring about an amicable arrangement, but to no purpose, being in a minority; while the Pope's party, and the Pope himself, were resolute in holding out to the last.

On March 24, 1870, there occurred an incident at Pavia which, so far as we know, has not been related by any Italian writer; and yet, though none of Victor Emmanuel's biographers have thought it of sufficient importance to mention, 'read by the light of subsequent events,' it has a certain significance. Since the attempted assassination of the reigning sovereign, and the consequent agitation for the suppression of disloyal societies, the public has heard a good deal about the *Circoli Barsanti*. What was the origin of the associations, and who was Barsanti? the inquiring foreigner asks; and in reply he hears all sorts of romantic stories—none of them true and most of them absolutely false. It is curious that a public event which happened only eight years ago should be so shrouded in mystery that hardly any Italian can tell the facts of the case. Even Signor Lanza, who was then Minister of the Interior, in lately contradicting a false version in the 'Italie,' himself gave an inaccurate account of the affair. The journals have had every variety of story but the true one. Some said Barsanti was a sergeant, who in a republican riot turned treacherously upon his commanding officer and killed him; others that he was a corporal, and had only drawn upon or slightly wounded his superior, under extenuating circumstances. Others again excited the sympathies of the sentimental by describing Barsanti as a most attractive young hero, who, having somehow mistaken his duty, was cruelly sacrificed by the government of the day, who would not permit the petitioners for royal clemency to approach the king. That Barsanti was twenty years of age, golden-haired, and had a mother, seemed convincing arguments in his favour; and last December one deputy in his place in the Chamber pronounced the execution of this renegade soldier 'an infamy.' It is true he was called to order by the president for the expression; but the fact of a member of Parliament being so ignorant of the merits of the case as such an opinion implies, seems strange to us. It can only be accounted for in this way. The Italians not being yet habituated to the use of a free press, have not brought theirs quite up to the mark; journalists have not a sufficient sense of their responsibilities, and private individuals shrink from telling what they know, because they object to be quoted as authorities. It is the cautious, secretive habit engendered by oppressive governments, now happily passed away.

A writer in the 'Nazione' of Florence, a respectable and trustworthy daily paper, at last undertook to clear up the disputed question; and on December 16 there appeared an article in that journal, entitled 'Who was Pietro Barsanti?' in which the accusation and sentence were reproduced in their entirety, and the testimony cited of the officers and men of Barsanti's regiment. All goes to prove the baselessness of the theory that he was an ill-used hero. According to the 'Nazione' the story of the riot in which he took part is briefly this:—

There was much discontent because of the corn-grinding tax, and the republicans thought it a good opportunity to stir up a rebellion; so they organised an attempt on the two barracks of Pavia, on the night of March 24. Inside of both these barracks there were several accomplices of the conspirators, and one of these perjured soldiers was Corporal Barsanti, a young man who in no way corresponded to the ideal picture drawn by his adherents. He was not blonde, but dark-complexioned, coarse and ordinary in appearance, and so dull of intellect that he was incapable of passing the examination to become a sergeant. On the night of the attack he kept two sergeants locked in a room to prevent them lending assistance in repulsing the attempt, menacing with a revolver a soldier who wished to release them, and endeavouring in every way to seduce his companions from their duty. He did not, however, kill or wound anyone. The young officer Vegezzi was in command of a detachment in the other barrack when he was wounded by a shot from a traitor soldier.

They were all tried by court-martial, and Barsanti was shot like the rest; a petition, got up chiefly by ladies, on the ground of his youth, being firmly repulsed by the ministry. The republicans immediately elected him as a 'martyr of the idea,' and endowed him with all the requisite qualities for a hero—the golden hair included. We confess it is not quite clear to us why a blonde traitor should be dealt with more leniently than a brown one. But as the *bella testa bionda* has been insisted on by Barsanti's admirers, so the iconoclastic writer above quoted sweeps away this myth with the other fictitious attractions of the republican martyr. This was the origin of the *Circoli Barsanti* to which belonged the assassin Passanante.

The Emperor Napoleon had sacrificed the Italian alliance by persisting in holding his army in the Roman State. He declared war against Prussia without consulting or acquainting Victor Emmanuel with his intentions; the news reached the king when he was chamois-hunting in the Alps, and hot upon it came the tidings of French disasters. It then becoming a matter of necessity to France to call all her available forces into the field, the army was withdrawn from Rome and the Pope left to his own devices. At the same time an appeal was made to the Italian Government for help.

It was Victor Emmanuel's generous impulse to aid France, in spite of the coldness that had arisen on the Roman question. France had once befriended Italy, and now she was in distress; that was enough to establish a claim upon his sympathy. But he found his government utterly averse to any interference in the quarrel. Italy had suffered enough from war; her financial affairs were not in a satisfactory condition, nor was she in any way bound to aid France, seeing that France had not thought it necessary to take counsel with her on the subject. The king argued the matter vigorously in the council, listened to the objections and combated them with perseverance but good temper, trying hard to win over his advisers to his opinion. But they stood firm, and of course he had to yield. He is reported to have said to the French ambassador—'I am ready to go to the aid of the emperor, but I do not expect to return here as King of Italy.' His ministers, however, convinced him that such quixotic friendship, though permissible in private life, did not become a sovereign who had the destinies of a nation depending on him, and he remembered that his first duty was to his country; being pledged to Italy, he had no right to throw himself away. The surrender of Sedan was a great shock to him.

When the news of the revolution in Paris arrived, Victor Emmanuel naturally thought of his daughter, and sent in haste an escort to conduct her home. But the Princess Clotilde refused to leave her adopted country in its hour of trial. She wrote a letter to her father to thank him for his anxiety about her, and saying that it was impossible for her to abandon Paris at such a moment. She owed it to her husband, her children, her adopted country, her native country, to remain at her post, no matter what might happen. Her brothers or her sister would do the same in the same position, and she knew her father would approve of her resolution. Victor Emmanuel read this letter to his councillors with a proud and flashing eye. He let Clotilde have her way, thinking she was the best judge of what was right under the circumstances.

The Romans had been very much excited from the time the war broke out; and when it became known that the emperor had surrendered himself and his army, and that there was a likelihood of a speedy settlement of the quarrel, they believed they would be abandoned once more to their fate, and got into a state of convulsive agitation. They sent one more thrilling appeal to Victor Emmanuel to come and take them before the favourable moment should have passed. Had he been deaf to this last petition it is probable that the despair of the Romans would have led to consequences still more serious than Mentana. But he was at last permitted to listen to the *grido di dolore* that came from the Eternal City. The decisive moment had arrived. As soon as the resolution was taken, an envoy was despatched to Paris to acquaint the provisional government with the intentions of the king. They replied in effect, 'You may do it because we have no longer the power to hinder you.' The truth is that republican France, strange and inconsistent as it seems, was more opposed to Italian unity than the emperor.

Just at the moment when preparations were being made to go to Rome, the Minister of War, General Govone, retired from office, being attacked by a fatal illness which soon after carried him off. He left behind him a grateful memory of the most devoted and single-minded patriotism, united with the charming qualities which are comprised in the Italian word *simpatico*.

While General Cadorna was preparing to conduct the Italian troops over the papal frontier, Victor Emmanuel, whose heart still yearned for a reconciliation with Pio Nono, addressed a private and confidential letter to him, in which he explained his sentiments, and entreated the holy father, for the sake of that Italy which he once loved, to make peace before it was too late. Nothing could be further from his desire than to embitter his old age; he was ready to abdicate if that would spare him pain, but his successor would be constrained to act as he was doing; the national aspirations must be satisfied.

It is said that the Pope was moved by this letter; but if so the impression was transitory—as was that which the words of the Conte di San Martino had produced on him at Gaeta. The same Conte di San Martino was now the bearer of an official letter from the King of Italy to the holy father.

Victor Emmanuel to Pius IX.

Most Blessed Father,—With the affection of a son, with the faith of a Catholic, with the soul of an Italian, I address myself now, as on former occasions, to the heart of your holiness.

A flood of dangers threatens Europe. Profiting by the war which desolates the centre of the Continent, the cosmopolitan revolutionary party increases in boldness and audacity, and is planning, especially in that part of Italy ruled by your holiness, the direst offences against the monarchy and the papacy.

I know that the greatness of your soul will not be less than the greatness of events; but I, being a Catholic king and Italian, and, as such, guardian by the disposition of Providence and the national will of the destinies of all the Italians, I feel it my duty to take, in the face of Europe and Catholicity, the responsibility of maintaining order in the peninsula and the safety of the Holy See.

At the present moment, Holy Father, the state of mind of the Roman populations, and the presence among them of foreign troops come from different countries with divers intentions, foments the agitation and the danger. A boiling over of the passions may lead to the effusion of blood, and this blood is mine.

Your duty is to avoid and prevent this; and I see the immediate necessity for the safety of Italy and the Holy See that my troops, now placed near the frontier, shall occupy certain positions for the security of your holiness and the maintenance of order. Your holiness will not see in this precaution an act of hostility. My government and my forces will restrain themselves absolutely within the conservative limits of maintaining and guarding the rights of the Roman people, easily reconciled with the inviolability of the Supreme Pontiff, his spiritual authority, and the independence of the Holy See.

If your holiness, which I do not doubt—as your sacred character and the benignity of your soul gives me the right to hope—feels the same desire as I do to avoid a conflict and fly the dangers of violence, you can with the Count San Martino, who bears this letter, take counsel concerning the matter now under the consideration of government.

Permit me, your holiness, again to say that the present moment is a solemn one for Italy and the Church. Let the popehood add efficacy to the spirit of inextinguishable benevolence in your soul towards this land, which is also *your* country, and the sentiments of conciliation which I have always studied to translate into acts, that, satisfying the national aspirations, the Head of Catholicity, surrounded by the devotion of the Italian people, should preserve on the banks of the Tiber a glorious seat, independent of every human sovereignty.

Your holiness, by liberating Rome from foreign troops, will take from her the constant danger of being the battle-ground of subversive parties. You will accomplish a marvellous work, restore peace to the Church, and show Europe, aghast at the horrors of war, how one can win great battles and obtain immortal victories by an act of justice—by one sole word of affection.

I pray your holiness to impart to me your Apostolic benediction, and to accept my sentiments of profound respect.

Your holiness's most humble, most obedient, and devoted

VICTOR EMMANUEL.

Florence, Sept. 8, 1870.

Pio Nono received San Martino courteously, and discussed the situation calmly with him. He listened to his assurances that his supreme spiritual authority, his income, his palaces and villas, should be all guaranteed to him by stringent laws. There was nothing his majesty's government would not do to please his holiness—short of abstaining from entering Rome, which could no longer be delayed without risking the existence of the nation.

'Signor conte,' said the Pope, 'I am not a prophet nor the son of a prophet; but I dare to foretell that the Italian troops shall not enter Rome.'

The count lowered his eyes that the Pope should not see him smile at this extraordinary faith, and replied that neither was he a prophet, nor did he pretend to have any relationship with prophets, but he boldly ventured to assert that the Italian army should enter Rome before long. He then consigned the king's letter to him. When he had read it, he turned wrathfully on the envoy. 'What is the use of this hypocrisy?' he exclaimed. 'Cannot he say at once that he wishes to despoil me of my kingdom?'

San Martino replied that if he had had the composition of that letter he would have used less circumlocution, and said plainly and shortly that Italy, recognising the state of Rome as indispensable to her national being, claimed it as a right.

This frankness made Pio Nono smile, for his humour was variable as a woman's. He said, 'You talk of the aspirations of the Romans: you see with your own eyes that the city is quite tranquil.'

'Your holiness,' replied the outspoken count, 'I may

claim some credit for this tranquillity. The citizens wished to make me a demonstration on my arrival, but I prevented it.'

Pius IX. to Victor Emmanuel.

Your Majesty,—The Count Ponza di San Martino has consigned to me a letter which your majesty has been pleased to address to me; but it is not worthy of an affectionate son who boasts himself a professor of the Catholic faith, and who glories in a kingly loyalty. I will not enter into the particulars of that letter, not to renew the pain the first reading occasioned me. But I bless God, who has suffered, your majesty to fill with bitterness the last period of life.

For the rest, I cannot admit the demands of your letter, nor accept the principles contained therein. I address myself to God, and place my cause in His hands, for it is entirely His. I pray Him to concede abundant grace to your majesty, deliver you from every peril, and render you a participator in all the mercies of which you may have need.

PIUS PP. IX.

From the Vatican, Sept. 11, 1870.

The day this letter was written General Cadorna had orders to march. He was received with ovations in all the small towns of the Roman State, and took up his quarters outside the capital in the Villa Spada. Here the Prussian ambassador, Count Arnim, visited him to beg that he would suspend hostilities till the diplomatic body should try mediation with the Pope. Next day he informed the general by letter that the attempt had been fruitless. The Pope was resolved to make a feint of defending the city, to show the world that it had been taken by violence. Early in the morning the attack was begun at the Leonine Gate, and at ten o'clock the Pia Gate gave way before the artillery. A breach was opened in the wall, and the infantry threw themselves into it, while the defenders poured grapeshot from the bastions. It was not much of a fight, but some killed and wounded there were, and, seeing how utterly futile the resistance was, the foreign ambassadors thought it a pity that one life should be lost, and entreated the Pope to send out a flag of truce. He did not yield at first; not till he heard the invaders were inside the walls. When the white flag was hoisted on St. Peter's the diplomatic body drove in haste to ask General Cadorna to put a stop to the conflict. All the male inhabitants of the city were in the streets; they now rushed to the Capitol, where the royal troops were disarming the last papal Zouaves. The great bell rang out while the tricolour was hoisted on the palace, and the multitude broke into rapturous applause. They could hardly yet believe that the temporal power was fallen. No more foreign legions, no more spies, no more Holy Offices! Castel Sant' Angelo and San Michele opened to let out the political prisoners! All this effected in five hours, after so many years of heartburning and bitterness, and fruitless conspiracies! It seemed a dream, so easily was Rome lost and won at the last. But September 20, 1870, marks a great epoch in the history of the world.

The Pope bore this last blow, as all the preceding ones, with wonderful fortitude. He was a brave old man, and, strong in the faith that his cause was just, he never yielded an inch. 'I cede only to force,' he had said in 1848; and now, at eighty years of age, he presented the same resolute front to all persuasions and remonstrances.

The vote of the Romans was taken as follows:—

For the King	40,785
For the Pope	46

This vote was enough to satisfy Victor Emmanuel's highest expectations. The dream of his life was accomplished, and in a manner most flattering to a monarch's pride. Yet this rose was not without its thorn either. To be all sweetness he should have had Pio Nono's blessing, and be crowned, like Charlemagne, by the hands of the venerable Pontiff in that city of glorious memories where he was henceforth to reign. But he grasped the rose, thorn and all, with the memorable exclamation, 'A Roma ci siamo e ci resteremo!'

CHAPTER XXXI.

M. THIERS' APPEAL TO THE KING.—AMEDEO ACCEPTS THE CROWN OF SPAIN.—LAST PARLIAMENT IN FLORENCE. A.D. 1870.

THE provisional government of Paris had sent an ambassador to Florence, M. Sénard, to whom the king had shown such deep feeling for the misfortunes of France that M. Thiers was encouraged to make a journey to Italy to appeal to the king for help for his unhappy country. He had never been friendly to the House of Savoy, and had always opposed Italian unity; so he felt the mission a trying and painful one. It is needless to say that Victor Emmanuel was not influenced by what the Frenchman had said about him when he met his appeal by a negative. He received him kindly, and explained that the reasons of state which prevented him aiding the emperor must prevent him aiding the Republic. 'You have been a constitutional minister,' said the king, 'and you know what are the duties of a constitutional monarch.' And he defined those duties with such precision and discernment that Thiers was much struck by his cleverness. He related to a friend what passed in the interview.

> The king [he said] avoided disagreeable allusions, but he let me know delicately, that he had not forgotten what I had said of him in the tribune. He discussed politics with the most elevated views, and as a man who understands the profession. I thought I should have to do with a soldier, but I found an accomplished statesman.

Spain, still in an unsettled state, with a provisional government, once more thought of applying to Italy for a king. Victor Emmanuel considered the task of rescuing Spain from anarchy, and putting her on the road of civilisation and progress, would be one worthy of a prince of Savoy. He had thought of his nephew, the Duke of Genoa, but his extreme youth was an objection, and he finally decided on sending Amedeo. Some Italian statesmen opposed the idea, urging that the prince would be uselessly sacrificed, that Spain was so hopelessly divided and torn by factions, there were so many pretenders to the throne, that the dangers and difficulties would be insurmountable. But the king replied that he knew one of his family would only yield to impossibilities, and he would like to make the trial. Amedeo shrank from the undertaking with a repugnance which seemed prophetic of disaster, and it took all Victor Emmanuel's influence to persuade his son to accept the proffered crown.

As soon as it was known in Spain that he had consented, a deputation from the Cortes, headed by the president, Señor Zorilla, came to Florence to make a formal offer of the throne of Spain, in the name of the nation. The deputation was received in state, in the presence of all the court, the ministers, and foreign ambassadors. In a very complimentary address the king's consent was asked to his son's acceptance of the office.

Victor Emmanuel's Reply to the Cortes.

By this your request, gentlemen, you do honour to my dynasty and to Italy, and you ask a sacrifice of my heart. I accord to my beloved son my consent to accept the glorious throne to which the wish of the Spanish nation calls him. I trust that, with the aid of Divine Providence and the confidence of your noble nation, he shall be able to accomplish his mission for the prosperity and the greatness of Spain.

The president then turned to the prince, who in a

voice tremulous with emotion signified his acceptance of the honour. He had not yet learned the truth of the poet's words—

> Uneasy lies the head that wears a crown,

but his good sense must have told him that a king with a conscience has a hard road to travel, particularly in a country degraded by ages of misrule and distracted by recent revolutions. He was not dazzled by the prospect; but in obedience to his father's wishes he resolved to make the trial of restoring order to Spain and establishing a settled government.

Though Victor Emmanuel's ambition was gratified by this arrangement, he felt that he was in a manner sacrificing his son. In a private interview with Zorilla he revealed his paternal feelings, and talked in such a way about Amedeo that the Spaniard came out from the audience in tears, and said to the Italian minister, whom he met at the door—'The king has confided his son to me; I will be a faithful subject.' In the last days of the year 1870 the young King of Spain sailed from Spezia, amidst the mingled joy and grief, smiles and tears, of his countrymen.

The last Parliament held in Florence was opened December 5.

The King's Speech.

Gentlemen Senators,—Gentlemen Deputies,—The year that now closes has astonished the world by the greatness of the events which have come to pass and which no human judgment could have foretold. Our opinion about Rome we have always loudly proclaimed. And in face of the late resolution to which my love of country has conducted me, I have thought it my duty to convoke the national assembly.

With Rome the capital of Italy I have fulfilled my promise, and crowned the undertaking which twenty-three years ago was initiated by my magnanimous parent. As a king and as a son, I feel in my heart a solemn joy in saluting here assembled the representatives of our beloved country, and in pronouncing these words—Italy is free and one. Now it depends on us to make her great and happy.

Whilst we celebrate this solemn inauguration of Italy complete, two great peoples of this Continent, glorious representatives of modern civilisation, are torn by a terrible struggle. Bound both to France and to Prussia by memories of recent and beneficial alliances, we are obliged to observe a rigorous neutrality, which is also imposed upon us by the duty of not increasing the strife, and that we may be able to interpose an impartial word between the belligerents. This duty, dictated by humanity and friendship, we will not fail to fulfil, adding our efforts to those of the other neutral powers to put an end to a war which ought never to have broken out between two nations whose greatness is equally necessary to the civilised world.

Public opinion, approving by its support this policy, has shown once more that Italy free and united is for Europe an element of order, of liberty, and of peace.

This attitude facilitated our task, when, for the defence of the national territory, and to restore to the Romans the arbitrament of their own destinies, my soldiers, expected as brothers, welcomed as liberators, entered Rome. Rome, reclaimed by the love and by the veneration of the Italians, was thus restored to herself, to Italy, and to the modern world. We entered Rome in the name of the national right, in the name of the compact' which binds all Italians to national unity. We shall hold to this, maintaining the promises that we have solemnly made to ourselves.

Liberty of the Church, of the Pontifical See in the exercise of its religious ministry, in its relations with the Catholic world—on these bases, and within the limit of its powers, my government has initiated the necessary provisions; but to conduct the great work to an end there is required all the authority, all the sense of Parliament.

A few days after the opening of Parliament a fearful inundation of the Tiber immersed a considerable part of Rome, reducing hundreds of families to the direst distress. Victor Emmanuel went to the aid of the sufferers, and the first sight the Romans had of their new king was in the character of a private philanthropist, assisting at relief committees, and alleviating the distress of the poor by every means in his power. With regard to the Pope, it was the least offensive mode of entering the capital that he could have chosen. As soon as he arrived he sent an aide-de-camp with a letter to Pius IX., acquainting him of his presence and repeating his expressions of reverence and affection. Cardinal Antonelli received the messenger, and would not admit him to the Pope's presence.

Meantime the Guarantee Laws were discussed and passed, and arrangements were made for the transfer of the capital to the Eternal City. The king, during a residence of six years, had grown very fond of the beautiful city of Florence, and he left it with regret, but nothing like what he suffered when tearing himself away from Turin. Florence behaved admirably on the occasion. The great expense the city had been at to worthily maintain the position of capital of United Italy made the loss of the court very much felt, and this added to other causes has reduced her to great poverty these late years. Nevertheless she rejoiced at the taking of Rome, and applauded enthusiastically the melancholy king as he said farewell to the city representatives at the railway station. 'You rejoice to send me away,' he said with a sad smile. It excites the more sympathy for the present suffering of that most interesting city, that her patriotism and loyalty have undergone no change, as recent events have shown. In the beautiful and touching address which her citizens presented to king Umberto on December 8, 1878, in that exquisite *lingua Toscana* that it is a pity to translate, they say—'Florence was crowned with joy when the great Father of his Country installed his palace in this fostering mother, Rome. Florence experienced a loss then, but she rejoiced always, because her misfortunes were a glory for Italy.' And they conclude with the declaration that 'as long as there is an arm able to carry a sword, or a drop of blood in the veins of her people, Florence will be always faithful to her plébiscite.'

CHAPTER XXXII.

ITALIAN UNITY FINALLY ACCOMPLISHED. A.D. 1871–76.

VICTOR EMMANUEL delayed his entry into Rome for nearly nine months after his troops had taken possession of it. When he left Florence he went to Naples for a time, and did not seem in any hurry to install himself in the city he had desired so intensely to unite to his kingdom. But he had got to make a public entry; he could not sneak into his capital like a thief who had no right to come there; so on June 2 he made his ingress in state, with immense demonstrations of enthusiasm. Soon after he went to the opening of the Mont Cenis Railway, and then had the happiness of being fêted by his own Turin with more than ordinary warmth.

This summer the Pope was celebrating the twenty-fifth year of his reign, the longest recorded in the history of the Papacy, and all the sovereigns sent their congratulations. Victor would not be behind the rest, and sent a general in state to the Vatican. He was received as before by Cardinal Antonelli, who said the holy father was exhausted and could not receive any more that day, but he desired him to thank his majesty.

On November 27 the first Parliament which represented Italy in her entirety was opened in the Palazzo Monte Citorio in Rome, more than a year after the entrance of the national army. The senators and deputies assembled in the midst of a joyous agitation, and Victor Emmanuel took his seat on the throne with a feeling of proud satisfaction. The first words that fell from the royal lips, 'The work to which we have consecrated our life is accomplished,' awoke such a response from the hearers as shook the house. The cheers in Parliament were heard and re-echoed in the piazza and along the streets.

On the same day a deputation of the clerical party prostrated themselves at the feet of the Pope with expressions of adoration which might have become a deity to accept, and in equally unmeasured language reprobated the Spoliator, who was just then congratulating himself and his hearers that the great crime of his life was consummated.

The King's Speech.

Gentlemen Senators,—Gentlemen Deputies,—The work to which we consecrated our lives is accomplished. After long expiatory trials, Italy is restored to herself and to Rome. Here, where our people, scattered for so many centuries, find themselves for the first time reassembled in the majesty of their representatives, here, where we recognise the home of our thoughts, everything speaks to us of grandeur, but at the same time everything reminds us of our duties. The joy of these days will not make us forget them. We have reconquered our position in the world, defending the rights of the nation. Now that the national unity is accomplished and a new era is opened in the history of Italy, we will not fall away from our principles. We have arisen in the name of liberty, and in liberty and order we ought to seek the secret of strength and conciliation.

We have proclaimed the separation of Church and State, and recognising the full independence of the Spiritual Authority, we ought to believe that Rome, capital of Italy, can continue to be the peaceful and respected seat of the pontificate. Thus shall we succeed in tranquillising the consciences of our people, as with a firmness of purpose equalled by the moderation of our measures, we have known how to accomplish the unity of the nation while maintaining unaltered our friendly relations with foreign powers. The legislative measures that will be presented to you for regulating the condition of ecclesiastical affairs, forming themselves on that same principle of liberty, will only relate to the legal representation, and the nature of possessions, leaving intact those religious institutions that form a part of the government of the Universal Church. Besides this grave question, economical and financial matters principally require your attention. Now that Italy is constructed, we ought to think of making her prosperous by the settlement of her finances, and this we cannot fail to do unless the virtue and perseverance which have given life to the nation should become less. Prosperous finances will give us the means of reinforcing the military ranks. My most earnest prayers are for peace, and there is no reason to fear its being disturbed; but to reinforce the army and navy, and to renew the arms and defensive works of the national territory, requires long and mature study, and the future may call us to a severe account for any imprudent delay. You will examine the provisions for that object which will be presented to you by my government. There will not fail to be other questions of grave moment, such as that relating to the government of the municipalities and of the provinces, the decentralising of the administration in such measure as not to diminish the strength of the state; those for making a single penal code, for the reformation of juries, and for increasing uniformity and efficacy in the administration of justice. In this way we will provide for public security, without which even the benefits of liberty are dangerous.

Gentlemen Senators,—Gentlemen Deputies,—A vast field of labour lies before you. The national unity accomplished, the struggle of parties will be, I hope, less violent, or they will rival each other only in exciting the development of the productive forces of the nation, and my heart rejoices to perceive already many indications of the increasing industry of our populations.

On the political revival follows closely the revival of economy; savings-banks, commercial associations, industry, and art exhibitions, public literary meetings, all multiply. The government and parliament should second this fruitful movement by enlarging and strengthening professional and scientific instruction, and by opening up new roads of communication and new outlets for commerce. The marvellous work of the Monte Cenis tunnel is accomplished, and that of St. Gothard is about to be undertaken: the world's road that traverses Italy to Brindisi, and thus unites Europe with India, will have three openings in the Alps for railroad travelling. Celerity of travelling and facility of intercourse will increase the friendly relations that already bind us to the transalpine peoples, and will revive a noble rivalry in industry and civilisation. The future opens before us rich in happy promise; it is for us to respond to the favours of Providence, by showing ourselves worthy to represent amongst the great nations of the earth the glorious part of Italy and of Rome.

On New Year's day, 1872, Victor Emmanuel sent an envoy with the compliments of the season to the Pope. He was treated in the same manner as before; the holy father did not receive him, but returned the compliments through his minister.

The chief source of anxiety the king had at this time was the unsatisfactory state in which Spain continued. The young king had set himself energetically to his arduous task in a straightforward and soldierlike manner. Like his father, he disliked court pomp and pageantry, and lived almost as plainly as a private gentleman. When he was conducted over the magnificent apartments of the palace, and heard that he, the queen, and the little prince were all expected to have separate households, he said simply, 'I live with my family;' which must have shocked the nerves of the Spanish courtiers not a little. The young king and queen went their own way—he given up to state affairs, she to charitable works, and improving the condition of the poor of Madrid—examples of devotion to duty and domestic virtues to which their subjects were unaccustomed, and which they did not know how to appreciate.

The war of parties went on raging throughout the country. There were the moderate Liberals who had put Amedeo on the throne; the Reactionists or friends of the fallen dynasty, to which belonged the clergy and many of the old nobility; the Carlists, the Republicans, and still another important section of society which the existence of all these generated—the brigands.

General Prim had already fallen a victim to the vengeance of some of these malcontents, and now an attempt was made upon the life of the sovereign while he was driving through the streets of Madrid with his wife. It was midsummer, and Victor Emmanuel was in the mountains of Savoy when he received the announcement.

To the King of Italy.

I advise your majesty that this evening we have been the object of an attempt. Thank God, we are quite safe.

AMEDEO.

Madrid, July 18.

When the king had recovered from the agitation into which the first shock threw him, he experienced a feeling of intense anger against the perpetrator of the crime. He hastened to the nearest telegraph office to let off the steam in a communication to his son.

After three inquiet and unhappy years of sovereign power, Amedeo resolved to abdicate, February 1873, because he would not betray the constitution to which he had sworn, nor shed blood for the establishment of his dynasty. It was pleasant to see the welcome the fallen king got on his return to Italy. The Turin people received him with rapture. He went to Florence to meet his father, and arranged to arrive in the dead of the night, so as to avoid a demonstration. But the Florentines were too clever for him. They waited all night in bitter winter weather at the station, and escorted him with a torchlight procession and bands of music to the Pitti Palace with the warmest display of affection. From a house opposite the palace we were witness of this hearty and spontaneous demonstration of the generous Florentines, which, under the circumstances, had something touching in it. Victor Emmanuel was grieved and disappointed, but he did not estimate his son's merit by his success; Amedeo had failed because, like himself, he would not be other than a *Rè galantuomo*, and he received him with open arms.

The Emperor Napoleon died on January 9 of this year, and Victor Emmanuel was really grieved at the event, for he had never forgotten the campaign of 1859, and the kindly feeling it had engendered survived all subsequent trials. In May Manzoni died at an advanced age. Milan decreed him a public funeral, and the king sent his sons and cousin to assist at the ceremony. In June another public loss followed in the death of Rattazzi; though not a brilliant statesman, the king mourned for him as a zealous servant of the crown and an attached personal friend.

Hosts of distinguished visitors came to Rome these first years of Victor Emmanuel's residence there; there was hardly a country in Europe which had not sent a royal prince to salute the King of Italy in his new capital. Amongst these were three English princes, a prince of Prussia, and an Austrian archduke. Nothing could be kinder than the feeling that now existed between the Houses of Hapsburg and Savoy, and the King of Italy accepted a very pressing invitation to visit Vienna on the occasion of the Exhibition. Accompanied by his ministers, Minghetti and Visconti Venosta, and a large following, he arrived in Vienna on September 17, 1873.

Victor Emmanuel had so completely sunk all personal considerations in the patriot king, that no one suspected, during the years of division with Austria, that this hostility cost him any sacrifice of feeling—at least after the death of his wife. But the intense pleasure he showed at the recovered friendship revealed the fact that the relationship of his adversaries had added to the bitterness of the struggle.

As the train approached the station a flood of painful memories rushed across his mind; it seemed almost a dream that he was the honoured guest of Francis Joseph, against whom he had been waging war ever since he came to the throne. In a few minutes he would be face to face with this strange brother whom he had never met; and an extraordinary agitation seized him, which sent the blood from his face to his heart. The Emperor and the King embraced with an emotion which attested the sincerity of their feelings. When Francis Joseph presented his brothers, even in that moment of confusion a gentlemanly instinct made Victor Emmanuel single out for special notice the Archduke Albert, who had distinguished himself on the two fields of Novara and Custoza—pregnant with painful memories to every Italian, but especially to the king. He walked up to him, and taking both his hands, shook them repeatedly. The emotion which Victor Emmanuel experienced in this reconciliation was brought to a climax when, in the salon of the Archduke Ranieri, he saw the portrait of his late queen, taken when she was a girl. Thinking how happy she would have been in this reunion with her long-divided relations, he could not restrain his tears.

Victor Emmanuel was painfully anxious to avoid any unpleasant allusion to past differences. He had removed from his travelling hat a representation of the Iron Crown of Lombardy; and when he was told that in proposing the Emperor's health he should also call him *King of Hungary*, he objected, saying that it recalled disagreeable memories, and he would not remind the emperor of them. But he was finally convinced that Francis Joseph was proud of the double title, and he gave the toast as etiquette demanded. In bestowing decorations he did not offer the *Corona d' Italia* to any Austrian unless he had some secret intimation that it was specially desired.

After four days of the most profuse and graceful hospitality on the part of the emperor, Victor Emmanuel set out for Berlin, where his reception by sovereign and people was cordial in the extreme. Nothing could exceed the Emperor Francis Joseph's kindness, but the welcome the Prussians gave *il Rè Galantuomo* was even more thorough and hearty than that of the Austrians. The Emperor William said he had never seen his subjects so excited by the presence of a foreign sovereign. Victor also won the hearts of all the royal princes and princesses by his frank simplicity of manners, his humour and *bonhomie*; and the crown prince and he became greater friends than ever. While he was at Berlin a characteristic incident occurred. At a court dinner Victor Emmanuel was seated at the emperor's right hand, and many distinguished guests, Italians and Prussians, were present, when he suddenly said, 'You know I would have made war on you only for these gentlemen,' pointing to his ministers, who listened in confused silence to this declaration. He then explained frankly that such had been his personal regard for Napoleon, and his grateful remembrance of past services, that he would certainly have gone to his aid had not his duty as constitutional sovereign compelled him to bow to the will of the government and nation. But now that the quarrel was ended he was proud to be the sincere friend of united Germany and her glorious emperor. The old emperor was charmed with this candour. He took Victor's hand and pressed it, saying, 'I thank your majesty for your frankness.'

On Victor Emmanuel's return to his own country he stopped in Turin to inaugurate a monument to Cavour on November 8, and on the 13th of the same month he opened the Parliament, in a long speech, chiefly on the relations of Church and State, which continued to occupy the attention of the government.

> I rejoice to tell you (he said), that our relations with the foreign powers are friendly. These good relations received a solemn confirmation on the occasion of the visit that I have just made to the Emperor of Austria and the Emperor of Germany. The demonstrations of cordial sympathy that I have received from those two sovereigns and from their peoples were meant for regenerated Italy, which has known how to take her place among civilised nations. Austria and Italy have been old adversaries on the field of battle. The cause of their long contest removed, there remains only confidence in their common interests and in the advantages of sincere friendship. This friendship is all the more grateful to me because it is associated with those family affections which a higher and more imperious duty has been able to dominate, but could not extinguish in my heart.

These words had been put in at the king's express desire. France, as usual, pretending a devotion to the Church, took umbrage at the proceedings of the Italian government, and recalled her representative. Victor Emmanuel, who liked the ambassador, spoke very frankly to him when he came to take his leave. 'It is a great pity,' he said, 'to use religious scruples as a pretext for political objects. Religion is a grand, a sublime thing; we all feel the need of it, and it is the duty of us all not to compromise it—not to use it as a cloak.' A just rebuke.

The year 1874 was the twenty-fifth of Victor Emmanuel's reign, and it was celebrated as a great national fête. On the morning of March 23, an immense assemblage thronged to the Quirinal, consisting of deputations representing all classes and bodies of the state, who wished to present loyal addresses to the king. The foreign ambassadors also came in the name of their sovereigns to offer their congratulations. It was a very warm demonstration, and Victor Emmanuel was much gratified by it. He exhausted himself in suitable replies to the addresses, but they are too numerous to quote.

About this time the French Government removed the old ship of war *Orénoque*, which had remained at Civitavecchia as a *protection* to the holy father, or a means of escape in case of danger.

In this year several eminent Italians died; amongst them the Marchese Gualterio, one of the most devoted friends of the House of Savoy, and the Cavaliere Desambrois, who had presided in the councils of Charles Albert at the promulgation of the *Statuto*. The 'makers' of Italy were fast disappearing, and Victor Emmanuel was left almost the only one of the noble band who had rallied round his throne in the time of trial and danger. He felt it deeply. 'I am not yet old, and all the friends of my youth are passing away,' he said sadly. La Marmora and the king had become estranged in the days of prosperity and peace, having clung to each other faithfully in the time of misfortune. We do not pretend to say whose fault it was, but it must have saddened the last few years of these two gallant warm-hearted soldiers, who had made the campaign of life together, to be divided at the end.

In 1876 the two emperors returned the visit the King of Italy had made them three years before. In consideration for the Pope's feelings Victor Emmanuel could not receive his visitors in Rome, so they were asked to select whatever other city in the kingdom they liked. The Emperor of Austria, with 'exquisite courtesy,' chose Venice as the spot of Italian soil on which to renew his pledge of friendship to Victor Emmanuel. If he went to Rome the Pope would be offended, if to Florence or Naples he would hurt the feelings of his dispossessed relations. Choosing Venice he hurt nobody but himself. Victor Emmanuel was quite touched by this magnanimity, because he knew Francis Joseph had selected Venice of a set purpose. There was Turin in which the king could have received his guest without awakening any unpleasant recollections. 'It is an act of self-abnegation,' he said, 'of which I do not believe I should be capable.'

All the more warm was the welcome he wished to give him in the city of the Lagunes. He felt a little uneasy lest the reception of the emperor by the Venetians should not be all he wished, but there was no need of anxiety on this point. The king walked up and down the platform with feverish impatience, looking up the line every few minutes. When the train stopped, and the emperor sprang out, the first face that presented itself was that of his 'dear friend, ally, and brother.' The sovereigns kissed each other on the lips, and walked arm in arm out of the station. Wherever they appeared they seemed anxious to show the people what sincere confiding friends old enemies can become when once reconciled. And the Venetians left nothing undone on their part that might please and honour the guest of their king. The city authorities spared no expense, and the people received the emperor, who had been to them the personification of the *Straniero* so long hated, with loud and hearty applause. Did the Kaiser remember all the hard names he was called in those days when the king and he exchanged messages of fierce defiance? If so, the memory was quickly drowned in the uproarious rejoicings with which he was now welcomed as a guest in that city over which he once ruled. The Italian tricolour which floated from the towers and windows was intertwined with the yellow and black of Austria; the bands played the national tunes of both countries, and various emblematical devices expressed a complete wiping out of the old feud, and cordial reconciliation.

In the October of the same year the Emperor William came to visit Italy, and stopped in Milan. With him there were no awkward reminiscences to be thrust in the background. Milan was devoted to King Victor, and was proud of the opportunity of displaying her loyalty by doing honour to his illustrious guest; and the king was proud of 'his Milanese, who always did things with spirit.' When driving from the station he ordered the soldiers not to impede the crowd from approaching the royal carriage, that the emperor and the people might see each other; and at a review where they were on horseback, the military gave way and allowed the multitude to surround the sovereigns, whom they greeted with enthusiastic cheers, which were very cordially responded to by both.

On November 8, 1876, after a lingering illness of three years, died, at San Remo, Vittoria, Duchess of Aosta, to the inexpressible grief of her husband and the deep regret of all the royal family.

There had been a general election, and the new Parliament opened on the 20th, the court being in deep mourning on the occasion, and the king delivered his last speech from the throne, from which we take the opening paragraph :—

Gentlemen Senators,—Gentlemen Deputies,—Afflicted by a domestic sorrow, in which I see with gratitude my people warmly share, I come to-day to seek the best consolation in the fulfilment of my duty. And in truth I never have to inaugurate this solemnity without feeling increase in my heart faith in the destinies of Italy, and in the future of the free institutions to which we are sworn.

The speech, which is very long, concludes with these words :—

For six years we have celebrated in Rome the fête of national unity. Our complete unity has borne fruits of glory and proofs of wisdom. Much has been done, but much remains to do. There remains the work which requires the greatest patience in labour and the greatest harmony of will, that of consolidating, and, where necessary, correcting, the whole edifice of government. In this we can only succeed by emulating one another in laboriousness and steadiness of purpose. I indicate the way to you, and I feel sure that also in these battles for our civil regeneration, my voice will find a response in noble sacrifices and glorious victories.

This was the last time that the voice of *il Rè Galantuomo* was heard to resound in the Legislative Assembly.

CHAPTER XXXIII.

VICTOR EMMANUEL IN PRIVATE LIFE. A.D. 1877.

VICTOR EMMANUEL had always been a man of the simplest tastes and habits, and his residence in Rome had in no way changed his mode of life. He rose at a little past four o'clock summer and winter, and took a small cup of coffee before going out for his morning walk. In the shooting season he never went without his gun and dogs; his favourite of the canine species being an English terrier called 'Milord,' a creature of extraordinary sagacity and devotion, and as a protection to his master as good as a regiment of soldiers. When the king died the poor dog, tied up in his house, sent forth the most pitiful cries, and refusing his food almost perished of hunger. On returning from the country the king transacted business of various kinds until his simple breakfast between eleven and twelve o'clock, which was also his dinner, for he tasted nothing more till he took a light supper at a late hour. He then rested for an hour or two, reading and smoking, and afterwards resumed his multifarious duties, of answering correspondence public and private, and giving audiences to all sorts and conditions of men, from foreign princes and statesmen down to the meanest artisan in the city. In the afternoon he generally drove through the town and appeared at the fashionable promenade on the Pincian Hill; after which more business was gone through, and late in the evening he drove to the Villa Mirafiore, a beautiful house a short distance from Rome, which he had built for his countess, on whom he bestowed every luxury. It is said that Victor Emmanuel repented of his union with this lady when he recovered from the fever. Be this as it may, after the ceremony of marriage had taken place, though it was in no way legally binding, he always spoke of her and regarded her as his wife. Unless the king were detained at the theatre or a reception or family reunion at the Quirinal, he generally passed the evening with one or two intimate friends at his country home. He supped about ten or eleven o'clock, retired at midnight, was up at the dawn, had two or three hours hard exercise, and was installed in his city palace, ready for work, before many of his subjects had opened their eyes.

A small plainly furnished suite of apartments on the ground floor was all Victor Emmanuel occupied of the magnificent palace of the Quirinal, except on state occasions. With the exception of his military uniforms, which were of necessity handsome, his wardrobe was the scantiest which a gentleman could be supposed to manage with by rigid economy. He wore the same cloth, colour, and texture all the year round—grey for morning and black for evening. He seldom had more than one suit of each, and wore them till they were shabby, which caused a Neapolitan boy to remark, 'The ministry load us with taxes, and yet they have not the heart to buy Vittorio a new pair of pantaloons!' The king laughed heartily when he heard the observation. The only thing he was particular about was his linen, and of that he liked a great quantity and fine quality. When he was going to Berlin and Vienna, his gentlemen-in-waiting told him that his wardrobe required replenishing. The king replied, 'Very well; order what is necessary.' 'But your majesty *must* have your measure taken this time, for they are very elegant at Berlin and Vienna.' 'What a nuisance! Ask Baron —— to be kind enough to have his measure taken for me; he is about my size,' was the response. He never wore gloves but when he was *en grande toilette*.

Going to the theatre one night in a grey coat, the king observed that the daughter of the Emperor of Russia and the Princess Margherita were in the house. He must pay a visit to the foreign princess, and it was too late to return to the Quirinal to change his dress. 'I am all black but the coat,' he said to his attendants; 'if some one would lend me a coat!' He espied a young marquis, one of his aides-de-camp, near, and sent for him. The coat was quickly exchanged, but a white tie was still wanting. The marquis offered his, but Victor Emmanuel, seeing one of his servants at the door of the box with a fresher one, walked up to him, and silently took off his tie and fastened it on himself; then brushing his hair at the glass he said, 'Do I look King of Italy?'

This familiarity, in which he occasionally indulged, did not involve a loss of dignity, for he knew how to check any undue presumption. Once a Roman noble, whose sympathies were rather with the old *régime* than the new, said, 'I wonder your majesty drives in the Corso; we Roman princes do not go.'

'And we, King of Italy, go;' replied Victor Emmanuel, with a stately dignity which he could assume when occasion required.

He was excessively punctual in all his engagements, having his time portioned out for every separate duty, and he could not tolerate the want of punctuality in others. One evening an engineer kept him waiting ten minutes, during which period his impatient temper got the better of him. He was just despatching a messenger to know if anything had happened, when the engineer made his appearance. The king walked up to him, watch in hand, saying, 'Bravo! you are ten minutes late!' The delinquent was so crushed that he could not find a word of apology. The good-natured king, seeing this, thought his rebuke had been too sharp, and hastened to add, 'Well, I am sure it was not your fault, and I will take care that it does not occur again.' He went into the adjoining room and brought out a handsome watch, saying, 'This goes exactly with mine, so in future there shall be no difference in our time.' 'Pardon,' murmured the engineer, 'your majesty, I am so confused——' 'Enough, the incident is forgotten; let us talk of more important things,' said the king.

King Victor was wont to quote the words of Henry of Navarre, 'A court without a queen is like spring-time without flowers;' and certainly his court suffered a heavy loss in the early death of his queen, who is described by everyone who knew her as quite an ideal character. The deep attachment and respect which her husband felt for her could not have failed to have a powerful influence on his life had she been spared to him. Unhappily the removal of his guardian angel—for as such he regarded Adelaide — released Victor Emmanuel, already too much disposed to disregard the *convenances*, from the wholesome restraints of family and court life; for a court without a queen, presided over by a king who hated ceremony and etiquette, must have been wanting in some important elements. The result of this excessive liberty on a temperament such as his may be imagined. But when all has been said in just condemnation of Victor Emmanuel's irregularities, the undoubted fact remains that public duty was never neglected nor postponed for private interest or pleasure, and that no back-door influence was permitted to bear upon state affairs; for no ideal prince, not even the British Arthur, could have a loftier sense of his kingly responsibility, or a more conscientious regard for the honour and welfare of his country.

Everyone has heard of King Victor's inordinate love of horses, of which he had a rare supply, and spent on them much more than he could afford. We have heard that his successor, who would not sell anything that had belonged to his father, had given some hundreds of these animals as presents to cavalry officers. He also refused to allow the nation to pay the late king's debts—which in the moment of sorrowful enthusiasm she would gladly have done—reserving that duty to himself. The king's debts, says an enthusiastic admirer, 'so far from being a blot, are much to his credit, inasmuch as the head of every state has an opportunity of amassing a large fortune if he will; and Victor Emmanuel not only did not do this, but spent much of his private patrimony, his civil list being insufficient even for a miserly sovereign, while it could not possibly be enough for a very generous one.'

The worry that all sovereigns have to support of incessant applications for help in various ways, Victor Emmanuel suffered from in an extraordinary degree. Petitioners lay in wait for him at his palace door, on his promenades, at the church door, at the door of the theatre—every place where they could catch sight of him and throw a paper into his carriage. Every post brought bushels of letters, some of them registered, containing the most pitiful tales of want, and misery, and despair, and everything that could touch a man's heart and excite his interest and curiosity. Many of these were genuine cases of distress, but many were also ingeniously devised plots to extort money from the softhearted king, or trap him into an intrigue. The *éclat* attaching to his public career, his well-known generosity, and—it must be owned—his reputation for gallantry, which his enemies had spread and exaggerated beyond his deserts, made him a target for this sort of persecution to a degree above the common lot of princes. It was in vain that his faithful servants unmasked impostors, and cautioned and warned him against lending too ready an ear to every applicant; he could not turn a petitioner away unheard, and if undeserving persons sometimes got what they had no right to, on the other hand hundreds of miserable beings were relieved and sustained through some difficult crisis. Here is one of the many authentic anecdotes of Victor Emmanuel's charity:—

One evening, at the door of the theatre, a man rushed at the royal carriage with a paper in his hand crying, '*Maestà, grazia.*' The king stopped the carriage, and put out his hand to take the petition.

'Permit me one word, your majesty,' said the man.

'Even two; let us hear them,' was the gracious reply.

'Your majesty does not know me?'

'Really I have not that pleasure,' said the king.

'Sire, I am a professor in the orchestra of the Politeama, where I play the horn close to your majesty's box.'

'This gives me much pleasure, but let us come to the moral.'

'Here it is, sire. My landlord intimates that I must pay my arrears of rent, or be turned out. Imagine it, with a wife and five children. To-morrow I am to appear before the Tribunal to hear myself condemned. Your majesty, I say no more; here is the citation.'

'Well, well, I understand; and do you want me to go to the *prefettura* instead of you?' asked Victor smiling.

'Oh no, your majesty, I will go; but going, I should like to be able to say, "here is the money, and I owe it to the generosity of my king."'

'Very well; we will provide it.'

The grateful musician kissed the liberal hand which saved him from ruin, and the king entered his box and related the incident to his friends.

'Ah,' said Count Castellengo, the Minister of the Household, whose life was a constant struggle to check his master's extravagance, 'if he makes this public to-morrow, everyone who has rent to pay will come to the Quirinal for it.'

The king shrugged his shoulders, and next day the player of the horn received 300 francs.

It was not on the battle-field alone that Victor Emmanuel was always ready to expose his life for the sake of his people. Whenever a town was visited by any violent epidemic, the king, besides contributing largely to the relief of the sufferers, hastened thither to assist personally in the work.

In 1865 the cholera was raging in Naples, and the inhabitants, seized with a panic, were migrating in hundreds from the city. So much depends in this disease on the state of mind, that the terror caused by the panic increased the pestilence tenfold. It was then that the king, wishing to give courage to his afflicted subjects by an example of utter fearlessness, arrived in Naples, and hastened, in company with the syndic and the prefect, to visit all the poor districts, which were most infected because of the dirt and squalor in which the inhabitants lived, 'where in the memory of man the least shadow of a king had never been seen,' says the narrator. A great number of the lower classes held the person of a sovereign in a sort of superstitious awe, as endowed with more than human power for good or ill; and so the presence of the benevolent king had a very efficacious effect.

In visiting the hospitals he stood beside the sick beds, and spoke encouragingly to the patients. Before one of these, already marked for death, the king stopped, and taking his frozen, damp hand, he pressed it, saying, 'Take courage, poor man, and try to recover soon.' The warm grasp of the hand, the strong cheerful voice, the recognition of the king's face, had an agitating effect on the dying man. That evening the syndic visited the king and said: 'Your majesty's coming is a joyful omen. I am happy to tell you that the doctors report a diminution of the disease in the course of the day, and your majesty has unawares worked a miracle. The man you saw this morning stretched for death, is out of danger this evening. The doctors say that the excitement of your presence caused a salutary crisis.'

'I am so glad. But what fun! If they spread the report that I work miracles I am afraid the Neapolitans will divide me in pieces in order to reduce me to relics,' said the king.

Victor Emmanuel had a droll humorous way of relating little anecdotes, which amused his friends more from the manner of telling them than the matter. One day when he was on a journey the train stopped for a few minutes at a little country station in a very remote district, where probably the shadow of a king had never been seen. On the platform the syndic appeared, elegantly 'got up' for the occasion. The king, seeing the good man 'exhausting himself in bows,' beckoned him to approach the carriage-window.

'I presume, signore, that you are the syndic. I congratulate you,' said his majesty; and after some further remarks he opened his huge cigar-case, which he had always at hand, and offered him one of his havannahs.

'No, sire, I never could have the boldness to put my hand in your majesty's cigar-case.'

'I pray you accept; do me the pleasure,' said the king persuasively, taking out a cigar and putting it into the hand of the modest syndic.

'Sire,' said he, kissing the royal hand, 'this cigar shall be the chief glory of my *comune*. I shall smoke this cigar the rest of my life.'

Victor was a great smoker. In the Summer Theatre at Naples there was put up once a prohibition against smoking, which displeased the king, and he ordered it to be taken down. Then he lit a cigar, and offered some to his suite; whereupon all the men in the theatre began to smoke.

'Behold, sire,' observed one of the courtiers, 'how quickly the example of royalty is followed.'

'When it is a bad example, yes,' was the keen rejoinder.

Victor Emmanuel had a passion for hunting; he never seemed in such good spirits as when he was inhaling the keen mountain air, and clambering over Alpine snows, where he outdid everyone in daring feats of agility. He never could be persuaded to wear flannel, or put on an overcoat or mantle. In these mountain excursions he slept under canvas in the severest weather, regardless of all discomforts. On Sundays a priest was brought from the nearest village, and a little temporary altar erected in the king's tent for religious service, in which he expected all his following to assist; for Victor Emmanuel was not, as he once said to the French ambassador, a *mauvais chrétien*. He reverenced everything sacred, he never used profane language, and we are told by one who knew him intimately, that 'it hurt his nerves to hear anyone swear.'

The king used to send the produce of the chase as

presents to strangers in the neighbourhood; and once there was assembled not far off from the mountain in which the royal hunting-party were stationed, a number of young artists and authors, who on receiving a gift from the king thanked him in comic verse and sketches, which pleased him much. He invited them all to spend a day or two with him, and received them with such a hearty hospitality, such *bonhomie*, such fun and wit, that the guests will never forget the pleasure of that mountain excursion. When thus set free from the cares of state and the irksome conventionalities of court life, Victor Emmanuel was like a schoolboy in vacation; no danger could daunt him, no fatigue could depress his spirits. He has often gone the whole day without food, having taken nothing but a cup of coffee early in the morning, and not returned to supper till a late hour in the evening.

Senator Plezza relates an amusing little anecdote which is characteristic of Victor Emmanuel. Just at the beginning of the war of 1859 Signor Plezza was appointed governor of Alessandria; but, on hearing that the Emperor of the French was expected to call there, begged to be excused, on the plea that he was unfit to receive a foreign sovereign. Count Cavour said he had need of him in that post, and refused to cancel the appointment. Plezza then appealed to the king, saying that he understood nothing of etiquette, and could not represent his sovereign.

'Is it possible?' said Victor Emmanuel.

'It is true, your majesty; I never come to court but on public business, and I am quite ignorant of the etiquette necessary for such an occasion.'

'You understand absolutely nothing of etiquette?' asked the king again.

'Nothing, sire.'

'Then since it is so, give me your hand. You are entirely fitted to represent me, for neither did I ever understand etiquette.'

One day one of his ministers spoke of an appointment he had just made to some public office. The king took up a publication in which the newly-appointed gentleman, writing in the Republican interest, had formerly attacked the king in a satirical poem. 'Did you know that he was the author of this?' he asked, showing the production.

'No, your majesty; of course not. I will cancel the appointment.'

But it was not in Victor Emmanuel's leonine nature to take such a paltry revenge on the ex-republican.

'No, we will cancel the poem rather,' he said with a smile; 'let the poor devil stand.'

There was a patrician family reduced to poverty by the gambling propensities of the father, and some friend of the house introduced one of the children into the king's presence. He patted her head, kissed her, and put a small gift in her hand. Then looking round to see that no one was observing him, he took notes for a large sum and fastened them in the child's plaits, saying, 'Let no one unpin your hair but mamma; you understand, dear?'

A young French officer, maimed so as to render him unfit for service, had been nursed in the house of a gentleman at Ferrara, and during his convalescence he and the daughter of the house had fallen desperately in love; but as neither the lady nor the gentleman had any provision for the future, the case seemed hopeless. The romantic story being told to the king, he gave the officer a pension and the girl a small *dote*, to enable them to marry.

But our space is running short and we must stop, though we could relate many more anecdotes illustrative of Victor Emmanuel's character in its strong and weak points. The more one studies it, the more one appreciates the just and well-balanced mind, the simple sincerity, the large-hearted humanity, of the man Victor Emmanuel, apart from his qualities as king, in which the world has acknowledged his merit.

CHAPTER XXXIV.

DRAWING TO A CLOSE. A.D. 1877.

VICTOR EMMANUEL had been now seven years reigning in Rome, and notwithstanding the difficult relations between Church and State, and other trials which the young nation had to struggle against, public affairs had gone on with wonderful order and tranquillity. The heads of the Church and State reigned in their respective palaces of the Vatican and the Quirinal, each living in his world apart, as if they had been in different hemispheres.

Pius IX., after an unusually stirring, eventful career, for a churchman, had sunk into political insignificance, and the world heard little of him, if we except the small commotion caused by an occasional flock of pilgrims in the Eternal City, or the reception of a number of foreign visitors desirous of seeing with their own eyes that most interesting personage called the Prisoner of the Vatican. The holy father received these visitors benignly, talked pleasantly with them, gave them his benediction, and his small white hand to kiss.

Hundreds of anecdotes were afloat as to how serenely—nay gaily—the good old man bore his imprisonment; and many of his witticisms relate to his own peculiar position, as when he remarked on Garibaldi's arrival in Rome, 'We were *two*; now we are *three*.' These *bon mots*, and an occasional allocution, were all that was heard of the Pope after the Italians took possession of the ancient capital. The bitterness of the pastorals and his private gaiety—the contrast between the ideal martyr-pope lying on a bed of straw, and the charming courtly gentleman whose green old age reposed in a home which the proudest monarch in Europe might envy, had a rather irritating effect on the Italian public mind. Pio Nono, however, was not wilfully false or deceptive, but he had a dual character: as Pope he felt it his duty to cry out about the persecutions of the Church, while as a man he was gentle and amiable, and did not feel towards Victor Emmanuel the animosity with which he was accredited. He sometimes, to the king's friends, spoke kindly of him as a *buon figliuolo*, and wrote, when occasion required, in a not unfriendly spirit. One instance will serve to show that it was as much from the influence of those around him as from principle, that Pius IX. refused all intercourse with the King of Italy. In 1872 the Pope, wishing to suppress some scandal of which he had become cognisant, wrote in his own hand, without consulting Antonelli, a letter to the king, asking him to use his authority for the removal of the said abuse. One of the Noble Guards arrived at the Quirinal, saying he had orders from the Pope to consign the letter into his majesty's hands. The king was pleased to recognise the Pope's own characters, and pleased also with the contents; for in that letter he acknowledged him as a constitutional sovereign, telling him to use his power as far as it went, and 'consult his ministers.' It concluded with these words, 'Full of paternal affection, I pray God for your majesty, I pray Him for Italy, and I pray Him for the Church.'

Thus in private Pio Nono's kind heart sometimes spoke, in spite of the constant guard he kept upon it. His public denunciations were for the edification of the Catholic world, which must also have been edified by the Christian humility with which Victor Emmanuel bore these public denunciations and private snubbings from the Vatican, never failing in deferential respect towards the holy father. And from a heretic point of view there seems something noble in the meekness with which the proud conqueror bowed before his aged and impotent foe, pleading for his friendship, and saying he was ready to abdicate if that could spare him pain. Pius IX. would have been more (or less) than man if he had not been touched by the attitude of Victor Emmanuel towards him personally; and there is no doubt that he was, though his court was at great pains to conceal the fact.

The liberation of Rome by the monarchy had silenced those restless spirits who had so long made it their war-cry; and Garibaldi, after sulking for years, and making common cause with the republicans, was elected deputy to the national Parliament, took a solemn oath of allegiance to the King of Italy, and in a long private audience all differences were explained away and the heroes reconciled. In presence of the great national triumph there was a general truce to the hostilities of party, all uniting in testimonies of admiration and gratitude to the sovereign whose brave, firm hand had guided the ship of state into port. It is sometimes said of constitutional sovereigns that they *reign* but do not *govern.* Victor Emmanuel never was a royal puppet of this sort. As head of the state, he exercised his authority judiciously, and assisted his ministers with his wise, moderate counsels, balancing the extremes of opinion. Not long ago he was asked by a distinguished foreigner if his ministers were not Radical. To which he replied with a smile, 'And if they were, what matter? Am I not here? If, instead of *Radicals*, as you say, I had a ministry of *Cardinals*, things should go on in the same way.' And when some one hoped that on the occasion of the expected conclave, public matters would be conducted with tolerance and moderation, he said, 'Be tranquil; all will go well. Remember that the leader of the choir is always the same.'

Victor Emmanuel was now at the zenith of his glory; his utmost ambition was attained. He had found Italy oppressed by a host of petty tyrants, dominated by Austria, torn by lawless combinations, misjudged and condemned by the other countries of Europe. She was now a free united nation, tranquil and law-abiding, respected everywhere. At peace with all the world, beloved and honoured by his people, what was left for him to desire? He might say with the poet—

> I have touched the highest point of all my greatness.

But he was not happy; and during the last few months he had been subject to unaccountable fits of melancholy. That this gloom had its origin in a feeling of dissatisfaction with himself is very probable. Notwithstanding his long and resolute struggle against clerical pretensions, Victor Emmanuel had preserved a simple child-like faith in the religion he had been taught at his mother's knee: and through all the stormy passions of his fitful career he had preserved sacred the image of his pure young wife, whose memory he revered as that of a saint. In Turin, where he passed the autumn of this year, having gone there to inaugurate a monument to his brother, the Duke of Genoa, he was heard to say more than once, 'I am not a good man, but I cannot die a bad death; she who is in heaven would not permit it.'

In the middle of November the king returned to the capital for the reopening of Parliament. Then in December he made a hasty journey to Turin to see the Countess Mirafiore, who was ill, and returned for the festivities of Christmas and New Year's day, with the intention of going back as soon as they were over. On the last day of the year 1877 Victor Emmanuel received all the foreign ministers who waited on him to exchange the compliments of the season in the name of their respective sovereigns. The following day he gave audience to deputations from both Houses of Parliament and others who presented congratulatory addresses. The king spoke cheerfully and hopefully of the future, and bade his ministers trust always in the star of Italy.

'The star of Italy is your majesty,' replied Signor Depretis, at which the king smiled sadly.

They did not dream that it was his last New Year's day; but he was even then feeling indisposed, and in nine days after he was dead.

CHAPTER XXXV.

THE LAST DAYS OF VICTOR EMMANUEL. A.D. 1878.

ON New Year's day the king had not felt well; on the 4th he was decidedly ill. On the 5th the news of General La Marmora's death arriving, gave him a great shock, and he wrote a telegram of condolence to the family, the last words he ever penned. Violent fever set in, accompanied by inflammation of the lungs, which was aggravated by his own imprudence in having got out of bed at night and gone on the balcony to cool himself. Every day the disease took more alarming proportions. Prince Umberto and the Princess Margherita were the only members of the royal family then at the Quirinal. Telegrams were sent in every direction to summon the absent ones, but too late. On the morning of the 9th the king was decidedly worse; the utmost consternation reigned throughout the palace. The grief of the prince and princess was indescribable; the latter had earnestly entreated to be allowed to sit all night with the patient, but her husband would not permit it. At an early hour a cardinal had come from the Vatican with kind inquiries from the Pope about the health of the royal patient. After being bled there was a slight amelioration in the king's state, and Prince Umberto had a long interview with him, in which he talked so clearly and calmly that his son was inspired with a hope that the case was not so bad as the doctors believed. But very soon after the miliary eruption breaking out, the physicians judged recovery impossible, and Dr. Bruno was deputed to break the fatal intelligence to the patient. With much hesitation he made the announcement, saying that the symptoms were such that he felt it his duty to warn his majesty not to lose time in fulfilling his religious obligations. The king was propped in a half-sitting posture, with his hands folded, twirling his thumbs. He looked a little surprised, but nowise disconcerted; he did not even cease to twirl his thumbs, and never took his unflinching eye off the doctor, as he said in Piedmontese, 'Are we come to that?' (*Siamo lì?*) 'Very well, I will do as you say. Call the chaplain at once.'

The court chaplain having received the king's confession, was obliged to apply to the parish priest for the Sacrament, and he would not dare to give it without permission from the Vatican, which was immediately granted; later a cardinal came with the special benediction of the holy father, whose good feeling at last triumphed over ecclesiastical prejudices.

As the day advanced the patient grew worse, and the time spent in obtaining the sacrament brought him very near death. He spent the interval in taking leave of his ministers and household, and then asked to be alone with his children, Umberto and Margherita. After a private interview the attendants were recalled, and all remained present at the administration of the communion. When the priest entered with the Host, the king, who was suffering terribly, his right lung being quite destroyed, raised himself with a violent effort to a sitting posture, and inclined his head reverently. After this his strength sank rapidly, and his chest was so oppressed that he had no voice for further conversation.

There was no hope of the Queen of Portugal or the Princess Clotilde coming in time to receive their father's last farewell, but Prince Amedeo and the king's cousin, Prince Carignano, of whom he was very fond, were on their way from Turin, and expected to arrive in the evening; death, however, travelled faster than they counted for, and they came all too late. The king asked again to see Umberto, and when he approached the bedside weeping, he gazed long and fondly at him, put out his hand and murmured the one word '*Addio!*' The prince kissed the hand, kneeling, and covered it with tears. During the day the sick man had muttered broken sentences about his beloved Turin, where he had wished to die. His last words were, '*I figli, i figli!*'

At the final moment, Prince Umberto was kneeling

at one side of the bed, and Count Mirafiore at the other, while the friends and attendants knelt round the chamber, and also in the anteroom, weeping silently. Dr. Bruno, who was supporting the patient's head, bent down and put his ear to his heart; it had ceased to beat. In a voice broken with emotion he made the announcement—

'The first King of Italy is no more!'

Convulsive sobs broke from all present; and Umberto remained kneeling in an agony of grief for nearly half-an-hour, till one of the doctors drew his arm in his and led him out of the room.

The fatal news fell like a thunderbolt on the city, and for a moment it was not credited. Groups of people gathered in the streets with pale, frightened faces, and hundreds of others were seen rushing from all parts to the Quirinal Palace, where a dense, agitated crowd filled the piazza from four o'clock in the afternoon till a late hour at night. Soon, however, all doubt was at an end, and before the winter sun had set every shop was closed, and the grand old city bore an aspect of deepest mourning as for some great public calamity.

While the poor prince was still stunned by the unexpected blow, he had to attend to public business. The diplomatic body came to offer their condolences, the ministry came to tender their resignations, and being reappointed, hastened to issue a proclamation officially announcing the death of Vittorio Emanuele II., and the accession of Umberto I. to the throne of Italy. Late in the evening a proclamation from the new king appeared.

Italians,— An immense calamity has befallen us. Vittorio Emanuele, the founder and uniter of the kingdom of Italy, has been taken from us. I received his last sigh, which was for the nation, and his last wishes, which were for the happiness of his people. His voice, which will always resound in my heart, imposes on me the task of vanquishing my sorrow, and points out to me my duty. At this moment there is but one consolation possible for us, that is, to show ourselves worthy of him : I, by following in his footsteps ; you, by remaining devoted to those civic virtues by the aid of which he succeeded in accomplishing the difficult task of rendering Italy great and united. I shall be mindful of the grand example he gave me of devotion to our country, love of progress, and faith in Liberal institutions, which are the pride of my house. My sole ambition will be to deserve the love of my people.

Italians,—Your first king is dead. His successor will prove to you that constitutions do not die. Let us unite in this hour of great sorrow, and let us strengthen that concord which has heretofore been the salvation of Italy.

UMBERTO.

Victor Emmanuel's failings are as well known as his virtues ; he was a man who scorned hypocrisy, and

> That fierce light which beats upon a throne

struck with a more sinister glare on the throne of Italy than that of older monarchies, laying bare remorselessly to the eyes of the world the faults of the sovereign, faults which his clerical detractors loved to dwell on and magnify, but which his people forgave, remembering all they owed him. Nor is it to be wondered at that nothing but hymns of praise should be raised over the lately closed tomb upon which a nation still mourns with heartfelt sorrow the liberator and father of his country.

CHAPTER XXXVI.

THE FUNERAL.

THE Pope is reported to have said that Victor Emmanuel died like a *cristiano, rè, e galantuomo* ; and certain it is that the clerical organs generally supposed to express the sentiments of the Vatican breathed nothing but

Christian charity in the notices of the king's death, while the popular journals poured forth the most passionate laments. One clerical paper in Venice ventured on some offensive comment, which caused the populace to break into the office and destroy the printing-press.

The grief of the other cities and provinces was not less than that felt in the capital. In Piedmont it was deeper; for Victor Emmanuel, liberator and regenerator of all Italy, and as such beloved and revered, never could be to all the Italians what he was to his faithful Subalpines, who had known him from infancy, and shared all the struggles of his early manhood.

Telegrams expressing the most ardent sympathy with the royal family poured in from every town in Italy, and everywhere the demonstrations of national grief were solemn and touching. On the 16th Parliament met, and the aged minister, Signor Depretis, announced to a crowded and agitated House the public misfortune. Again and again the old man's speech was interrupted by tears; and in those painful pauses in which the words seemed to choke him, the deputies were also overpowered with emotion.

If in history there exists a sovereign who has merited the title of *Padre della Patria*, that sovereign is without doubt Victor Emmanuel. Member of his Parliament since he ascended the throne, thrice member of his council, I had rather that my life had not been prolonged to see the dreadful day when the great author of Italian independence disappears in the darkness of the tomb. . . . I cannot now speak of the great, the inimitable qualities of the deceased; but I will say that a death more serene, more confident and manly, it is impossible to imagine. The body succumbed, but the soul remained, the soul of patriot and soldier; the last look he rested on our faces was so calm!

Here the speaker broke down; and many of the deputies and many occupants of the crowded galleries, were seen to wipe away their tears. In the Senate Chamber a similar scene took place. When the president began to speak all the senators rose to their feet and remained standing, while he delivered a brief but often interrupted eulogium on the dead, in the midst of a profound emotion. 'The lips are mute,' he said, 'but the heart bleeds. On the remains of the father of his country I can but weep as Italy weeps.'

Senators, deputies, and soldiers, who only knew Victor Emmanuel as king, wept his loss: but the grief felt by his household and intimate friends was still deeper. It was touching to see the heart-broken faces of the officers who guarded the remains of their dead sovereign when he lay in state in the chapel of the Quirinal; and General Medici, the king's aide-de-camp, was so overpowered with grief on the morning of the funeral, that he had to be assisted to his horse, to take his place in the procession. What Victor Emmanuel's own children experienced may be better imagined than described—and none felt the blow so heavily as the heir to the throne. We never saw a man so broken down by grief as he was when he went to receive the allegiance of the troops and to take the oath to the Constitution, the only occasions on which he appeared in public for a month after the death of his father.

Great diversity of opinion existed as to the place of interment, the royal family and ministers being much divided on the subject. Most of them, however, were of opinion that the first King of Italy ought to be buried in the capital, and the Romans were clamorous to have him sepulchred in the Pantheon. On the other hand King Victor loved Turin, and was loved by his Piedmontese subjects with the romantic loyalty of bygone days; it was hard to slight them for the Romans. Rome conquered however; and the citizens of the favoured capital sent an address to the citizens of Turin, asking them, for the sake of united Italy, for which they had already made so many sacrifices, to make this sacrifice also, and waive their claims. The Turin people were not softened; they had been deprived of their king in life, and in death they thought he ought to have been theirs; he was their fellow-citizen, reared amongst them; he was the descendant of their ancient line of princes, who were all buried at Superga, and no city had a prior claim to Turin. They rose in a wild demonstration of grief and anger, and compelled the authorities to send a deputation to Rome to demand the body of their late sovereign. The young king was gratified, but at the same time embarrassed by these passionate demonstrations of affection for his father. He was deeply moved by the address of the deputation, and explained in broken accents, that the Romans had asked, and must have, the king's body: it was a heavy sacrifice to him and all his family, to give up the idea of carrying their father's remains to the tomb of their ancestors; but private feelings must yield to national interests. He would bestow on the city of Turin the king's sword, helmet, and medals. Immediately after the funeral, Prince Amedeo carried these precious relics to Turin; they were received by the syndic and municipality with tears of gratitude, and the following day seventeen thousand persons went to look at them.

During the eight days that elapsed before the funeral, all business was suspended in Rome; the shops and offices were closed, and from almost every house the tricolour bound with crape was hung out. In the streets were vast crowds of people dressed in mourning; some eagerly reading the black-bordered journals and proclamations, and others gathered in knots conversing in low sad tones. The one all-absorbing theme was Victor Emmanuel; nothing else could be spoken of or thought of during that week of intense excitement and agitation.

On January 17, at ten o'clock, the funeral *cortège* left the Quirinal, its departure being announced by the firing of cannon. As early as seven o'clock the streets were lined with military, and the crowds were gathering so densely that it was with difficulty one could push through them to the Corso. All along the line of march every window, door, and balcony was draped in mourning, the tricolour with its crape pendant drooping sadly from the different storeys of the houses and public buildings. The crowds of ladies and gentlemen who filled the windows and balconies were dressed in black, and provided with wreaths and bouquets of rarest flowers to throw upon the hearse. At the cross streets where carriages had to break up the crowds, the *Bersaglieri* stood three deep with drawn swords; but the behaviour of the multitude was admirable.

After two hours' waiting the procession came in view at the far end of the Corso, moving slowly to the sound of a funeral march, composed especially for the occasion. A battalion of infantry with its band passed, then a body of cavalry, and after that there was a break of fifteen minutes or so, when the procession reappeared in a never-ending flood of military. Regiment after regiment poured into the street, and moved slowly past, in all their different varieties of uniform, making a brilliant spectacle: dark blue slashed with red, light blue with silver cord, gold and silver epaulettes, shining helmets, plumes of white ostrich feathers, of cock's feathers, of white horse-hair, of black horse-hair — plumes of every colour and variety.

The men did not walk abreast, but in a loose broken mass, which rather heightened the brilliant effect. They were from all parts of Italy, of every age and rank: grizzled veterans[1] who had fought with King Charles Albert and the Duke of Savoy in 1848-9, whose medals, doubtless, covered honourable scars; men in the prime of life also adorned with military decorations, and beardless cadets who had their honours yet to win.

After the military came the syndics of Rome and Turin, with the civil functionaries; then followed the representatives of the schools of arts and sciences, all in plain black; four hundred deputies and two hundred senators next made their appearance; and then an imposing group of commanding officers of land and sea, the uniforms and decorations, which are strikingly picturesque, contrasting with the mass of black-coated gentlemen in front. Very fine also were the judges in

---

[1] Amongst the old officers we saw General Durando, the brave commander who led the papal army in '48.

their crimson velvet togas. The clergy, eighteen in number, preceded by a white cross on a black field, then appeared; and were followed by the gorgeous display of the foreign ambassadors, and the not less striking habiliments of the knights of the Santissima Annunziata —crimson velvet mantles trimmed with ermine.

When this blaze of gorgeous colouring had passed, a solitary horseman appeared, holding aloft a drawn sword, on which was inscribed, '*Viva Carlo Alberto!* 1848.'

There was a look of settled sorrow in the old officer's face, but he sat his splendid charger with grace and dignity. It was General Medici, bearing the dead hero's battle-blade, the same which he had wielded in many a hard-fought field in the cause of Italian independence— and the sight went home to the hearts of the people. The interest of the spectators heightened, and tears rose to many eyes when the line of princes passed, with Amedeo in the midst—Amedeo who had never recovered the brightness of youth since his ill-starred sovereignty in Spain, who had lately lost a dear wife, and who, in this last affliction, had not the consolation of receiving his father's final farewell. '*Povero Amedeo!*' was the exclamation that went round as the crowd caught sight of the pale sad face of the young general. Beside him walked the Archduke Ranieri of Austria; there was also the Prince Imperial of Prussia, whose friendship for the royal family of Italy was shown by his warm sympathy in their sorrow; there was the Prince Napoleon, the Prince of Baden, and the Crown Prince of Portugal, King Victor's little grandson, a boy of fourteen.

Two outriders in black, mounted on black horses, rode forward; and the funeral car approached and stopped for a short space, while a thrill of deep emotion shot through every heart. The multitude uncovered their heads, and the ladies and gentlemen on the balconies and in the windows bent forward to throw with trembling hands the garlands they had prepared. The hearse was an imposing sight—of enormous dimensions, with gold ornamentation on the black field, and the arms of Savoy painted on the panels; it was open at the sides, showing the coffin, on which were laid the crown and sceptre of the defunct monarch, and the garlands sent by the Queen of England and the Emperor of Germany. Fastened on to the back of the car were wreaths of rarest flowers, tied with crape and tricoloured ribbons, while the roof was an enormous mass of verdure and flowers, contributed from the balconies on the line of march. The hearse was drawn by eight black horses covered with crape, with white and black plumes from their heads, each led by a groom. This great car moved on slowly, followed by wistful eyes; and immediately after came a groom leading an aged warhorse covered with crape. ' It was thirty years old, and had seen many an eventful day, for it was that horse that the young Duke of Savoy mounted on the joyful occasion when his father gave Piedmont a constitution, and it was consequently called *il cavallo dello Statuto*.

A cavalier with the Iron Crown of Lombardy on a cushion came next, and was followed by the municipality of Monza, where this precious relic is kept; then a body of ensigns bearing the colours of the different regiments. At this moment it was a splendid spectacle; in front the funeral car with its following of officers of the royal household, and behind, as far as the eye could reach along the Corso, one sea of waving banners, the brilliant tricolour all draped with crape. Next came the scientific bodies; they were followed by 450 Turinese students, then Roman students, then municipal bodies from the provinces. These last would have made a respectable funeral procession in themselves, and it was a strong testimony to the sentiments of the nation that every remote mountain village, in spite of the poverty of the times, subscribed funds and sent its representatives with handsome banners and wreaths to the funeral of the great king.

There were not less than 200 civic flags from the provinces. Many magnificent garlands were borne on the tops of the flagstaffs, but the masterpiece of beauty was one carried by the Roman shopkeepers, of enormous dimensions, composed of the rarest white flowers, bordered with green, and tied with gold cord and tassels mingled with crape; it was attached to a broad banner on which was embroidered in huge letters—

ALLA SACRA MEMORIA DEL RÈ GALANTUOMO.

The piazza in front of the church presented a grand *coup d'œil*, with all the houses hung in black and white, the national colours waving from the balconies, great flagstaffs planted as thick as forest trees all round the square, which was lined with a picked body of military, among which were the king's Life Guards in their picturesque white uniform with mail breastplates and helmets. These formed a hollow square round the processionists as the principal bodies filed into the church, and the rest who could not enter filled the great piazza to overflowing.

A fabulous sum had been spent on the decorations of the Pantheon for the occasion, and the result was beyond all doubt impressive in a high degree, notwithstanding that the severe simplicity of the architecture of this vast temple rendered a tasteful ornamentation difficult. On the top of the façade was a huge spread eagle flanked by two winged figures of Fame blowing trumpets; the front was all covered with paintings in imitation of bas-reliefs in bronze; the roof of the portico, from which hung great bronze lamps, was covered with black cloth starred with silver, and the sides adorned with arms of all sorts. Over the great door in large gold letters was the inscription :—

A VITTORIO EMANUELE II. PADRE DELLA PATRIA.

Underneath—

ITALIA CON ORGOGLIO DI MADRE, CON DOLORE
DI FIGLIA, PREGA AL GRAN RÈ,
CHE FU CITTADINO FEDELE, E SOLDATO
VITTORIOSO, L'IMMORTALITÀ DEI GIUSTI
E DEGLI EROI.

In the middle of the great circular temple rose the enormous catafalque, square in form, divided into three storeys, each one a degree smaller as they went up, the top one being covered with a crimson cloth and surrounded by six grand figures, which the Italian authorities wished to represent the chief cities of Italy, but which the clergy insisted on being called cardinal virtues. After some discussion they were named as follows: Magnanimity, Fortitude, Justice, Liberty, Prudence, Loyalty; qualities to which, in the abstract, no one could take exception. At the corners of the basement were lions couchant, and on each division of the structure were placed immense *candelabri* lit up with wax-tapers. The catafalque reached almost to the lofty dome, and all the sides of it were covered with exquisitely wrought garlands of every description, presented by the different cities and provinces of Italy. The walls of the church were draped in black with gold ornamentation. At each side of the altars, over a base on which were emblazoned the arms of Savoy, were large *candelabri*. The great circular window in the centre of the vault was veiled over with a transparency in the midst of which shone the star of Savoy, the surrounding roof being black, spangled with transparent stars. The effect of the whole was indescribably grand and impressive.

At the door of the church the priests received the coffin and accompanied it up the steps of the catafalque till it was deposited on the summit, the crown, sword, and sceptre, which had been carried with the defunct monarch, being laid upon it; and beside these emblems of sovereignty was placed the garland sent by Queen Victoria to be laid on the bier of her old ally. When the funeral *cortége* departed the great surging multitude were permitted to enter and look their last at the remains of the man who had given them national life and liberty.

In the evening the church was closed, and at 10 o'clock the ministers and officers of state assembled privately to lay their king in his last resting-place. There was a profound stillness in the church. The priests stood at the high altar beside the open tomb, in front of which was a silent group of mourners. The officers and men who guarded Victor Emmanuel in this last watch stood round the catafalque, motionless as statues, till the order was given to 'ground arms,' when the clash of the weapons on the pavement broke the awful silence which reigned in the church. When the coffin was placed in the grave all knelt while the priests chanted the burial service. A silence followed, broken only by the click of the mason's trowel walling in the tomb. Then the benediction was said and the mourners departed, leaving *il Rè Galantuomo* to sleep in peace.

King Humbert said in a proclamation, 'Romans, I commit to your charge what I hold most sacred on earth; prove yourselves worthy of the trust.' And the Romans replied with one voice, 'It is as sacred to us as to you; we will be worthy.'

> We believe [said the *Popolo Romano*], that we are interpreting a sentiment which will remain indelible in the souls of the Romans, that is, gratitude. Rome, even though she was the last to enter in the great family, after having witnessed the immense affection that the Italians bear to the king and to his dynasty, knows what a sacred deposit is confided to her, and she has the conscience to preserve it scrupulously. Though the last in time, she shall be first from this day henceforth in the love that binds all Italy to her king, and of this love she has yesterday given ample proofs before Europe.

In the loyal demonstrations which the attempted assassination of Humbert last November called forth, there was one little incident expressive of popular sentiment in Rome worthy of remark. The city had been suffering from a severe inundation, the Tiber had left its deposit of yellow mud in the streets, and the Pantheon was still more or less surrounded by water, the weather was bitterly cold, when about fifty or sixty thousand Romans who had assembled to make a loyal demonstration expressive of their horror and indignation at the attempted crime, marched through the streets nearly all night, with bands playing the royal march, etc.; and when they had gone from the Quirinal to the Capitol, where the syndic brought out the king's bust to please the excited crowd and made a speech to them, they all turned with one accord, and without any preconcerted arrangement, to the Pantheon to do honour to the memory of the dead king, and walked round the church in solemn silence.

We do not believe there ever was a monarch whose death called forth such spontaneous demonstrations of loyal affection, or who was followed to the grave by such profound sorrow. With the exception of Garibaldi, he was the last of that noble band of patriots who initiated in North Italy the work of Italian independence. And with the death of her chivalrous king the nation feels the romance of her youth is passed. She now enters on a new and more prosaic era—let us hope a happier and more peaceful one—under a sovereign who has already proved himself a worthy successor of *il Rè Galantuomo*. And though the heart of the Italian nation is still 'in the coffir there with Cæsar,' it is the just inheritance of Cæsar's son.

May he live to deserve it, and enjoy it!

INDEX.

ABERCROMBIE, Sir Ralph, interview with King Victor Emmanuel II., 49
Abruzzi, people of, petition for annexation, 227
Adelaide Princess, *see* Maria Adelaide
Alessandria, Italian subscription for cannons for, 117
Alfieri, Countess, niece of Cavour, 95
Alpine peasants and Victor Emmanuel II., 79
Amedeo, Prince, wounded, 270; marries Maria Vittoria, 281; birth of his son Emanuele Filiberto, Duke of Puglia, 301; made king of Spain, 318; deputation from the Cortes, to Victor Emmanuel II. thereon, 318; attempt on his life, 326; abdicates, February 1873, 326; returns to Italy, 327.
Ancona, visit of Victor Emmanuel II. to the Holy House of Loreto, 225; to the Jesuits' College, 225
Anglo-Austrian alliance, 122
Anglo-French alliance, 1854, 92; Sardinia proposes to join in, 92; joined by Sardinia, 96
Antonelli, Cardinal, and the Naples revolution, 210
Aosta, Vittoria, Duchess of, death, 333
Appony, Count, the Austrian ambassador at the court of Turin, 75; and the Neapolitan ambassador, 84; leaves Turin, 88
Aspromonte, the battle of, 249
Austria, and the Jesuits, 17; and the Liberal party in Italy, 23; occupies Ferrara, 26; the Sardinian war of 1848 with Austria, 35; battle of Goito, 36; Pio Nono's part in the war, 39; Ferdinand's proclamation on, 39; the Duke of Tuscany's proclamation on, 40; collapse of the Neapolitan army, 41; disputes among the Lombards, 42; Pio Nono's indecision, 42; the battle of Sommacampagna, 43; victory of Staffala, 43; the defeat at Custoza, 43; Charles Albert occupies Milan, 44; renewal of the war, March 20, 1849, 44; treachery of General Ramorino, 45; defeat at Sforzesca, 45; victory at Mortara, 45; victory at Novara, 44; an armistice demanded by the Italians, 47, 49; concluded, 50; negotiations for peace, 56, 72; treaty of peace signed August 6, 1849, 73; amicable relations established between Austria and Sardinia, 75; bitterness between, and Piedmont, 88; continued disagreements with Piedmont, 118; severance of diplomatic relations with Piedmont, 123; tour of the emperor through his Italian provinces, 123; the war of 1859, 138; military preparations, 141; Count

Buol's despatch to the English ambassador, 142; endeavours to make Sardinia disarm, 143; the proposed European Congress, 143; endeavours to exclude Piedmont from the Congress, 144; Count Cavour's reply thereto, 144; ultimatum to Piedmont, 146; declaration of war, 146; the Austrians cross the Ticino, 152; attempt to retake Palestro, 155; collects more troops and returns to the combat, 162; quarrels with Prussia, 266; proposes to cede Venice, 267; Archduke Albert commands the forces, 270; battle of Custoza, 270; victory of Prussia over, 271; asks mediation of Napoleon III., and offers to cede him Venice, 271; the defeat of Sadowa, 271; treaty of peace signed at Vienna, October 2, 1866, 272; visit of Victor Emmanuel II., 328; Emperor of, returns visit of Victor Emmanuel II., 331

Austrian prisons, death of Silvio Pellico, author of book on, 92

Avete, Count, on the *Statuto*, 77

Azeglio, Massimo d', *I Miei Ricordi*, 19; his scheme for the unification of Italy, 20, 23; his interview with the King, Charles Albert, 21; his interview with Pio Nono, 23; advice to King Charles Albert, after the defeat at Custoza, 43; made chief minister, 57; on Pio Nono, 62; on the trial of General Ramorino, 71; letter to, from Victor Emmanuel II., 78; his pamphlet on the papal government, 82; his remarks on the interview between Victor Emmanuel and the Cavaliere Ramirez, 84; disagreement with Cavour, 87; resigns office, 87; accompanies Victor Emmanuel II. to Paris, 108; his reception by the emperor and empress, 108; arrives in England, 108; sent as governor to Bologna, 167; made governor of Milan, 188; letter to Farini on death of Cavour, 242; his death, 265; anecdotes of, his character, 265

BALBO, Count Cesare, sent on a mission to Pio Nono by Victor Emmanuel II., 68; utter failure of the mission, 69; death of, June 3, 1853, 88

Barsanti, the true story of, 307

Bartolucci, General, and the siege of Rome, 67

Belgiojoso, Count, 176

Benedek, General, 162

Berold (Humbert of the White Hand), founder of the Sabaud family, 1; Count Moriana, title borne by, 2

Berry, Duchess de, marries Emmanuel Philibert, 3

Bersezio's *I Contemporanei Italiani*, 50; on Victor Emmanuel II., 150

Bologna, governor sent to, 168

Bonghi's opinion of Cavour, 89

Bourbon power in Italy, overthrow of, 6

Bourbon race, the, in the Two Sicilies, 67

Brigands in Naples, 246, 251; seizure of, from a French vessel at Civitavecchia, 251; controversy with the French thereon, 252

Brofferio, his attacks on Cavour, 89, 90, 121, 235

CADORNA, General, Victor Emmanuel's minister, 52; suppresses the insurrection in Sicily, 272; marches on Rome, 315

Cairoli commands the Roman rebels, 289; his death, 289

Capital punishment in Italy, 297

Capponi, Gino, member of the new Italian Parliament, 205; first to welcome Victor Emmanuel II. to Florence, 208; receives order of SS. Annunziata, 259

INDEX.

CAR

Carbonari, the, 9
Carignano, Charles Albert, prince of (afterwards King of Sardinia), 8; his education, 8; his religion and character, 9; marries daughter of the Grand Duke of Tuscany, 9; proposal of the federates that he should sever himself from Austria, 10; proclaims the constitution, 14; ordered by the king to quit Turin, 14; receives a commission to serve in the Spanish War, 15; recalled to Sardinia by the king, 15; ascends the throne, 15; is asked by Mazzini to lead the Liberal cause, 16; interview with D'Azeglio, 21; proclaims a constitution, 27; the Mazzinians and, 42, 44; defeated at Sommacampagna, 43; victorious at Staffala, 43; defeated at Custoza, 43; occupies Milan, 44; escapes from Milan, 44; renews the war, March 20, 1849, 44; treachery of General Ramorino, 45; victorious at Sforzesca, 45; defeated at Mortara, 45; utterly defeated at battle of Novara, 44; broken-hearted, 45; demands an armistice, 47; abdicates, 47; appoints his son Victor Emmanuel king, 47; retires to Oporto, 48; death of, 73; celebration of the tenth anniversary of his death by the Lombards, 176

Carignano, Prince of (cousin of Victor Emmanuel II.), becomes prince regent, 147; appointed Viceroy of Central Italy, 185; made Viceroy of Naples, 231; proclamation of Victor Emmanuel II. thereon, 231; appointed regent in 1866, 268

Casalmonferrato, Bishop of, offers to pay certain clerical dues, 103

Castelar on the influence of Rome over the Italian mind, 235

Cavour, Camillo, 55; appointed Minister of Agriculture, 82; disagreement with D'Azeglio, 87; resigns office, 87; resumes office, 88; feeling against, 89; attacked

CAV

by Brofferio, 89; his nickname of 'Lord Camillo,' 89; his admiration of England, 89; Bonghi's opinion of him, 89; his oratory, 90; called an ultra-Moderate by Brofferio, 90; his reply thereto, 90; has an interview with Victor Emmanuel II. on the treaty, 96; appointed Minister of Foreign Affairs, 96; resignation of, 96; recalled to office, 104; maligned by the clergy, 103; President of the Council, April 1855, 104; accompanies Victor Emmanuel II. to Paris, 108; his reception by the emperor and empress, 108; plenipotentiary at the Congress, 111; makes the wrongs of Italy known at the Congress, 111; the discussion in the Congress thereon, 112; visits Lord Clarendon, 114; returns to Turin, 115; receives the Order of the Santissima Annunziata, 116; defends Victor Emmanuel and his policy, 120; his reply to Brofferio, 121; on public affairs in 1857, 125; on the crisis, 128; on exiling political offenders, 128; interview with Napoleon III., 132; and the marriage of Princess Clotilde to Prince Napoleon Jerome, 139; is presented with a ring by Victor Emmanuel II., 142; letter to Earl Derby on the Italian-Austrian question, 143; his reply respecting the endeavour of Austria to exclude Piedmont from the Congress, 144; visits Napoleon III., 145; returns to Turin and receives an ovation, 145; is summoned to the camp, 167; his view of the armistice of July 1859, 170; his immense labours, 171; his interview with Napoleon III., 172; his interview with Victor Emmanuel, 172; returns to Turin, 172; resigns office with his colleagues, 173; on the situation of Italy, 177; appointed plenipotentiary to the European Congress, November 1859, 185; discussion

CHA

with the ministry on the Congress, 186; resolves to retire to Leri, 186; visits Sir James Hudson, 187; sends his last conditions to the ministry, 187; Sir James Hudson writes them from his dictation, 187; consequent resignation of General La Marmora, 187; sent for by Victor Emmanuel II., 187; composes a new cabinet, January 21, 1860, 187; annoyance of the *Codini* at his return to office, 188; accompanies Victor Emmanuel II. to Lombardy, February 1860, 188; letter to La Farina, 214; messages from, to Garibaldi, 216; jealousy between, and Garibaldi, 219; resigns office, 234; is recalled, 235; resolves to have Rome for the capital, 235; attack of Garibaldi on, concerning the cession of Nice and Savoy, 236; his reply thereto, 236; reconciliation with Garibaldi, 237; on the severance of the temporal power from the Papacy, 238; on Free Church and Free State in Italy, 239; illness of, 241; visit of Victor Emmanuel II. to, 241; death, 242; letter of D'Azeglio to Farini on death of, 242; his burial, 243; his last words, 243; monument to, 329

Chabron, Colonel de, letter from Victor Emmanuel II. to, 156

Chamber of Deputies, dissolution of, in 1849, 55; general election of, July 15, 1849, 72; opening of, July 30, 1849, 72; representation of *Giovane Italia* in, 73; dissolution of, 73; royal proclamation thereon, 74; opening of, December 20, 1849, 75; new ministry formed, 104; opened by Victor Emmanuel II., 106; the king's speech, 106; dissolution of Parliament, 1857, 124; general election, 124; speech of Victor Emmanuel at opening of Parliament, 125; Parliament opens January 10, 1859, 133; comments

CIA

of the *Codini* and the *Liberali* on speech of Victor Emmanuel II., 138; election of members for the new provinces, 202; opening of, on April 2, 1860, 205; general elections, 232; new Parliament (February 1861) opens, 232; speech of Victor Emmanuel II., 232; kingdom of Italy proclaimed, 234; new ministry appointed, 243; opening of, May 1863, 250; speech of Victor Emmanuel II. at, 251; new Parliament, 279; Victor Emmanuel II.'s address to, 279; opening of, December 15, 1866, 275; dissolves, 279; discussion of the Roman question, December 1867, 262; resignation of the ministry, 293; the last Florence Parliament, 319; first Parliament in Rome, 322; speech of Victor Emmanuel II. thereat, 323; general election, 333; last speech of Victor Emmanuel II. 333; Parliament meets on January 16, 1878, 352; death of Victor Emmanuel II. announced, 352; speech of Signor Depretis on, 352

Chambéry, the school of the Sacred Heart in, 124

Charles Albert, *see* Carignano

Charles Albert (son of Victor Emmanuel II.), death of, 91

Charles Emmanuel IV., 7; abdicates, 7; turns monk, 7

Charles Felix succeeds Victor Emmanuel as King of Sardinia, 8, 13; takes possession of the capital, 14; death of, 15

Charvaz, Monsignor, the king's preceptor, 86; made Archbishop of Genoa, 86; visits Victor Emmanuel II. on the death of the queen, 100

Chassepots at Mentana, 289

Cholera epidemic in the Riviera and Genoa, 91

Cialdini, General, 154; takes Ancona, 221; besieges Gaeta, 232; commands the royal troops at Aspromonte, 249; receives the

order of the SS. Annunziata, 273
Cibrario, Count, Minister of Foreign Affairs, April 1855, 104; conversation with Victor Emmanuel II., 135
Circoli Barsanti, 307
Civil marriages, 87
Civitavecchia, landing of the French at, 67
Civitella, fortress of, taken by the Italians, 232
Clarendon, Lord, defies Count Buol at the Congress, 114; visited by Count Cavour, 114; conveys a message from Victor Emmanuel II. to Pio Nono, 293
Clergy, wealth of, in Sardinia, 101; proposed confiscation of part of, 102; Rattazzi's Clerical Bill, 102; complaints of, 224; on Victor Emmanuel II. 260
Clotilde, Princess, proposed marriage with Prince Napoleon Jerome, 139; married, January 29, 1859, 140; refuses to leave Paris during the Franco-Prussian war, 310
Codini, the comments of the, on Victor Emmanuel's speech at the opening of Parliament, January 10, 1859, 138; annoyance of the, at the return of Cavour to office, 188; Rome the headquarters of the, 240
Concordia, 24
Congress at Paris on the Crimean War, 111; Count Cavour raises a discussion on Italy, 112
Congress, European, proposed, on the Italian question, 185
Consulta, address to the Pope from the, 60
Corsi, Cardinal, and the marriage of Victor Emmanuel II. with Countess Mirafiore, 305; anecdote of, 305
Courmayeur, Victor Emmanuel's first visit to, 80
Crimean War: Shall Sardinia go to the Crimea? 95; starting of the troops, 102; the victory of Tchernaya, 105; fall of Sebastopol, 110; the Congress, 110; return and review of the troops, 116
Cushion, the lady of the, and Victor Emmanuel II., 298
Custoza, battles of, 43, 270

DABORMIDA, General, his letter on the dangerous illness of Victor Emmanuel II., 69; letter from Victor Emmanuel II. on Anglo-French alliance, 1854, 93; his opposition to Sardinia joining the alliance, 94; resigns office, 96; takes office, 174
Delaunay, General, forms a new ministry for Victor Emmanuel II., 55; its dissolution, 56
Depretis, Signor, speech in Parliament on death of Victor Emmanuel II., 352
Desambrois, Cavaliere Luigi, appointed plenipotentiary to the proposed European Congress of November 1859, 185; death of, 331
Devincenzi, Signor, accompanies Victor Emmanuel II. on his southward journey, 227
Dickens, Charles, on exiled politicians, 215
Dino, Duke of, 37
Durando, General, appointed minister of war, April 1855, 104

ECUMENICAL Council, 307
Elizabeth of Saxony, her marriage to Duke of Genoa, 80
Elizabeth Tudor, offered in marriage to Emmanuel Philibert, 3
Emilia, *see* Italy, Central.
Emilian provinces, Signor Farini made dictator of, 183
England and the House of Savoy, 83
England, Cavour's opinion of, 89; visited by Victor Emmanuel II., 108

FAN

FANTI, General, 154, 158; takes office as Minister of War, January 21, 1860, 187; presents banner from Victor Emmanuel II. to the army, 382

Farini, '*Lo Stato Romano dal 1815 al 1850,*' 41; made dictator of the Emilian provinces, 183; letter to Victor Emmanuel II., giving up his dictatorship of Emilia, 200; Victor Emmanuel II. replies to him, 200; receives the order of the SS. Annunziata, 202; made Minister of the Interior, 202, 205; resigns office as Viceroy of Naples, 231; letter to, from D'Azeglio, on the death of Cavour, 241; takes office, 250; resigns, 250

Ferdinand of Savoy, 67

Ferdinand II. (of Naples), character of, 17; his proclamation on the war of independence, 39; Pio Nono takes refuge with, at Gaeta, 62; opinion of, by Victor Emmanuel II., 228

Fiorentino's '*La Vita di Pio Nono,*' 66

Five days' struggle, the, 42

Florence, proposed removal of capital to, 256; remark thereon by De Lhuys, 256; La Marmora's opinion thereof, 257; Marquis Pepoli's opinion thereon, 257; Visconti Venosta thereon, 258; consternation in Turin thereat, 258; the last Parliament of, 258; address of the citizens to Umberto, December 1878, 321

'Forced Recruit,' the origin of the poem, 343

Foro Ecclesiastico, 76; the Jesuits and the, 77; abolition of, 77, 78

France, the French besiege and take Rome, 68; letter of thanks from Pio Nono to their General, Oudinot, 69; cession of Savoy and Nice to, 141, 203; signing of the treaty, March 24, 1860, 204; French fleet withdrawn from the coast of Naples, 232

Francis II., alliance offered to by

GAR

Victor Emmanuel II., 169, 210; and Count of Syracuse, 210; appeals to Victor Emmanuel II., 212; takes up his abode at Rome, 240

Franco-Prussian War, 309; Princess Clotilde refuses to leave Paris, 310; excitement in Rome on, 311; France appeals to Victor Emmanuel II. for aid, 317

GAETA, King Ferdinand's court at, 62, 64; besieged by Cialdini and Menabrea, 232; is taken, 232

Galletti accepts office under the Roman Republic, 65

Garibaldi, in Rome, 63; his influence in, 65; and the Neapolitan insurgents, 67; defends Rome from the French, 67; joins the Italian army against Austria, 141; successes of, and his volunteers, 154; receives the military medal from Victor Emmanuel II., 161; proposes to make war on the Marches, 184; refrains on the advice of Victor Emmanuel II., 185; prepares to take command of the rebel army in Sicily, 211; indignation of Prussia, Austria, and Germany thereat, 212; his successes in Sicily, 214; enthusiasm for, 216; message of Victor Emmanuel II. to, 217; Cavour's message to, 217; enters Calabria, 218; takes possession of the capital, 218; is elected dictator, 219; jealousy between, and Cavour, 219; submits to the Chamber of Deputies, 226; meeting of Victor Emmanuel II. in Naples, 229; resigns his dictatorship, 229; retires to Caprera, 230; on the cession of Nice and Savoy, 236; his attack on Cavour, 236; his reconciliation with Cavour, 237; proposed amalgamation of his troops with the Italian army, 247; and his troops march for Rome, 248; fight at Aspromonte between the royal troops and the Garibaldians, 249; and his troops threaten to invade Rome, 283; is arrested, 284; Italian troops cross the frontier, 288; his '*Rule of the Monk*,' 288; escapes from Caprera, 289; Menotti Garibaldi at the head of his troops enters the Papal State, 289; arrive at Rome, 288; desperate encounter at the Gate of St. Paul, 288; victory at Monterotundo, 289; reaches Mentana, 289; defeated by the French army, 289; sent prisoners to the fortress of Varignano, 291; is sent to Caprera, 292; elected a deputy, 346; is reconciled to Victor Emmanuel II., 346

Gavazzi, the Barnabite *frate*, 61

Genoa, insurrection in, 56; cholera epidemic in, 91; Victor Emmanuel II. visits, 91

Genoa, Duke of, fills place of Victor Emmanuel II. during his illness, 71; opens the Novara Railway, 91; marriage to Elizabeth of Saxony, 80; illness of, 132; death of, February 10, 1855, 99; his character, 99

Germany, Emperor of, visits Victor Emmanuel II., 332

Gioberti's book against the Jesuits, 61; his letter to Gaeta on Pio Nono, 64; his '*Rinnovamento Civile d' Italia*,' 85

Giovane Italia, society founded by Mazzini, 16; becomes republican, 17, 25; representation of, in the Chamber of Deputies, 73; demands Rome for the capital of Italy, 239

Giusti's poem 'The Boot,' 19

Goito, battle of, 36; description of, 37

Govone, General, death of, 311

Govone, General Giuseppe, concludes treaty of 1866 with Prussia, 267

Gramont, Duke of, French ambassador, has an interview with Victor Emmanuel II., concerning the Anglo-French alliance, 1854, 93; his second interview, 95

Grido di dolore, 135

Grifeo, Count, his recall from the court of Turin, 84

Gualterio, Marquis, made governor of Perugia, 222; death of, 331

Guarantee laws, 321

Guildhall, London, Victor Emmanuel II. attends a banquet at, 109

HAPSBURG family, Victor Emmanuel II.'s friendship for, 302

Hilliers, Marshal, 163, 164

Hudson, Sir James, English ambassador at Turin, 92; on the Papal temporal power, 168; interview with Victor Emmanuel II., 173; visit of Cavour to, 187; the consequences thereof, 187

Huguenots, war of extermination against the, by Victor Amadeus, 6

Humbert of the White Hand (Berold), 2

Humbert, Prince, made captain, 129; marries Princess Margherita, 294; anecdote of, 296; birth of a son, Vittorio Emanuele, Prince of Naples, 306; succeeds to the throne of Italy, 350; his proclamation, 350; proclamation at the funeral of Victor Emmanuel II., 360

INQUISITION, the, 58; abolition of, 65; thrown open to the public, 65; account of, by a prisoner, 66; in Rome, 282

Italian subscription for cannons, for fortress of Alessandria, 117

Italy, the war of 1848, 26; battle of Goito, 36; Pio Nono's part in it, 39; Ferdinand's proclamation on, 40; the Duke of Tuscany's proclamation on, 40; collapse of the Neapolitan army, 41; disputes among the Lombards, 42; Pio Nono's indecision, 42; the battle of Sommacampagna, 43; victory at Staffala, 43; the defeat at Custoza, 43; Charles Albert occupies Milan, 44; renewal of the war, March 20, 1849, 44; treachery of General Ramorino, 45; Victory at Sforzesca, 45; defeat at Mortara, 45; battle of Novara, utter defeat, 45; an armistice demanded by the Italians, 47; negotiations for the armistice, 49; conclusion, 50; negotiations for peace, 55, 72; treaty of peace signed, August 6, 1849, 73; a mere 'geographical expression,' 119; the Anglo-Austrian alliance, 122; the war of 1859, 139; preparations for, 139, 141; proposal for a European Congress, 143; Austria's ultimatum to Piedmont, 146; declaration of war, 147; proclamation to the people by Victor Emmanuel II. 147; the king's address to the soldiers, 149; the Sardinian army at San. Salvador, 151; Napoleon III. lands at Genoa, 151; the Austrians cross the Ticino, 152; Turin armed for defence, 153; successes of Garibaldi and his volunteers, 154; victories of Montebello and Palestro, 154; royal proclamation thereon, 154; the victory of Magenta, 159; triumphal entry into Milan, 160; proclamation of Victor Emmanuel II. to the Lombards, 160; the double victories of Solferino and San Martino, 162; the central provinces eager for union, 167; governors sent to Tuscany, Parma, Modena, Bologna, 167; an armistice proposed and concluded, 169; dissatisfaction of the disputed provinces thereat, 170; peace signed at Villafranca, 173; presentation of banners to Italian army, by Victor Emmanuel II., through General Fanti, 237; Russia and Prussia acknowledge Italian unity, 244; war declared with Austria, June 20, 1866, 267; La Marmora leads the army northwards, 267; Victor Emmanuel II. and his sons start for the seat of war, 268; battle of Custoza, 270; defeat at Lissa, 270; Venice restored to Italy by Napoleon III., 272; treaty of peace signed at Vienna, 272; financial state of, 1867, 280; Italian troops cross the papal frontier, 288

Italy, Central, offers itself to Victor Emmanuel II., 179; his reply to the Tuscans, 180; Prince of Carignano made Viceroy of, 185; annexed with North Italy, 189; address from Victor Emmanuel II. to the people of, 202

JESUITS, and political feeling in Italy, 17; popular feeling in Rome against the, 61; Gioberti's book against, 61; Austrian, and Pio Nono, 63; and the *Foro Ecclesiastico*, 76

Journalism in Italy in 1849, 71

LA MARMORA, General Alfonzo, rescues King Charles Albert from the Milanese, 44; sent to quell the insurrection in Genoa, 56; his opposition to joining the Anglo-French alliance, 94; his able generalship, 105; promotion of, 117; resumes his seat in the cabinet, 118; remonstrates on the king's rashness, 151; takes office, 174; resigns, 187; his opinion on the removal of the capital to Florence, 257; forms a ministry in 1864, 258; forms a new ministry in 1866, 267; leads the army northward, 267; and the armistice with Austria, 272; estrangement of, 331

Lambruschini, popular feeling against, 61
Lamoricière, General, takes command of the army of Pio Nono, 217
Lanza, Minister of Public Instruction, discussion with the king, 126; forms a ministry, November 1869, 306
Lhuys, de, opinion on removal of capital to Florence, 256
Liberals, on Victor Emmanuel II., 261; on Victor Emmanuel's speech at the opening of Parliament, Jan. 10, 1859, 138
Lissa, Italians defeated at, 270
Lo Straniero, 266, 272
Lombardo-Venetian provinces, 83
Lombards propose to join the Anglo-French alliance, 95; amnesty to the banished, 122
Lombardy, begs to be joined to Piedmont, 159; proclamation of Victor Emmanuel II. to, 160; visited by Victor Emmanuel II. and Cavour, 188
'Lord Camillo,' nickname of Cavour, 89

MAGENTA, the battle of, 159
Mamiani, Count, made Minister of Public Instruction, January 21, 1860, 187, 205; description of tour with Victor Emmanuel II. through his new dominions, 207
Manzoni, interview of Victor Emmanuel II. with, 177; his remarks on Victor Emmanuel II., 177; member of Chamber of Deputies, 205; death of, 327
Marches, Signor Valerio made governor of, 222
Margherita, Princess (of Genoa), marries Prince Humbert, 294; her character, 294
Maria Adelaide, Princess, 32; marries Victor Emmanuel II., 33; her boundless charity, 34; education of her children, 34; cause of her death, 34; her appearance in the Chamber of Deputies, 75; illness of, 95; death of, 98; her funeral at Superga, 100
Maria Pia (daughter of Victor Emmanuel II.), marries King of Portugal, 244; receives a deputation from the senators and deputies on her departure, 244
Maria Vittoria marries Prince Amedeo, 281
Marriage laws of Sardinia, 87
Martino, de, and the Neapolitan Government, 211
Massari, on the friendship between England and the House of Savoy, 83; on King Ferdinand of Naples, 83; his '*La Vita ed il Regno*,' 93; on the treaty with England and France, 96; his remarks on Victor Emmanuel's speech at the opening of Parliament, January 10, 1859, 138; remarks on the armistice of July 8, 1859, 172; his account of marriage of Victor Emmanuel II. with Countess Mirafiore, 304
Mauri, Achilles, on the proposal to join the Anglo-French alliance of 1854, 95
Maximilian, Archduke, made Viceroy of Lombardy, 122, 130
Mazzini, founder of the society *Giovane Italia*, 16; writes to the king, Charles Albert, asking him to lead the Liberal cause, 16; his followers and the king, Charles Albert, 42, 44; his influence in Rome, 65; insurrection at Genoa headed by, 123
Medici, General, bears sword of Victor Emmanuel II. at his funeral, 356
Menabrea, General, narrow escape from death of, 54; besieges Gaeta, 232; receives the order of SS. Annunziata, 273; forms a new ministry, 285; forms a new ministry, December 1867, 293
Mentana, battle of, 289; chassepots at, 289
Messina, fortress of, taken by the Italians, 232

MET

Metternich, Prince, his definition of Italy, 119
Milan, rebellion in, 1853, 88; the peace, 133; triumphant entry of the troops into, 160; Massimo d'Azeglio appointed governor of, 188
Minghetti, ministry, 250; and taxation, 250; letter from Victor Emmanuel II. on the same, 250; resigns office, 258
Mirafiore, Countess, Victor Emmanuel's connection with, 98; marries Victor Emmanuel II., 304; her villa, 334
Modena, Duke of, conspiracy against, 18; leaves Modena, 166; governor sent to, 167; inhabitants resolve to become subjects of Victor Emmanuel II., 179; reply of Victor Emmanuel II. thereto, 181
Mollard, General, 162, 163
Monferrat, Duke of, death of, 265
Mont Cenis pass, opening of, 124
Montebello, battle of, 154
Moriana, Berold's castle, 2; title borne by Berold, 2
Mortara, battle of, 45
Motley, the historian, on Emmanuel Philibert, 4, 5

NAPLES, revolution of, 1860, 210; the treatment of political prisoners in, 215; visit of Victor Emmanuel II. to, 230; brigandage in, 246, 251; seizure of brigands from a French vessel at Civitavecchia, 251; the cholera in, 262; Prince of (son of Prince Humbert), 306
Napoleon III., his reception of Victor Emmanuel II., 108; Orsini's attempt on his life, 126; English feeling against him, 127; is appealed to by Victor Emmanuel II., 128; has an interview with Count Cavour, 132; lands at Genoa, 151; his interview with Count Cavour, 172; and

PAP

Rome as the capital, 240; his friendship with Victor Emmanuel II., 152; demands an armistice from the Austrians, 169; Marshal Vaillant's remonstrance thereon, 170; attacked for aiding Victor Emmanuel II., 183; a congress proposed to, at Savona, by Victor Emmanuel II., 287; Pepoli's letter to, 289, 290; declares war against Prussia, 309; death of, 327
Napoleon Jerome, proposed marriage with Princess Clotilde, 139; married, January 29, 1859, 142; visits Victor Emmanuel II. in state, 246
Neapolitan Government and De Martino, 211
Niccolini, the poet, his address to Victor Emmanuel II., 209
Nice and Savoy, cession to France, 141, 203
Nigra, Count, takes charge of the children and household of Victor Emmanuel II., 149; the king's instructions thereon, 149
Novara, battle of, 44
Novara railway, opening of the, 91

ODONE (Duke of Monferrat), death of, 265
Orsini, Felice, attempts to assassinate the French Emperor, 126; letter to Napoleon III., 128
Otho III., 2
Oudinot, General, enters Rome, 68

PALEOCAPA, the blind Venetian minister, 173; receives the order of SS. Annunziata, 273
Palermo, insurrection in, 212
Palestro, battle of, 154
Pantheon, decorations of, at funeral of Victor Emmanuel II., 358
Papal government, D'Azeglio's pamphlet attacking the, 82
Papal States, absence of railways in, 245

INDEX.

PAR

Pareto, Marchese, insurgent at Genoa, 56; pardon of, 56; elected deputy, 72

Paris, visited by Victor Emmanuel II., 108

Parliament, *see* Chamber of Deputies

Parma, Duchess of, leaves Parma, 166; governor sent to, 167; the people of, become subjects of Victor Emmanuel II., 181

Peace, Treaty of, of August 6, 1849, 73

Pellico, Silvio, author of book on Austrian prisons, dies, 1854, 92

Pepoli, Marquis, 167; on the Peace of Villafranca, 175; made Governor of Umbria, 222; his opinion on proposed removal of capital to Florence, 257; arrives from Paris, 289; writes to Napoleon III., 289, 290

Perugia, Marquis Gualterio made governor of, 222; Bishop of, 222

Pettinengo, General, Minister of War, 267; resigns ministry of war, 276; letter of Victor Emmanuel II. thereon, 276

Piedmont, financial difficulties, 89; increased taxation, 89; military preparations in, 92; starting of the troops, 102; return and review of troops, 116; continued disagreement with Austria, 162; severance of diplomatic relations with Austria, 123; preparations for war with Austria, 141; Lombardy begs to be joined to, 159. *See also* Sardinia

Piedmont and Savoy, invasion of, 2

Pinelli, Minister of the Interior, in 1849, 52

Pio Nono, accession of, to the Papal throne, 23; popularity of, 24; and Austria, 26; and the war with Austria, 39; his indecision therein, 42; and the papal power, 58; his relations with Austria, 59; receives an address from the Consulta, 60; his hesitation in sending the papal army to the war, 60; disaffection created

PIO

thereby, 61; bombardment of Quirinal Palace, 62; leaves Rome secretly and takes refuge at Gaeta, 62; the Austrian Jesuits and, 63; is visited by Conte di San Martino, envoy of Victor Emmanuel II., 63; resolution of Parliament, that he has fallen from temporal power, 65; Fiorentino's '*La Vita di Pio Nono*,' 66; thanks the French General Oudinot for the taking of Rome, 68; and the death warrants of the traitors, 68; receives Count Cesare Balbo on a mission from Victor Emmanuel II., 69; receives Count Siccardi as an embassy from Victor Emmanuel II. on the revision of *The Statuto*, 78; letter from Victor Emmanuel II. on the insolence of the clergy, 82; letter to Victor Emmanuel II. on the licence of the press, 82; sends a letter to Victor Emmanuel II., 167; letter from Victor Emmanuel II., 189; public character of, 189; letter to Victor Emmanuel II., 193; letter from Victor Emmanuel II. on annexation of Central Italy, 194; excommunicates Victor Emmanuel II. and all his subjects, 196; letter to Victor Emmanuel II., 197; threatens to place an interdict on the kingdom of Italy, 237; letter to Victor Emmanuel concerning certain bishoprics, 262; raises a foreign legion, 277; relations between Victor Emmanuel II. and, 278; Lord Clarendon conveys a message to, from Victor Emmanuel II., 293; his reply thereto, 293; calls an Ecumenical Council, 307; letter to, from Victor Emmanuel II. on his decision to annex Rome, 312; his conversation with Count San Martino thereon, 314; his reply to Victor Emmanuel II., 315; yields to Victor Emmanuel II., 316; celebrates the twenty-fifth year of his reign, 322; deputation of the clericals to, 323;

PIS

receives greetings, January 1, 1872, from Victor Emmanuel II., 325; his relations with Victor Emmanuel II., 345
Pisanelli, Signor, bill for the suppression of religious houses, 252; remarks of Victor Emmanuel II. thereon, 252
Philibert, Emmanuel, surnamed Testa di Ferro, 2; offered the hand of Elizabeth Tudor of England, 3; marriage with Duchess de Berry, 3; Ricotti, the historian, on, 4; Motley, the historian, on, 4
Plezza, Senator, anecdote of, 342
Poerio, Baron Carlo, 169; elected a deputy, 205; his sufferings in prison, 215; Victor Emmanuel II.'s opinion of, 228; advises Victor Emmanuel II. to recall Cavour, 235; death of, 281
Popolo Romano, on the death of Victor Emmanuel II., 360
Portugal, King of, marries Princess Maria Pia, of Italy, 244
Prim, General, assassination of, 326
Prussia, quarrels with Austria, 266; alliance with Italy, 267; victorious over Austria, 271; the victory of Sadowa, 271
Puglia, Duke of (son of Prince Amedeo), 301

QUIRINAL Palace bombarded, 62

RADETSKY, Marshal, head of the Austrian army, 42; interview with Victor Emmanuel II., 49; his offer of soldiers to, 75
Railway communication, in Sardinia, 91; opening of the Novara line, 91; objection of the Popes to, 245; opening of the Bologna and Ancona railway, 245; the Pescara and Foggia railway opened, 254
Ramirez, Cavaliere, appointed by Ferdinand II. ambassador to

ROM

the court of Turin, 84; his interview with Victor Emmanuel II., 84
Ramorino, General, is tried by court-martial, 71; sentenced to death and shot, 71; D'Azeglio's comments thereon, 71
Rattazzi, his opposition to joining the Anglo-French alliance, 95; Minister of the Interior, April 1855, 104; his Clerical Bill, 102; passing of the same, 104; forms a new ministry, 174; forms a new ministry, 246; unpopularity of his ministry, 247; resigns office, 250; forms a new ministry, 281; he resigns, 284; death of, 327
'Red Shirts,' the, Garibaldi's soldiers, 229
Ricasoli, Baron, made Dictator of Tuscany, 183; gives up his Dictatorship of Tuscany, 200; reply of Victor Emmanuel II. thereto, 201; receives the order of the SS. Annunziata, 202; made Governor of Tuscany, 202, 205; forms a new ministry on death of Cavour, 243; resigns office, 246; visited by Victor Emmanuel II., 253; appointed La Marmora's deputy in the Council, 267; resigns office, 280
Ricotti, the historian, on Emmanuel Philibert, 4
Riviera, cholera epidemic in, 91
Romagnuoli, reply of Victor Emmanuel II. to the, 182
Rome, 58; nationalist feeling in, 59; sympathy with the Piedmontese troops, 60; the address of the Consulta to the Pope, 60; disaffection in, 61; bombardment of the Quirinal Palace, 62; Pio Nono leaves secretly, 62; Garibaldi in, 63; inauguration of a republic, 65; Galletti accepts office, 65; abolition of the Inquisition, 65; Garibaldi and Bartolucci defend Rome, 67; capitulation of, 68; to be capital of Italy, 235, 238, 240; Francis II.

takes up his abode in, 240; the French to evacuate in 1866, 257; evacuation of the French troops, 275; conspiracy against the Pope, 278; Inquisition in, 282; Garibaldi threatens to invade, 283; French troops sent to Civitavecchia, 283; occupation of, by French soldiers, 306; Victor Emmanuel II. decides to annex, 312; General Cadorna marches on, 315; attack on, 315; Pio Nono yields to Victor Emmanuel II., 316; visit of Victor Emmanuel II., on the inundation of the Tiber, 321; the first Parliament in, November 27, 1871, 322; public entry of Victor Emmanuel II. into, 322; royal visitors to, 327; in mourning for Victor Emmanuel II., 354

Rossi, Pellegrini, comes into office, 61; brutal murder of, 62

Ruffini's '*Doctor Antonio*,' 216

'*Rule of the Monk*,' the, by Garibaldi, 288

Russia, increasing friendship of, for Piedmont, 123

Russia and Sardinia, ill feeling between, 92; reconciliation of, 116

SABAUD family, introductory notice of the, 1; end of the Sabaud monarchy, 2

Sadowa, battle of, 271

San Martino, battle of, 162; Conte di, visits the Pope at Gaeta, 63; the Austrian and Bavarian ambassadors and, 63; bears a letter to Pio Nono from Victor Emmanuel II., 312; his conversation with Pio Nono, 314

San Salvador, the Sardinian army at, 151

Santa Rosa, death of, 81; brutal outrage upon, 81

Santa Rosa, Count Santorre, leader of the Carbonari, 10, 11; on the abdication of Victor Emmanuel I., 12

Sardinia and Austria, amicable relations established between, 75

Sardinia, the marriage laws of, 87; proposes to join Anglo-French alliance, 92; ill-feeling with Russia, 92; joins the alliance, 96; reconciliation with Russia, 116; Sardinian army ordered to the Marches and Umbria, 220; engagement with the Papal troops at Castelfidardo, 221; takes Ancona, 221. *See* Italy. *See also* Piedmont

Savona, a congress at, proposed to Napoleon III. by Victor Emmanuel II., 287

Savoy, the Dukes of, 2

Savoy and Nice, cession to France, 141, 203

Savoy and Piedmont, invasion of, 2

Saxony, visit of the King of, to Victor Emmanuel II., 124

Sclopis on the *Statuto*, 77

Seven Weeks' War, 267, 268, 271

Sforzesca, battle of, 45

Siccardi, Count, and the revision of the *Statuto*, 77; sent on an embassy to Pio Nono concerning the revision of the *Statuto*, 77; Cardinal Antonelli's reply thereto, 77; accompanies Victor Emmanuel II. on a tour in the Alps, 78; death of, 126

Sicilies, the Two, rebellion in, 67

Sicily, rebellion in, 210, 272

Solferino, battle of, 162

Sommacampagna, battle of, 43

Sonnaz, General de, letter from Victor Emmanuel to, 153

Spain, revolution of 1868, 300; Amedeo made king, 318; deputation of the Cortes to Victor Emmanuel II. thereon, 318; unsettled state of, 325; sends an ambassador to Florence, 262

Spezia, narrow escape of Victor Emmanuel II. and his family from drowning at, 91

Staffala, battle of, 43

Statuto, the, 54, 72, 74, 75; protest by the clergy against the revision of, 77; Count Siccardi

STE

and the revision of, 77; Count Siccardi sent on an embassy to Pio Nono concerning the revision of, 77; the anniversary of, 237
Sterbini abolishes the Inquisition, 66
Straniero, lo, 162
Superga, the church, 7
Sweden, Crown Prince of, visits Victor Emmanuel II., 246
Syracuse, Count of, and Francis II., 210; takes refuge with Victor Emmanuel II., 218

THIERS, M., appeals to Victor Emmanuel II. for aid in Franco-Prussian War, 317
Thomas, fifth son of Charles Emmanuel I., made Prince of Carignano, 8
Tiber, inundation of the, 321
'Times,' The, on Victor Emmanuel's visit to England, 109
Tommasi, Dr., accompanies Victor Emmanuel II. on his southward journey, 227; conversation of Victor Emmanuel II. with, 257
Treaty of peace of August 6, 1849, 73
Turin, outbreak amongst the university students of, 10; outbreak of students, the military and citizens, 15; rebellion in, on the abdication of Victor Emmanuel I., 13; punishment of the rebels, 14; the court of, Count Appony the Austrian ambassador at, 75; put in a state of defence, 153; consternation in, on proposed removal of capital to Florence, 258; demonstrations in, 259; inhabitants of, send an address to Victor Emmanuel II., 260; deputation from, asking that Victor Emmanuel II. may be buried there, 354; relics of Victor Emmanuel II. deposited at Turin, 354; visit of Victor Emmanuel II. to, 230
Tuscany, Duke of, his proclamation on the War of Independence, 40

VIC

Tuscany, the people demand a constitution, 166; the grand duke leaves the country, 166; governor sent to, 167; the people of, resolve to become subjects of Victor Emmanuel II., 179; Baron Ricasoli made dictator of, 183. *See also* Italy, Central

UMBERTO, King, *see* Humbert
Umbria, Marquis Pepoli made Governor of, 222

VAILLANT, Marshal, his remonstrance on Napoleon III. demanding an armistice with Austria, 170
Valerio, Signor, made Governor of the Marches, 222; on the unjust attacks of the clergy and clerical press, 224; answer of Victor Emmanuel II. thereon, 224
Venice, the impending struggle for, 266; restored to Italy by Napoleon III., 272; deputation from, to Victor Emmanuel II., 272; his reply thereto, 273; Victor Emmanuel II. enters, 274
Venosta, Visconti, on removal of capital to Florence, 258
Verdi, the composer, 181
Victor Amadeus, first King of Savoy, 6; marries niece of Louis XIV., 6; declares war with France, 6; made king of Sicily, 6; erects the church of Superga, 7; his war of extermination with the Huguenots and Waldensians, 7
Victor Emmanuel I. succeeds Charles Emmanuel IV., 7; persecuted by Napoleon, 7; exiled to Sardinia, 7; returns to his capital, 7; abdicates, 12; agitation in Turin, 13
Victor Emmanuel II., birth and early days, 28; fatality to his nurse, 28; education, 29; military studies of, 34; marries Maria Adelaide, daughter of the Archduke Ranieri, 32; anecdote

VIC

of, 35; is given a command, 36; his first taste of war, 36; at the victory of Goito, 43; made King of Sardinia on the abdication of his father, 47; his negotiations for an armistice, 49; interview with Marshal Radetsky, 49; conclusion of the armistice, 50; popular indignation thereon, 51; reception by the citizens at Turin, 51; his proclamation to the people, 52; reception of the armistice by the Chamber of Deputies, 52; deputation to, from the Chamber, 53; narrow escape from death, 53; takes the oath to the constitution, 54; his speech thereon, 54; dissolves Chamber of Deputies in 1849, 55; interview with the ambassadors of France and England, 56; interview with D'Azeglio, 57; his title of '*Rè Galantuomo*,' 58; his envoy Conte di San Martino visits Pio Nono at Gaeta, 63; sends Count Cesare Balbo on a mission to Pio Nono at Gaeta, 68; utter failure of the mission, 69; dangerous illness of, 69; General Dabormida's letter thereon, 69; the Duke of Genoa fills his place, 71; his recovery, 71; issues a proclamation to the people, 71; his welcome at the Chamber of Deputies, 72; death of Charles Albert, his father, 73; his proclamation on the dissolution of the Chambers, 73; visits the Alps, 78; writes to D'Azeglio, 78; his success in the chase, 78; *Barba Vittorio* (Uncle Victor), 79; anecdotes of, and the peasantry, 79; tour through Savoy to meet the Duke and Duchess of Genoa, 80; letter to Pio Nono, on the insolence of the clergy, 82; Pio Nono's letter to, on the licence of the press, 82; and the Lombardo-Venetian provinces, 83; enmity of King Ferdinand to, 83; his opinion of Gioberti's '*Rinnovamento Civile d"Italia*,' 85; his

VIC

magnanimity, 85; his religious belief, 85; memorandum to Austria, 88; his active part in the cabinet, 90; narrow escape with his family from drowning, 91; death of his son Charles Albert, 91; visits Genoa during the cholera epidemic, 91; letter to the Minister of Foreign Affairs concerning the Anglo-French alliance, 93; his interview with the French ambassador on the Anglo-French alliance 1854, 93; illness of his mother and his wife, 95, 97; interview on the treaty with Cavour, 96; death of his mother, January 12, 1855, 98; his connection with Countess Mirafiore, 98; death of his wife, January 20, 1855, 98; public announcement on the loss of his mother, wife, and brother, 99; reviews troops about to leave for the seat of war, 102; speech to the troops starting for the war, 103; maligned by the clergy, 104; illness of, 105; proposes to visit England and France, 105; opens the Legislative Assembly, 1855, 106; his speech, 106; starts for Paris with Cavour and D'Azeglio, 108; his reception by the emperor and empress, 108; arrives in England, 108; the '*Times*' on his visit, 109; receives the order of the Garter, 109; attends a banquet at the Guildhall, 109; returns to Turin, 110; addresses the troops on their return from the war, 117; interview of La Marmora, 117; his plan for the unification of Italy, 119; visited by brothers of the Czar of Russia, 123; visited by the King of Saxony, 124; receives a deputation on female education, 124; his speech on the opening of Parliament, 125; conversation with Lanza, 126; his appeal to Napoleon III., 128; is again visited by the royal family of Russia, 132; receives deputa-

C C

VIC

tions on January 1, 1859, 134; his remark to the magistrates, 134; his speech at the opening of Parliament, January 10, 1859, 135, 136; 'Grido di dolore,' 135; his remark to Ciprario thereon, 135; Massari's remarks on his speech, 138; proposed marriage between Princess Clotilde and Prince Napoleon Jerome, 139; his repugnance thereto, 139; his present of a ring to Count Cavour, 140; his walks incognito, 145; anecdote of, and his wife, 146; appointed supreme commander of the Italian forces, 147; Prince Eugenio appointed regent, 147; his proclamation to the people, 147; his address to the people, 148; confides his children to Count Nigra, 149; his instructions to him, 149; description of, by a French officer, 150; his friendship with Napoleon III., 152; letter to General de Sonnaz, 153; Royal proclamation on the battle of Montebello, 154; his gallantry at Palestro, 155; made captain of the Zouaves, 156; his letter to Colonel de Chabron, 156; issues another proclamation, 157; meeting of, and Garibaldi, 161; at the battles of Solferino and San Martino, 162; his message to Marshal Hilliers, 163, 164; issues another proclamation on the late victories, 164; receives a letter from the Pope, 167; offers his alliance to Francis II., 169; his interview with Count Cavour, 172; returns to Turin, 173; his interview with Sir James Hudson, 173; interview with the Marquis Pepoli, 175; his letter to Count Belgiojoso on the service at Milan in memory of his father, 176; visits Lombardy privately, 177; visits Manzoni, 177; Manzoni's remarks on, 177; the inhabitants of Modena resolve to become subjects of, 179; Central

VIC

Italy offers itself to him, 179; his reply to the Tuscans, 180; to Modena, 181; to the Romagnuoli, 182; sends for Count Cavour, 187; visits Lombardy, February 1860, 188; letter to Pio Nono, 189; letter from Pio Nono, 193; letter to Pio Nono on annexation of Central Italy, 194; is excommunicated by Pio Nono, 196; letter from Pio Nono, 197; efforts for reconciliation with Pio Nono, 199; address to Signor Farini on giving up the dictatorship of Emilia, 200; address to Baron Ricasoli on giving up the dictatorship of Tuscany, 201; address to the people of Central Italy, 202; address to inhabitants of Nice and Savoy on their cession to France, 204; speech at the opening of Parliament, April 2, 1860, 205; makes a tour through his new dominions accompanied by Count Mamiani, 207; is welcomed to Florence by Capponi, 208; address of Niccolini the poet to, 209; message from, to Garibaldi, 217; Count of Syracuse takes refuge with, 218; is appealed to by Francis II., 218; his address to the soldiers on leaving for the Marches, 220; commands his soldiers to be considerate with the Clericali and the prisoners, 222; and the foreign powers, 223; visits new provinces, 223; enthusiastic reception at Ancona, 223; address to the soldiers, 223; address to the marines, 224; answer to Signor Valerio on clerical complaints, 224; visits the Holy House of Loreto, 225; visits the Jesuits' College, 225; his tenderness for the wounded, 225; anecdotes thereon, 225; his address to the people of South Italy, 226; his journey through the Southern States, 227; is called to Naples, 227; his daily routine of work,

VIC

227; his opinion of Poerio, 228; his opinion of Ferdinand II., 228; meeting with Garibaldi in Naples, 229; his reception in Naples, 230; arrives in Turin, December 29, 1860, 231; his proclamation on Prince of Carignano as Viceroy of Naples, 231; his speech at opening of Parliament, February 1861, 232; proclaimed King of Italy, 234; presents new banners to the army through General Fanti, 237; his address thereon, 237; his notes for the use of the Paris envoy, 243; his letter to Count San Martino, 244; visited by Crown Prince of Sweden, 246; visits Naples, 246; receives a visit from Prince Napoleon, 246; telegram to Napoleon III. thereon, 246; proclamation on the crisis in Rome, 248; his grief on the battle of Aspromonte, 249; letter to Minghetti on finance, 250; his remarks on the bill for suppression of religious houses, 252; and the Republican writers, 253; anecdote thereon, 253; travels through the central provinces, 253; visits Ricasoli at Broglio, 253; opens a railway between Pescara and Foggia, 253; his remarks on proposed removal of capital to Florence, 257; his conversation with Dr. Tommasi, 257; sets out for Florence, January 31, 1865, 259; his reception, 259; retires to Villa San Rossore, near Pisa, 259; receives an address from Turin, 260; surrenders a fifth of his civil list to avoid taxing the country, 261; the Clericals and the Liberals on, 261; receives letter from Pio Nono concerning certain bishoprics, 262; visits Naples, 262; opens the first Florence Parliament, 262; his speech thereat, 262; death of his third son Odone, the Duke of Monferrat, 265; anecdote

VIC

thereon, 265; goes to seat of war of 1866 with his sons, 268; his addresses to the people, national guards, and soldiers, 268, 269; his letter to Napoleon III. on the war, 269; the emperor's reply thereto, 269; his son Amedeo wounded, 270; resolves on an armistice with Austria, 271; deputation to, from Venice, 272; his reply to the Venetians, 273; entry into Venice, 274; returns to Florence, November 21, 1866, 274; his speech to the Chamber, December 15, 1866, 275; letter to General Pettinengo on his resignation as Minister of War, 276; relations between, and Pio Nono, 278; address to new Parliament, March 22, 1867, 279; proclamation on the insurrection in Rome, 285; telegram to Marquis Pepoli on the crisis, 286; proposes to Napoleon III. a congress at Savona, 287; on the chassepots at Mentana, 289; a message conveyed from, to Pio Nono, by Lord Clarendon, 293; institutes a new order of knighthood, *la Corona d' Italia*, 296; anecdotes of his deeds of charity, 297; presented with a cushion, 299; address to, on birth of Amedeo's son, 301; his reply thereto, 301; receives visits from Russians and Austrians, 302; receives Empress of French at Venice, 302; growing friendship between, and Emperor of Austria, 302; severe illness of, 303; marries Countess Mirafiore, 304; his recovery, 304; and the Clericals, 305; decides to annex Rome, 311; his letter to Pio Nono thereon, 312; Thiers appeals for aid in Franco-Prussian war, 317; deputation from the Cortes on Amedeo becoming King of Spain, 318; his reply thereto, 318; his speech at the last Florence Parliament, 319;

VIC

goes to Rome on inundation of the Tiber, 321; makes his public entry into Rome, June 2, 1871, 322; attends opening of Mont Cenis railway, 322; his speech on opening of first Parliament in Rome, 322; on January 1, 1872, sends greetings to Pio Nono, 325; grief at Amedeo's abdication, 326; pays a visit to Austria, 327; meets Austrian emperor, 328; visits Germany, 329; meets the emperor, 329; returns to Italy, 329; inaugurates a monument to Cavour, 329; his speech on opening of Parliament, November 13, 1873, 330; celebration of twenty-fifth year of his reign, 330; estrangement from La Marmora, 331; a return visit from Emperor of Austria, 331; visit from Emperor of Germany, 332; his last speech in Parliament, 333; his private life, 334; anecdotes about his dress, 335; his punctuality, 336; his love of horses, 337; his reputation for gallantry, 338; and the horn player, 339; his love of smoking, 341; his love of hunting, 341; his last illness, 348; his dying words, 349; 'the first King of Italy is no more,' 350; his death announced in Parliament, 352; speech of Signor Depretis thereon, 352; his funeral, 354; decorations of the Pantheon at his funeral, 358; a tribute to his memory, 361

Vienna, court of, memorandum from Victor Emmanuel to, 89; Sardinian ambassador leaves, 88

Villafranca, peace signed at, July 1859, 173; conference at Zurich for formal settlement of the Peace of, 178

Villamarina, Marquis, appointed plenipotentiary to the Congress, 111

Vittoria, Duchess of Aosta, death of, 333

W ALDENSIANS, persecutions of, 3; war of extermination against the, by Victor Amadeus, 7

Z ORILLA, Señor, 318

THE END.

www.ingramcontent.com/pod-product-compliance
Lightning Source LLC
Chambersburg PA
CBHW051247300426
44114CB00011B/928